'David Fowler's new book is one of the most illuminating books on twentieth-century youth culture I have ever read. From the youth cults of the Edwardian era to the Mods of the Sixties, he looks behind the stereotypes and has unearthed some fascinating material. Based on years of archival research and written with an admirable eye for detail and perspective, this is bound to become essential reading for anyone interested in the social and cultural history of the last century.' – **Dominic Sandbrook**, *University of Oxford*

'An ideal text for students: always clear and accessible, with a good eye for detailed examples that are amusing and memorable, even gripping in their opening up of the issues.' – **Alastair Reid**, *Girton College, Cambridge*

'David Fowler offers us an iconoclastic account of the history of youth culture, enlivened by telling examples (the 1960s civil servant earnestly reading Herbert Marcuse's *One-Dimensional Man*) and challenging arguments which force us to re-examine our comfortable assumptions.' – **John Street**, *University of East Anglia*

Historians and sociologists invariably view youth culture as a by-product of the affluent 1950s and 'Swinging Sixties'. However, this highly readable new study challenges received wisdom on the subject. David Fowler locates the roots of British youth culture in the student communities of the interwar years and traces its history through to the more familiar world of youth communities and pop culture.

Youth Culture in Modern Britain, c. 1920-c.1970:

- draws on extensive original research across the British Isles
- explores the individuals, institutions and ideas that have shaped youth culture, both among the middle classes and among urban working-class communities
- argues that 'Ivory Tower' universities were the prime movers in the development of the notion of youth culture, from where it spread not just across Britain, but across Europe and further afield
- offers a new revisionist interpretation of postwar youth cults such as the Mods, and of the so-called youth culture decade of the 1960s.

Including tables, illustrations, chronologies and a comprehensive Bibliography of primary and secondary sources, this approachable and informative text is essential reading for students and scholars of Modern History and Sociology.

D0218176

David Fowler teaches Modern British History at the University of Cambridge where he also lectures on the history of youth cultures in modern Britain and is a Senior Member of Clare Hall. He is the author of *The First Teenagers: The Lifestyle of Young Wage-earners in Interwar Britain* (1995) and the forthcoming *The Youth Apostle: A Life of Rolf Gardiner*, and of several scholarly articles on modern British youth history and cultural history.

Also by the author:

The First Teenagers: The Lifestyle of Young Wage-earners in Interwar Britain (1995)

The Youth Apostle: A Life of Rolf Gardiner (forthcoming, 2009)

Youth Culture in Modern Britain, *c.*1920–*c.*1970

From Ivory Tower to Global Movement – A New History

David Fowler

University of Cambridge

First published 2008 by
PALGRAVE MACMILLAN

Palgrave Macmillan in the UK is an imprint of Macmillan Publishers Limited, registered in England, company number 785998, of Houndmills, Basingstoke, Hampshire RG21 6XS.

Palgrave Macmillan in the US is a division of St Martin's Press LLC, 175 Fifth Avenue, New York, NY 10010.

Palgrave Macmillan is the global academic imprint of the above companies and has companies and representatives throughout the world.

Palgrave® and Macmillan® are registered trademarks in the United States, the United Kingdom, Europe and other countries.

ISBN-13: 978 0–333–59921–1 hardback
ISBN-10: 0–333–59921–7 hardback
ISBN-13: 978 0–333–59922–8 paperback
ISBN-10: 0–333–59922–5 paperback

This book is printed on paper suitable for recycling and made from fully managed and sustained forest sources. Logging, pulping and manufacturing processes are expected to conform to the environmental regulations of the country of origin.

A catalogue record for this book is available from the British Library.

A catalog record for this book is available from the Library of Congress.

10   9   8   7   6   5   4   3   2   1
17   16   15   14   13   12   11   10   09   08

Printed and bound in Great Britain by CPI Antony Rowe, Chippenham and Eastbourne

To Andrew Martin, a great friend, who encouraged, cajoled and inspired

Contents

List of Tables

Appendix tables

List of Figures

Preface

I began my research on the history of Youth and Youth Cultures during the 1980s – in the Thatcher decade. I lived at the time in that renowned city of youth, Manchester; the city that in the 1990s became 'Madchester' when its youth culture became linked with recreational drugs such as ecstasy, with 'drug wars' and with exciting but troubled pop groups such as the Stone Roses and Happy Mondays. I left Manchester in 1988 and eventually moved, in 1993, to the relatively tranquil and godly city of Belfast, where I spent almost ten years as Lecturer and Research Fellow in Modern History in The Queen's University of Belfast. The first thing I noticed in my new university was a statue of Churchill at the main entrance. Apart from that, there were lots of churches – gloomy Presbyterian churches – with few windows; there were nightly reports of deaths and punishment beatings on the local news; the local opinion formers were politicians and churchmen (very few were women), and there did not appear to be a youth culture of any kind.

In my student years during the 1980s I would visit The Hacienda and The Venue, two Manchester clubs literally next door to each other. The Hacienda was then a nationally known centre of youth culture, where for about £2 one could spend three hours experiencing a counterculture of sorts; hearing very subversive music you never heard anywhere else – 'Niggers are Scared of Revolution' was a record I was shocked by.[1] But in those days all you had to do if the sentiments of records were alien to you was walk downstairs to a quiet haven called The Gay Traitor (after the Cambridge spy Anthony Blunt). There, in relative peace, you could hear the dreamier tunes of an earlier counterculture such as 'Lucy in the Sky with Diamonds' or 'I'm Fixing a Hole where the Rain Gets in to Stop My Mind from Wandering' and you thought about how untroubled the youth cultures of the 1960s must have been. In short, you became depressed at how risible was the youth culture of the 1980s with its cacophonous drumbeats on the latest House music from 'the ghettoes' of New York City, spliced with the latest grim sound from the Mancunian pop group New Order, who were worshipped by the Hacienda crowd but left me feeling sapped of all my natural gaiety.

The Hacienda was a spartan warehouse environment. But, on the positive side, it at least stirred my interest in youth cultures and it was in that draughty place that I liked to talk about the forerunners of the hip-hop dancers upstairs; namely the teenage wage-earners of the interwar years who were the focus of my Ph.D. thesis, 'The Lifestyle of the Young Wage-earner in Interwar Manchester', which no one, not even the great A.J.P. Taylor, had written about.

A. J. P. Taylor once wrote that Manchester 'is the only British city that can look London in the eye' and I still think this is the case. Taylor grew up in Southport, a small coastal town in south Lancashire renowned as the safest Conservative seat in England during the 1980s, but his first academic post was as Lecturer in Modern History at Manchester University, from 1930 to 1938. In Taylor's day the University died at 5 p.m. when all the lecturers and university administrators went home, and the only entertainment for a young don, so he claimed, was the Hallé Orchestra about two miles from the University at the other end of Oxford Road; a thirty-minute walk at least. During the 1980s I was discovering that there was also a youth culture in Manchester during the 1930s that touched the life of the University even in Taylor's day. But A.J.P. Taylor simply did not notice it. Either that, or he did not feel it was worth commenting on in his autobiography, *A Personal History* (1983), or in his other essays on Manchester.[2]

I now realise that there were several youth cultures in Britain in the first half of the twentieth century – visible not only in Manchester, for example, but in London, Dublin and Cambridge as well. The following study is an attempt to explore how youth culture evolved in British society and 'across the water' in Ireland both before and after the Beatles put British youth culture on the global map in the early 1960s. It is well known, indeed a cliché, that the Beatles made British politicians take notice of youth. They became very rich very quickly, earning over £6 million for themselves in their first two years, 1963–5.[3] The Prime Minister when the group first emerged, Alec Douglas-Home, referred to them as 'my secret weapon' as their colossal global earnings by early 1964 had significantly reduced Britain's international debts. Moreover, the new Labour Prime Minister, Harold Wilson, awarded the group MBEs in 1965. But the Beatles' impact on British youth culture, rather than on the country's coffers, is an interesting research question that has never been properly explored.[4] Moreover, the development of youth culture in Britain before the Beatles has never been properly researched, from archival sources, either.[5]

The following study draws on extensive archival research conducted in Britain and Northern Ireland (and also includes material on youth culture in the Irish Republic). The net is cast far wider than my earlier work and explores the development of youth culture in the universities as well as in the urban working-class neighbourhoods of British, and Northern Irish, towns and cities. Moreover, the book also explores the pioneering investigations of British youth culture undertaken from the late 1950s by middle-class intellectuals such as Richard Hoggart and Colin MacInnes, and assesses the merits and drawbacks of this work (see Chapter 6). Surprisingly little has been written on the impact of youth culture in British universities, and hardly anything on the youth cultures and youth communities of Northern Ireland or, for that matter, the Irish Republic, and it has taken me several years to grasp what was going on before the 1960s, and indeed during the 1960s. This book is, therefore, an attempt to uncover a history that is largely hidden before the Second World War, and it asks new questions about the youth culture that came to prominence in Britain during the 1960s. Were the Beatles beneficial for British youth culture? Was youth culture in Northern Ireland a threat to the social and political stability of the region even before the onset of 'The Troubles' in the late 1960s? Did the student protesters in British universities in the late 1960s pose a serious threat to the Labour government of the period?

I was commissioned to write this book at the start of my period in Northern Ireland. The historian who asked me to write it was Professor Jeremy Black, an electric presence and inspirational scholar, who sent me off to Belfast to write it with the cheery words: 'Make sure you avoid the bombs.' I am grateful to my friend and former colleague at the University of East Anglia, Professor John Charmley, for introducing me to Jeremy Black, and especially grateful to Professor Black for setting me the challenging but mammoth task of researching youth culture since 1900 and for leaving me to get on with it.

The thesis of this book is that there were several youth cultures in Britain that predated the Beatles and the teenage culture of the 1950s and 1960s and, in essence, it is university students who have shaped British youth culture as a creative force in the twentieth century for much of the time. I had no notion of this when I wrote my first book, *The First Teenagers: The Lifestyle of Young Wage-earners in Interwar Britain* (1995). What now seems clear to me after digging deeply into the archives for material on youth culture before the Beatles and the 'Swinging Sixties' is that, in Britain at least, a way of life described at the time as 'Youth Culture' was developed by youth 'enthusiasts' in the universities such as Rolf Gardiner (see Chapter 2). Sometimes it was hinted at over a political issue such as the 'King and Country' debate of the 1930s, which galvanised student opinion across Britain against the Baldwin government's drift towards another European war. Then there were the solitary youths who sat in their lodgings and in the time off from their academic studies wrote novels about 'youth'. They created a new genre of fiction between the Wars: the 'Undergraduate Novel'.

In a sense, these interwar students not only developed youth culture; they invented it. The term 'Youth Culture' was unknown in Britain in 1900, except in medical circles.[6] But by the 1920s it was well known in Weimar

Germany (*JugendKultur*), where it was associated with hiking and youth hostelling and the mass membership youth movements that had emerged in Germany after the end of the First World War. Moreover, the concept of 'youth culture' was also introduced into British universities during the 1920s. How it was introduced into British universities, and how it was developed in an era before mass advertising and pop music, is explored in Chapter 2. We normally think of the 1950s as the pioneering decade for youth culture in Britain. Mark Abrams first identified the teenage market for manufacturers in 1959; the first British pop stars Tommy Steele and Cliff Richard appeared in the late 1950s, and Colin MacInnes wrote the first British novel about teenagers: *Absolute Beginners* (published in 1959). It now seems that the advertising industry and media industries were very slow to identify the youth market in Britain. A youth market for leisure and consumer goods existed in the 1930s, but it was hardly targeted at national level until much later. Why? Were manufacturers and advertisers incompetent or were there sound reasons for ignoring the young consumer before the 1950s?

The development of youth culture in Britain over the twentieth century long predated the era of the teenager (1950s) and the Beatles (1960s). Perhaps surprisingly, given its cloistered image and reputation as a meeting place for Bloomsbury intellectuals during the 1920s, the University of Cambridge has a central role in the development of British youth culture (see Chapter 2). A whole world of youth and youth culture existed in interwar Cambridge. It can be glimpsed both in the student periodicals of the period and in the rich archival material available. Some of the ideas generated by the University's youth culture enthusiasts, cultural and political ideas, were disseminated not just across Cambridge, but across Britain and beyond Britain; reaching Europe, the United States and even India. A prime mover in this process was Rolf Gardiner, a pivotal figure in the development of Youth Culture and youth communities in the period between the Two World Wars; not only in Britain but across Northern Europe (see Chapter 2).

One of my former students at Queen's, Belfast, once remarked with great panache and brevity in a tutorial: 'Youth culture got bigger and better' over the course of the twentieth century. This was in the mid-1990s and I thought it was probably an accurate summary. Greater affluence must have improved youth culture immeasurably from its interwar days and made it less sexist, more international, and less racist. But after researching this study I now believe that the heroic days of youth culture were the decade of the 1920s (for middle-class youth), the 1930s (for urban working-class youth cultures) and the 1960s (for student youth) and that the youth culture of the 1990s, the Brit Pop moment and the Rave cult, were less significant than these earlier decades. As will be shown, youth culture was an important cultural phenomenon that reshaped communities, institutions and values in the period between about 1920 and the late 1960s. Modern youth generations would find it impossible to shape youth culture in such diverse ways as their predecessors documented in this study managed to do. With no access to modern media such as television, the internet and text messaging, these earlier generations took their ideas about youth culture from the universities to the cathedral and university cities of Northern Europe, the rural regions of eastern Germany and even, via the journals they produced, to India, Canada and the United States. At the heart of youth culture before the Second World War was the concept of a literary culture. After the Second World War its focus shifted from literature and travel to pop music and spending.

Modern youth generations would find the creative impulses of their predecessors baffling; not least because they pursued many different forms of creativity – writing novels and poetry, performing folk dances, conducting political debates, undertaking foreign travel and making cultural contact with youth of other countries, consumerism, hiking, sightseeing, mountaineering, and performing plays. One of these interwar youth culture pioneers was Katherine ('Kitty') Trevelyan, a Northerner, who was a student at Girton College, Cambridge, during the 1920s (and the niece of the Cambridge historian G. M. Trevelyan). In her early twenties she trekked 2000 miles across Canada, alone, and then wrote a book about her experiences.[7] Subsequently, she joined a folk dance team of male and female students who toured Northern European towns and cities during the 1930s, trying to promote cultural links between Britain and Northern Europe (especially with young Germans). She then married a young German, went to live in eastern Germany and helped establish a cultural centre for the progressive arts aimed at youth. She and her collaborator Rolf Gardiner were in a sense, therefore, as much the pioneers of Youth Culture, though micro- or organic youth cultures, as later youth pop stars such as Mick Jagger. Would modern youth generations in Britain feel any of this activity was worth the effort? The many cases of youthful endeavour discussed in this book may inspire some to think that youth culture does matter and did matter in earlier decades.

Note on terms used in the text

The term 'Youth Culture' is capitalized where a specific version is being discussed, e.g. Rolf Gardiner's appropriation of the term during the 1920s, or 'the Youth Culture' of the 1960s as discussed by sociologists such as Bryan Wilson. Elsewhere, when used generically it is given a lower case. All named youth cults, e.g. Teddy Boys, Mods, the Flapper cult, are capitalized following the *Oxford English Dictionary*'s usage.

Acknowledgements

I was commissioned to write this survey while I was teaching at The Queen's University of Belfast during the 1990s, and I consider it a privilege to have been a Lecturer and then Research Fellow there from 1993 to 2002. The extensive primary research I conducted for this study would not have been possible without the beneficence of Queen's and I thank, first, the School of Social Sciences there for awarding me research funding to conduct research in London, and the Institute of Irish Studies for electing me to a Research Fellowship in Irish Studies in 1999–2000, which made possible detailed archival research on youth culture and youth crime in Northern Ireland since c.1922. Among former colleagues at Queen's, I thank for stimulating discussions and fellowship: Professor Ken Brown, the late Professor Peter Jupp, Professor Leslie Clarkson, Professor Alvin Jackson, Professor Liam Kennedy, the late David Johnson and Professor Brian Walker. After Queen's, I had a year in the superb School of History back at my old university, the University of Manchester. I thank Dr Stuart Jones for his support during this period, and some wonderful students who took my Third-Year course 'Cultures and Communities in Twentieth-Century Britain'.

Since 2003, I have been teaching and researching at the University of Cambridge and I would like to express my thanks to Wolfson College, Cambridge, for electing me to a Visiting Fellowship from 2004 to 2005 and Clare Hall, Cambridge, for offering me a permanent research base since 2005. I have tested out many of the ideas in this work in 'supervisions' at Cambridge and my students have shown a real engagement with the subject of youth culture. I thank especially Caroline Potter, Andrew Lord, Jamie Martin, Adam Child, Fiona Henderson and Ed Thomas. I thank Dr Alastair Reid of Girton College, Cambridge, and Professor William Lubenow of Richard Stockton College, New Jersey, for commenting on draft chapters of the book; Professor Martin Daunton for his inspirational example and serious interest in my work over a number of years; Professor Eamon Duffy for his stimulating Research Seminar at Cambridge on 'Irish Studies', and several friends and fellow Modern British historians who have offered encouragement: Professor Peter Clarke, Dr Ben Griffin, Dr Jacqui Faulkner, Dr Richard Toye, Dr Patrick Zutshi and Dr John Walker.

For permission to quote from the Rolf Gardiner papers held in Cambridge University Library, Manuscripts Department, I thank Mrs Rosalind Richards, Gardiner's daughter and copyright holder; and Dr Patrick Zutshi, Keeper of Manuscripts at Cambridge University Library, for his continuing

ACKNOWLEDGEMENTS **xvii**

interest in my forthcoming biography of Rolf Gardiner, *The Youth Apostle: A Life of Rolf Gardiner*. For inviting me to give research papers on themes covered in this book I thank: Dr John Davis of Queen's College, Oxford, for the opportunity to deliver a paper on 'Rolf Gardiner and English Youth Movements' in the Modern British History Research Seminar at Oxford, in May 2004; Dr Alan Sked of the London School of Economics for inviting me to give a paper to his International History Seminar on the theme '1968: the LSE, the New Left and the International Student Revolts', in January 2006; the Institute for Contemporary British History in the Institute of Historical Research, London, for inviting me to talk on 'The YMCAs and Youth Culture in Twentieth-Century Ireland', in June 2006; Professor Gary MacCulloch, convenor of the History of Education Research Seminar at the Institute of Historical Research, for inviting me to deliver a paper on 'Rolf Gardiner, Education and Anglo-German Youth Movements Between the Wars', in March 2007; King's College, Cambridge, for inviting me to address a Symposium on 'The Life and Work of Edward Dent' on the theme 'Edward Dent, Rolf Gardiner and English Folk Dance Between the Two World Wars', in June 2007; and Birkbeck College, London, for inviting me to give a paper on 'Anti-Semitism and British Youth Culture Between the Wars' at an International Conference on Anti-Semitism and English Culture, in June 2007. Finally, I would like to acknowledge the encouragement and support of my parents, and some close friends – Andrew Martin, John Walker, Richard Toye and Penny Croxson.

List of Abbreviations

CCCS	Centre for Contemporary Cultural Studies, Birmingham University
CUL	Cambridge University Library
CWC	Child Welfare Council, Northern Ireland
EFDS	English Folk Dance Society
GAA	Gaelic Athletic Association
JC	Juvenile Courts
KKK	Kibbo Kift Kindred Youth Movement
LSE	London School of Economics and Political Science
MHA	Ministry of Home Affairs, Northern Ireland
NA	National Archives, Kew
NSL	*New Survey of London Life and Labour*
NUS	National Union of Students
ODNB	*Oxford Dictionary of National Biography*
PD	People's Democracy Student Movement, Northern Ireland
PRONI	Public Record Office of Northern Ireland
RSA	Radical Students Alliance
RSG	*Ready, Steady, Go!*, TV programme, 1960s
RSSF	Revolutionary Socialist Students Federation
RUC	Royal Ulster Constabulary
SDS	Students for a Democratic Society (US)
SDS	(Germany) *Sozialistischer Deutscher Studentenbund* (Socialist German Student Union)
SUS	Scottish Union of Students
VSC	Vietnam Solidarity Campaign
WEA	Workers' Educational Association
YMCA	Young Men's Christian Association

Introduction

The roots of British youth culture

It was an American sociologist Talcott Parsons who coined the phrase 'youth culture' in 1942; but, appearing in a learned journal in the United States, and at a time when the youth of Europe were being conscripted into military units and taking part in a monumental European and global war, the term does not seem to have reached Britain for over twenty years. In this country it was first taken up by sociologists; most notably, Bryan Wilson, a Fellow of All Souls College, Oxford, who pioneered discussion of British youth culture in a series of newspaper articles that appeared in the mid-1960s.[1] What Wilson meant by the term was the autonomous behaviour of the young and his definition was so broad (and imprecise) that it included various categories of working-class youth (Mods and Rockers, and teenagers, for example), as well as middle-class students. It is tempting to say his use of the term was so elastic because it enabled him to include whichever groups of youth he wanted to write about that week.

There were other sociologists at the time who were drawn to this subject and, like Wilson, were trying to extract from newspaper and other media reports of youth activity deeper meaning and wider significance. The most celebrated group of pioneering 'youth culture' researchers were based at the University of Birmingham in a new Department, an offshoot of the English Department, called The Centre for Contemporary Cultural Studies (CCCS). Set up in 1962 by a new Professor, Richard Hoggart, whose own roots lay in working-class Hunslet, a suburb of Leeds, it recruited as its first Research Fellow a schoolteacher who hailed from the West Indies and who had written articles on 'teenagers' for leftist periodicals like *Socialist Commentary*. His name was Stuart Hall. Together, Hoggart and his understudy Hall proceeded to recruit a growing body of postgraduate researchers to work on such innovative research topics as Pop Music with special reference to Birmingham; Women's Magazines; Student Protest; Hippy Culture; and Skinheads.[2]

It was sociologists, therefore, who pioneered the study of youth culture in Britain during the 1960s and the nature of this research was very amorphous and, it appears, highly influenced by reports in the media. Graduate students at Birmingham, for example, were asked to analyse contemporary newspaper accounts of the student protests of the era and to construct dissertations from these impressionistic sources.[3] Already by the late 1960s

1

journalists were generating escalating column inches on Mods, Rockers, the Beatles, Swinging London, Hippies, the Rolling Stones, student protest at the London School of Economics (LSE) and other universities; and even some historians were getting in on the act. The Regius Professor of Modern History at Cambridge, Herbert Butterfield, wrote scholarly articles on youth culture – for example, 'The Discontinuities between the Generations in History: their Effect on the Transmission of Political Experience', first delivered as the Rede Lecture in Cambridge in 1971.[4] Another Cambridge historian, J. H. Plumb, whose main research was on eighteenth-century political history, toured America in the late 1960s and wrote about Hippies.[5] Cambridge was, in fact, brimming with scholars who were intrigued by youth culture. Besides Butterfield and Plumb there was Philip Abrams, a sociologist at Peterhouse who wrote learned articles on the concept of 'generations', which included discussion of youth culture.[6] Professor Denis Brogan, a Professor of Politics at Cambridge and a Fellow of Peterhouse, wrote a regular column in *The Spectator*, in which he frequently ruminated on youth culture. His topics ranged from the Paris students' revolt of May '68 to Cambridge students' lifestyles and 'morals'.[7] Even the austere constitutional historian Professor Geoffrey Elton, who was disturbed by the student protests of the late 1960s, was moved to write letters to *The Times* on the subject and to allude to youth culture in his lectures and books.[8]

Beyond the Ivory Towers of Cambridge and Birmingham during the 1960s youth culture had embedded itself in people's minds, and was projected before the public not only in newspapers but on television. Everyone in Britain who could read or had access to a television set knew about youth culture.[9] To contemporaries, it meant the Beatles, who emerged in 1963 and generated a form of fan worship not seen in Britain before or since.[10] Crowds of teenage girls queued at airport terminals in Britain, and in the United States, to wave to their pop heroes and to scream at them. Stadiums in the United States were so packed with screaming fans that the band could not hear themselves play and, exasperated, they retired from touring altogether in 1966. British Beatle fans were not as noisy as American teenagers, and there was no fanatical response to the Beatles here as there was in the United States, where the Ku Klux Klan started burning their records during an American tour in 1966 when John Lennon told a journalist that the Beatles were bigger than Jesus Christ.[11] Even so, British Beatlemania did generate some disturbing behaviour. At several concert venues they played during 1963 and 1964, it was discovered afterwards that the seats were stained with urine.[12]

Shortly after the Beatles, in 1964, came another manifestation of the 'new' youth culture: the Mod culture. It started in north London suburbs like Stamford Hill and Stoke Newington. But between 1964 and 1967 it was transformed into a national youth cult stretching from Stoke New-ington to Scotland and touching great provincial cities like Manchester, where the Mods wore their hair long to distinguish themselves from the southern Mods on display every week in the teen pop programme *Ready Steady Go!*[13] Arguably, the Mods were a more important cultural phe-nomenon than the Beatles because they generated the first geographically mobile, national youth movement that empowered thousands of youths and young females. In essence, these Mod youths were trying to create new youth communities by the sea, well away from the postwar suburbs their parents had been relocated to after the Blitz. Certainly, the Mods were an organic youth movement that emerged from working-class communi-ties, including ethnic communities (the pioneers were young Jewish boys like Mark Feld, who transformed himself from a cheeky teenage Mod of north London *c*.1960 into the first Glam rock superstar of the 1970s, Marc Bolan).[14] Moreover, it could be argued that the Beatles did not generate a youth culture at all; merely a youth audience of passive teenage (mainly female) fans who became superfluous when the group stopped touring Britain in 1965.[15]

By the late sixties, British youth culture had become synonymous with drug use, promiscuity, and student unrest. In London, the London School of Economics was forced to close for over three weeks in early 1969 when student demonstrators occupied its buildings, and, two years earlier, a porter had died during one confrontation there.[16] There was even a debate in the House of Commons on the 'trouble' at the LSE in 1969, after two of its lecturers had been sacked and following further outbreaks of student discontent.[17] The 'Establishment' were so worried about youth culture they decided to interview one of its leaders in July 1967. The interview was filmed and shown in a peak-time slot one Monday evening. It appeared on ITV's award-winning current affairs programme *World in Action* and the 30-minute interview was with a 23-year-old pop star who, in fact, had been a student at the London School of Economics in the early 1960s. When he left after just two years, one of his tutors told a colleague: 'J . . . came to see me today. He says he's leaving the LSE and wants to join a Rhythm and Blues band. A pity. He's a bright student. Can't see there's any money in that.'[18] But the student in question was a millionaire when he met the new Editor of *The Times*, William Rees-Mogg, two church leaders and a senior politician in July 1967. He flew into the meeting, held on the lawn of a country house in Essex, by helicopter. He was regarded by those who questioned him as a leader of the 'new youth culture' and they wanted to find out whether it was a threat to the stability, and institutions, of British society. His name was Mick Jagger and several million TV viewers watched and listened on that Monday evening in July 1967, as he expounded his views on the new youth culture.[19]

Historians and British Youth Culture

How have historians defined youth culture? It has to be said at the outset that several historians of early twentieth-century Britain have tended to shy away from using the term 'youth culture'; no doubt because it is linked so closely with the decades of affluence and classlessness, the 1950s and 1960s, in scholarly surveys of postwar Britain.[20] Thus, while historians of early twentieth-century Britain have undertaken pioneering research on youth – primarily working-class youth – and have shed light on their labour market behaviour, work cultures, spending behaviour (though not their saving patterns), youth movements, delinquency, smoking habits, gang life and so on,[21] they have not explored how far youth culture transcended class experiences; and how far it represents new ways of living pursued by different categories of youth; students and young workers, for example. Indeed, during the 1920s and 1930s, youth of different social classes in Britain were involved in creative collaborations with each other. These interactions strongly suggest there was a conscious attempt during these years to construct a youth culture well away from the conventional youth arenas of cinemas and dance halls.[22]

The following study, therefore, takes a different tack from existing historical and sociological research on twentieth-century youth culture by identifying and tracing two strands in twentieth-century youth history. Firstly, the book charts the emergence of youth lifestyles in mainstream society that were shaped by material changes in society – the expansion of white-collar work, for example, between the Wars, helped generate female youth lifestyles such as the Flapper.[23] Much later, during the 1960s, the vibrant cultural world of 'Swinging London' generated, though not in the ways conventionally argued, the Mod culture of London and the provinces.[24] Secondly, there is a more subterranean world of youth culture largely hidden from conventional social histories of twentieth-century Britain; namely, the world of middle-class or elite youth, who were often shaping youth culture as a conscious pursuit of 'new ways of living'. This involved extensive travel, cultural contact with youth of other nations and other social classes, and a highly innovative marrying of high culture and folk culture (intellectual discussions were combined with arduous hikes; performances of choral music with folk dance; Morris dances in genteel Cotswold villages with folk dance tours of working-class communities in Northern England).[25] Is it fanciful to draw a distinction between urban youth lifestyles and a broader category of youth activity involving a pursuit of 'new ways of living'?[26] The following study will attempt to draw out the differences between these two manifestations of twentieth-century British youth culture, by surveying a wealth of evidence which does seem to suggest two enduring and meaningful pathways through the bricolage of twentieth-century youth culture. Certainly, it is far too crude to regard all youth experiences as being shaped by class, region, gender, and work. The history of twentieth-century youth culture cannot be conceptualised using such blunt categories without losing a strong sense of the dynamics and vibrancy within youth communities, even in a decade such as the 1920s when class divisions in British society were well defined.[27]

The central aspect of twentieth-century youth culture explored in this survey, therefore, is the creativity underpinning modern British youth cultures.[28] As will be revealed, highly creative student movements have shaped youth culture at certain periods (the 1920s, for example); but youth movements run by adults, such as the Boy Scouts or Boys' Brigade, do not appear in this study as they were targeted at adolescents and one of the central claims of this book is that youth culture is largely shaped by 18–25-year-olds.[29] It is not simply a story of the young controlling and promoting their own 'ways of living'. In certain environments youth culture was held back – in Northern Ireland, for example – by the patriarchal nature of the society and by the ubiquitous religious influences being targeted at the young. But, as Chapter 4 argues, even in traditional societies like early twentieth-century Northern Ireland youth were endeavouring to define and pursue a culture of their own, and, indeed, were hijacking institutions run by adults to pursue their own preoccupations and lifestyles.

Youth culture, this study suggests, transcends class; but age caused fractures within British youth culture at certain periods. The concept of generation is a slippery one. Bryan Wilson wrote of the youth culture of the 1960s as a 'War of the Generations' and this was echoed by politicians and journalists during the decade, some of whom saw youth pop stars such as Mick Jagger as harbingers of a new generational divide in British society.[30] It is also the case, however, that in the universities a generation lasted just three years. Moreover, within the student body there could be quite distinct generations at a given period. The Ex-Service students who entered British universities in 1919 are a case in point. The tensions between these students who had been in the First World War and the students who arrived straight from school in 1919 were significant and are explored in Chapter 2.[31]

The chronology and themes of the book

The following study will establish that the history of youth culture in twentieth-century Britain has a definite beginning around 1920. At this stage, there were youth cultures rather than a youth culture; but those who organised youth clearly had ideas and visions and they have left a significant amount of material for the archival historian to probe. Much of this material will be utilised for the first time in this study.[32] The book is a thematic study concerned with what Arthur Marwick has neatly called 'youth as agent, not as object'.[33] Its protagonists include university students as well as the working-class youths who have received most attention from social historians. The prime focus is on the 18–25 age-group and, moreover, those who were single; but it is not primarily a study of working-class youth; nor of the teenager, though individual chapters cover these subjects.[34] The core of the book probes the individuals, institutions and cults that have shaped the lives of the under 25s in Britain during the period from *c*.1920 down to the late Sixties – a secret world, in many respects, before the Second World War.[35]

Social commentators of the 1950s and 1960s seem to have been oblivious of developments in youth culture, especially in the universities, before the Second World War. By the mid-1950s youth culture meant Elvis Presley and the Teddy Boy and was seen as synonymous with popular music, and delinquency. As John Lennon once observed: 'Before Elvis there was nothing.'[36] But learned academics ought to have known better. Moreover, they only seem to have scratched the surface of the youth culture of their own day. Richard Hoggart, for example (the focus of Chapter 6), wrote about the Teddy Boy in his classic book *The Uses of Literacy* (1957); but in a severely critical way. Hoggart depicted Teddy Boys as mindless yobs who spent all their free time in coffee bars and whose only contribution to society was to tip money into jukeboxes and, occasionally, to wiggle their hips to a song they liked.[37] Hoggart, a pioneering 'cultural studies' scholar, saw youth culture as an alien presence in Britain; an unwelcome aspect of the so-called 'Americanisation' of British society during the 1950s. But this was far from the truth. It had a lineage in Britain stretching back to the 1920s, and the youths he observed in milk bars during the Fifties were far less liberated than he suggested. As they dropped their spending money into the jukeboxes they were probably thinking sombre thoughts. These were the unfortunate youths who were drafted into the armed services at 18 and were sent all over the world to undertake their two years of compulsory military service; a feature of their lives that Hoggart totally ignored.[38] How they coped with this experience and how it shaped their lives subsequently, and indeed how the National Service experience altered Youth Culture, are themes Hoggart never addresses in his celebrated account of working-class life.

Colin MacInnes, an acute writer on youth culture of the late 1950s and 1960s, assumed its history only went back to the early 1950s. He is often cited by cultural studies academics as a pioneer in the study of youth cultures;[39] but he had a limited grasp of the history of youth culture in Britain. He had only moved to England permanently in the late 1940s (he was in his mid-forties, in fact, when his teenager novel *Absolute Beginners* was published in 1959).[40] Although he was born in England in August 1914 (the month the First World War began), he emigrated to Australia with his mother and brother in 1919. His own youth during the 'Roaring Twenties' was spent living in a Melbourne suburb and staying at sheep stations in rural Australia where he and his brother Graham were surrounded by wilderness.[41] MacInnes's insights into late 1950s' London teenagers deserve attention – but he admitted himself that the teenagers in his novel *Absolute Beginners* were fantasy teenagers dreamed up in his mind.[42] He undertook no archival research on British teenage lifestyles of the 1950s.[43] Moreover, Colin MacInnes is an acquired taste. The teenage 'speak' he employs in *Absolute Beginners* grates with some readers. One recent British historian of the Fifties and Sixties, Dominic Sandbrook, who has written two hugely entertaining and comprehensive surveys of the period from 1956 to 1970, finds MacInnes's novel thoroughly unconvincing.[44] It is undeniably derivative, aping the 'beat' novels of the American 1950s – J. D. Salinger's *Catcher in the Rye* (1951) especially. But Sandbrook's judgement on MacInnes as a feeble chronicler of British youth culture is too harsh. He entirely ignores, for example, MacInnes's journalism and it is here, especially in his weekly *New Society* column 'Out of the Way', that the evolution of his thoughts on youth culture and 'the Permissive Society' of the 1960s are to be found rather than in his novels.[45]

Another widely cited but entirely unhistorical source on British youth culture is Mark Abrams; the pioneer market researcher who published two slim pamphlets on teenage consumers in the late 1950s and early 1960s.[46] He tried to measure the economic worth of the teenager for advertisers; but he was not interested in more complex questions such as what teenagers thought – either about politics, the Monarchy, their work, or National Service, for example. He entirely ignored regional patterns of teenage spending and, furthermore, he did not consult historical records on teenage consumerism, but generated his own data in the form of questionnaires and social surveys.[47] His work is widely quoted by cultural studies academics but historians are more sceptical of its superficial findings.[48]

The historian of youth culture, therefore, has a difficult task. The history of youth culture since the 1950s has been written, very largely, by sociologists or literary writers such as Richard Hoggart and Colin MacInnes, whose work is, to say the least, problematic for the historian. Chapter 6, below, focuses on an analysis of Hoggart's writings on British Youth Culture and it reveals that even a perceptive social commentator, and pioneer of the cultural studies approach to youth culture, had a very superficial and unhistorical understanding of the subject. The sociology of youth cultures and youth subcultures is also of limited value to the social historian because, with one or two exceptions, it does not utilise historical evidence, and for this reason it does not feature prominently in this study.[49]

The scope of this work is therefore both ambitious and uncharted. Thus far, in the work of social historians, youth culture is essentially taken to be working-class youth cultures in provincial England, and among the key concepts explored are their lifestyles, gender experiences, and how far class, poverty and affluence have 'shaped' British youth culture.[50] But, as will be revealed, there is far more to be said about the history of British youth culture. It began, as we will discover, as an experiment in new ways of living and among elite youth in the universities, not in the dance halls or cinemas of interwar Manchester or Salford. It will be argued below that youth culture was a very protracted development in Britain. We are dealing with a concept that, initially, took root in the Universities between the Wars, and could exist in the minds of a generation long before it was noticed and measured by market researchers in the 1950s.[51]

There are several key themes that need to be explored in relation to youth culture in Britain; some familiar, others not. So much of the story of youth culture in twentieth-century Britain is still unknown, but not unknowable. Historians have studied the teenage consumer from the 1920s down to the late 1950s;[52] but hardly any detailed research has been conducted on the Flapper Cult of early twentieth-century Britain, a cult that was widely debated in the House of Commons during the Twenties when Baldwin's Conservative Party were pushing through legislation that in 1928 enfranchised 'the Flapper' – young females of 21 to 30 (females over 30 having been given the vote in 1918). Chapter 3 explores the development of the Flapper lifestyle in early twentieth-century Britain. There are sociological surveys of the history of juvenile delinquency in England, most notably Geoffrey Pearson's *Hooligan: A History of Respectable Fears* (1983), Stephen Humphries' *Hooligans or Rebels? An Oral History of Working-Class Childhood and Youth, 1889–1939* (1981), and Stanley Cohen's *Folk Devils and Moral Panics* (1972), on the Mods and Rockers. But far less is known about the history of juvenile and youth delinquency in Northern Ireland, which is discussed in detail below.[53]

Any history of British youth culture must confront the theme of rebellion, whether in the urban gangs of late Victorian and Edwardian Salford or among the Mods and Rockers of the 1960s.[54] But the idea of rebellion in British youth culture is probably less significant over the twentieth century than the idea of community.[55] It is interesting, for example, that many of the Mods and Rockers of the 1960s were products of new London suburbs. In pursuit of new communities of their own, they escaped these concrete postwar suburbs at weekends and on public holidays. So much of the existing work on the Mods stresses their affluence, but this has been greatly exaggerated. The Mods were, in fact, largely excluded from the cultural environment of 'Swinging London', which centred on the discotheques of London's West End.[56]

The idea of community as a central concept shaping youth culture in twentieth-century Britain emerges strongly at several points in this story. It was crucial to the pioneers of youth culture in Cambridge during the 1920s, like Rolf Gardiner. Moreover, the different youth communities of even a single university town such as Cambridge are depicted in the undergraduate novels of the interwar years, which emerged as a new genre of British fiction between the Wars.[57] What mattered to these interwar student cultures were personal relationships, travel and the search for new youth communities.[58] These were powerful dynamics in the lives of British students between the Wars. Moreover, in Northern Ireland the idea of serving communities, especially working-class communities, has underpinned student culture for much of the twentieth century. Even the students of the late 1960s maintained ties with working-class communities throughout their university years and served these communities in their protests at university.[59]

The intellectual currents in youth culture form a significant theme in this study. Youth culture actually developed as a philosophy of life in early twentieth-century Britain.[60] It can be probed through an exploration of the literature its pioneers, university students, generated: articles in student periodicals, poems, their diaries, undergraduate novels and other sources. These are neglected sources and they are of fundamental importance if historians are ever to understand the minds behind the development of youth culture in twentieth-century Britain.[61] Social investigators and sociologists have, at various points over the twentieth century, tried to gauge the attitudes of youth to all sorts of subjects – their work, courtship, sex, politics, the Monarchy, and politicians: from Pearl Jephcott's surveys of girl factory workers in the 1940s to Ferdynand Zweig's interviews with university students in the early 1960s.[62] These works rarely provide insights into the creativity of youth, which has always been the central dynamic in youth culture. One of the central arguments of this work will be that youth culture in Britain has always involved creativity; whether the focus is university students developing their ideas about youth culture in Ivory Towers, or youth pop groups emerging from Northern cities during the late 1950s and early 1960s.[63]

The history of British youth culture over the twentieth century has been significantly shaped by youth of the middle classes; which is a neglected theme in existing histories of youth.[64] They were the prime movers in the development of youth culture in the first half of the twentieth century; or, to be more precise, it was middle-class students in a limited number of universities who were the prime movers. Cambridge was, perhaps, the most significant city for Youth Culture between the Wars in that the pioneers of British youth culture, Rolf Gardiner for example, studied at Cambridge. Moreover, even after the Second World War the city continued to influence British youth culture. It produced the most celebrated psychedelic pop group of the 1960s, Pink Floyd; youth entrepreneurs such as John Dunbar (who married Marianne Faithfull); the student pop star and subsequent media and youth entrepreneur Jonathan King (who had a Number 1 single in Britain in 1967 when he was still an undergraduate at Trinity College, Cambridge); and, in more recent times, Cambridge has produced the author of the definitive book on Punk Rock, Jon Savage, and the brilliant young music and pop-culture journalist Simon Reynolds.[65]

It should not be forgotten that there were far more students from working-class backgrounds in British universities between the Wars than is often recognised; and Oxford and Cambridge educated 50 per cent of the 27,000 Ex-Service students who entered the universities in 1919, a staggering social transformation in the British university system that has never been properly investigated.[66] But it remains the case that the students who pioneered youth culture in Britain were middle-class and upper middle-class youths such as Rolf Gardiner.[67] The history of youth culture, at least in Britain, is therefore not only a story about the juvenile delinquent, the Teddy Boy and the birth of 'the teenager', as is often argued.[68] Youth culture has evolved, by and large, through the efforts of middle-class youth. Indeed, individuals from middle-class and even upper middle-class families have been, over the course of the twentieth century, among the most active youth culture enthusiasts: from the middle-class youths who pioneered youth culture in the early 1920s down to middle-class youth pop stars of the Sixties and beyond, such as Mick Jagger, the Pink Floyd, and the latest pop icons of the early twenty-first century, the public school-educated teen pop group 'Keane', named after the nanny who looked after the group's lead singer Tom Chaplin in childhood.[69]

Finally, it will emerge in this historical survey that, at certain periods over the course of the twentieth century, youth cultures have existed, or were developing, in extremely close proximity to some of the twentieth century's most eminent historians. A. J. P. Taylor was a young Lecturer at Manchester University during the 1930s when the city's youth would have been flooding into dance halls such as the Ritz, just off Oxford Road and close to the University where Taylor worked.[70] Hugh Trevor-Roper was researching his first book, a biography of Archbishop Laud (1940), when the Hitler Youth were at their peak, and his second book, *The Last Days of Hitler*, when a neo-Nazi youth movement had appeared in postwar Germany.[71] J. H. Plumb and Geoffrey Elton were teaching at Cambridge during the student protests of the late 1960s; which, in Cambridge, culminated in the Garden House riot of 1970. It ended in a high-profile, and protracted, court case in which six Cambridge undergraduates were sent to prison for up to two years and two others were sent to borstal.[72] Given, therefore, that youth were involved in important contemporary events, and indeed even generating them, the question arises: why did these eminent British historians not study youth culture and consider whether it had a role in shaping history?

Youth culture was certainly not ignored by contemporaries even as early as the 1930s. The classic example is the 'King and Country' debate held in the Oxford Union in February 1933. The Oxford students who attended that debate voted decisively not to support their King and Country in the event of a European war. It was reported at the time that Hitler paid close attention to the event and to the public outcry in the British national press afterwards. Churchill, at the time a backbench Conservative MP, was so alarmed by the message it sent out to Europe that he refused to visit Oxford University for several years.[73]

Then there was the case of Artur Axmann, the Head of the Hitler Youth, who did not shape History but at least survived to tell it. In April 1945 the young Oxford historian Hugh Trevor-Roper (then only 31) was sent to Germany to piece together the final stages of the War in Berlin. He established that one of the last people summoned to Hitler's Bunker just before he committed suicide, in April 1945, was Artur Axmann, who had replaced Baldur von Schirach as the Head of the Hitler Youth in 1941. Axmann managed to escape from Berlin in April 1945 and when he was eventually arrested, in March 1946, he was found with several other members of a new neo-Nazi youth movement.[74]

These examples of youth involvement in political events, both prior to and after 1945, strongly suggest that the development of youth culture and its impact on British society, and its impact on British universities such as Cambridge University during the 1960s, is a significant theme in Modern British History. Moreover, a comprehensive history of British youth culture needs to deal not just with consumerism and fashion; with youth delinquency and 'class resistance' to bourgeois institutions such as schools and youth movements, and other sociological themes; but also with the individuals who have shaped British youth culture as a cultural movement.[75] The following study places the cultural movements of the young at the core of the history of British youth culture between c.1920 and c.1970 in order to explain a phenomenon – youth culture – that mattered to large numbers of young people over this period.

Edwardian Cults of Youth, c.1900–1914

For a youth culture to exist in any society there needs to be a dynamic. Susan Brigden has suggested that there was a distinct youth culture in early modern England, in the form of young trade apprentices reacting against the Catholic Church.[1] Another imaginative approach to the subject sees the apprentices of seventeenth-century London – in service from their early teens until their mid-twenties – as a distinct group with their own rituals, literature, and values.[2] And, given that half the population in early modern England were under 20, these arguments are not farfetched.[3] Moreover, youth communities existed elsewhere in the seventeenth century – at Harvard College, for example, where a Dutchman visiting in July 1680 encountered a room full of young male students puffing tobacco and speaking Latin.[4] The historian who wants to identify youth cultures thus has at least four centuries to choose from and some innovative scholarship to draw on.

Boy labourers: an Edwardian subculture or embryonic youth culture?

An American historian, Michael J. Childs, has argued that the boy labourers of Edwardian Britain had their own culture.[5] Indeed, some Edwardian commentators made the same claim; Sidney Webb, for example, told a Government inquiry in 1910 that the boy labourer was 'indisciplined … precocious in evil, earning at 17 or 18 more wages than suffice to keep him, independent of home control and yet unsteadied by a man's responsibilities'.[6] In the same vein, numerous critics of Edwardian boy labour wrote books, pamphlets and countless articles on how depraved boy labourers were – youth leaders like Charles Russell; clergymen such as Reverend Spencer J. Gibb; the headmaster of Manchester Grammar School, J. L. Paton, and polemical journalists like E. J. Urwick and Arnold Freeman.[7] Few of these boy labour critics had any involvement with working-class youth. Russell had set up a Lads' Club in Manchester in the 1890s, but by the Edwardian period he was the Chief Inspector of Reformatory and Industrial Schools at the Home Office in London.[8] Not a single boy labour critic was an employer and only Freeman bothered to talk to city youths to discover their interests; whether they were interested in politics; what they read; what they thought and what they did outside work.[9]

The lives of Edwardian boy labourers, to judge from Freeman's detailed case-study of Birmingham boy metalworkers, were highly regimented, a little dreary, certainly not affluent and not irresponsible either. Freeman persuaded a number of 17-year-olds to keep diaries for a week during 1914 and they are very informative. They all rose for work, whether they were apprentices or labourers, between 6 a.m. and 7 a.m. and some had started work by 7 a.m. 'I got up at 6.15 and went to work at 6.50', one unskilled youth wrote in his diary.[10] 'I do hinge making and grinding on Emery wheel. It requires no intelligence it can be picked up in a few minutes. Not so hard but very monot.' He worked until 8 p.m. during the week and a half-day on Saturdays.[11] A boy apprentice in a silversmith's workshop began at 9 a.m. and worked until 7 p.m. each weekday and worked a half-day on Saturdays. Another, who worked for a furniture manufacturer, stated proudly that he began work at 'ten minutes to eight' and worked until 8 p.m. normally – evidently loving making wire handles for pans and even sweeping up: 'FRIDAY – I done about an hour's wire-cutting and then went to clean the factory yard of course it took me about an hour and a half. I then went on with my own work.'[12] All of these youths were thoughtful and, despite only receiving full-time education to age 14, they read newspapers and followed current affairs.

On Tuesday evenings the young wire-cutter read the *Birmingham Daily Mail* and during the week in question he had read about Captain Scott's expedition to the South Pole. He wrote in his diary: 'It was stated that Scott who was the leader and his band of explorers reached the Pole but it was on their return Journey that they Perished.' He was also following the Women's Suffrage debate and on the Friday he recorded in his diary: 'Went home at 8 o'clock. After supper I had a wash and began to read the *Mail*. One of the chief things I took interest (in) was a Suffrage incident which occurred in the House of Commons while Mr. Mills was speaking a man in the Strangers [*sic*] gallery shouted: "I protest against your brutal treatment to women" the man was seized by private detectives and carried out.'[13] The entry ends there – poignantly. But we have learned something about this boy's character and interests from his random jottings. He was a punctual and diligent worker. He was thoughtful, deferential, liked stories of heroism and was probably a supporter of women's suffrage. (He would hardly have bothered to record the debate in his diary if he was indifferent to it.)

The music halls and cinemas hardly feature in the Birmingham boy labourer's week. The boy wire-cutter cited his weekly budget and it reveals that he made no visits to either a cinema or a music hall; his only two outings being to a football match (Birmingham v. Preston North End) and a coffee house. His wages were 10s 2d and after subscriptions were deducted he 'Took home' only 7s.[14] The phrase suggests that he gave his parents his wage packet. He received very little of this for his own use (less than 2s) and his total weekly expenditure comprised: a football match (6d), a coffee house visit (4d), fruit (4d), and a football sweep (4d).[15] The boy apprentice who supplied details of his weekly expenditure was even worse off than the boy wire-cutter. He earned just half the boy labourer's wage – 5s. He had just 1s for pocket money and this went on 'fares' (4d), cigarettes (2d) and two visits to cinemas (6d). He also contributed a ½d to a collection – coyly omitting to mention it in his weekly budget.[16]

Freeman did a great disservice to these diligent and creative youths (one played a banjo, for example) when he discussed their ideas. He was himself an MA, a BLitt and a Fellow of the Royal Historical Society[17] and seems to have enjoyed embarrassing the Birmingham youths he spoke to by posing difficult questions about the role of the House of Lords in government legislation and Mr Bonar Law's status. He even expected them to know that Sir Oliver Lodge was 'the distinguished Chancellor of Birmingham University'.[18] But they were not the ignoramuses he portrayed them as. One talked to him at length about politics and told him Parliament was: 'A kind of place where they have Acts made out to stop little lads smoking.'[19] He was thus well aware of the Children Act of 1908 and he also knew how legislation proceeded through Parliament – or just about: ' 'Ouse of Lords first, then the 'Ouse of Commons, and then the King signs 'is name, and it's an Act.'[20] They knew that Edison had developed the cinema and the gramophone; they all knew what votes for women 'meant' and they had all heard of Lloyd-George and Asquith (though one only hesitantly suggested that the latter was 'an M.P').[21] When he asked them about Tennyson and Dickens they were not always sure. One was 'ignorant of the names of Tennyson and Dickens, Columbus, Edison, and Gladstone' and he thought Shakespeare was 'the head of an army' – but he was an unusual case. He had been educated in a Catholic church school and had then immediately joined the army.[22] The point Freeman was trying to emphasise was that these poorly-informed youths would be voting in four years' time and most would also be heads of households. He did not blame them for their slippery grasp of political facts and thought the education provision in Britain was at fault.

When Freeman turned to the subjects that interested the boy labourers of Birmingham he discovered they had creative interests and were not just passive consumers of music halls. One unskilled lad who had had ten jobs in three years told Freeman he did not visit the music hall, or attend football matches and only occasionally visited cinemas. He preferred reading about the Arabian Nights.[23] Another did visit the cinema to see 'Travel Pictures' mainly. He visited the music halls and liked the dancing and singing; he liked football and he was reading a book about the Dreadnought.[24] Another read sheet music and played the banjo. He recorded in his diary: 'SATURDAY – Had to work hard this morning to finish a contract ordor [*sic*]. Had dinner at 1 p.m. Read the *Birmingham Daily Post* till 2.30 then rote to London for a list of Banjo music....' He played his banjo most evenings and even in his lunch hour.[25] Even the cinema was a creative experience for other youths. One learned about Hell there. He told Freeman 'there are red-hot stones raining down' and 'men walking about with a little pair of knicks on and no shirt nor nothing; they have to row in boats and men prod them on; and then they get poked in holes upside-down with just their ankles showing'.[26] Freeman also learned that even those who went to the music halls were discerning youths. The young banjo player told him of one visit: 'The top of the bill was George Mozart in his thumb-nail sketches, I think he was very good, as I take great interest in acting. Most of his sketches were different characters on the race course.'[27] Freeman thought music halls were harmful to boy labourers; supplying them, he believed, with their 'ideas about life'[28] – presumably a euphemism for sex. But the only evidence these boy labourers provided on the salaciousness of music halls was one boy's reference in his diary to his favourite song: 'Everybody's Doin It', Irving Berlin's Ragtime song, which the boy labourer sang at work.[29]

The proposition Freeman was exploring in Birmingham in 1914 was that boy labourers became poorer as they entered their late teens and early twenties.[30] Numerous authorities on boy labour had suggested before Government committees, and in print, that occupations that attracted large numbers of juveniles, such as van boy work and messenger work, were classic 'blind-alley' occupations that dispensed with juveniles en masse at 18.[31] The important question was: what happened to youths in the years between 18 and 22? In essence, Freeman wanted to learn whether they formed a distinct youth culture – too old and expensive for juvenile occupations and unable to secure employment as adult workers. Were there, as he put it, 'vast armies of young men loafing at corners or holding unemployed demonstrations about the streets'?[32]

In Birmingham, the reverse was the case. There were not enough juveniles and youths to fill the vacancies advertised at the Juvenile Employment Exchanges. In 1911–12, the Birmingham Juvenile Employment Exchange advertised 6271 vacancies for 14- to 17-year-olds and only managed to fill 3965.[33] In other large industrial cities – London, Glasgow and Manchester, for example – there was an 'insatiable' demand for juveniles and youths.[34] But in the case of youths between 18 and 22 this could not be demonstrated statistically as they were treated as adult workers. Cyril Jackson had undertaken his own survey of the industrial careers of a miscellaneous collection of 135 Birmingham juveniles and youths. He found that in various employments the percentage of 20-year-olds was about the same as the percentage of 14-year-olds. In low-skilled factory jobs, 20-year-olds comprised 19.4 per cent of the workforce and 14-year-olds 20 per cent; in general labouring jobs, 20-year-olds comprised 23.8 per cent of the labour force and 14-year-olds 23 per cent. In skilled trades there were significantly more 20-year-olds (28.4 per cent of the workforce) than 14-year-olds (8.1 per cent). In errand boy work, 14-year-olds comprised 30.4 per cent of errand boys in Birmingham but there were no errand boys of 20. Jackson assumed that the errand boys became the skilled workers of 20. Freeman accepted this conclusion with the words 'this is well known to be true'.[35] The point, however, seemed to be that many former errand boys – comprising about half of all juvenile workers in Birmingham – were forced to change jobs between 18 and 22 and they were under greater pressure than workers under 18 to find secure employment.

Freeman knew there was far more competition in the adult labour market from casual workers; and from youths who had migrated from other towns and cities to Birmingham. And there was evidence that they did not all find jobs. 'The proof lies in the records of the young men who apply to the Distress Committee and the Recruiting Sergeant.'[36] He did not follow this up in depth, but he thought that for every 95 vacancies in industry in Birmingham in 1914 there were 100 applicants.[37] He knew from Jackson's own survey that there were 'numbers of youths' earning only boy's wages (referred to in Birmingham as 'kid's wages') and unable to secure adult wages. Moreover, his own survey of 74 boy labourers randomly chosen from the Birmingham Juvenile Employment Exchange's register had revealed that 21 were likely to become 'unemployable'.[38]

Freeman's survey of boy labour in Birmingham on the eve of the First World War illustrates why there was no youth culture among urban youths – at any rate in that city. The boy labourers of Birmingham worked in almost exclusively male workshops and in their diaries they never refer to girls.[39] Only occasionally did they mention other boys at their workplace; but, invariably, they visited the music halls and cinemas alone.[40] They had creative interests but with 12-hour working days and a limited budget they were too busy and too poor for youth culture. All the boy labourers in Freeman's survey walked to work, but they all lived within ten minutes of their work and they returned to their homes for their lunch. Psychologically, they were like schoolchildren. One gave an account of his lunch hour thus: 'TUESDAY – Dinner time 1 till 2. I have ten minutes walk home, have a wash, twenty minutes to have my dinner, a talk (with) my mother . . . a tune on the Banjo, till ten minutes to two and then back to work.'[41] Another wrote: 'MONDAY – At about ten minutes to one I went . . . home. I got there about five minutes after one when I got home I found my dinner waiting for me after dinner I went and played football until 1.50 and then went to work.'[42]

Freeman had no interest in the subject of youth culture, but he did want to liberate boy labourers from industrial employment and working-class culture. He had a programme for doing this. First, all boys should be in full-time education until they were 15. Second, they should be prohibited from wage-earning until 15. Third, he favoured a drastic reduction in the working week of 15- to 18-year-olds – to a maximum of thirty hours. Fourth, he advocated Continuation Classes for juveniles 'up to the dawn of manhood' (18?). The subjects, he thought, should be military and physical training; gardening; sex education; public speaking; letter writing; reading (nurturing an interest in good novels, biographies, and history) and citizenship training.[43] His ideas were greatly influenced by what the War Minister Lord Haldane was advocating. He wanted urban youths to undertake part-time education courses to pursue their dreams. He told a Workers' Education Association meeting in April 1913 that education made youths 'citizens of the highest type ... and shows them in the common life of the city something that causes them to put forward the utmost endeavour that is in them'.[44] Freeman thought that 'Continuation Classes' would teach urban youths about politics, cure their ignorance and, looking beyond the three years they would spend in Continuation Classes, he recommended a test on political questions, that youths could sit before they were given the vote.[45]

The boy labourers of pre-World War One Birmingham led lives not radically different from those of London apprentices in the sixteenth century. Both groups were literate, curious and driven by a strong desire to improve their economic prospects.[46] In fact, the pursuit of status was as important to some boy labourers as to apprentices and one of the 'unskilled' boy labourers in Freeman's study was attending a technical school three evenings a week to improve his work skills.[47] In both cases adults controlled their lives. True, boy labourers were not prevented from marrying and were not sent to the stake for holding heretical views about religion. But they were pushed into the labour market to sink or swim at 14; they were required by law to work at least 55 hours a week (including Saturdays); they were likely to be searching for new employment in their late teens; they were unlikely to be entitled to any unemployment benefits (the scheme introduced in 1911 only included shipbuilding and engineering trades) and they could not vote until they reached 21. The London apprentices who faced similar dire economic prospects rebelled in the 1530s and '40s – against their employers; migrant workers; the government that banned May Day amusements, and religious leaders.[48] But the boy labourers of Edwardian Birmingham seem to have been remarkably quiescent down to the outbreak of the First World War. Why?

The obvious answer is that they continued to live with their families until they married, whereas apprentices in early modern London left their families in their early teens.[49] Boy wage-earners, whether labourers or apprentices, continued to live with their parents well beyond 1914 and in fact down to the 1950s when compulsory National Service forced them to leave not only their families but their home towns and cities and in many cases Britain.[50] Youth culture could never develop properly in circumstances where youths from different regions never met each other and where they were still tied emotionally and physically to their parents. In early modern London most apprentices were living independently of their parents and were migrants. They established their own communities after they arrived.[51] In Edwardian Britain young workers invariably worked in the towns and cities where they were born. In Cambridge, for example, 437 boys left the city's elementary schools between July 1908 and July 1910. They were all still in the city in October 1910.[52] Moreover, the local authority was endeavouring to keep them there by helping them to find work. A Juvenile Registry, an employment exchange for the under-17s, had been established 'to assist boys and girls under the age of 17 in finding suitable work, give information about evening classes, and in various ways ... to assist them in starting well on their careers'.[53]

Cambridge was not an ideal environment for young people with ambitions and aspirations looking for work at 14. There were no big employers (apart from the university) and restricted job choices for apprentices. In some ways, the University was responsible for young workers being forced to take errand boy work at 14 and to delay apprenticeships. Whereas, in Oldham, people carried their own parcels and, consequently, only 1 per cent of boy workers in Oldham were errand boys or van boys; in Cambridge no one carried their own parcels and two-thirds of boys who left school at 14 were employed as errand boys.[54] Few were able to find apprenticeships for at least two years after leaving school. Some gave up trying: 'ambition is inclined to slip away in the simple, free life spent largely in the streets'. But those who were not able to secure an apprenticeship in Cambridge were not resentful. 'These young men', one contemporary investigator concluded, 'rarely bear a grudge to anyone – to their parents for not seeing that they received a training, or to the commercial conditions of which they have been the victims. They merely have a vague feeling that they have been unlucky'.[55] They also stayed in Cambridge.

The middle classes and Edwardian youth

In 1880 a London doctor, J. Mortimer-Granville, whose previous books had included *Sleep and Sleeplessness*, *The Secret of a Clear Head*, and *The Care and Cure of the Insane*, published a book entitled *Youth. Its Care and Culture: An Outline of Principles for Parents and Guardians.*[56] It cost 2s 6d and was obviously aimed at middle-class parents because its author assumed that those who read it would employ servants. 'Parents', he wrote, 'do not adequately realise the extent or permanency of the mischief done by leaving the management of their children to coarse, and, as it often happens, lascivious servants.'[57] He wasted no time in telling them. The 'girl-youth' needed to be watched at all times, even during the night, since:

> paroxysmal disturbances – ... fits, faintings, outbursts of temper, moodiness, and the nocturnal teethgrindings, nightmares, and sleep-walking phenomena – incidental to this period of life, are the effects of disorderly activity in the organism ...[58]

He thought that girls and boys in their teens ought to be kept at home during their leisure hours until they married, and a system of 'girl management' should be introduced into the home. This consisted of simple food at regular times, some exercise, no 'undue excitement', some study and hardly anything that would make them emotional. He believed that a teenage girl's main emotional engagement was with books, rather than boys, and romantic novels really upset them. 'Books of fiction abounding in word pictures of love-making, and describing or portraying the passions under a flimsy disguise, are the bane of female youth,' he reported.[59] This is an interesting observation. He assumed that middle-class girls in their teens, in the capital city, did not visit the theatre frequently and did not have a culture of their own outside the home. Was this the case?

He also thought that male youths in middle-class families were largely confined to their homes in the evenings; keeping their mothers company while their fathers were 'in the counting-house', at a club, or 'in a box at opera or play [which] takes the father of a family frequently from home in the evening'.[60] The boy, if he was fortunate, might have access to a billiard table. 'No private house in which a large family is resident ought to be without its billiard room and full-size table', he advised; and he also recommended 'a little tobacco' for 'elderly youths' and some alcohol to steady their hands while playing billiards. 'I have not a word to say against a little tobacco for elderly youths. The fragrant weed has done nothing to cause it to be tabooed in society, nor is there anything to be urged against stimulants ...'[61]

In essence, then, youth culture was first identified with middle-class families in Britain and it was associated with Darwinian ideas. Mortimer-Granville even referred to youths in his study as 'organisms' that, as it were, needed to be protected, reared properly and controlled – almost like plants.[62] Mortimer-Granville's analysis of youth culture was, therefore, very much a study of youth as object.

The middle-classes of late Victorian and Edwardian London were not only interested in their own young; in 1887, Katherine Price Hughes, and her husband, a Protestant clergyman, opened a club for factory girls in West London, off the Tottenham Court Road. The girls it attracted led difficult lives. They left school at 12. They earned between 7s and 8s a week in the clothing trades and could not afford to pay 8s a week for a single room in the district. So they continued living with their parents until they married. According to Emmeline Pethick-Lawrence, the Edwardian suffragette who worked at the club before the First World War, the girls had no disposable incomes, even for clothes and shoes. 'They never had new clothes or new boots', she wrote in her autobiography: 'They wore the bedraggled garments which in those days were the badge of the workers.'[63] She described the girls at the West London Mission as 'those half-starved and over-worked young people'. Many of the girls had never seen the sea or the countryside. When the club took a party into the country in 1892 some of the girls were confused when they heard a cuckoo and started looking in the trees for a cuckoo clock. One girl saw a skylark and reported: 'Here's a bis that's got a fit! It can't go up and it can't come down!' Cows terrified them. When two cows were seen 'whispering together' the girls thought they were going to be attacked.[64]

Outside the club their favourite amusement was funerals. Two of the club's members watched a funeral whilst on a Sunday School trip to Brighton and were asked to recall the experience one evening in the club. One reported:

> No sooner had we come out of the station than we saw a lovely funeral. Bella and me, we followed the funeral and we cried and cried. I cried a lot, but Bella cried more than me. Then we went and sat on the beach, and presently along comes a man wot had buried his uncle in the morning. He comes up to us and begins to talk and he says to Bella: 'You're a good girl', he says, 'you cried more for me uncle than I did myself. Here's a shilling for you!' Then we spent the shilling in donkey rides and ginger pop.[65]

The girls at the West London Mission were fascinated by macabre murders. They spent one evening discussing the Crippen murders and, on another evening, they heard several accounts of fathers beating their wives. One girl told her club leader she would never marry after what she had seen of it. She confessed: 'I ain't going to be married. I know too much about it. Before you're married, you can 'ave this and 'ave that, but afterwards if you don't belong to 'im body and soul, you gets it on the 'ead.'[66] Another subject on these girls' minds was serious illness. Only one member, however, contracted a serious illness – tuberculosis – before 1914 and after a three-month period convalescing in the country (which the club paid for) she recovered.[67]

But the truly fascinating story in the West London Mission's work with factory girls was its role promoting folk music. This began in 1905 when Mary Neal, one of the club's leaders who knew Cecil Sharp, invited a group of Morris dancers from Oxford to the club to teach the factory girls their dances. Neal discovered that the two old men who turned up at the club only knew one word to describe the girls' movements – 'perpendicular'. Neal recalled: 'this word had to do duty many times during the evening. We were told we must "dance perpendicular to one another", "perpendicular to the music", and, finally, that we had got the dance "quite perpendicular". But the event was a great success.'[68] Cecil Sharp, who was there, remembered:

> The first dance that was set before the Londoners... was Bean-setting. It represents the setting of the seed in spring-time. Of course, the music, its lilt and the steps that their [the Morris dancers'] forefathers had footed to in the olden time, were as little known to these, the London born, as the tongue and ceremonial of old Peru.... Within half-an-hour of the coming of these Morris men we saw the Bean-setting – its thumping and clashing of staves, its intricate figures and steps hitherto unknown – in full swing upon a London floor. And ... we saw it perfect in execution to the least particular. It was even so with the other dances...[69]

After two days, the girls knew four dances and soon they were giving public performances. They performed at a Settlement in London in 1905 and from 1906 they began touring the provinces; travelling as far north as Yorkshire and south to Sussex.[70] By 1909, they were giving dance classes in every county of England – in villages, towns, schools, clubs and factories. The Morris dancing craze they started resulted in legislation. In 1909 the President of the Board of Education, Sir George Newman, included Morris dancing as a subject in the physical training programme he recommended for elementary schools.[71]

The factory girls who performed these dances were empowered by the experience. One girl from the West London Mission was able to pursue her dance career in the United States. Those who became dance teachers were invited to country houses to perform and one taught Mrs Herbert Gladstone. This girl wrote back to her club leader in 1912:

> I am staying at Lady Muriel Paget's house this week and am having a lovely time. In the afternoon I teach the children games, and in the morning I have a class of grown-ups, amongst others Mrs. Herbert Gladstone, to whom I am teaching dances and songs. I have my meals with Lady Muriel in the dining-room.... There are three men to wait at table – I do feel swagger. I have my breakfast in bed.[72]

We do not learn from the existing accounts of the West London Mission's work exactly how many factory girls were able to develop careers as teachers. Mrs Pethick-Lawrence's account mentions only three cases of girls who travelled outside London to perform and teach; but many more taught elementary school teachers the Morris in London and performed regularly in large venues such as the Queen's Hall.[73] Moreover, the craze undoubtedly made an impact nationally. The satirical magazine *Punch* carried a full-page advertisement showing boys and girls Morris dancing along a village street, led by Mr Punch playing a pipe and holding a drum.[74] Mary Neal herself was given national recognition for her Morris dancing work with the factory girls of West London when she was made a Commander of the British Empire (CBE) in Coronation year, 1938.[75]

The Morris or folk dance craze survived into the interwar years[76] – and it was especially popular in working girls' clubs. The Federation of Working Girls' Clubs, which oversaw numerous clubs all over London – in East London, Fulham, Hanover Square (central London), Hackney, Stepney, and Paddington – strongly recommended Morris dancing in a *Handbook* produced in 1921. They argued that it was cheap (girls who performed Morris dances only needed sun bonnets and pinafore dresses). There were, in fact, folk dance classes now being run at several venues in London. A textbook had even been produced which girls were encouraged to purchase from the English Folk Dance Association.[77] But by the early 1920s the trips to country houses seem to have ceased. There was no mention of these in the official literature on working girls' clubs.[78] In 1922, however, a young Cambridge undergraduate – who will be introduced later in this study – took up the Morris and toured Europe with his student Morris and country dancers, males and females; reaching an international audience that Cecil Sharp (who died in 1924) and Mary Neal, who became friendly with the young enthusiast, never envisaged.[79]

Thus in obscure publications – biographies, periodicals, working girls' clubs literature – held in the British Library we can identify working girls' musical cultures that long predate the Spice Girls. But the Edwardian working girls of West London were not the forerunners of the Spice Girls. Their leisure was being shaped by adults and their performances were usually for adults. Moreover, their specialism of Morris dancing was hardly youth music; the two dancers from Oxfordshire who taught them the dances were in their sixties and Mary Neal had met them in a village pub when she arranged for them to visit the girls in London. Nonetheless, the fact that some of the working girls of the West London Mission became professional dance teachers suggests that working-class girls were empowered by music in this earlier period, and this was the case despite their inauspicious beginnings in families experiencing poverty. More research on the Edwardian and interwar folk dance craze among working-class girls would no doubt uncover further examples of young females transcending lives 'shaped' by family poverty. Certainly the evidence available in official literature does suggest that folk dance had tapped a national youth audience by the early 1920s, and it is highly likely that more examples of female youth empowerment would be uncovered by further research.

The cult of Youth in Edwardian Cambridge: Rupert Brooke

Cambridge's popular image is of a city that for centuries has been culturally conservative. It was a Royalist city in the English Civil War of the seventeenth century. It has produced over 30 Nobel Prize Winners in the twentieth century. Some of its most senior academics are appointed directly by the Queen – the Master of Trinity College, for example; the Master of Churchill College, a newer college set up in the 1960s; and the Regius Professor of Modern History is appointed by the Monarch in consultation with the British Prime Minister. In essence, then, any historian of cultural change has to confront the obvious links that Cambridge has had historically with the British Establishment. The present Archbishop of Canterbury, Rowan Williams, is even a product of Cambridge. He studied at Christ's College. In effect, therefore, at the heart of Cambridge culture over the last one hundred years since *c*.1900 lie the Monarchy, the Church, the historic colleges (the oldest, Peterhouse, being nearly 800 years old) and college events and rituals such as May Balls and High Tables that have not changed for a very long time.[80]

If we consider, briefly, Cambridge's popular media image over the last thirty years or so, we think of the annual Carol Service held at King's College on Christmas Eve, which is shown on the BBC every Christmas Eve. There is the annual Boat Race in London, which has been held most years since 1829. In the press, the most frequent images of Cambridge are of May Balls held every year; not in May, in fact, but by custom in June. A front-page photograph that appeared in the *Daily Telegraph* in June 2006 showed three sozzled female students making their way along a cobbled street in the city centre at around 6 a.m.[81] Postcards of Cambridge invariably show its magnificent colleges either bathed in sunshine or lightly sprinkled with snow; or images of honey-coloured stone or immaculate lawns.

Superficially, it seems highly implausible that Cambridge has produced significant youth cultures over the last century; but, as it turns out, its ancient university has played a major role in shaping British youth culture over the course of the twentieth century. In the Edwardian period Cambridge was the home of an embryonic youth community led by one of its undergraduates – the poet Rupert Brooke. Members of this embryonic youth culture began to advocate, in print and in their behaviour, new lifestyles that set them apart from their contemporaries.[82]

Before we examine the ideas and influence of Rupert Brooke, however, it is first necessary to outline the cultural environment of Cambridge in the period *c*.1900–1914. First of all, Cambridge culture of these years was shaped by an 'intellectual aristocracy' of a few families. These families were upper middle-class families rather than upper-class families (few owned large amounts of land); but, it seems, these families had a virtual stranglehold on the colleges of Cambridge and on the ideas that circulated in these colleges. In essence, then, it was families, very distinguished intellectual families, rather than cultural institutions such as music halls, museums and art galleries, that were the source of cultural ideas in late Victorian and Edwardian Cambridge.[83]

This 'intellectual aristocracy' had only emerged in Cambridge since the 1880s. This 'new class' in late Victorian Cambridge was made possible by the liberalisation of the laws governing College Fellowships. Before the 1880s, all Cambridge dons had to resign their Fellowships when they married. But, during the 1880s, this law was abolished and it meant that Cambridge dons who did marry could now continue to live and work in Cambridge. It was in the 1880s that intermarriage between academic families began to increase markedly and brought about the emergence of a 'new class' in Britain – the 'intellectual aristocracy' in Noel Annan's celebrated phrase.[84] If we look at the family tree of one of these families, the Trevelyans, we can see what happened. At the heart of the Trevelyan family tree is Professor G. M. Trevelyan. He became Regius Professor of Modern History at Cambridge in 1927 and Master of Trinity College in 1940. During his long career in Cambridge – he began as a student at Trinity in 1893 and was Master of Trinity until 1951 – Trevelyan became the most widely read historian in the English language. The house he lived in is still standing on the corner of West Road, close to the History Faculty.

What is evident in the family tree of the Trevelyans is that its members had roots across generations not only in Cambridge, but in politics, the arts and in the public schools. Dr Thomas Arnold, for example, the Headmaster of Rugby School in the Victorian period, was a distant relation of G. M. Trevelyan's wife Janet Penrose Ward. Moreover, G. M. Trevelyan's brother, Charles Trevelyan, was a politician and Labour Minister for Education in the 1920s. There were also novelists in the family. G. M. Trevelyan's brother-in-law was the novelist Aldous Huxley, who was a student at Cambridge. If we move to the next generation after G. M. Trevelyan, we see that his son became a Fellow of King's College Cambridge and his nephew was Julian Trevelyan, the painter who married into the Darwin family.[85]

So, from this one example, we can see that ties of kinship drew together families who were involved in politics, the universities and the arts, and members of these families – G. M. Trevelyan being a good example – became important cultural figures through their writings and other activities. G. M. Trevelyan, besides being the most popular historian of his generation, was also active in setting up the National Trust. He was President of the Historical Association from 1947 and he was even elected High Steward of the Borough of Cambridge in 1946.[86]

G. M. Trevelyan is a quintessential Cambridge figure who rose within the political and social Establishment. Rupert Brooke's cultural path was somewhat different. Let us now consider Brooke's time in Cambridge before the First World War. Rupert Brooke was born on 3 August 1887 and, in some ways, he was born into the intellectual aristocracy of middle-class families we have just identified; even though his mother came from Scotland. Brooke's father, William Parker Brooke, was the son of a clergyman and had studied Classics at King's College, Cambridge, where he sent his son Rupert in 1906. Indeed, not only was Rupert sent to the same Cambridge college as his father; he read the same subject. At the time he entered King's College, Cambridge, in 1906, Rupert Brooke's uncle, Alan Brooke, was the Dean of the College. His father was a teacher at Rugby School, one of Britain's major public schools, where Rupert Brooke was a pupil; and where his father had taught Classics since 1880. This places Brooke firmly in the late Victorian and Edwardian upper middle-class. But the college he entered in 1906 had undergone quite radical changes since the late nineteenth century. For much of its history, down to 1906, King's College, Cambridge, had drawn its students exclusively from one public school-Eton. The formal links between the two institutions still lived on through dons who taught there in Rupert Brooke's time. A standard career path for a King's student in the late nineteenth century would be to have been to Eton; studied at King's; become a Fellow of the College; and then to have returned to Eton as a school-teacher. One of the King's dons during Rupert Brooke's time was Oscar Browning. He had diverged from the normal career path from Eton to King's and back to Eton by ending up back at King's. Why? He had been a teacher at Eton after studying at King's, but had then been dismissed from his job for gross misconduct. He had conducted affairs with his boy students. When Rupert Brooke arrived at King's College he found that his rooms were just across a corridor from Oscar Browning's.[87]

King's College Cambridge had a reputation for being a liberal college in the early twentieth century, and still does have this reputation. There was undoubtedly an insipient homosexual culture at the college during Brooke's time and into the 1920s. We know this from a visit D. H. Lawrence made to King's in 1915 when he was horrified to discover that Fellows he encountered there, such as the Bursar J. M. Keynes, openly enjoyed homosexual friendships with each other.[88] But what is most notable about Rupert Brooke's period at King's between 1906 and 1914 is that he pioneered a new cultural lifestyle within Cambridge, which one of his contemporaries, Virginia Woolf, christened 'Neo-Pagan'. What did it involve and where did this culture come from?

Rupert Brooke became a Neo-Pagan in the summer of 1908 and he announced his transformation in a letter to a friend. He wrote that he was 'becoming a wild rough elementalist'.[89] What did this mean? Essentially, it meant going back to nature; to a primitive state. For Rupert Brooke, it meant spending his vacations going camping and on reading parties to Cornwall and other rural environments. It was a liberating culture in that it was undertaken by male and female students together without chaperones (an essential requirement in Cambridge for meetings between the sexes). It therefore made possible friendships that were hard to establish in the male environment of the Cambridge colleges. It could be argued that the Neo-Pagans were a sort of 'New Age' alternative to the Cambridge Apostles. The latter were an elite intellectual society in Cambridge, exclusively for male students and male Fellows and restricted by custom to only 12 active members at any one time.[90] Brooke is a fascinating countercultural figure because he was both a member of the Apostles (he was elected into the Society in January 1908) and a Neo-Pagan. It meant that he moved freely between two Cambridge cultural worlds – an elite male intellectual society which had weekly debates on Philosophical subjects, where members read out a paper, always referred to each other as 'brothers' and held an annual dinner in London for members and former members; and, secondly, he belonged to a circle of friends who were not all students at Cambridge and who, in their own words, were undertaking an experiment in new ways of living.[91]

We can gain a flavour of the Neo-Pagan camps Rupert Brooke participated in from the photographs its members took. The impression they leave is that Brooke's circle (the female members at any rate) modelled themselves on peasants or gypsies. They wore gypsy headscarves or Pagan robes like Roman women. On certain occasions, they wore nothing at all.[92] The males looked more genteel. Rupert Brooke wore cricket pullovers, and in one photograph was even wearing a tie. But, regardless of how they dressed, the purpose of the Neo-Pagan camps was to lead the Simple Life. The two sexes cooked together and they slept in tents on hard ground.

What inspired this cult of back-to-the-land or Neo-Paganism in Edwardian Cambridge? This is an interesting and intriguing question. It is clear that the cult had a mentor: a man called Edward Carpenter who was 80 years old by the time Rupert Brooke took up the Neo-Pagan life. Carpenter had written about his philosophy in a book published in 1906 and entitled *Civilisation: its Cause and Cure*. Put simply, Carpenter's creed can be summed up in three words: nudity, sunbathing and sandals. Who was Edward Carpenter?

Edward Carpenter had been a Fellow of Trinity Hall, Cambridge, in the 1860s. In 1880, before Rupert Brooke was even born, he resigned his Fellowship and decided to make contact with working-class communities in the Midlands and later in the North of England (Sheffield). He became an extra-mural lecturer in the Midlands for seven years. He became a vegetarian. He undertook manual work and, finally, he went to live in a rural community near Sheffield; in a village called Totley. He lived there with a scythe-maker called Albert Fearnehough in a *ménage à trois*. Fearnehough had a wife and two children; but it seems that he also enjoyed a homosexual relationship with Carpenter. In 1883 Carpenter started a new community at Millthorpe in Derbyshire. He supported himself by growing vegetables and by writing. He wore home-made leather sandals as an alternative to shoes, which he called 'leather coffins'. He sunbathed and swam, nude, in the river at the end of his garden. He also wrote books denouncing urban life and the industrial revolution and he entertained many visitors. In fact, Millthorpe became a colony for young men still at Cambridge to visit and Carpenter became a celebrity for having bravely resigned his Fellowship. His visitors included two young Cambridge students who were dons at King's when Rupert Brooke was a student there: Goldsworthy Lowes Dickinson and the novelist E. M. Forster. Carpenter inspired others to establish progressive communities of their own. One school teacher who stayed at Millthorpe was Cecil Reddie. He went on to found a progressive boys' school called Abbotsholme. He did so partly with money provided by Edward Carpenter.[93]

It is unclear how Rupert Brooke became interested in Neo-Paganism. What is clear, however, is that he never used the term. It was first used by Virginia Woolf, in 1911, whom he did know and who attended camps with Brooke. So, Brooke was never consciously promoting the cult of Neo-Paganism. Also, he never met Edward Carpenter, who had given lectures on Neo-Paganism, though Brooke had presumably read Carpenter's books outlining the philosophy. What seems to have happened is that female members of Rupert Brooke's circle of friends spread the idea. Among these were four sisters called the Oliviers, whose cousin was Laurence Olivier. These girls had received all their education at home rather than at one of the new progressive schools such as Abbotsholme or Bedales. The father of the Olivier sisters was Sydney Olivier, a civil servant in the Colonial Office who moved his family out to a cottage in rural Surrey, where the four daughters were tutored at home and where they spent hours and indeed years roaming the Surrey Downs and climbing trees. All four sisters became very fast cross-country runners, outrunning most of the males they knew. One of their male friends described their upbringing in Surrey as like something from ancient Sparta.[94]

It is important to grasp not just what the back-to-nature philosophy of the Cambridge Neo-Pagans did involve; but also what it did not involve. Neo-Pagans did not believe in free love. In essence, it was a cult that believed that its female members should be chaste until marriage and Rupert Brooke subscribed to this idea. Secondly, the Neo-Pagans were not early feminists. They did not even support the female suffrage campaign in Edwardian Britain and Brooke himself was anti-women's rights.[95] When they were not in camps during University vacations, the Cambridge 'Neo-Pagans' spent their evenings planning and producing plays. In 1908 Rupert Brooke produced and acted in a play that received notices in national newspapers and periodicals including the *Spectator* published in London. It was the first event that brought him to the attention of people beyond Cambridge and it happened well before he became widely known to the public as a romantic War poet.

The play was Milton's *Comus*. It was a play about a young virgin who gets lost in a forest; is accosted and then is saved by a Spirit, played by Rupert Brooke. Milton had been a student at Cambridge and, in fact, the play was sponsored by his old college, Christ's, to celebrate the tercentenary of his birth. Brooke's adaptation of *Comus* was an example of how the Neo-Pagan cult could still exist even in the rule-bound environment of the Cambridge colleges. If the play had been performed during term-time the female actors would have been forbidden from playing female roles. But, craftily, Brooke staged the play during the summer vacation of 1908 – enabling him to use female actors in female parts – and two performances were given in the New Theatre of Cambridge on 10 and 11 July 1908.[96] Brooke used many of his Neo-Pagan friends in the production. It has even been suggested by the American historian Paul Delany that the production actually created the Neo-Pagans of Cambridge by bringing a set of like-minded males and females into contact with each.[97] Some of Brooke's friends were even active behind the scenes, making costumes for the production.[98] Rupert Brooke certainly seems to have used the play to pass on some of his philosophy of life to his friends. He told all the cast, for example, at the outset that they should all promise not to marry within six months of the performance.[99]

What conclusions can be drawn about Rupert Brooke's Neo-Pagan youth cult in Edwardian Cambridge? The first is that Brooke was not initiating a youth cult himself, as later youth culture enthusiasts in Cambridge, like Rolf Gardiner, were to do.[100] Moreover, it is probably more accurate to describe Brooke's cult as a small subculture within Edwardian Cambridge, consisting of a tightly-knit circle of friends, rather than a youth cult that was consciously being promoted to enlist outsiders. Finally, the Neo-Pagans of Cambridge left a rather troubled legacy. Several of the cults' members, including Rupert Brooke himself, had nervous breakdowns – Frances Darwin, who saw Brooke in the play *Comus* and christened him 'Young Apollo'; Gwen Darwin, Justin Brooke (not related to Rupert Brooke but a fellow thespian), Katherine Cox and one of the Olivier sisters, Daphne. In Rupert Brooke's case there was one further negative legacy of devoting so much of his free time to acting in, and producing, plays. His academic work suffered and in the summer of 1909 he graduated from King's with only a Second in Classics, and almost took a Third. His father had taken a First in the same subject. In June 1909 Rupert Brooke left Cambridge and went to live in Grantchester, a nearby village, to try to rescue his academic credentials by producing a thesis. This thesis, which he eventually completed, and which won Brooke a Fellowship at King's College, Cambridge, had a cultural theme: the plays of the Elizabethan dramatist John Webster. Rupert Brooke's Neo-Pagan youth cult phase came to an end around 1912 and, thereafter, he played no further part in promoting youth culture. But Cambridge continued to be preoccupied with youth culture long after 1914 – producing a pioneer of Anglo-European student and youth movements during the Twenties (Rolf Gardiner); a celebrated student novelist, Rosamond Lehmann, whose first novel *Dusty Answer* (1927) was partly set in Girton College, Cambridge; and, somewhat later, a series of individuals who were prime movers in the pop culture of the 'Swinging' Sixties.[101]

2 Rolf Gardiner, Cambridge and the Birth of Youth Culture between the Two World Wars*

Rolf Gardiner is a neglected figure in the history of British Youth Culture. This chapter will argue that he was one of the prime movers in the development of Youth Culture in British universities between the Two World Wars. Drawing on his rich personal papers, published essays and on contemporary perceptions of Rolf Gardiner, the chapter will chart Rolf Gardiner's extraordinary influence as a shaper of ideas about youth culture and youth activity in the era of cinema, the Jazz Age and the rise of Nazism on the European Continent.[1]

Gardiner is a gift for the social historian of the interwar years because he was at the forefront of the development of youth movements in Britain, and beyond Britain. Moreover, his extensive correspondence with other youth enthusiasts reveals that he was interested in developing a youth culture in an era which, certainly in Britain, has been seen to lack a distinct youth culture.[2] This chapter introduces some of the rich archival material held in Cambridge, documenting Rolf Gardiner's pioneering role as a prime mover in the development of Youth Culture in the early twentieth century, both in Britain and across Europe. Moreover, it seeks to demonstrate Gardiner's credentials as an interwar pioneer of British youth culture; a neglected theme in the growing secondary literature that views him, essentially, as a British Nazi sympathiser of the 1930s.[3] Indeed, from his late teens and on into his undergraduate years Gardiner developed a serious interest in youth culture; editing a student periodical at Cambridge, when he was a student at St John's from 1921 to 1924, and which he gave the weighty title *Youth: An Expression of Progressive University Thought*.[4] Moreover, he believed that youth movements were not leisure organisations for adolescents; but, potentially, intellectual movements for galvanising the thoughts and aspirations of young, articulate, educated youth in the universities, such as himself: essentially, the 18–25 age-group. What distinguishes Gardiner from his contemporaries in the universities, some of whom also started cults of youth (Harold Acton and Brian Howard being the most celebrated examples), is that Gardiner's cultural movements developed well beyond the Ivory Towers of Oxford and Cambridge; as, uniquely for this period, he set about establishing student movements that linked English and European students in an exercise in cultural fusions and an exploration of new ways of living.[5]

It will emerge below that Rolf Gardiner's pursuit of new ways of living for student communities, and indeed his whole fascination with youth culture as a concept worth taking seriously, are unique for the period between the Two World Wars. Reflecting in 1931 on his efforts to build an Anglo-European youth culture during the 1920s, he told a friend:

> For me the (folk dance) tours have proved stepping stones to wider and more ambitious fields of action . . . it was these wider activities which I was seeking and aiming at when we started the 'Travelling Morrice' (a Cambridge folk dance team) together. I hoped that the tours would lead to a new vision determining our work as a generation in England, not merely stop at folk-dancing.[6]

But Rolf Gardiner's youthful visions have been largely forgotten. When he died in November 1971 the Cambridge college where he studied, St John's, knew hardly anything about him. The college magazine, *The Eagle*, recorded simply that Rolf Gardiner, 'forester', had died.[7] Rolf Gardiner evidently thought that a biography would eventually be written about him. He would not have kept such meticulous records going back to his school reports if he did not and he would not have asked his closest friends and associates to return all his letters to them. Moreover, he thought from his early twenties that he was a significant cultural figure and confided in his diary that the person who researched his life would find the important intellectual currents in his thinking and activities in the letters he wrote.[8]

He was aware, at this early stage of his life, that he did not have the discipline to complete books and make all his various activities and ideas immediately accessible to future academics. Nonetheless, Rolf Gardiner has left a vast collection of letters, many handwritten and some quite lengthy – the longest so far discovered was a 12-page defence of his philosophy on life to his close friend and fellow Morris dancer Arthur Heffer, an Oxford graduate of the Twenties and, subsequently, a Cambridge bookseller.[9] Gardiner's letters are written with a steady hand and are, invariably, literary efforts. Heffer, for example, chided him for being too influenced by D. H. Lawrence's writing style; saying far too much about his moods and feelings, the weather, drawing attention to people's foibles, and enthusing about the miners of the north-east of England and their sword dances.[10]

Much of Rolf Gardiner's voluminous correspondence is brilliantly written, once one gets used to his florid writing style. Moreover, even influential historians can develop arguments in a florid style – Simon Schama springs to mind.[11] Gardiner's letters touch on all sorts of things: people, the books that he was reading, youth movements, cultural enthusiasms, relationships, his philosophy of life, politicians, and Hitler and Nazi Germany. He also wrote many articles for literary journals such as *New English Weekly*, *The Times Literary Supplement*, *Encounter*, and *The Listener*. He wrote several letters that were published in *The Times*. He wrote two books: *England Herself: Ventures in Rural Restoration* (published by Faber and Faber in 1943) and *World Without End: Politics and the Younger Generation* (1932); published, interestingly, around the same time as A. L. Rowse's first book with a very similar title, *Politics and the Younger Generation* (1931).[12] Intriguingly, Rowse had talked in this work about the pro-German youth enthusiasts of the early Twenties, so he may have been aware of Gardiner.[13] Rolf Gardiner also co-edited a volume of essays, *Britain and Germany* (1928), and he wrote an essay on English youth in a book published by Harvard University Press in 1940, which Eleanor Roosevelt wrote the Foreword for. She praised Gardiner's essay for its foresight and so, in a sense, he had gained a global reputation as a youth culture enthusiast by the early years of the Second World War; something not stressed in the existing historical literature.[14] Towards the end of his life, Rolf Gardiner was commissioned to write a further book on landscape, predating Simon Schama's book *Landscape and Memory* (1995) by almost thirty years, but he did not live to complete it.[15]

There is a short entry on Rolf Gardiner in the new *Oxford Dictionary of National Biography*, but it hardly touches on his central role as a prime mover in the development of youth culture.[16] Nor does it offer any conceptual models of how Rolf Gardiner's life should be studied by historians. That said, Rolf Gardiner is probably best seen as a countercultural figure in British cultural life between the Wars rather than as a British Nazi. We will see this through a focus on four themes: his home background and years at Cambridge between 1921 and 1924; his brief association with one of the established English youth movements of the 1920s, the Kibbo Kift Kindred, from 1923 to 1925; his own attempts to establish new youth movements in Britain, in which university students made contact with working-class communities in the north-east of England and Scotland, and with rural communities in the south-east; and, fourthly, Rolf Gardiner's extraordinary efforts to bring about cultural contact between young Britons (not exclusively middle-class university students, but young workers as well) and young Germans in the aftermath of the First World War. His first international folk dance tour of Germany took place in 1922 and these international ventures continued throughout the 1920s and into the 1930s. We can see this in the record he kept of his yearly activities (reproduced in Appendix 1). Indeed, Rolf Gardiner had a significant impact in intellectual circles, and in the quality press of the period, as an advocate of 'internationalism'.

The issues for historians to grapple with in Gardiner's early life (some of which are addressed below) are: to what extent was he self-consciously motivated by a concept of youth culture? To what extent was he influential in the development of youth culture? How representative of other student cultures at Cambridge in the early 1920s is Gardiner's enthusiasm for youth culture? Was he trying to introduce German ideas about youth culture and youth movements into Britain? Or was he trying to export English culture, as he saw it, to Germany?[17]

Rolf Gardiner's early life

Henry Rolf Gardiner was born on 5 November 1902 in Kensington, West London. A myth has developed in the historical literature – principally in the work of Richard Moore-Colyer – that Gardiner was a product of rural England, active in Dorset and always naturally disposed to peddle anti-urban sentiments in his writings.[18] In fact, he was from a very cosmopolitan family based in Holland Park, West London, and his parents regularly entertained intellectual types from the universities, writers from Europe and Ireland and, in a word, liberal-minded people interested in the arts.[19] In essence, Rolf Gardiner grew up in a family that were on the fringes of Bloomsbury and his criticisms of intellectuals in his later writings would have been forged early on when he witnessed groups of adults invading his home and depriving him of his parents' attention. In his early twenties, he developed an extreme contempt for academic types; referring to them as the 'Metallic people of Bloomsbury and King's'. He had in mind people like J. M. Keynes, the economist, Virginia Woolf, E. M. Forster and the other 'brainy writers', as he put it, who all left him cold. His parents were austere people and he seems to have seen very little of them in his childhood. His father, Alan Gardiner, was an Oxford-educated Egyptologist who was sent to Egypt to inspect Tutankhamen's tomb in 1921 and Rolf reported seeing him on a Newsreel. Gardiner's mother, Hedwig, was from an Austro-Hungarian aristocratic family and frequently travelled abroad. The large number of letters in the Gardiner archive to and from his parents, dating from his early childhood, is a strong indication that he did not see much of them.[20]

Rolf Gardiner's upbringing was extremely privileged. His birth was officially announced in *The Times* on Saturday 8 November 1902 and early photographs provide glimpses of a genteel and upper middle-class childhood. One photograph from his childhood, in the Rolf Gardiner archive, shows him and his sister Margaret (born 1904, and who lived to be 100), in their playroom in Holland Park. The room is vast and the ceiling not even visible. Rolf Gardiner is leaning on a rocking horse and both children are with their nanny. Other photographs reveal that the children were fond of dressing up. One taken in the Isle of Wight shows Rolf, Margaret and two Edwardian nannies both wearing fancy hats, and Rolf dressed as a musketeer in a dark velvet suit, knickerbockers and long white stockings. Another shows the two children astride two real horses.[21]

Rolf Gardiner received a very progressive education before he went to Cambridge in 1921. Both of his parents were learned, but they were constantly entertaining guests or travelling abroad (Alan Gardiner was a scholar of independent means), which meant that Rolf's early education was left in the hands of his nannies, who sent formal reports to his parents on his progress. This was the case until he went to West Downs, a preparatory school in rural Hampshire, just before the outbreak of the First World War.[22]

His first cultural interest at school was the Boy Scouts. He became a very active Scout at West Downs (he was the first 'King's Scout' at the school), and he talked of little else in his letters to his parents, who became concerned that he was not being taught enough. The school does seem to have built scouting into the curriculum. In October 1914, for example, when he was almost 12, his lessons consisted of the following: 'Friday: games all day – Swedish drill, signalling, shooting and boxing in the evening. Saturday: scouting on the Downs, a sing song with the scouts and a lecture from a retired naval officer on the war.' There was basically a lack of teachers at the school from the start of the First World War and four of Rolf's teachers had joined up within the first two months of the war. The teacher he was closest to was Roland Phillips, who ran the School's Scout Troop. Rolf Gardiner heaped praise on him in a letter to his parents written in February 1916. 'One of the best if not the best and keen scouts in England', he reported. 'He has given his life up for scouting ideals and is by far the kindest and nicest man I have met so far.' He too enlisted shortly afterwards and was killed in action in July 1916.[23]

Rolf Gardiner was very much a patriotic Scout at his first school. He did war work with his school troop, scrubbing floors at Euston Station, and gave talks to the school's pupils on the benefits of scout life.[24] On one occasion when he was only 10 his nanny attended a Scout event at the school. The Scouts were being presented with a prize and Rolf had to make a speech. She noted that the other boys 'beamed with pride' as he spoke.[25] His Scouting days culminated at an early age. Baden- Powell visited West Downs in November 1915 and Rolf was chosen to show him round the school.[26] He would have been just 13 at the time. West Downs is primarily of interest to historians because it was a deeply patriotic school during the war years and because it introduced him to the Scout movement, which was his first cultural interest. His mind was so preoccupied with the movement at this school he would tell his parents at the end of each letter home: 'Be Prepared'. He, unquestionably, wanted England to defeat Germany in the war, even though he was ribbed at school for having an Austrian mother. He also took a close interest in the logistics of the war and had a column in his diary called 'War News', where he recorded how many ships had been lost (British and German). 'Never mind,' he told his nanny, 'when the Boy Scouts grow up they will build up all that has been lost now'.[27]

His interests began to broaden at his next school, Rugby, which he entered in October 1916; but he was only there for two years. He took an instant dislike to Rugby and was chastised for being a Boy Scout. He wrote to his parents in a distressed state in February 1917:

> In class I can't do my work because someone punches me or flips my ears. They take away my food from me at meals and bag my books and belongings. They stuff snow down my neck so that my back freezes and I am not able to change my clothes and so have to go about wet. They bombard me with snow when I am playing squash. And question me the whole day long in knots and signals to try and catch me (out). Well it's a bit too much for me and I can't stick at it much longer... It is all because I'm a scout and talk scouting.[28]

He remained loyal to the Scout movement at Rugby, despite being bullied about it, and was even given responsibility for running his own troop. But he began to pursue new creative interests that were less conventional, and even daring. He attended life-drawing classes, took up horticulture and went driving in a Morgan sports car. He began to sing classical music (Rolf was an Alto) and became a serious reader on a wide range of subjects. In a two-week period in April 1918, he read Macaulay's essays, 100 pages of a book on plant life, a study of Classical Greece, a political memoir, *Lord Mosley's Recollections,* and a Life of Rousseau. He now had conventional interests (Scouting), daring interests (painting nude women), and contentious interests; for example, he was developing a real interest in the Irish question and this may have come from his mother. (She was the organiser of an Irish Festival.) From being someone who opposed Home Rule at West Downs, purely because he wanted to join the British Army there, he had decided by the age of 16 at Rugby that Ireland deserved Home Rule because the Irish had their own culture and a sense of national identity. He wrote to his mother, clearly engrossed in the subject:

> I read a very interesting article on the men of County Clare Ireland. Apparently they have got a national character (good character) in them. In fact, I don't know whether the best thing for Ireland would be to settle her own disputes by herself; that is, giving her freedom from English rule.[29]

He began to look further afield than Ireland and started to take an interest in European countries, such as Finland. He wanted to learn about the civil war there and he wrote a paper on the theme 'The Finnish Revolution' at age 15. He began reading a journal entitled *New Europe,* describing it as 'extremely good'. He also liked books on English history, and he was a discerning reader, delivering a very balanced judgement on G. K. Chesterton's *The Short History of the English People*: 'It is most amusing, for although it is wonderfully written and is extremely clever it is quite inaccurate and is not a history at all.'[30]

Rolf was removed from Rugby in July 1918 and sent to Bedales, a progressive co-educational school. Bedales was a very unconventional school. It had boy and girl pupils and they were allowed to roam freely for hours at weekends. It allowed its pupils to develop interests as part of their daytime education and there were no examinations. Ostensibly mainstream subjects, such as English, could be taught in highly unusual ways. One of Rolf Gardiner's 'English' essays was on the nebulous theme 'Atmospheres'. He was given no question to address, just this odd title. Another of his English essays carried the title 'Dreams'. Rolf Gardiner flourished under such a loose curriculum. He wrote about whatever came into his head, very eloquently; but the danger of this method was that he would never know how to sift what was relevant from what was not relevant to a question. He flourished at being free to write essays on his enthusiasms, but they were airy essays, and they lacked any sense of rigour. They were like random jottings in a diary and his teachers awarded him high marks (usually A or A-).[31]

He wrote one of his essays on the history of popular culture in England and Europe since the Elizabethan era. It was written when he was 17 but it discusses ideas he would subsequently develop in his twenties and indeed into his later years. His central argument was that culture – which he defined as drama, literature and opera – ought to be available to the working-classes and he thought that certain theatres in London were drawing in the working-classes. The Old Vic, he thought, was doing just what he wanted: bringing Shakespeare to the masses. 'This theatre', he wrote:

> situated in one of the most squalid ugly streets of London across the bridges, for night after night, year in and year out, has drawn audiences of the working-classes to see Shakespeare or hear classic operas. The Old Vic has grafted a sincere love for Shakespeare in the hearts of the workers.[32]

He had very broad tastes in theatre and opera. He liked Gilbert and Sullivan because they were anti-Establishment; he liked Irish Plays, especially Yeats and Synge, and liked their anti-English agenda:

> This school is characteristically Irish and have tried to explain to the English public the true character of the Irishman, which they (the English) have failed to understand throughout centuries of mutual misunderstanding.[33]

We see clearly, then, that Gardiner's growing affinities in his late teens were with the underdog and especially the English working-classes and the Irish in general. What is interesting is that he saw plays as a vehicle for expressing political ideas and his idea that culture must be used to improve the social worlds of the poor is a very radical notion for someone who had had no direct experience of working-class people up to this point. We can also see from the ideas expressed in this essay that Rolf Gardiner had no interest in middle-class theatregoers' tastes; only in how the theatre could serve the working-classes. This is what makes him a countercultural figure. He was from a middle-class background, but he was to distance himself from this social world in quite dramatic ways.

Rolf Gardiner at Cambridge, 1921–4

Rolf Gardiner was preparing to go to university in 1919 and he could not decide which university to go to, or even which subject to study. He was attracted to the idea of Oxford because he thought it was a progressive university. He had two friends at Balliol College and told his parents: 'Oxford seems to be a much more interesting and broad-minded place now than before the War. Such a large number of soldiers have come back and ideas are flooding in from far more varied circles.'[34] This is a very revealing statement. What he may have been referring to were the thousands of Ex-Servicemen who went to university under the Fisher Education Act of 1918. Fisher recorded in his autobiography that 27,000 Ex-Service students were admitted to English universities between 1919 and 1922 and they doubled the university population from its pre-War level. Fisher also pointed out that he had personally looked at every application from the Ex-Service students and was convinced that the vast majority were from working-class and lower middle-class backgrounds and these students would not have gone to university before the First World War.[35]

Gardiner was picking up on the idea that Oxford was attracting students from far more diverse class backgrounds after the First World War, giving rise to a broadening of cultural tastes and an infusion of new ideas, which appealed to him. When he visited Oxford in December 1919 to sit for a Brackenbury Scholarship at Balliol College, he found the students he met extremely creative and colourful. He met student journalists who wore 'canary-coloured' waistcoats and edited student journals with names like *The Sport*.[36] But his initial impressions were modified when he went to a party and met the student novelist Beverley Nichols. Gardiner thought Nichols was frivolous. He was reading from a play he had written and Gardiner thought it 'silly'. It was about a Bishop who wore red pyjamas. After listening to much 'pseudo-brilliant and bawdy talk till the early hours of the morning', Gardiner left Oxford with the impression that its students, or the ones he encountered, were superficial. He was not offered a place in any case; but he came close, being placed fifth for a Brackenbury Scholarship in a competition that attracted around 50 candidates.[37] There followed a brief period when he went abroad to northern Italy (the

Tyrol) to work on a farm with Italian peasants. He then applied to Cambridge but had no idea which subject he would specialise in. He thought he might study History, Political Science, Literature or 'similar subjects'. In the end, he was accepted to read Economics, but he soon changed to Modern Languages, specialising in German, French and Italian.[38]

Gardiner's countercultural phase really begins at Cambridge. In the beginning he was just unconventional. He wore brightly coloured clothes, including a sky blue coat, wore his hair quite long, and he claimed he bathed naked in the River Cam – which was only odd because he did this in the winter months.[39] He became a countercultural figure when he took on the Editorship of a journal called *Youth* in 1923, which up to that point had been a socialist journal covering strikes, industrial relations and wage levels. Gardiner knew that for a counterculture, or indeed a culture, to develop it needed a spokesperson or sage. There were other people establishing cultural journals at this period and discussing new ideas, especially psychology. One was A. D. Orage who edited a cultural journal called *New Age*. Orage had no interest in youth affairs, however, and was chiefly interested in discussing Freudian ideas in psychology and appealing to medical professionals.[40] Another voice in the cultural field was John Middleton Murry, the Editor of *The Adelphi*, who was married to the novelist Kathleen Mansfield and had been a close friend of D. H. Lawrence. But he and Orage were both middle-aged. Rolf Gardiner was only 21 when he became the Editor of *Youth* and he turned the paper into a vehicle for promoting the concept of an international youth culture (see Figure 1).[41]

Rolf Gardiner was aware of youth culture before it existed in Britain. He had read about a youth culture in Germany and the term 'Jugendkultur' was widely used in the early 1920s.[42] What Gardiner meant by youth culture was, essentially, youth movements such as the pre-War Wandervogel and he thought there had to be some element of protest in youth culture. He developed this theme in essays he wrote on the German youth movements, while studying at Cambridge. They appeared in his own journal *Youth*, in other Cambridge journals such as *The Gownsman* and *New Cambridge* and in a national student paper called *The University* started in 1924. He also gave talks on the German Youth Movements at Cambridge during 1923. Gardiner believed the pre-World War I Wandervogel were reacting against the militarisation of pre-War German society and he noted in his diary that 3000 members of the German youth movement were killed in action during the First World War and this had literally killed off the Wandervogel altogether. He also thought they were a reaction against the state education system in pre-War Germany, which, he argued, was very regimented. He liked the idea that the Wandervogel was a classless youth movement, appealing to both university students and factory workers and apprentices. He also liked the tone of the movement; a mixture of physical and intellectual endeavour. The Wandervogel were urban workers but they would go on hikes into the countryside. They stayed in castles that had been converted into youth hostels and they discussed political ideas, literature, and philosophers such as Goethe.[43]

Gardiner was attracted to the idea of youth communities and he was, of course, used to living in youth communities himself, as a boarder at West Downs, Rugby and Bedales. He committed his ideas on these youth communities to paper in his diary for August and September 1923 under the heading: 'Youth-A Culture'.[44] The notes are only fragments; but they suggest he was thinking of trying to develop a youth culture in Britain. 'Culture is the work of Youth', he wrote. He defined culture as two things: 'power' and 'spirit'. He talked of youth culture as 'a creative impulse'. He thought that religion, or rather 'spiritual education', should be a feature of these youth communities. He said some quite perceptive things. Youth culture was only possible, he thought, in isolated communities where youth lived together. The only reference to a country that had a youth culture, as he defined it, was to Germany. But he had latched onto an idea that he would later put into practice.

Gardiner was viewed by his contemporaries at Cambridge, and indeed by some of the dons, as a sort of sage. *The Gownsman* referred to him reverently as 'the brilliant Editor of *Youth*'; J. M. Keynes, the economist and Fellow of King's, wrote to congratulate him on his paper *Youth* and another Fellow at King's, Edward Dent, a musicologist, became a close friend and put Gardiner in contact with young Germans.[45] He had many admirers, especially females, and his female friends included an Irish girl from Belfast who went horse-riding with him; Kathleen Trevelyan, a student at Girton College who was the daughter of the Labour Education Minister Charles Trevelyan and the niece of the historian G. M. Trevelyan; and Sydney Courtauld, a rich heiress who was a folk dancer and toured Europe with him (and later married Gardiner's Cambridge contemporary Rab Butler, a student at Pembroke College, Cambridge, from 1921 to 1924).[46] Rolf Gardiner seemed to attract people because of his looks, his self-assurance and his uninhibited conversation. One of the female members of the Kibbo Kift Kindred youth movement, which he made contact with in his second year at Cambridge, recalled years afterwards the striking impression he made on that movement:

> Rolf Gardiner was a very gorgeous and magnificent young man. He brought to us something of what the Wandervogel were doing . . . the breaking of various taboos: the taboo against discussing sex, the taboo against throwing off your clothes in camp and the taboo against discussing anyone else's religion.[47]

In the cloistered world of St John's College, Cambridge, Rolf Gardiner was part of a progressive social circle whose members discussed 'free love' and students from the women's colleges of Girton and Newnham would attend these meetings. When the college learned of the meetings, they were banned.[48] He had no interest in conventional student societies at Cambridge such as the Cambridge Union. The leading light in the Union during Gardiner's years was Rab Butler and a comparison of the two would reveal their very different philosophies on youth and youth culture. Butler was extremely conventional and eager to work within existing institutions and, in a sense, eager to institutionalise all youth activity.[49] Gardiner was a far more original, questioning and mildly anti-Establishment spirit. Gardiner eschewed conventional Cambridge undergraduate societies and instead joined avant-garde groups such as The Heretics and The Socratics; societies whose members included free-spirited females such as Jane Harrison, the Classics don, who was a member of The Heretics and corresponded with Rolf Gardiner.[50] Female students his own age from the women's colleges could also become members of The Heretics.[51] The Socratics was a very secretive and intriguing society which held its meetings in the rooms of one of the dons at St John's College: G. G. Coulton, a Medievalist who specialised in cultural, social and religious history (and hated the Catholic Church). Gardiner was on the committee of this society and gave a talk on the educational aspects of the German Youth Movements. The Socratics were, basically, socialists who heard papers on workers' cooperatives and working-class education; a forerunner of the History Workshop movement of the 1970s. Gardiner himself was not politically active as a socialist at Cambridge, but he had several socialist friends who shared his interests: the lives of the working-classes, education, and culture.[52]

One of Gardiner's best friends at Cambridge was a young Communist historian, Maurice Dobb, who was teaching at The London School of Economics but lived in Cambridge and had been a student at Cambridge. Both were members of a socialist club in London called 'The 1917 Club'; a bohemian environment where, according to one of Gardiner's friends, it was unsafe to leave your coat, and whose members included celebrated Bloomsbury figures such as Lytton Strachey. Dobb, who was a couple of years older than Gardiner, thought Gardiner was full of vitality. He told him in May 1922, looking back to Gardiner's arrival at the university in October 1921: 'Your freshness and vitality came like a new breath of life.'[53]

Gardiner never thought that youth culture and youth movements were only for youth. He was never ageist and never wished to develop an anti-adult agenda. At Cambridge he felt superior to people his own age because he thought they lacked what he called 'intellectual wisdom'.[54] His whole approach to culture and social movements was to draw in young people and their elders. His whole vision was that culture ought to unify people and bridge tensions between the generations, tensions between different classes and different communities, and tensions between countries.

At Cambridge he was friendly with students who had fought in the First World War. Among these friends was J. B. Priestley, who had gone to Cambridge under the Fisher scheme for Ex-Servicemen and smoked a pipe. He was a very sedentary individual who would sit in an armchair and try to disarm Rolf Gardiner's enthusiasm for youth movements with the words: 'Young man all ye want is a few reforms'; delivered in a pronounced regional accent (he was from Bradford).[55] The younger students distanced themselves from the Ex-Service students because they were older and were seen to be excessively diligent; but Gardiner befriended them, possibly drawn to them by their 'wisdom' and leadership qualities. When Rolf Gardiner arrived at Cambridge in October 1921 there were several Ex-Service students at his college. They were the students who ran college societies and they were always present at the college debates.[56] They were culturally a very conservative group, tending to support motions on maintaining the British Navy intact, agreeing that Germany should pay for the costs of the War, and showing no interest in cultural subjects.

There were, in effect, three generations in the Universities in the early 1920s (and this was especially the case in Oxford and Cambridge, which had absorbed significantly more Ex-Service students than other British universities).[57] There was, first of all, the War Generation; namely, the Ex-Service students such as Priestley. Secondly, there was the Postwar Generation; those like Gardiner who had been at school during the War. Thirdly, there was the Prewar Generation (the dons). In Cambridge the dons even had their own journal, *Old Cambridge*; an alternative to *New Cambridge* for the young undergraduates. The dons also contributed to *The Cambridge Review*, which was a very donnish periodical focusing very largely on matters of importance to the University, rather than to its students. To the younger students, the university must have seemed a very adult environment before Rolf Gardiner launched his various youth crusades. When the ex-soldiers left in the summer of 1922 the Cambridge student journal *The Gownsman* reported on its front page that Cambridge could now 'return to normal'. Their readers were glad to be rid of these older men and they were acidly depicted in illustrations in the student magazines as miserable outsiders who smoked pipes, and stood in isolated groups in the quadrangles looking on reprovingly at the younger students.[58] They were not really welcomed by Cambridge colleges. In the records of St John's College's student debates the Service students are not even referred to by their names, when the other students were.[59] Thus, when Gardiner arrived in Cambridge the student body was severely fractured: by age, war experience, and temperament. When he became Editor of *Youth* in July 1923, all the ex-soldiers had gone and it was an opportune time for a youth enthusiast to be launching a new idea.

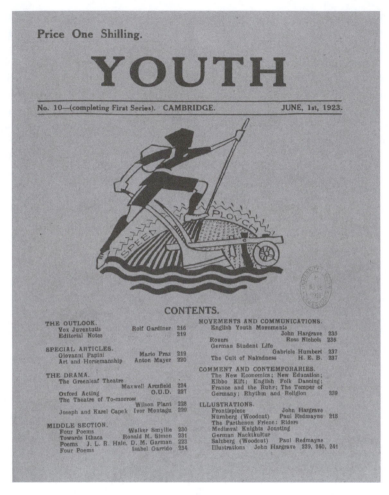

Figure 1 Front cover of *Youth*, 1 June 1923, Rolf Gardiner's pioneering 'youth culture' periodical.
Source: Cambridge University Library.

Youth had first appeared in the middle of a coal strike in May 1920, and was initially a vehicle for the Labour Party in Cambridge. Its features tended to be on industrial themes with dreary titles such as 'The Conduct of the Coal Industry' and the paper was not greatly interested in social subjects. In fact, it was not about youth at all but merely wanted its 'youth' readers to debate grown-up issues of the day – 'the various local, national, social, political, and religious questions of the day' in its words.[60] Moreover, it was a sexist paper before Gardiner became its Editor. It thought female students at Cambridge should not be allowed to become members of the

Cambridge Union: 'The Union is a club for men and should remain so,' it told its readers in its first issue of May 1920.[61] This was the sort of thing the Ex-Service students would support and it is no surprise to learn that its first Editor, William A. Harris, had fought in the First World War. His first Editorial was all about the War and he stressed that youth should know their place and not question their elders:

> The young people of the rising generation must supply new leaven to 'ginger up' the old world, but they must never lose sight of the sentiment, 'For those good things that we have received, our religion, our prestige, our Constitution, let us be truly thankful'. Youth must always respect its elders, must respect tradition. Nor must it in its position of small responsibility overshoot its mark...Youth must realise its limitations.[62]

We can see from this that the paper was misleadingly called 'an organ of progressive university thought' and it must have struck the younger students of postwar Cambridge as patronising and uninspiring.

Rolf Gardiner transformed *Youth* into a vibrant cultural, almost lifestyle, journal, that ran features on female folk dancers, and German body culture (including an article with a photograph of naked youths running across a German plain plunging into a lake – see Figure 1), and he also made it a vehicle for his own enthusiasms – D. H. Lawrence, the poets of the First World War, the Woodcraft youth movements in England and the German youth movements.[63] Its themes were a mixture of Neo-Paganism, youth culturism and internationalism and it made a major impact in Cambridge, and acquired a readership well beyond Cambridge. His paper had inspired one reader in Hertfordshire, who had decided to try to start his own youth movement: 'I am glad to see that the Editor is trying to make *Youth* a general organ of the Youth Movement.... One comes across a number of little groups of folks who have caught the spirit of the Jugendbewegung (the German Youth Movement). I want to see it grow in this county, but at present they all seem quite ignorant of what other people are doing along similar lines.'[64] Another reader, Dr Stanton Coit of 'The Ethical Church' in Bayswater, London, found the paper 'stimulating'. He felt compelled to now read D. H. Lawrence's novels and a young novelist Rolf Gardiner had enthused about, Robert Nichols, author of a novel called *Guilty Souls*.[65] A reader based in Chelsea liked the fact that it was 'youthful' and told the Editor not to ask people over 30 to contribute articles. Even T. S. Eliot, Editor of *The Criterion*, was moved to write to Gardiner, saying he found it 'interesting'. He was subsequently to publish Rolf Gardiner's first book, *England Herself*, when he became Editor at Faber and Faber.[66]

Gardiner had set about marketing the paper in London by using his parents' address and distributing the paper from there. He also had advertisements placed in other Cambridge student papers such as *The Gownsman* and *New Cambridge* and he cheekily wrote to John Hargrave of the Kibbo Kift Kindred, based in Hertfordshire, asking if he would advertise *Youth* in the Kibbo Kift's journal *The Nomad*. He must also have sent a copy to *The Times* because the paper gave it a short review in October 1924, describing it as: 'the organ of a sect called Kibbo Kift'.[67] In reality, Gardiner was using the name of the Kibbo Kift, a national youth movement with offices in London, to promote his own ideas. He managed to persuade Hargrave and the Kibbo Kift's London secretary Moya Jowitt to conduct his business for him and by 1924 the Kibbo Kift's office in London was distributing hundreds of copies of *Youth* around the world. The paper was being sent to Germany, the United States and even to countries in South America.[68]

In private correspondence, Rolf Gardiner admitted he was using the Kibbo Kift to promote his own distinctive ideas. He told one correspondent:

> And who are we?...Well we are a number of individuals and groups of Individuals, in central Europe very definite corporate bodies such as the Youth movements, encamped in their various settlements, workshops, craft centres and school communities, in England...such as Kibbo Kift, who do see European civilisation poisoned and rotten...and who feel it their responsibility to...accomplish through action...a culture or let us say a way of living....That this can only be done on a comparatively small scale I am convinced...[69]

He wrote this in April 1924 and the central point he was making was that he had turned *Youth* from a journal for Cambridge undergraduates into an international journal that just happened to be published in Cambridge. Gardiner hinted at the fact that the European readers in Germany and Scandinavia wanted the paper to be even more European. For example, they wanted its articles to be translated into two or three languages.[70] Gardiner translated all the articles himself and did everything himself except distribute it – organising the printing, keeping its accounts, and answering correspondence. He claimed that the paper was attracting 'a colossal correspondence' by 1924; but hardly any of it is deposited in the Rolf Gardiner archive and there is no record of the readership figures for *Youth*. Rolf Gardiner claimed it had a readership of 4000 and had readers in India, South Africa, Germany, the United States, Australia and Britain. He paid for some of the printing costs himself. In January 1924, for example, he ran up debts of £90 to have one issue, 'a German issue', printed in Germany. He had told his grandfather, who frequently gave him money, that the costs should have been no more than £15. This suggests his paper sold well in Germany, but his grandfather, who had to pay for the venture, was livid with him. Rolf reported to his parents: 'he was so angry that I had to leave the house'.[71]

He only edited the paper for one year, but a measure of its success is that when he left Cambridge in 1924 he applied for rights to keep the copyright of the title.[72] He knew he was onto something and wished to keep the brand name and to possibly revive the paper in the future. For, what he had done was effectively appropriate a Cambridge student paper, establish contacts with people beyond Cambridge and use it as a vehicle for promoting ideas he would pursue after he left Cambridge in June 1924. As his statement about *Youth*'s philosophy 'Who we are' suggests, he had no pro-German agenda at this stage of his life; just vague thoughts about promoting a '(new) way of living'. But his vision about the communities he wished to create – and it was repeated in several of his articles in the paper – was an attempt to make people interested in his schemes and to make them want to participate in them. This strategy, as we shall discover, drew into his schemes many young people who had no connection with Cambridge and some who had not been to university at all.

Just before he left Cambridge Rolf Gardiner wrote to his mother and told her his thoughts on the University. He reflected:

> Cambridge, [has] been completely unreal to me – you will remember, or Daddy will, how I prophesied to Rivers [a family friend], when he first tried to persuade me to come here, that it would be so – I have virtually led my life outside it . . .[73]

This was not in fact true, as his various activities discussed above have indicated. It would be truer to say that Gardiner had led his life as a countercultural figure within Cambridge University. His various activities at Cambridge, editing *Youth*, establishing the Cambridge Morris and a Folk Dance movement within the University and his international ventures such as the Folk Dance Tour to Germany in September 1922 (discussed below), were at one level examples of his various cultural enthusiasms; but at a deeper level they were also attempts to subvert the collegial traditions of Cambridge life. Gareth Stedman Jones wrote a very perceptive essay on the differences between student life in the 1920s in England and student life in the late 1960s. He argued that the concept of an autonomous 'student' body or student culture was not known in the 1920s; whereas in the late 1960s students were more autonomous and more disembodied, as it were, from their universities.[74] In Oxford and Cambridge, at any rate, there were undergraduates and dons (and a few postgraduates) in the 1920s and 1930s. These universities were very hierarchical and very collegial. Brian Harrison has made the same point in his fascinating chapter on 'College Life Between the Wars' in the Twentieth Century volume of the *History of Oxford University*. In Harrison's judgement there was no 'student culture' in interwar Oxford.[75] A good example of this is the way Oxford undergraduates instinctively sided with the authorities in the General Strike of 1926.[76] By the late 1960s students were, it appears, far more autonomous and were involved in student protests at LSE, Essex, East Anglia, Oxford and briefly at Cambridge.[77] How does Gardiner fit into this model?

Rolf Gardiner's years at Cambridge suggest that he was trying to develop within the University, and beyond it, a significant cultural movement which would liberate students from the watchful eyes of their elders. Youth movements would be the vehicle for Gardiner's cultural ideas, and undergraduates would be among the participants. But his youth movements would be just one expression of a wider movement with a new language. He talked of a culture for 'youth'; not for 'undergraduates'. Indeed, he avoided ever using the term 'undergraduates' in his journal *Youth* and in his correspondence; a subversive idea in itself. The concept of 'Youth' seems quaint now but in the early 1920s a 'cult of youth' would have seemed a subversive idea even to undergraduates at Cambridge and certainly a challenge to the university's patriarchal and collegial environment. In Oxford a 'cult of youth' seems to have been more closely associated with a few individuals from bohemian upper-class backgrounds such as Harold Acton and Brian Howard; at least according to Martin Green's fascinating book *Children of the Sun: A Narrative of Decadence in England since 1918*.[78] Rolf Gardiner did not transform student life in Cambridge and seems to have operated on the margins of his college. Moreover, he was not in any sense ageist or anti-adult and seems to have socialised with his elders as much as with people his own age. Possibly, the students of the late 1960s were no different; but they seem to have been more disposed to rebel than students in interwar Britain and the shifts in student values and behaviour between the 1920s and the late 1960s are an intriguing issue for future researchers. Gardiner was, then, a countercultural figure within early 1920s' Cambridge and had a slightly subversive agenda also. His brief involvement with the Kibbo Kift youth movement, from 1923 to 1925, shows his deepening opposition to established youth movements.

Rolf Gardiner and the Kibbo Kift youth movement

John Hargrave was 29 when Gardiner made contact with him in 1923. He had established the Kibbo Kift Kindred in August 1920 at a meeting in London. He drew its initial members from ex-Scouts. He himself had left the Scout movement for two reasons: its alleged militarism and its close links with the Church of England (Hargrave was a Methodist).[79] The Kibbo Kift Kindred (KKK) developed its own programme along Methodist lines, emphasising its pacifism and interest in 'world peace', temperance, and the first play its members performed was about the Methodist preacher William Penn – called 'William Penn and the Indians'.[80] It was a tiny movement, only 200 people attending its annual meeting (or 'Al-Thing') in 1922 and most of its members lived in the Home Counties.[81]

Rolf Gardiner wrote to Hargrave in April 1923 when he was in his second year at Cambridge and wanted Hargrave to publicise his new journal *Youth*. He also wanted Hargrave to put him in touch with youth leaders in Europe and Hargrave – who was internationally known as a prominent former Scout leader and a successful author of *The Great War Brings it Home* (he had fought in the First World War in the Mediterranean) – put Gardiner in contact with a youth leader in Germany and mentioned that the KKK also had branches in Russia, Czechoslovakia, Italy, Holland and France.[82] Rolf Gardiner spent several months corresponding with Hargrave, and Hargrave supplied two articles and some illustrations for *Youth* (see Figure 1 for examples of some of his work); but Gardiner did not become a member of the Kibbo Kift. He had heard from Hargrave's secretary Moya Jowitt that Hargrave was bossy. He was certainly an odd individual. When Gardiner became a roving ambassador for the KKK in Europe, during 1924, Hargrave insisted that he must wear the KKK's uniform when conducting its business.[83] He wrote very dogmatic letters to Gardiner and sounded like a schoolmaster:

> As for yourself and KK, we will speak of this. But you may have got an exaggerated impression of the terrific dictatorship idea from Miss Jowitt [the KK's secretary] who is having special treatment owing to her special tendencies. I want Individualists. I have no wish to 'boss it' over anyone. I ask for one thing only – work. Show results.[84]

Hargrave had christened himself 'Head Man' of the KKK and gave Rolf Gardiner a new name when he started to do European work for the Movement – 'Rolf the Ranger'. Rolf's parents must have been baffled when they picked up letters in Holland Park, West London, addressed to 'Kinsman Rolf Gardiner' or 'Rolf the Ranger'. If they read any further they would have been even more confused by the arcane lingo Hargrave used. He would start a letter with the word 'Greeting' and sign them with such phrases as 'Peace and Smooth Trailing' or 'Peace Huh!' and his signature took the form of an image of a skull. Gardiner, who was a sophisticated and eloquent young man and a brilliant letter writer, would have winced at such puerile literary endeavour.[85]

Hargrave claimed he was interested in developing contacts with youth movements in Europe; but in reality he was quite anti-European and certainly anti-German. When Gardiner tried to persuade him to write to the British Ambassador in Berlin and invite young Germans to a KKK camp he refused. He thought all the German youth movements were right-wing nationalistic movements, 'springing from a more-or-less defeated people' as he put it, and forecast that flag-flying and talk about a Fatherland, the Soil, Knights and blood rites would eventually lead to another European War.[86] Gardiner was only wanting to invite members of a young German choir to

England. But Hargrave resisted all of Gardiner's schemes, describing his cultural exchanges of English student Morris dancers and German classical singers exchanging visits to each other's country as 'a sort of Cook's tours for young Germans visiting England'.[87]

Rolf Gardiner had had very little contact with Germans, or any young Europeans, before Hargrave appointed him the KKK's European representative in 1924. He had been in the German Society at Cambridge; not surprisingly, as he was reading German as part of his Degree. On one occasion he had organised a German evening. He wore Bavarian shorts and ankle-less stockings and performed folk dances. His German Professor, Professor Breul, was there and Rolf pronounced it 'an outstanding success'.[88] But a careful reading of his articles on German themes published during his Cambridge years reveals that he was very critical of sophisticated young Germans, and preferred peasant cultures of southern Germany. He visited Oberammergau in 1922 to attend the Passion Plays and he wrote about the visit in one of his articles.[89] He warmed to the peasant farmers he met who were busy preparing to act in the Passion Plays. But the young Germans he met on the train coming down from Munich to Oberammergau he loathed. He described them as 'pallid-looking students from Munich' who were travelling from a so-called civilised city to watch the peasant farmers performing in the plays. He thought the peasants were extremely industrious and versatile. They farmed, they acted, they sang and danced and they were devout churchgoers. They had their own culture, in other words. He thought the young Germans he met were boring to talk to. 'With the Germans there exists nothing but issues', he remarked.[90]

In November 1924 after he had left Cambridge and was wondering what to do with his life, Rolf Gardiner went to Austria – to a mountain top in Austria to be precise – and he began working on an autobiographical novel in which he played the Biblical figure 'David' who was preparing to slay the giant Goliath (representing intellectual life in England). He was also working on a book of poems and had had poems published even before he went to Cambridge, including one on the Irish Republican Terence McSwiney who died on hunger strike in Brixton Prison, and Gardiner, along with some friends, had sent money to his widow.[91] In Austria, Gardiner began sending Hargrave reports on youth activity in Europe, for no obvious purpose; but some were quite detailed. The youth leaders he came into contact with were highly educated university types who had written books, or were influenced by people who had written books. One, Eberling, was in the *Jungnationaler Bund* – a nationalist youth movement that wanted to revive the German aristocracy. Eberling had read a two-volume history of the early Wandervogel by Hans Bluher, who had written other books on sex, education and religion. Another, Fritz Klatt, had a lodge where he taught working-class boys from Berlin the value of the countryside. He had written books on the political ideas of the younger generation. A third, Heinz Rocholl, was attending lectures at Berlin University on philosophy, political science and economics and was working as a part-time youth leader with 150 boys and men in Berlin. Gardiner, who knew about the pre-War Wandervogel, became engrossed in the German youth movements active in postwar Germany and wrote copious letters to Hargrave who was not at all interested in the arcane world of the Deutsche Freischar, Jungnationaler Bund and other such organisations.[92]

Gardiner told Hargrave he had seen German Boy Scouts wearing the KKK's symbol – a cross – on their wooden sticks as they walked through the streets of Regensburg. He claimed he had seen more KKK symbols in Regensburg than in the streets of London. He even accompanied a group of German Scouts in their late teens and early twenties (they were older than Scouts in England) on a hike into a Bavarian forest. Gardiner was 22 at this point. After their hike they stripped and spent an hour throwing javelins, practising archery and running through the forest pelting each other with fir cones. They then made a fire and Rolf Gardiner told them all about the KKK youth movement in England. This was followed by a German hymn, some verse, and then they all walked back in silence to Regensburg.[93]

Hargrave was interested in very few of Gardiner's ideas. He did not like too much creative expression in his movement and he had banned books and pens altogether. He did not really care for youth who were highly educated. He had left school himself at 12 and was self-taught, and in his book *The Confessions of the Kibbo Kift* (published in 1927), about the KKK's methods and philosophy, he wrote:

> He may be an LL.D., D.Sc., F.R.S., K.C.B., or what-not, but if he cannot find his way across country, cannot light a fire quickly and skilfully, cannot cook his own 'grub', and make and pitch his own shelter, he is ranked as a 'greenhorn' who must now go to the school of the woods, as a little child, and graduate in the University of the Open Air.[94]

Rolf Gardiner could do all of these practical things and he also wanted to discuss new ways of living with other like-minded young people; but he was isolated in the KKK and he was the only graduate in the organisation in 1924. He severed all contact with the movement in 1925.[95]

Rolf Gardiner was one of very few educated middle-class youths interested in starting youth movements in the early 1920s. Hargrave's Kibbo Kift was not a youth movement at all and admitted children as young as five and adult men and women, as well as the 18–25s.[96] Moreover, the structure of Hargrave's movement mirrored the life-cycle: there were children's groups, adolescent groups and family groups and the most senior members were adult males.[97] Hargrave claimed he was the pioneer of youth movements in England and was under the impression that all the other youth movements in London were run by middle-aged women. This was possibly true. As we saw in Chapter 1, Mrs Pethick-Lawrence had been running girls' clubs in London in the 1890s, and was still active in the Woodcraft groups during the mid-1920s; Mary Neal had worked with Cecil Sharp teaching folk dances to female clothing workers in Tottenham Court Road before the War and was still active, and a 'Mrs English' wanted to establish a British Youth Movement with an Internationalist flavour in London. There were various pacifist youth groups such as the 'No More War Group', but there was no one with the broad cultural interests Gardiner was developing.[98] So what would he do once he had severed his links with the Kibbo Kift Kindred?

Rolf Gardiner and folk dance

The remainder of this chapter will focus on two events in Rolf Gardiner's early life – his first international Folk Dance Tour to Germany in 1922 and a tour of Yorkshire he made with young English dancers and young German singers in 1931. Both events illustrate Gardiner's neglected role as an internationalist between the Wars. In the historical literature, Rolf Gardiner stands condemned for being only interested in developing cultural links with Germans and for having been photographed with the Nazi Agriculture Minister in the late 1930s, Walther Darre.[99] This seems a very narrowly conceived view of Gardiner's cultural world and if we look back to his activities in the 1920s we see that he corresponded with all sorts of Europeans – Dutch folklorists, young Norwegians, young German folk dancers, the Prussian Minister of Culture in the Weimar Republic, Carl Becker, a young German puppeteer and members of the German Youth Movements.[100] The main purpose of his trips to Europe in the early 1920s, it seems, was to introduce Germans and Austrians to English culture. His chosen method for establishing cultural links with Europeans could not have been more quintessentially English. He was fascinated to learn that in the Elizabethan period – England's cultural highpoint, in his view, when even the illiterate poor saw Shakespeare's plays performed – many English musicians travelled to Europe performing at fairs to audiences of thousands. Rolf Gardiner, who had been a keen Morris dancer since his school days, thought that a novel idea would be a Morris dance tour with some of his Cambridge friends to Germany; part holiday in the free-spirited cities of the Weimar Republic (the 'Swinging Weimar Republic' as Arthur Marwick has memorably labelled it) and part humanitarian gesture towards all the impoverished German and Austrian students he had read about.[101] The tour was an extremely controversial event in Britain, attracting criticism within middle-class circles among people who thought it was too soon after the War and would send the wrong message to Germany; and it infuriated Cecil Sharp and the folk dance establishment in London who thought Gardiner's dancers lacked technical ability and would damage the reputation of English folk dance abroad.[102] Gardiner received several damning letters from members of the English Folk Dance Society (EFDS) and his former teacher at Bedales even tried to dissuade him from going; arguing it would damage the school's reputation – 'what will the society (EFDS) think of our Bedales ways of playing the game?' – and claiming that Gardiner should have consulted Cecil Sharp first.[103] Winifred Shuldhamshaw of Chelsea, one of Sharp's dancers, was asked to go on the tour and declined the invitation. She thought Gardiner's dancers would lack 'meticulous accuracy' and 'historical truth'.[104] Sharp himself did not disapprove of the tour, but he wanted Gardiner to avoid performances in major cities and to confine himself to villages. He thought it would be 'calamitous' if Rolf's dancers gave performances in cities.[105]

The Gardiner Folk Dance Tour of Germany went ahead in September of 1922 and he took a team of 15 dancers – 7 males and 8 females.[106] He decided to ignore Cecil Sharp's advice and concentrate on the major cities. They gave performances in: Cologne, Frankfurt, Rothenburg, Dresden, and several other cities. All the dances were performed in large theatres or halls. In Cologne they performed at the Deutsches Theatre in an evening show that consisted of 10 dance movements (in some movements there were three or four dances), and they paid an orchestra to accompany them.[107] The Cologne Programme was printed in English and all the dances were English traditional dances – folk dances, country dances, and jigs. In Dresden they performed at a bohemian theatre with beer garden attached, described by one of Gardiner's friends as: 'the artistic dance centre and general Bohemian garden city village of all Germany'.[108] All the dancers found it an exhilarating experience. 'Bill', a participant who stayed on in Germany when the tour ended, wrote to Gardiner after the tour, saying: 'We enjoyed the tour immensely and felt sorry when it was over.' Sarah Waites described it as 'a most unique and delightful experience'. Claire Vintcombe reported that she 'loved the whole trip, every minute of it and hope it will be repeated'.[109]

It seems to have been a very English affair. The dancers sang and played English folk songs such as 'Oranges and Lemons', 'Helston Processional' and country jigs such as 'Ladies' Pleasure' and 'Rigs of Marlow'. They also performed sword dances and at the end of the evening the English National Anthem was played – a highly provocative gesture it would seem.[110] The tour received reviews in the press of Frankfurt, Dresden and Cologne and as the tour progressed they were invited to give additional concerts in Mainz, Wiesbaden, Darmstadt, Jena and Weimar. Rolf Gardiner sent a circular to all the participants after the tour claiming: 'We have blazed a trail,' but the participants made little contact with Germans. Only one of those who wrote to Gardiner after the tour mentioned that the tour would improve 'relationships between England and Germany'. Interestingly, the author of this statement, one of the female dancers, did not mention that personal contacts had been established between the English dancers and any young Germans.[111]

Rolf Gardiner himself used the trip to write some articles and submit them to German newspapers. He had one published in English in the *Cologne Post* on the theme 'English Folk Dance and Song'. It was a piece of folk music propaganda that did not mention Germany once. Instead he used the opportunity to explain to Germans what English culture meant. They must not think the English were only interested in American mass culture – in jazz music and the cinema; or, as he put it more eloquently:

> We may try to forget our worries in the foxtrot and the jazz, in an hour's surrender to the charms of 'The Dolly Sisters', or in following the romantic adventures of Douglas Fairbanks or Mary Pickford on the screen . . . but these things . . . have very little to do with England.[112]

He argued that folk dances had far deeper roots in English communities, even urban communities, than mass culture. He noted that miners in Northumberland danced folk dances, and so did people in the suburbs of Sheffield, farmworkers in Oxfordshire and middle-class people in London. He was edging, it seems, towards a highly original attempt to solve the North–South divide in interwar Britain, singlehandedly, but it is not clear why he was using the German press to work out his ideas. He possibly needed the money as the tour was running at a loss; not because of poor ticket sales, but because halls had to be hired, costumes prepared, posters produced and programmes printed. The tour ended with debts of £35, which seems to have been largely due to the hyperinflation rather than poor attendance at the performances. The price of the programmes alone came to £10 and the price had risen by 350 per cent from between when they were ordered in July, and when they were paid for in September.[113]

It is not clear from the records of the tour where the dancers lived or indeed whether they were all students. They were not all at Cambridge University. One of the female dancers was based in Withington in Manchester.[114] Rolf Gardiner began to keep more comprehensive records as his various cultural exchanges developed during the 1920s. The overall impression left by this first venture was that its participants were all middle-class and a civilised and decorous group of young people. No romantic or sexual liaisons between the dancers were reported, which seems surprising given that there were no older adults on the tour and all the participants would have been in their late teens and early twenties.

Rolf Gardiner came back from the tour a hero in the eyes of some prominent public figures. Mary Neal and Mrs Pethick-Lawrence were dying to meet him. Neal wrote a spirited letter to him after the tour, though the two had never met, and described Gardiner's dispute with Sharp as a generational struggle between 'youth, growth, life, joy and beauty and age, decay, pedantry and death'.[115] Sharp was in his 60s at the time and was to die two years later, coincidentally when Rolf Gardiner was on a folk dance tour of the Cotswolds with the Travelling Morrice.

In Cambridge, Rolf acquired an influential fan, Dr Edward Dent, a Fellow of King's and the Professor of Music at Cambridge from 1927. He was much older than Gardiner (he was in his mid-forties at the time of Gardiner's first dance tour), but he emerged as a key figure in Gardiner's international ventures. He had backed the 1922 tour, passing a reassuring verdict on the efficacy of the tour: 'I am sure that a group of young people like yourself with friendly connections in Germany (and the Wandervogel connection is very important) would have every chance of success, whereas Cecil Sharp with patriotic tub-thumping and a great send off from the *Morning Post* and *Daily Mail* would be a complete failure, except at the YMCA in Cologne, and would do more harm than good.'[116] Dent was a frequent visitor to Germany and saw his role as promoting Cambridge's image abroad rather than England's. He toured Germany with Cambridge choirs along with his friend Dennis Arundel, who ran the Trinity Madrigal Choir. Dent was not an internationalist at all, but a Little Englander, and Gardiner found his attempts to promote Cambridge culture abroad vulgar. Dent told Gardiner: 'I think it is desirable that foreigners should get it well rubbed into them that Cambridge is the intellectual leader of all that is best in English life.' His own version of Cambridge culture, however, was far more elitist than Gardiner's. He was not interested in folk music, only in classical music; but he publicised Gardiner's folk dances abroad. 'Munster is very much interested in you and your folk dancers', he told Gardiner in 1926, 'and if you are bringing them to Germany again this year, you must certainly arrange for a show there.'[117]

In 1928, Dent wrote from Germany again, inviting Gardiner over to perform sword dances in Essen. He frequently discussed Gardiner's cultural work not only with Germans but with his fellow dons in the common rooms of Cambridge. In 1931 Dent attended a tea party at Trinity College where Rolf Gardiner's recent Baltic Tour was discussed, though Gardiner was not present. Dent wanted Gardiner to develop closer links again with Cambridge and to conduct his foreign tours through Cambridge's musical societies. This is significant because it suggests that Rolf Gardiner was a more influential figure abroad than Dent by 1931. This had not been the case in the mid-1920s, when the *Daily Telegraph* had described Dent as 'our Ambassador of Music'.[118] Gardiner never took up this offer, however.

He saw Cambridge as an 'official body', just like the EFDS, and the close friendship between Dent and Gardiner seems to have been severed for several years after Gardiner's refusal to cooperate with Dent and Cambridge in 1931.[119]

Rolf Gardiner's European visits were numerous during the 1920s and into the early 1930s and they were covered in the national and international press. But one of the most intriguing of his musical tours was undertaken in September 1931, one of the worst years of the interwar Depression, when Gardiner made contact with working-class communities in Yorkshire (see Figure 2). Gardiner was a well-known national figure by 1931. W. H. Auden had learned of his cultural work and had invited Rolf up to Scotland in 1930 and a journalist on the *Manchester Guardian*, David Ayerst, was keen to join Gardiner's tour of Yorkshire. He also wanted Gardiner to meet his friend, a young composer called Michael Tippett.[120] The Yorkshire tour of 1931 brought Gardiner into contact not only with working-class communities in the North, but with many young music enthusiasts around the country who applied to join the tour. Rolf selected all the people who applied and took 50 people – 25 English participants were to be joined half-way through the tour by 25 Germans travelling on a ferry from Hamburg to Hull. His English group were a very broad cross-section of 18 to 25 year-olds, from music students who could sing and play an instrument to others who were clueless about music but keen. He had people from rural England and young sophisticated people from central London.

They were all of a liberal disposition and some had already worked with working-class communities. Virginia Coit, of London, was one of Rolf Gardiner's closest friends. She was 27, lived in London and had been researching working-class education in Germany, and had worked among the unemployed communities of South Wales, where she read to women and their infants the poetry of John Keats and W. B. Yeats. She was a very liberal-minded spirit who hated the Nazis and found, to her relief, that the young men she talked to in Germany did too.[121] Another female on the tour was Dorothy Collingham, aged 24, who worked for the Women's Institute in Farnham, Buckinghamshire. She was also one of Gardiner's friends and was obviously irritated at having to complete the application form. She wrote impatiently: 'Dancing Experience: Varied; anyway you know more or less'.[122] Joan Brocklebank of Dorset, who did not give her age, was new to Gardiner. She was a friend of the Trevelyan family and wrote hesitantly: 'my accomplishments are not very many. I haven't got much voice, but I can sing in tune ... I can't play any musical instrument.' She was still selected for the tour. At the other extreme, musically, were Elizabeth Chetwynd, aged 23, from London, a music student who played the violin; and Muriel Cracknell, aged 25, from Grimsby, a singer and dancer who described her dancing ability as 'Advanced'. There were undergraduates on the tour such as Sophie Hopkinson, 19, a student at Cambridge, who could sing well, and there were young farmers with a limited education. For many of the southerners it was an adventure into the unknown and Yorkshire was as foreign to them as it was for the young Germans. A teacher at Stowe School remarked: 'Yorkshire is very nearly a foreign country and we came all the fresher to it for that'.[123]

What was the purpose of Rolf Gardiner's Yorkshire tour? He described his purpose to the Lord Mayor of Hull as 'experiments in living'. He also wanted to achieve a second objective: 'communion with places and people'.[124] How did he set about achieving these aims? He began by making English and Germans share rooms, but the tour party were not living among the people of Yorkshire. They were staying at a large country house on the outskirts of Middlesbrough, Ormesby Hall. Relations between the young English and Germans were very strained. The English would play croquet while the Germans watched and in the actual performances they would perform separately. In Middlesbrough Town Hall the English singers sat at the back of the stage while the Germans sang madrigals. The English singers then sang Purcell alone. The performances mixed high culture and popular culture and this must have seemed refreshing to the audiences. An English folk dance such as 'The Nutting Girl' would be immediately followed by the Germans singing a canon. Rolf Gardiner performed alone at some points – dancing a jig – then an orchestra would play Mozart.[125]

The group did make contact with places and people, even if they could not understand each other. Rolf Gardiner took male dancers off to dance sword dances with unemployed miners and, in the first folk dance performance at Stokesley, miners performed alongside the male student folk dancers. The student participants visited factories in Leeds and York. At Burton's, in Leeds, they sang and danced in front of factory workers and were clapped 'very loudly'. At York, they visited Rowntree's chocolate manufacturers and put on a 45-minute dance on the lawns for female factory workers, and were invited to stay for lunch. Christopher Scaife, Rolf's musical director, and a future Professor at the Hebrew University in Cairo, was far more succinct than Rolf in summing up the purpose of the tour. It projected three main messages: 'Counterpoint, Beer and Good Fellowship'.[126]

Rolf Gardiner's own profile was significantly enhanced by the tour. A Leeds reporter was captivated by Gardiner's presence and wrote: 'He is the most lively and enthusiastic of any student who ever came out of Cambridge.'[127] Even *The Times* reported the tour and spoke of Gardiner's 'crucial role' in promoting Anglo-German relations.[128] The participants were filmed in Ripon by Movietone News and watched themselves in a cinema at York later on.[129] But the event does seem to have been slightly surreal and dreamlike. It came at a transitional phase in Rolf Gardiner's

Figure 2 Rolf Gardiner's Folk Dance Group 'on tour' in Yorkshire, 1931. Gardiner is in the foreground.

Source: Rolf Gardiner Papers, Cambridge University Library.

own life and he did not really know what his Yorkshire tour set out to do and whether it achieved anything. He told his future wife Marabel, who was on the tour, that it had achieved nothing.[130] Certainly, the vision he articulated to the press sounded very dreamy and almost childlike. 'He believes', the *Leeds Mercury* reported, 'that a revival of the happier spirit of former times can be attained through a revival of the songs and dances of the village greens of England.'[131] This must have sounded very odd in a major industrial city like Leeds. The reporters who covered the tour were largely bemused by the performances. The reporter in Middlesbrough watched one of the Morris dances and had no other word for it than 'interesting', which seemed to mean baffling.[132] The dancers wore rustic costumes. The females wore lemon-coloured dresses, and ribbons dangling from their waists whirled round as they danced. The young males wore white flannels, blue baldrics, ribbons on the sides of their trousers and cloth balls hanging from their legs. The participants were extremely versatile. They performed folk dances in the open air during the day and gave concerts of sacred music in churches in the evenings. The young Germans joined the English in the churches but they did not perform folk dances.[133]

At the church performances, the English and the Germans performed separately, and the dancers had minimal contact with Yorkshire people for most of the tour.[134] The genteel logkeeper, 'Phyllis', observed that many children who watched the outdoor performances had dirty faces. and in Middlesbrough they performed for a 'not over-clean crowd'. Her account of the tour was over 100 pages long but she did not mention a single conversation she had had with local people, or cite any remark by one of the Yorkshire inhabitants.[135] To a reporter in Durham who watched a performance at Durham Cathedral, the singers seemed detached. The females wore veils over their faces.[136] The tour came at an uncertain stage of Rolf Gardiner's own life. The press reported that he was a student, and his youthful demeanour may have given this impression. But he was not a student and had not been for seven years. He did not really have a career at this period. He had just taken up farming, and he evidently had lots of time on his hands.[137]

Conclusion

Rolf Gardiner is an intriguing cultural commentator and activist of the interwar years. He had many gifts and one of his most precious gifts was his ability to inspire people his own age to do things. He is primarily of interest during the 1920s as offering new ideas on how youth in Northern Europe could experiment with new ways of living.[138] He was a product of urban England and of a very comfortable upper middle-class upbringing, but his vision was to create cultural bonds between different social groups in Britain and in his work with European youth movements of the 1920s and 1930s. He exerted a benign influence on British cultural life during the 1920s and made a highly original contribution to youth affairs. He was noticed and widely admired by his elders and deserves to be considered an important thinker and activist in the field of youth cultures and youth movements during these years. It could be argued that there was no youth culture in Britain between the Wars, even when due acknowledgement has been given to Rolf Gardiner. There was no pop music, no Elvis Presley, no Beatles, no youth marketing industry to generate a youth culture; and no Spice Girls. But this would be incorrect. There was a youth culture that was taking shape in the universities, but it was not a consumer-oriented youth culture.[139] It was something far more communal and experimental. It was a youth culture rooted in outlook and rooted in relationships with like-minded people and also with communities different from one's own. If this culture had a dynamic it was not disposable income, as with the working-class youth cultures of the period, but travel: domestic travel and foreign travel. This offered excitement, opportunities to develop relationships with like-minded friends, and it offered the prospect of new experiences and contact with other social classes. Rolf Gardiner was a key figure in the development of this activity.

3

The Flapper Cult in Interwar Britain: Media Invention or the Spark that Ignited Girl Power?

In Hollywood films of the 1920s, and in the short stories and novels of F. Scott Fitzgerald, the flapper is a cigarette-smoking, dance-mad young female in her teens to early twenties. Her hair is 'bobbed' or 'shingled' and neatly tucked under a cloche hat; a sort of helmet that clasped the head like a bathing hat. She wears knee-length skirts and make-up. She is the most iconic figure of the American 'Roaring' Twenties; and the symbol of teenage emancipation.[1] The classic Hollywood flappers were Clara Bow, Colleen Moore and Louise Brooks; all very young actresses in their late teens to early twenties at their peak, who made era-defining films such as *It* (Clara Bow, 1927), *Flaming Youth* (Colleen Moore, 1923) and *Pandora's Box* (Louise Brooks, 1927).[2] The movie flapper outlasted these iconic silent film actresses and survived into the new era of Hollywood musicals. In 1929, for example, a Super Cinema in Manchester screened the film 'Movietone Follies of 1929'. It was advertised as a Hollywood musical about 'Youth with a capital Y' and featured a 'Jazz-mad Flapper' (played by Sue Carroll). It drew huge audiences and was screened at Manchester Hippodrome, a large city-centre cinema, for an unprecedented three-week period.[3]

Much is known about the Hollywood flappers of the 1920s. Clara Bow and Louise Brooks had only fleeting film careers. Clara Bow, the most famous of the flapper film stars of the Twenties, rose and fell from public approval before she passed her 25th birthday. She had emerged from an impoverished family in Brooklyn, New York, and by 1928 was receiving over 35,000 fan letters every month. But her Brooklyn accent was so strong that when the talkies came (in the late 1920s) she was unable to make the transition from silent films to talking films. Her private life also damaged her reputation. She was a flapper in reality as well as on screen. She pursued a highly promiscuous and hedonistic lifestyle and in 1931, at the age of just 25, her affair with a married man was revealed in a high profile court case. It ended her career.[4] Louise Brooks, meanwhile, a major Hollywood flapper star of the 1920s' silent film era, thereafter fell into total obscurity until she was discovered living in poverty in a New York apartment during the 1980s.[5]

The Hollywood flappers were fashion icons as well as young actresses. Clara Bow, the 22-year-old star of *It* (1927), and Colleen Moore, 23-year-old star of *Flaming Youth* (1923), made the 'bobbed' haircut the first global youth hairstyle.[6] But the flapper look signified much more than a boyish and chic hairstyle. Hollywood flappers also projected a lifestyle. *Flaming Youth*, one of the early flapper films, featured premarital sex, abortion, nude swimming parties, illegal drinking and an adolescent girl losing her virginity to an older man.[7] Clara Bow's film *It*, based on the best-selling novel by Elinor Glyn, was so sexually charged it drove one 14-year-old American Boy Scout who saw it to write in protest: 'I believe *It* with Clara Bow is entirely a menace to the community. Pictures of such sort should not be allowed in the community.' However, an older boy of 17 was more positive: 'I liked *It*. It was a wonderful interpretation of alluring women.'[8] In Britain the film was greeted with alarm by the *Daily Express*. '*It* is bilge', wrote the paper's film critic; who added: 'of the worst possible type, a six-reel lesson on sex attraction that would be funny if one could forget the hundreds of thousands of youths and flappers who will absorb Madame Glyn's sententious drivel and attempt to cultivate her definition of "It" as portrayed by Miss Bow.'[9]

There is a growing scholarly literature on the American flapper, and on the Flapper cult in Europe. Steven Zdatny, for example, has shown that in Paris during the 1920s the flapper image, christened the 'garçonne' look, was so pervasive among young females of all social classes that it fuelled an enormous expansion of the hairdressing trade.[10] The British flapper, however, languishes in almost total obscurity. Hardly anything is known about the cult in Britain. No scholarly monograph has appeared and all we have are sketchy details supplied in impressionistic 'social histories' of the interwar period such as Graves and Hodge's *The Long Weekend* and scattered references in secondary works.[11] Indeed, some recent historians even question whether there was a Flapper cult at all in interwar Britain. Sheila Rowbotham, for example, argues that it was at best a 'half-truth': an image concocted by the press and probably experienced as a lifestyle by only a tiny minority of middle-class young women in London.[12]

The following chapter is primarily a work of excavation, and surveys both primary and secondary material on the British flapper in an attempt to discover the answer to a basic question: did the British flapper exist? It also explores further questions not adequately addressed in current social histories of the period: for example, was the Flapper cult an invention of the tabloid press (most notably, the *Daily Mail*), or a female youth lifestyle in interwar Britain?[13] How far was the British flapper primarily a metropolitan phenomenon, largely restricted to a few hundred middle-class girls and young women in affluent districts of London such as Mayfair and Kensington? – an impression strongly suggested in novels and memoirs of the period; in both highbrow and tabloid newspapers; in working-class autobiographies, and in fleeting references to flappers made by recent historians.[14]

Several further questions arise from the rich array of sources available on the British flapper; namely, newspapers, memoirs, contemporary social surveys, flapper novels, student periodicals and other sources. Was there a provincial flapper? If so, how did the Flapper cult spread from metropolitan communities to provincial towns and cities? What did being a flapper signify? Was it a female youth cult and an expression of teenage empowerment, as in the United States?[15] Or is it best seen as an expression of the social aspirations of working-class and middle-class girls, perhaps seeking to emulate upper-class debutantes?[16] Was it, as two recent fashion historians have claimed, a challenge to the patriarchal nature of British society during the 1920s?[17] How central was sexuality to the Flapper cult in Britain? How far did a Flapper lifestyle permeate working-class communities and reach the mill girls of Northern England, as well as the middle-class typists of Kensington and Mayfair?[18]

Our exploration of this intriguing cultural phenomenon needs to begin by tracing the lineage of the term 'flapper'. Deirdre Beddoe, using Graves and Hodge's unreliable survey as her source, has suggested that the term 'flapper' first began to be used in Britain 'about 1912';[19] but this is erroneous. It actually goes back much further. The Cambridge student paper *Varsity* noted, for example, as early as 1906: 'Here we were in tight uniforms stepping out to raucous bugles beneath the eyes of many flappers.'[20] At this stage, it meant young girls with pigtails; and this meaning survives down to the First World War. The magazine *Home Chat* recorded in 1915: 'She was the jolliest flapper I had seen, with her long plait of hair down her back.'[21] By 1920, just five years later, 'a flapper' had ceased to mean an innocent schoolgirl. In Britain, as elsewhere, it now described fashion-conscious young women with bobbed hair; moreover, young women who were pleasure-seekers, who danced risqué Negro dances like the Charleston and the Black Bottom (energetic dances that involved much bodily contact between male and female partners) and who wore make-up.[22] How this happened is still shrouded in mystery in all the secondary sources that touch on the subject. But the impression given is that the first precocious, sexy flappers were the young munitions workers of the First World War period.[23]

Adrian Bingham, in a scholarly study of gender in the British popular press of the Twenties, touches on the subject of the flapper. But his focus is entirely on the 'Votes For Flappers' press campaign waged by the *Daily Mail* in the late 1920s.[24] This is a fascinating episode because it projected the flapper, by this time a generic term used in the popular press to describe all females between 21 and 30, before a national audience. Thus by 1928, the year young women of 21–9 were given the vote in Britain, everyone who read a newspaper would have been familiar with flappers; and probably seen pictorial images of them in newspapers like the *Daily Express* and *Daily Mail*, both mass circulation papers of the period.[25] But was there a Flapper cult in Britain before the press and Stanley Baldwin, the Prime Minister who granted votes for flappers, created the generic flapper voter?

It is clear from existing research that the British flapper has a low-key image compared with the flappers of France and the United States during the Twenties, but why? It is useful to begin with the circumstances that triggered the emergence of the Flapper cult in these latter countries, in order to identify why perhaps the flapper was a more muted phenomenon in Britain. In France the flapper image was first projected in the pages of a novel: Victor Margueritte's *La Garconne* (published in 1922). The focus of the story is a 19-year-old flapper called Monique who leaves home (after her fiancé has been unfaithful); cuts her hair short, dresses in men's clothes and pursues a series of lesbian affairs. The book was a bestseller (it sold over 750,000 copies in its first year of publication).[26] It also triggered a cultural revolution of a kind, bringing about a huge transformation in women's hairdressing in France as 'millions of francaises cut their hair "a la garconne"'.[27] In the United States, meanwhile, the flapper image also had a far-reaching social impact. It created a huge consumer market and especially in the centres of American youth culture during the Twenties, the elite universities. At Harvard, for example, 85 per cent of the total student population smoked cigarettes during the 1920s. At the University of Pennsylvania, female students bought, on average, each year: seven dresses, five sweaters, three skirts, one coat, three hats, four pairs of shoes, 25 pairs of stockings, 12 articles of lingerie, and four pairs of gloves.[28] The flapper style also trickled down from the elite universities to non-elite universities; with female college students purchasing tubular dresses (classic flapper style), yellow raincoats, silk stockings, bandanas tied at the head and waist (very flapper gear), and some female students even wore masculine clothes such as waistcoats, ties and knickerbockers.[29]

It seems that Hollywood films were the trigger for flapper wear on American campuses; and American university students were regular cinemagoers. Every student in the US visited a cinema, on average, once a week during the 1920s.[30] Moreover, there were Hollywood films made about university life in the United States; suggesting that university students were part of mainstream youth culture and not detached from it.[31] *The Plastic Age*, released in 1925, was based on a scandalous novel about American college students and starred the 20-year-old Clara Bow.[32] American college students were also keen on jazz, and jazz bands regularly played concerts at American universities.[33]

In Britain, if there was a Flapper culture it was hardly likely to be found in the universities, where male students dwarfed female students. In the elite British universities, Oxford and Cambridge, male students were in an overwhelming majority during the 1920s. In 1925 Oxford had 4353 students (only 820 of whom were females). Cambridge had 5203 (only 475 of whom were females). Indeed, after the Asquith Commission into Oxford and Cambridge in 1922, both universities set a ceiling on the number of female students they would admit: in Cambridge it was set at approximately one-tenth of the total student body (female students were not to exceed 500); in Oxford the five women's 'societies' (not yet permitted the status of colleges) were not to admit more than 840 students and the ratio there was 1 female student for every 6 male students by the late 1920s.[34]

In the United States there were roughly equal proportions of male and female students nationally and as around 30 per cent of 18-year-olds went to University they were a significant component of the youth population.[35] During the 1920s, however, less than 2 per cent of 18-year-olds in Britain attended universities, and this remained the case down to 1939.[36] Moreover, the vast majority of these students in British universities were males. In 1919, on the cusp of the emergence of discussion about Youth Culture in British universities,[37] the student population doubled. There was a massive influx of 27,000 Ex-Service students brought into the universities under the 1918 Education Act and they reached the universities for the first time in 1919.[38] But all of these 27,000 new students were males. Furthermore, 6 per cent of them were over 30 and 12 per cent were married – a situation hardly conducive to the creation of a Flapper student culture.[39] But while British universities were not, it seems, the primary sites of flapper styles in dress as in the United States, they were permeated by the Flapper ethos, and the evidence of this can be briefly considered.

In Cambridge flapper dresses and cloche hats were advertised in student papers, and these papers carried numerous photographs of young female undergraduate actresses with bobbed or shingled hair, and wearing slinky dresses. As early as November 1923 the *Cambridge Gownsman* ran a front-page advertisement for cloche hats and Turkish cigarettes. The hats were marketed at 'the flapper girl' and 'the dapper girl'. Moreover, the spirit of flapperdom is hinted at in the films shown locally in 1923: 'Jazzmania' was screened in November 1923 and was described in the *Gownsman* as 'almost too exciting'; and '*A Girl's Desire*' was shown in the same week.[40] The most celebrated flapper film, 'It', starring Clara Bow, was shown in Cambridge in November 1927. Bow was described in the student paper The *Cambridge Gownsman* as 'Hollywood's leading exponent of feminine S.A. [Sex Appeal]' and, in more risqué fashion, as 'positively top-heavy with It'. Indeed, the student reviewer of '*It*' liked the film and Clara Bow, reporting: 'It is an excellent film … Clara Bow … was not at all vulgar and, in fact, made a very life-like shop-girl.'[41] There is no doubt, there-fore, that the flapper image certainly reached Cambridge University during the 1920s. But behind the images of Cambridge as a sexually liberated city for females – the Turkish cigarette advertisements and photographs of glamorous flapper actresses in Cambridge – the reality was somewhat different. Female students in Cambridge during the 1920s had to have a chaperone with them at all times – even if they were visiting the river with their brother. Also, a female university student was not allowed to enter a cinema in Cambridge, except with a friend.[42]

In any case, as revealed in Chapter 2, youth culture in British universities during the Twenties was being driven forward not by images of American flappers and the commercialised youth culture of the Jazz Age, but by a more organic and European model of youth culture being developed by individuals like Rolf Gardiner. This form of youth culture was rooted not in cinemas and dance halls, the sources of the Flapper cult; but in a cult of asceticism involving strenuous hiking, lengthy and uncomfortable foreign travel in third-class train compartments, frenetic performances of English folk dance in open air marketplaces and, if possible, cultural contact with remote peasant communities in the Italian or Bavarian Alps.[43] Rolf Gardiner himself, the prime mover in so much of this vibrant organic youth culture of the Twenties, never attended the cinema so would probably not have encountered a Hollywood flapper.[44]

So, students can be largely discounted as agents of flapperdom in the British context. Moreover, the fragmentary glimpses of flappers we gain from newspaper reports suggest that there was no trigger in Britain such as a celebrated flapper novel or a highly publicised Hollywood film. There was at least one flapper film released in Britain – '*The Irresistible Flapper*', released in 1919; but it was not widely publicised at the time and certainly did not trigger a cultural movement such as the bobbed hair look in Paris following the publication of Victor Margueritte's novel.[45] In fact, the British flapper was hardly discussed in the British press of the early–mid-1920s, when thousands of young females in Paris were having their hair bobbed and the American flapper was being analysed in print by young writers like F. Scott Fitzgerald and his glamorous young wife Zelda.[46]

The British flapper was announced to the public in a highly unglam-orous fashion – by a medical doctor delivering a lecture at the Institute of Hygiene in London.[47] Dr R. Murray-Leslie was concerned about what he called 'the excess' of females in the population (over 1 million females who were unlikely to find husbands due to the demographic impact of the First World War). He was alarmed that young females of the 'middle and upper classes' were delaying marriage and pursuing a hedonistic lifestyle, which he associated with the emergence of the flapper. In a lecture that was intended only to reach a middle-class audience and politicians, Murray-Leslie drew attention to a new female cult. 'The social butterfly type has probably never been so prevalent as at present,' he asserted:

> It comprised the frivolous, scantily-clad, jazzing flapper, irresponsible and undisciplined, to whom a dance, a new hat, or a man with a car, are of more importance than the fate of nations.[48]

These comments on British flappers appeared in *The Times*, but they were also reported in the *Daily Mail* and even in provincial newspapers such as the *Manchester Evening News*.[49] At this stage, no details were given about where the Flapper cult was to be found. But it was not exclusively among middle- and upper-class girls, it appears. For instance, flappers were observed dancing to jazz music in broad daylight in Morecambe during August 1919: 'the couples are usually made up of flappers, who valiantly attempt the intricacies of the jazz-rolle in walking skirts and jumpers.'[50] For much of the period between 1919 and the Flapper Vote controversy in 1927–8, the British press could not decide whether the flapper was a working-class female or a middle-class female. *The Times* called an eclectic range of young females 'flappers' – young munitions workers (in October 1919); young women who liked horse racing and attended 'flapper race meetings' in Ireland (November 1919); young female clerical workers, who were referred to as 'flapper typists' (June 1920); young women who were flirts (July 1920) and young actresses who featured in plays in London's West End such as Noel Coward's *Hay Fever* (January 1926).[51] There was even a report of an 'Edinburgh flapper' (June 1922), who appeared in a novel by Rebecca West and was described as a feminist.[52] The BBC, meanwhile, broadcast 'flapper songs' (February 1924) and comedy sketches featuring flappers (November 1924).[53] It was only in 1927 that the flapper was given a fixed identity as a young female of 21 to 29 who lacked the vote and who was finally given it by Baldwin's Conservative Government in 1928.[54] Indeed Baldwin, a lifelong supporter of female suffrage who unveiled a statue of the suffragette leader Emmeline Pankhurst when he was Prime Minister and who admired the female novelist Mary Webb, more than any other individual brought the British flapper to national prominence.[55]

The British flapper seems to have been primarily a figure in literature rather than an important cultural phenomenon. There were a number of flapper novels on the British market by the late 1920s; some of which were originally published in the United States and featured American flappers.[56] The satirical magazine *Punch* carried cartoons of flappers, by Lewis Baumer; initially of scrawny androgenous female tennis players. But, by the late Twenties, Baumer's images of flappers were appearing regularly in the *Daily Express*. They depicted flappers as glamorous young females. One of these illustrations was of a smart and sophisticated young woman wearing a cloche hat, tubular dress and leaning nonchalantly against a stool, smoking a cigarette. Another portrayed Stanley Baldwin entranced by a young flapper applying make-up in a park.[57]

So far, these fragmentary media images of British flappers suggest that they were, overwhelmingly, genteel middle-class girls and young women. But this is probably a simplification. For example, in 1923 a young female factory worker from Willesden, north London, told a careers officer she wanted to be 'a flapper in an office'. She had seen pictures of flappers in *Punch* and wanted to be one.[58] This is a revealing piece of evidence. It suggests that the real generator of the flapper image in interwar Britain was not Hollywood, but the enormous expansion of clerical work for young females. Between the censuses of 1911 and 1931, in fact, the number of females employed in clerical work in Britain grew from 183,000 to 1.3 million.[59] Moreover, clerical work did generate new lifestyles. It was a magnet for young, single women; many of whom migrated long distances to commercial cities like Manchester and London during the 1920s, and into the 1930s, and effectively lived independent lives away from their parents.[60] During the 1920s, for example, thousands of teenage girls and young women were transferred to jobs in new cities under the Government Transference scheme (4000 in 1929 alone); and this was just the tip of the iceberg as the Juvenile Employment Bureaux active in big cities like Manchester also placed large numbers of young female and male migrants into jobs locally.[61]

There was also a café and restaurant culture linked to office work. At lunchtimes young office workers were observed sitting chatting and smoking in the cafés of London, for example, during the First World War; and by the late 1920s an American student visiting London was shocked to see so many young 'girls' sitting in restaurants and smoking. 'I was a bit surprised to see so many girls in London smoking in public', she recorded. 'It seems to be quite the custom for them to take out their cigarette-cases in restaurants and light up. You do not see so much of that in New York.'[62] Nerina Shute was one of these independent young women of the Twenties. She was just 19 in 1928 when she took up work as a typist in central London. She lived, initially, in lodgings in a hostel and then met a young bohemian couple who invited her to live in their luxurious flat at the grand location of 23 Carlton House Terrace. There, she met other young professionals and began attending parties; on one occasion a risqué party where the guests were dressed only in their underwear.[63] Shute then changed jobs and moved into journalism. She became a film reviewer for *Film Weekly* and wrote a novel; which received an unfavourable review from Rebecca West. 'Miss Shute writes, not so much badly as barbarously,' West wrote; adding, 'as if she had never read anything but a magazine . . .' Shute candidly admitted that this was true.[64]

Nerina Shute's memoir of life as a 'twenty-something' female living and working in central London during the 1920s is a valuable work; not least because our image of London youth culture in the 'Roaring Twenties' is still that of the effete upper-class youths down from Oxford, and labelled by the press at the time as the 'Bright Young Things'.[65] These were the party-going upper-class youths whose lives were chronicled in Evelyn Waugh's novel *Vile Bodies* and in the society pages of newspapers such as the *Daily Express* and *Daily Mail*. It has long been clear to historians that the Bright Young Things were not the forerunners of modern youth culture.[66] They had minimal contact with any social group outside their own circle and certainly no cultural contact with youths from the working-classes (as Rolf Gardiner in Cambridge did, for example).[67] Moreover, the two leading figures among the Bright Young Things, Harold Acton and Brian Howard, were both exotic characters. Acton was an aesthete primarily interested in art, who eventually emigrated to Italy. Brian Howard was a troubled young Oxford dandy who committed suicide in 1958.[68]

Shute's memoir is a valuable corrective to the media-driven image of the Bright Young Things of London in the Twenties. It throws much-needed light on the prosaic aspects of the lives of twenty-somethings: their attitude to sexual relationships, to marriage and, revealingly, to America. The impression Shute gives is that the young professionals she mixed with were not superficial or hedonistic youth, as Waugh suggested in his novel *Vile Bodies*. Far from being inspired by the hedonistic lifestyles portrayed in American flapper films, Shute's contemporaries were actually trying to resist the Americanisation of British cultural life. As she puts it:

> Gramophones ... Talkies and modern friendships were all designed to stop us from thinking.... The art of conversation died a long time ago, when the American mania for ... excitement was born.[69]

But, as Shute's memoir reveals, young professionals like her continued to value conversation and the art of conversation. They spoke of all sorts of things and frankly – sex, the novels of D. H. Lawrence (more sex), Aldous Huxley, Hemingway, Eugene O'Neill, Havelock Ellis, and current affairs.[70] It is perhaps debatable whether Nerina Shute would have liked to have been called a British flapper. Her independent lifestyle and occupation fit the media image of the flapper; but her anti-Americanism does not. She was only superficially a flapper in that she worked for the media industry as a film critic. In reality, she was a highbrow who was not influenced by films and did not talk about films in her leisure time. Moreover, her values were very traditional. She disliked risqué parties and, far from pursuing a life of singledom and hedonism, she desperately wanted to marry.[71]

So far, we have seen glimpses of a Flapper lifestyle in different parts of Britain during the 1920s; but mainly through fleeting references in contemporary newspapers. How far was there a Flapper culture that took root in communities and permeated working-class communities, as well as middle-class communities? No historian has probed this question directly; but if there was a Flapper culture that did take root and spread, it is likely that the prime medium for its dissemination was the dance halls or palais de danse.[72] The first of these was the Hammersmith Palais, in London, opened in 1919. But by the late 1920s there were dance halls in most British towns and cities; many were situated in working-class districts and they were patronised almost exclusively by young people between 15 and 25 – the prime flapper age-groups.[73] These temples of interwar youth culture certainly projected an image of glamour. At the Hammersmith Palais there were tables surrounding the huge dance floor (the venue held over a thousand) and the furnishings were exotic. Chinese lanterns hung from the ceiling above the dance floor and indecipherable Chinese handwriting decorated the ceiling.[74] When Horace Wyndham visited in the mid-1920s he noticed many young males dressed in dinner jackets ('the local Beau Brummels'), and many glamorous young females – especially Jewish girls. As he put it: 'There is certainly a preponderance of the Chosen among the assembled throng, for the building is full of black-eyed, olive-hued damsels and crimped-haired and Nero-coiffeured young men.'[75] There was an MC (a Master of Ceremonies) who watched over the dancers; occasionally rebuking them for too much intimacy with the words: 'None of that, if you please. We are not the Holborn Town Hall.'[76] The Hammersmith Palais might have been a notch or two above a town hall dance, but it was certainly not expensive entertainment for city youths and young females. The dances ran from 8 p.m. to 12 p.m. on six nights of the week and the entrance fee was a humble half-crown (2s 6d) in the mid-1920s.[77] Other London dance halls could be even cheaper. The Carlton Dance Hall in Camberwell (south London) charged just 1 shilling.[78] There must have been young people of all social backgrounds at the Hammersmith Palais because it served much of West London: from working-class Hammersmith with its migrant Irish communities to more prosperous districts like Putney, Fulham and West Kensington.[79] The social tone of the Hammersmith Palais was clearly aspirational. The young habitués were no doubt predominantly young wage-earners from working-class and lower middle-class backgrounds but they were imitating High Society debutante dances.[80]

There was much social mixing in the cafés and restaurant of Twenties' London, and the Lyons Corner House on The Strand, in central London, was a haven for flappers of all social backgrounds. There, young typists and shopgirls would eat alongside young businesswomen and a three-course meal could be purchased for just 2 shillings at lunchtimes; with the added attraction of dance music from a resident orchestra as they ate. As the journalist W. L. George put it: 'The public of the Strand Corner House is . . . the world.'[81] Moreover, The Strand Corner House was the height of modernity; a plate-glass building catering primarily for fashion-conscious young people. The young males wore shirts purchased in Regent Street; the 'girls' wore outré outfits bought at West End Department stores.[82] W. L. George was convinced that the clientele at The Strand Corner House were mainly working-class youth from the East End, who travelled into the city on the London Underground from Aldgate (in East London) into Charing Cross (in the centre). As he walked along The Strand, he encountered young female office workers wearing face powder and lipstick and munching chocolates.[83] Across the city in Covent Garden another social commentator noticed that the main habitués at the Covent Garden Opera House, which had been converted into a dance hall, were shopgirls and young office workers.[84]

It seems that the root of the Flapper lifestyle of Twenties' London was the expansion of clerical work and this is revealed at a statistical level by the findings of the *New Survey of London* (*NSL*), published in 1929; the highpoint of the Flapper cult in interwar Britain. The authors of the *NSL* found that the main beneficiaries of the expanding clerical sector between the Wars were working-class youths and girls. As their work demonstrated, large numbers of juveniles of both sexes entered office work during the 1920s; most straight from elementary schools at age 14. As Herbert Llewellyn Smith, the principal author, put it: 'a large proportion of present-day London clerks are of working-class origin, and a considerable percentage of them are actually members of and living in working-class families.'[85] He secured wages data from a sample of over 4000 young clerks. All were from working-class families and their wages ranged from 10s–15s for 14-year-olds (of both sexes); 25s–30s for 17–19-year-olds and 35s–40s for 20–24-year-olds. On closer inspection, his data reveals that female office workers earned more than boys at certain ages. For example, 14–16-year-old girl clerks earned 17s 6d–20s; whereas boys of the same age earned only 15s–17s 6d.[86] But these findings make clear that young clerical workers whose weekly earnings between 17 and 25 were between 25s and 40s would have been well able to afford regular trips to the cafés of The Strand for 2s and, in the evenings, a trip to a palais de danse for around 2s.[87]

Thus it appears that W. L. George was not exaggerating when he referred to: 'These great crowds of young people with a little money in their pockets and much zest in their hearts' in his *A London Mosaic* (1921).[88] There were even books published documenting the pleasures of the London dance halls; such as V. Macclure's *How to be Happy in London* (1926). But how far did the Flapper lifestyle reach provincial communities during the 1920s?

The evidence of Flapper culture in provincial Britain is patchy. There were flappers in Manchester by 1925. As one local resident reported:

> A great number of flappers do swear and smoke. Two cafés, not a stone's throw away from where I live, are every Sunday evening simply packed with this type of girl, joking and sipping coffee in the company of boys, and unless you have an unseemly joke or tale to tell there, you are considered dull.[89]

Cheryl Buckley and Hilary Fawcett have uncovered photographs of wage-earning girls of Newcastle-upon-Tyne dressed in flapper outfits and cloche hats and photographed in 1929.[90] Another shows young mill girls from Darlington in flapper dresses and sporting bobbed hair in the mid-1920s.[91] In Birmingham a family business (the Hodsons) operated from a small terraced house and sold rayon (artificial silk) dresses in flapper designs to local girls and young women by 1926.[92] All of this is clear evidence that the Flapper look had reached working-class neighbourhoods by the late 1920s and it is not difficult to understand why. Flapper dresses were simple, cylindrical designs and could be made up easily on a sewing machine and using the dress designs supplied in cheap magazines like *Mab's Fashions*. But even in Selfridge's, London, flapper dresses were modestly priced – just 10s in 1924; and on one day the store sold 300 such dresses in a thirty-minute period.[93]

All in all, British flappers of the Twenties seem distinctly tame compared with the cigarette-smoking, cocaine-snorting, night-clubbing flappers of the American 1920s. As Penny Tinkler has shown, there is very little evidence, even, of a cigarette-smoking young female in Britain during the 1920s. In 1920 female smokers were not deemed important enough to record in official statistics. Female smoking became more pronounced by the close of the interwar period with females aged 15 and older smoking, on average, 500 cigarettes a year in 1939 (less than two cigarettes a day).[94] In British girls' magazines of the 1920s, the message peddled was that it was unacceptable for girls in their teens to smoke; and the female smokers depicted in these magazines were not flappers but outcasts – tomboy schoolgirls, mannish lesbians and spinsters.[95] There is some evidence, however, of cigarettes being targeted at females in their twenties. An advertisement in the women's magazine *Britannia and Eve* in 1929 depicted a flapper with bobbed hair leaning over a chair, smoking a cigarette. The caption read: 'Our New Electorate', a reference to the new Flapper voter.[96]

It may be that a hidden world of sexually-liberated, hedonistic, drug-taking and chain-smoking British flappers lurks beneath the surface of the newspaper coverage and other primary material of the period. If so, it would most likely be centred on the nightclubs of Twenties London such as 'The 43'; Mrs Meyrick's establishment in Soho.[97] But in the mainstream youth establishments, the palais de danse, which existed in most British towns and cities by the late 1920s, the overwhelming impression given in contemporary sources is that the Flapper look was an aspirational lifestyle which probably thousands of young females, working-class and middle-class, were able to pursue in an effort to re-invent or 're-fashion' themselves. The Twenties marked a clear break from the Edwardian class society and dowdiness of women's fashions. Between 1918 and 1925 alone, 11,000 dance halls and nightclubs were opened in Britain, catering predominantly for the under 25s.[98] Moreover, thousands of young workers of both sexes migrated for work to the cosmopolitan cities of Britain during this period; whether to commercial and industrial cities like Manchester in the north-west, a magnet for migrant juvenile workers throughout the interwar decades; or to cities like London in the more prosperous south-east. The flapper image was not a subversive image in British popular culture, as in the United States; but an image associated with stylish, wage-earning, and aspirational city females. A Flapper lifestyle undoubtedly existed in cities like London and had cross-class appeal. Whether the British flapper was consciously challenging the patriarchal nature of British society is unclear. The evidence available in memoirs suggests that far from rejecting patriarchal institutions such as marriage, young women of the British 1920s were playfully exploring new ways of living, perhaps in lodgings, until marriage, but not rejecting marriage.

4 Youth Culture in Early Twentieth-Century Ireland

Bernadette Devlin, reflecting on the student unrest at the London School of Economics during 1968, expressed horror at what she saw on her television set. 'We looked upon them (the students in Paris and London)...as a bunch of weirdos – we didn't know what the hell was annoying them, she told an interviewer in 1988.'[1] She was a university student herself in the late 1960s, studying Psychology at The Queen's University of Belfast. She implied, in her reflections on the period, that student and youth empowerment were an anathema in Northern Irish society during the 1960s. The Oxford historian R. F. Foster agrees. In his sparkling survey *Modern Ireland, 1688–1988* (1988), he dismisses the concept of youth culture as inapplicable to Northern Ireland in a single sentence, remarking that youth in the Province 'have always followed their elders'.[2] Is this correct? Has Northern Ireland for much of the twentieth century been insulated from the likes of the Teddy Boy, the teenage consumers of 1930s' and 1950s' Britain, the youth pop groups of the 1950s and '60s and the student youth movements of the 1960s in Britain, the United States, France, Germany and elsewhere in Europe?

The historian who wants to try to explain the absence of a distinct youth culture in twentieth-century Ireland, or to identify one, has a lifetime's work ahead of them. The sources available on the institutions that shaped the lives of the young are very rich for the interwar years, the focus of this chapter. Yet much of this material has not been utilised by historians. Many government files on juvenile delinquency, for example, have been shifted to outhouses 20 miles from the Public Record Office of Northern Ireland (PRONI) where much of the archival research for this chapter, and the following chapter, was conducted. Indeed, researching youth culture in twentieth-century Northern Ireland, as a Research Fellow at The Queen's University of Belfast between 1999 and 2002, sometimes felt like being a medievalist. It was as if the period from the end of the First World War down to the emergence of the People's Democracy movement in the late 1960s, which began as a student movement, were a cultural 'Dark Age' and not a glimmer of an apprentice's memoir or a young typist's diary shines through any of the historical surveys of twentieth-century Ireland.[3]

The following chapter is a comparative study of youth culture in Northern Ireland and the Irish Republic from *c*.1922 down to 1939. Its two central themes are: first, the role and impact of the YMCA (The Young Men's Christian Association), especially in Northern Ireland during the interwar years; and, secondly, the intriguing debate that emerged in the Irish Republic during the same period about the public dance halls and their role in the lives of Irish youth. The outcome of this debate was a major piece of government legislation in the Irish Republic: the Public Dance Hall Act of 1935.[4]

Early twentieth-century Ireland was a very youth conscious society. Belfast newspapers covered youth affairs diligently during the 1920s, reporting on such arcane matters as a new club for Newspaper Boys (established in 1926). These were juvenile street traders in their early teens, many of whom were homeless. Their club was to be a social centre, but it also had beds for needy youths.[5] There were, in addition, articles about more affluent young workers – girls who worked in shops or services in the city centre who were terrible at cooking and yet living independent lives in lodgings. They were told they had to learn to cook to be able to entertain friends and attract potential husbands.[6] Furthermore, a Young People's Week in October of 1926 in Belfast was widely-reported in the Belfast press. This event was a platform for a Presbyterian minister's visit to Belfast, but it provided a useful opportunity for Belfast citizens to comment on the lives of Ulster's youth.[7]

The Minister in question was Dr Harry Miller, a lecturer at the University of Edinburgh and a Settlement Leader in a slum district in the city. It emerged during his visit that he had fought alongside young soldiers from Northern Ireland at the Somme, and entertained them.[8] They were stationed on a hill called Etaples 'in those feverish days of the Somme push, when that vast reinforcements camp on the hill was ever full to the limit with young lads passing up the front to fill the awful gaps...'[9] Miller showed the young soldiers films every Sunday evening in a hut and preached to them. During 1926 Miller was in Belfast to try to draw more youths into the church. The organisers of the Young People's Week were, in fact, a committee the local Presbyterian churches had established on 'the State of Religion'. Miller was not only interested in the concerns of the church, however. He preached on social problems and wanted educated youths in Belfast to do social work. 'In Edinburgh University', he told an audience, 'men and women give much more attention to these questions. Here, particularly among the men students, they do not seem to face social questions at all.'[10] Miller was thus primarily interested in how Ulster's youth could serve Belfast rather than in the lifestyles or preoccupations of youth, but he had raised the subject of Ulster youth and in a newspaper, the *Northern Whig*, which described itself as the 'Brightest and Best Morning Paper in Ulster'.[11]

Behind the scenes at Miller's sermons in the Assembly Hall, Belfast, during October 1926, Belfast citizens were already reading about Ulster's youth. A series of articles on the subject had appeared in the *Northern Whig* the week before Miller's visit.[12] The author, mysteriously named 'W.A.', implied that a generation of youths had appeared in Ulster society since the War with no interest in politics, local or national affairs, and untouched by youth organisations. 'There are twenty thousand lads', he reported, 'about the streets of Belfast who have left school and are unoccupied in the evenings . . . of girls there are a corresponding number. We have flourishing organisations, but with their existing staff they are unable to cope with a tithe of the youths.'[13] He claimed that the suburbs and parts of the city centre were bereft of youth organisations. He observed in another article on 'Youth and the Corporation' that Ulster's youth were not interested in local affairs and disliked Ulster politicians. 'One cannot but be struck', he reported,

> by the feelings of disgust which Ulster's youth often have for politics, whether municipal or Parliamentary. It is particularly noticeable among those who have served in the War. Among these are some of the finest young men of the Province. They are perfectly loyal to Crown, Constitution and Empire, and for these many offered their lives. When it comes to identifying them with politics, they will have nothing to do with it. One attends political meetings – they are not there. Their services are lost to the community.[14]

Are we, then, dealing with a 'Lost Generation' when we consider the youth of 1920s' Ulster – the Northern Irish equivalent of the rootless individuals in English universities during the 1920s who no longer respected their fathers' generation?[15]

The YMCAs and Northern Irish Youth Culture

There is little evidence suggesting that Ulster youth were rejecting their elders during the 1920s and 1930s. Belfast's youth, in fact, wanted to be patronised and this is very clear from the work of the YMCAs. In the early 1920s, the YMCA's membership was spread throughout Ireland, from big city branches such as Wellington Place and Mountpottinger in Belfast to remote rural areas such as Spike Island in County Cork. Its highest membership was in the cities – in Belfast, with 350 members at the Wellington Place branch in 1921 and 108 at its East Belfast branch, Mountpottinger; Dublin, with three YMCAs in 1921 and almost 200 members at its city branch; and Londonderry, with 283 members in 1921.[16] By 1935, the

YMCA's membership in Northern Ireland had risen markedly. Belfast's city branch at Wellington Place had a membership of almost 2000; Mountpottinger YMCA had 310 members; a new branch on Shankill Road had 372 members and, elsewhere in Northern Ireland, Londonderry YMCA had 479 members; Carrickfergus had 125 and Enniskillen had 96. Furthermore, the YMCA's membership in 1935 was predominantly youths aged 18 or older (they were eligible to be full members up to 21).[17] There is no sign in these statistics, then, of a generational rift alienating older youths from organisations they did not control.

For, the YMCA's leaders during the 1920s and 1930s were, in chronological age, almost as far removed from these youths in their teens as it was possible to be. The National Secretary in the early 1920s was William Wright, an MBE, who had been National Secretary for 25 years when he decided to retire in 1924 at the age of 65.[18] He had, despite his age, been an energetic National Secretary. He made six or seven visits to YMCA branches across Ireland every two to three months and then reported back on them to his Executive Committee in Belfast. The YMCA's meetings were held in three places – Belfast, Dublin and Cork – and Wright attended them all. Wright died shortly after retiring in 1924 and the YMCA's Executive wrote movingly in its minutes that the YMCA had been 'his life'.[19] How were such aged, if noble, youth leaders able to enrich the lives of youths in their teens?

A cursory glance at the YMCA's official records reveals an obvious answer. The YMCA's buildings were spacious, well-equipped and warm. Cork YMCA looked like a building where the Lord Mayor of Cork might live.[20] Mountpottinger YMCA on Albertbridge Road in East Belfast was the size of a factory.[21] Inside such buildings were rooms with billiard tables (Mountpottinger had six in 1923), music rooms, parlours for reading newspapers and for conversation, libraries, debating rooms, rooms for drama societies, table tennis and even badminton. Londonderry YMCA subscribed to 30 journals and weekly magazines in 1925. They included: *Nineteenth Century, Fortnightly Review, Strand Magazine, London Magazine, Boys' Own Paper, The Catholic, Great Thoughts, Punch, The Spectator, Tit-Bits, English Mechanic, British Weekly*, and *The Christian*. Religious journals were thus not prominent. By 1934 it had added to these titles *The Ontario Bulletin, The Pathfinder* and *South America*, indicating that there was an interest in the club in emigration, and two journals indicated an interest in Animal rights: *The Animal's Defender* and *Vegetarian Messenger*. It also stocked assorted British, Northern Irish, Irish and Scottish newspapers: *The Morning Post, Daily Sketch, Daily Mail, Irish Times, Belfast News-Letter, The Times, Financial Times, Irish Independent, Northern Whig, Glasgow Herald* and *Belfast Telegraph*.[22] These tantalising details do not tell us much, but we must assume that newspapers and periodicals that were bought by an organisation always conscious of its limited finances were read. The impression given is of a deliberate attempt to nurture aspirational youths, knowledgeable about current affairs, history, Catholicism even, and of an egalitarian environment where young mechanics and adolescents mingled with intellectual and urbane youth who read *The Spectator* and *Punch*.

Who joined the YMCA? During the First World War its main work had been serving British soldiers stationed in Ireland. The YMCA established huts for them providing meals, writing paper and desks for them to write their letters home, and musical concerts. There were even YMCA huts in France during the War.[23] Many of the YMCA's members during the War, throughout Ireland, were in the Forces and there was a high recruitment rate even in the south.[24] (There was, of course, no conscription in Ireland during the First World War.) Belfast, Dublin, Londonderry and even Cork had very high YMCA involvement in the War. Belfast City branch had 350 members in 1921 and they had all served in the War; Londonderry had 283 and 109 had been in the War; at Dublin City branch, 250 YMCA members fought in the War, the highest figure outside Belfast, and in Cork, 58 of its 98 members in 1921 were in H.M. Forces during the War. We thus have a recruitment rate of between 50 and 100 per cent at the city YMCAs in Ireland. Recruitment in the smaller rural YMCAs was also not insignificant. Ballymena (County Antrim) had 59 members in 1921 and 25 had been in the War; in the south, 50 of Waterford YMCA's 236 members and 4 out of 8 at Ennis YMCA (King's County). The YMCA's war record was not forgotten in the south. In July 1922 Dublin City YMCA was doused in petrol and set on fire. One of its leaders was in the building at the time and, though the premises were 'practically destroyed', he managed to save the club's records and to wire a message to the headquarters branch in Belfast saying: 'We are quite sure that the whole tragedy will be over-ruled for the furtherance of the Dublin work, and to the glory of God.'[25]

Protestant youth were thinly spread in the south of Ireland and after Partition in 1922 the YMCA endeavoured to develop its work in difficult circumstances. It was overzealous at times. In 1922, for example, it tried to establish a YMCA branch at the University of Galway, but was told by the University authorities the plan was doomed as there was only one Protestant student in the University.[26] In Dundalk the YMCA had established 'Association Rooms' for young clerks ('Protestant young men chiefly of the business class'). During October 1921 there were clashes between local Catholics and Protestants in Dundalk and one of the town's 'Protestant business houses' had been 'burnt to the ground'. By July 1922 the local YMCA had closed and its leaders were trying to sell the building. They had, apparently, received a letter pointing out that the building 'might be burnt down' and the young clerks who used it had been threatened.[27]

Tralee YMCA (County Kerry) was also in the thick of violence in the early 1920s. The National Secretary had wanted to visit the branch to attend its annual meeting in 1920 but he was sent a telegram instructing him not to 'as, owing to the terrible state of the town, the meeting could not be held'.[28] Meanwhile, a YMCA party on their way to Bantry in a car to perform a concert for British troops were stopped 'by a body of some seven or eight men' and their car was taken. (The car was later recovered and the men were apprehended.)[29] The YMCA still pressed on with its work in the south. New branches were opened specifically for Protestant youths in Ballymote (County Sligo) and Cootehill (County Cavan) during 1921. Their aim was to give the few Protestant youths in these districts access to books and 'equipment'. The Executive in Dublin sent books to Cootehill to enable them to open a small library.[30]

Elsewhere in the south, the YMCA tried to establish branches but failed. In Killarney the environment was hopeless. William Wright told his committee back in Belfast: 'At Killarney I conferred with . . . our Corresponding member regarding the possibility of reviving our little YMCA Branch. He says it is hopeless, as there are now not more than 5 Protestant young men in Killarney. There is a population of nearly 6,000.'[31] The YMCA was also fussy about who it would work with to develop youth work. At Bandon there was already a 'Young Men's Society' in existence when Wright visited the area in October 1920. He reported back sniffily to his committee: 'At Bandon I visited . . . a Young Men's Society . . . Though not on our basis, I thought it well to get in touch and was glad to meet the Secretary and other leading members.'[32]

He was alluding to the spiritual side of the YMCA's work and the YMCA Executive attached great importance to this. The branches developed their own ethos, however, and the trade apprentices and young clerks who joined the organisation were not always Christians and were more interested, frequently, in other matters anyway. Wright was angry when he visited Waterford YMCA in March 1921. He reported back to his committee: 'The Waterford Association has suffered the religious side of the work to fall to zero . . . the Association cannot be regarded as fulfilling its aim until the spiritual side of its programme is revived, and I urged that this should be done.'[33] The trouble was over dances that Waterford YMCA had been holding regularly for about a year. The Executive had been so concerned it had organised a 'special visit' to the town in March 1920. A small YMCA delegation began by meeting with the Bishop of Waterford to gain the facts. A conference on dances followed and five Waterford youth leaders were invited. They all argued that the dances were 'properly conducted' and 'undesirable persons' were excluded. They had even established a Dance Committee to supervise the dances. They also said the dances were serving a useful purpose – bringing young Protestant youths and girls together and preventing 'mixed marriages'. 'They urged that such dances among Protestant young men and women were a safeguard against mixed marriages in a community like Waterford [i.e. overwhelmingly Catholic].' The Executive decided to tolerate dances at YMCA branches in the south and felt that banning them 'might do as much harm as good'. In other words, the YMCA would lose members it could not afford to in order to survive in the south. It still hoped that dances 'will be discontinued when the present craze for dancing has subsided'.[34]

In the north the YMCA's programmes were no more spiritual during the 1920s than in the south even though the YMCA felt less threatened. Mountpottinger YMCA specialised in billiards and in August 1920 it was trying to recover its billiard tables from a group of military personnel who had occupied the top floor of its premises.[35] In August 1920 it bought three new billiard tables with the income it received from leasing rooms to the Boy Scouts and Boys' Brigade.[36] Billiards were often discussed at the committee's meetings. In February 1921 two members reported the need for 'Billiard Table covers and additional cues'.[37] The following month billiards were on the agenda again and the committee recorded: 'It was moved . . . and passed – That 6 New Cues be purchased for Billiard Room.'[38] Later in the same year, in September 1921, another discussion of billiards ended with a decision that 'supplies of tips and chalk were (to be) maintained in the Billiard Room'. The issue of billiards was so central to Mountpottinger YMCA that a 'Billiard Room Sub-Committee' was appointed in September 1921 and six new billiard tables were ordered. They were very expensive. Two were installed in September 1921 and cost £160. Mountpottinger YMCA was so proud of a new billiard hall at the club that it organised an official opening in November 1921. It was followed by an exhibition billiard match.[39] Then disaster struck.

In December 1921 a group of Special Constables working for the Ministry of Home Affairs occupied Mountpottinger YMCA for about six months. At the time, the YMCA claimed it was serving 'about a thousand' youths of East Belfast and drafted a resolution politely asking the Constables to at least let their young members use the billiard room. 'To these young men', it recorded, 'this is a very great hardship and we respectfully urge that . . . we should be allowed the use of the Billiard Room . . . in order to keep [in] touch with our members.'[40] Thus religion was very far from the centre of YMCA life in parts of Belfast.

Outside Belfast, the life of the YMCAs was generated by mainly secular pursuits. Ballymena YMCA (County Antrim) promoted 'enjoyment', which meant billiards, badminton and literary meetings during the winter months. These attracted average attendances of 200. A guest speaker in 1921 was a clergyman, Reverend Joseph Hocking, but he was introduced as 'the famous novelist'.[41] Banbridge YMCA had named itself 'Banbridge

YMCA and Literary Society' and was said to be 'in a very prosperous condition' in May 1921 with about 60 members and well attended debates
during the winter months. It stocked 'Almost every daily paper and periodical' and had just one billiard table.[42] Strabane YMCA had weekly literary
meetings and at Enniskillen YMCA (County Fermanagh) the emphasis was
on enabling youths to better themselves. Its programme for 1924–5 comprised lectures from 'educated' speakers on non-religious themes: 'Home
Life'; 'The Growth of the Merchant Service' and one on 'A Visit to London' illustrated with over 60 slides. There was a temperance night; an Essay
night; and a musical and elocution night for 'members and friends'.[43]

Only one YMCA in Northern Ireland in the interwar years could be
described as godly – Bessbrook YMCA, a village YMCA near Newry. Bessbrook's leaders spoke to each other in the manner of Archbishop Laud,
Archbishop of Canterbury during the early seventeenth century. They
wished each other 'God-speed' when saying goodbye or signing letters to
each other.[44] Bessbrook's founder was a local spinning manufacturer and
Quaker, Arthur Sidney Clibborn. He had started a Bible Class for 'banding
together young men converted and with a further purpose to strengthen
their religious fellowship', but that was in the nineteenth century.[45] By the
1920s it was still a very holy YMCA – fanatically so at times. In June 1926,
for example, it passed a resolution protesting at the sale of ice cream in
Bessbrook village on Sundays, thinking this was 'demoralising the young'.
It even wanted Sunday newspapers banned from the village.[46] Its talks were
always religious and sometimes frightening. In November 1929 a Salvation
Army official from Newry spoke on: 'An Object lesson on some samples
from the Devil's Dope Factory'. The talk's theme was drink and gambling.
On other occasions a religious talk would be followed by a solemn silence.
When they heard a talk on Oliver Cromwell it was on the religious influences in his life, and another on Tennyson focused on his thoughts on
'Death and Heaven'. Bessbrook YMCA was not a YMCA that promoted
enjoyment. The only time the phrase 'an enjoyable evening' appeared in
the minutes for the interwar years was at Christmas 1931.[47]

We cannot leave the YMCA on this sombre note. Lurgan YMCA was
an up-beat branch even during the unsettling period for YMCA work
in the early 1920s. Its members comprised working lads who mingled
with young professionals in a YMCA branch that focused on sport. It
had several football and cricket clubs – and the parents of the district
thought it 'a safe place of resort for their sons'.[48] Meanwhile, Mountpottinger YMCA regained its premises in January 1923 and immediately made
plans for its billiard room – for 're-wiring, new curtains, new lino'.[49] An
All-Night Dance was arranged for Easter Monday 1923 and later in
the year a group of members sent a deputation to the leaders' meeting
with a petition requesting further dances. A confrontation ensued. The

Chairman would not even peruse the petition containing a large number of members' and associates' signatures. He declared it 'out of order and without precedent'.[50] The youths were then ordered out of the room and the leaders had a discussion. They then passed a resolution noting: 'That dancing be not permitted in connection with the Association'. The committee had been divided on the issue and two of its members resigned. The Social Club Sub-Committee members who had presented the petition then decided to boycott the YMCA. They also summoned a local councillor to the club to address the Executive Committee in support of dances and he did so 'at considerable length'.[51] He argued that during 1920 and 1921 the YMCA had advertised dances in its programmes; that the Social Club Sub-Committee had raised £78 for the YMCA through holding dances in 1921 and that he would organise a public campaign for dances at the YMCA if necessary. The pressure worked and the Executive Committee agreed to hold a conference on dances, but the outcome is unclear since no records survive for the period after 1923 – except its list of members.[52]

Mountpottinger YMCA lost members during the 1920s, but they did not desert the club over its policy on dances. Its membership fell from 100 in 1921 to 84 in 1927, for two reasons: emigration and death. The figures are intriguing as almost as many members who 'left' died (8) as emigrated (9).[53] The deaths are never explained. The only remark made next to a member who had died was 'Deceased', which conveniently disguises whether they were accidentally killed, murdered or died naturally. Many people were killed by snipers in the Mountpottinger district of Belfast in the early 1920s and a number were youths walking over the Albertbridge from their work in the shipyard, Harland and Wolff.[54] The members who emigrated are sometimes easier to track. A David Coulter who paid a 5s subscription in 1921 and 1923, the rate for 18 to 21-year-olds, had next to his name a clear explanation for not paying his subscription in 1924. He had 'Gone to Canada'.[55]

Our story so far suggests strongly that the history of the YMCA in early twentieth-century Ireland is a case of the tail (the adolescent members) wagging the dog (the leaders). But what drove leaders such as William Wright to devote many years of their lives to recalcitrant adolescents? Wright himself is significant in the story. He was an Englishman who had settled in Belfast and singlehandedly held the Irish YMCAs together for over 20 years between 1901 and 1924. In some ways, the Northern Irish YMCAs were a deliberate and successful attempt at cultural conditioning of the young. The city YMCAs in Belfast and Londonderry were openly promoting Britishness and knowledge of English political affairs and literature in the journals and newspapers they held. They were also consciously insulating the YMCAs from almost anything Irish. It is not straining a point to say that either of these two YMCAs could have been in northern England

and if they had been in Manchester, say, the members would not have felt they were in a strange environment.

What of the religious work of the Irish YMCAs? Was this, as much of the evidence suggests, peripheral and even in some places irrelevant by the 1920s? It is necessary to recall that the YMCA was started in London by an evangelical youth who did not like the 'loose habits and behaviour' of the drapers' assistants he was forced to work with. He was called George Williams and he was only 14 at the time, in 1844.[56] He had moved to London from Somerset where his father was a farmer and he was thus living independently in lodgings and working in a large clothing store in central London. He formed a prayer circle with 12 young men. They recorded at their first meeting (in Williams' bedroom at the drapers) that their purpose was to 'spread the Redeemer's Kingdom among those by whom they are surrounded'. From the beginning, therefore, the organisation had a siege mentality. It had 150 members by 1845 and a salaried Secretary. In 1895 Williams was knighted by Queen Victoria. At his death in 1913 the YMCA had 700,000 members. By 1942 it had 2 million and 10,000 centres throughout the world. Williams was buried in St Paul's Cathedral in London.[57]

These details were still relevant to the work of the Irish YMCAs during the 1920s. London was still the headquarters of the movement in the British Isles and its London Secretary, Sir Arthur Yapp, was responsible for appointing Wright's successor in 1924.[58] Also, when an 'All Ireland' Conference was held in Dublin in 1924 Yapp attended.[59] More important still, London YMCA paid the salaries of the full-time secretaries in Ireland – even the salary of George Bird, Secretary of Cork YMCA, who was not a British citizen.[60] The Irish YMCAs were not linked to churches and distanced themselves from the church. In one of their publications, *The YMCA in Ireland* (Belfast, 1917), they asserted: 'Young Men's Christian Associations . . . earnestly disavow any intention or desire to enter upon functions proper to the churches.' Their aim instead was to reach 'a class of persons not easily reached by ordinary Church agencies.'[61] This vagueness enabled the Irish YMCAs to proceed pragmatically and adapt their recruitment policy to suit different circumstances. In the First World War period they were mainly interested in soldiers and, moreover, British soldiers far from their homes and churches. By 1917 Irish YMCAs had opened over 50 huts and centres for British soldiers in Ireland and they were all over Ireland – at Newtownards, Victoria Barracks, Belfast, and Randalstown (all in the north) and, in the south, Bere Island, Tralee, Bray, Blackrock and Dublin.[62] Moreover, the Irish YMCAs were very proud of their work with soldiers and often did it at their own expense. As they put it in one of their wartime publications: 'we have . . . gladly erected our Huts and done everything in our power to minister to the comfort and convenience of our brave soldier lads'.[63] There was another motive for this work. The huts were retreats from pubs and 'other forms of evil which are unfortunately never far away'. The huts were spartan places with newspapers, magazines, writing paper and maybe some games; places where 'Tommy Atkins can rest, read, enjoy simple recreations, and above all indulge his penchant for writing to the dear ones at home.'[64] They were, in other words, safe.

The Irish YMCAs were slow at winding down their war work with British soldiers. In 1920 there were still 40 YMCA huts in use for soldiers throughout Ireland. They were also swift in installing memorials in their branches to commemorate the YMCA members who had fought in the War.[65] A new YMCA Boys' Club in Manor Street, Belfast, in 1920 had a memorial commemorating 122 Belfast YMCA members who had fought in the War and 24 who had died.[66] The Belfast leaders also invited a guest speaker to address their members in 1920, an English evangelist named 'Gipsy Pat Smith'. He was a very accessible speaker and his name suggests he was charismatic. In Belfast 250 youths who heard him joined the YMCA immediately. When he preached in Dublin in 1923 the Dublin City YMCA, which held 1000, was 'packed'. 'The Gipsy's message is very simple', the YMCA Executive reported, 'and there is not much teaching, but he puts Jesus well in the front, and tells of His power to save and keep in an attractive way'. Many in the audience stayed behind afterwards to ask him questions.[67]

Religion did not draw large numbers of youths to the YMCAs in Northern Ireland during the 1920s. Branches that specialised in religious programmes such as Bessbrook and Omagh had small memberships. Omagh YMCA only met twice a week: once for a prayer meeting on Friday evenings and on Sundays for an evangelistic service. It had a select membership of 65 in 1924.[68] One of Bessbrook YMCA's leaders was so incensed at the absence of religion in the Province's YMCAs he wrote to the Executive to complain – three times. On one occasion he wrote to say he was withdrawing his support for the headquarters' work and told them why:

> The condition of the Belfast branch shows that their purpose has failed – the Belfast branch is the leading association in the country – the others naturally are in danger of following it.
> As to that branch it is not a question of want of spirituality but that, in my opinion, it has become a [sic] agency through its entertainments and ease-training for the destruction of young men.[69]

Another discontented YMCA official in County Kerry put it more succinctly. He found his members 'take the physical and reject the spiritual'.[70] Among the donors to the Belfast YMCA's funds during the 1920s, church leaders are not prominent. The most prominent are shopkeepers; some of whom ran YMCAs in Ireland, and others who sent money from England must have employed people who had been in the YMCA.[71] One intriguing donation of £10 around 1918 was sent from a hotel in Cannes. Fry's chocolate manufacturers in Bristol and Cadbury Brothers in Birmingham also sent money. Both were Quaker employers, who presumably thought temperance work was prominent at Belfast YMCA. A ginger ale manufacturer in Belfast who sent £3 3s in 1923 perhaps did so too – mistakenly.[72]

If one delves too deeply into the local YMCAs' activities one quickly becomes aware of how little the Executive Committee in Belfast knew about what went on and how far the branches had drifted from the headquarters' policy. Girls, for example, were ignored in the Executive Committee's meetings and assumed to be absent. They were not absent at Ballymena YMCA, where youths and 'young ladies' played badminton together and the leaders were endeavouring to buy a wireless set and to start a tennis or football club 'or any other form of amusement the boys might like to take up'.[73] They also had a billiard room – 'the great centre of attraction for their younger members' – but it is difficult to see how their professed aim of making youths 'aspire to a higher plane of living' would be achieved through potting billiard balls. Or were they trying to produce professional billiard players who could earn an income from the game? The Irish billiard champion visited the club in 1923.[74]

Girls and women drew youths to the secular events at YMCAs. At Shankill Road YMCA a weekly mixed evening on Sundays attracted 450 regulars in 1931; its devotional meetings were held only 'occasionally' and attracted a lowly 12 to 20.[75] Girls were never admitted as members at Irish YMCAs, and in some they were exploited; being charged the same rate as boys to play badminton at Mountpottinger, for example (7s 6d); or they were excluded altogether, as at Banbridge YMCA.[76] Elsewhere in rural areas they were admitted just to make up the numbers and to help subsidise the YMCA. At Cloughjordan YMCA (Tipperary): 'They join with us in the Bible class and ping pong.' They had to pay 2s to play ping pong, however.[77]

Money was something of an obsession to the leaders in the city YMCAs; far more than religion. At Belfast City YMCA the members paid a 5s subscription (apprentices paid 2s 6d) but there were countless other charges: 5s to join the radio club; 15s for the hockey club; 3s to play table tennis; 5s to join the camera club; 15s the boxing club; and 15s to use the gymnasium. The club had 450 members in 1929 who paid these charges.[78] Sandy Row YMCA in a poor suburb of Belfast, meanwhile, was attracting youths 'of a rather rough and careless class' who were neither aspirational nor affluent. They were catered for with billiards, a Bible class on Sunday afternoons, and occasional lectures and concerts. The Executive regarded them as an embarrassment.[79]

The YMCA's role in Northern Ireland during the 1920s confirms Foster's proposition that youths in Northern Irish society follow their elders, but only up to a point. In some ways the YMCAs of the 1920s were endeavouring, where possible, to prepare youths to leave the Province to pursue careers abroad. In 1924, Belfast YMCA interviewed 200 youths who wanted to emigrate to Australia. The Australian government was liaising with the YMCA to receive them.[80] Furthermore, the plethora of YMCA programmes in Northern Ireland suggests that the leaders were not fully in control of the YMCA. Did they tame youth? The YMCAs did attract potential and actual delinquents and they attracted large numbers of urban youths in a decade when the school-leaving age was 14 for 70 per cent of the youth population.[81] They were only serving the Protestant community in most cases, but they provided comfort and tried to develop the potential of large numbers of Protestant youths whose home circumstances were presumably less congenial.

Juvenile and youth unemployment in Northern Ireland

The picture presented above of the lives of those in their teens in Northern Ireland during the 1920s implies that most were not touched by poverty and unemployment. Is this correct or were the YMCAs serving only a section of Northern Irish society – upwardly mobile and sometimes quite affluent youth? We can gain a clearer impression of juvenile unemployment through public records. For most of the 1920s juvenile unemployment was not officially acknowledged in Northern Ireland. No juvenile unemployment centre existed to cater for unemployed juveniles (officially those between 14 and 18) or for youths (18–21s). The Northern Ireland Cabinet was content to let the Belfast Rotary Club organise camps for unemployed youth; but the implication was that there were few of them and they were only between jobs. In 1923, for example, a camp for unemployed boys at Clandeboye attracted just 40.[82] In any case, the benefit system for juveniles was keeping juveniles in the labour market looking for jobs. Fourteen- and fifteen-year-olds were not entitled to unemployment benefit until 1934; 16- and 17-year-olds were only entitled to a fraction of a juvenile wage (6 or 7 shillings, when a van boy, for example, could earn 31 shillings) and youths of 18 to 21 received just 15 shillings in 1923 when an adult manual wage was 50 to 60 shillings.[83] Those 40 unemployed youths who attended the camp at Clandeboye in 1923 were to give most of their benefit (10 shillings out of their 15 shillings) to the Rotary Club for expenses.[84]

A Juvenile Unemployment Centre was established in Belfast in February 1929, some three years after the Newspaper Boys of the city had been given a club.[85] The Committee that approved the scheme did not feel there was a serious juvenile unemployment problem in Northern Ireland. It reported in 1929 that 'the general state of employment among juveniles in Belfast was good', but many juveniles experienced short-term unemployment lasting for 'about three months'.[86] In January 1929, 330 insured juveniles (16- and 17-year-olds) were on the registers as unemployed in Belfast and 930 in the 14–18 age-group. These figures should not mislead. They represent about 5 per cent of the juvenile workforce and full employment allows for 3–4 per cent unemployment.[87] The idea behind the club was to make those few juveniles who experienced unemployment, who were in effect remedial juveniles given the favourable employment circumstances for juveniles in Northern Ireland, acquire work skills. They were to be taught handicrafts; the use of tools; physical training; arithmetic, and reading and writing, to give, as the committee who approved the centre put it: 'some facility in expressing themselves both in speech and in the written word'.[88] By 1938 the centre was admitting 18- to 21-year-olds who were unemployed, to justify the continued existence of the centre. It survived until May 1942 when juvenile unemployment vanished from Northern Ireland. As the centre's organiser, L. Allen, put it in a letter to the Northern Ireland Cabinet on 18 May 1942: 'The unemployed juveniles appear to have left the City for a while.'[89]

It is possible that the very low level of juvenile and youth unemployment in interwar Belfast disguised a more serious problem in the rural areas and in certain industries – shipbuilding, for example. Some impressionistic evidence was presented in the Northern Ireland Parliament during 1933 and 1934, but by a single individual who seems to have liked overstating his case. The MP in question, a Mr Henderson, claimed in October 1933 that 25,000 children left Northern Ireland's schools in 1933 and were 'without the slightest hope of securing employment'.[90] He went on to assert that apprentices in the local shipbuilding industry were being sacked at 16 'due to the serious depression through which Northern Ireland is passing' and felt 'there is no hope of getting them to a trade'. He claimed that 38,000 young people were unemployed in Northern Ireland in October 1933. The Minister of Labour, Mr Andrews, challenged these figures, but his own calculation – that there were 5621 14–21-year-olds registered at the employment exchanges – implied there was a problem; but it was mainly among 18- to 21-year-olds rather than juveniles. Of the 5621, 4122 were in the older age group. Many more adults in Northern Ireland were unemployed in October 1933 – some 61,991 were registered at the exchanges.[91]

Youth Culture in the Irish Republic

The early twentieth-century history of youth in the south of Ireland is better documented than in the north. Learned journals such as *Studies* and *Irish Ecclesiastical Record* published articles on youth during the 1920s and 1930s and treated the lifestyles of the young as a serious subject. One author, Arthur E. Clery, even argued that youths of 14 who were pushed into the labour market to find jobs ought to have the vote. They would then be in a position to influence whether they should leave school at 14; to question why there was little technical training for young workers, and to decide whether so-called 'blind-alley' jobs in which juveniles were hired at 14 and sacked at 18 were a good thing. More important still, if youths had the vote they could stop adults degrading youth. Youths, for example, were the only group in the population of Ireland who, in 1915, could be flogged (except procurers and garotters).[92] He had a point. Most boys in their teens throughout Ireland worked from the age of 14 during the 1920s and 1930s; many fought and died in the First World War, and others in the Irish Republican cause, but they could not vote until they reached 21.[93]

Was there a youth culture in the south? In theory, there ought to have been a youth culture. The marriage age was very late in early twentieth-century Ireland. Among males the average age at marriage in 1945 was 33. Few girls and young women married in their twenties. In 1936, 64 per cent of females in the 25–29 age group were single in the Irish Republic; only 40 per cent were in Britain; 42 per cent in Germany; 24 per cent in France and 21 per cent in the United States.[94] Young single people were thus a distinct group in Irish society well into their twenties and a youth lifestyle was observed. Eithne wrote in the mid-1920s: 'Look at the pleasure-mad crowds of boys and girls who jazz and fox-trot in our questionable dance halls, drunk with excitement and champaigne. Catholics also.'[95] She disapproved strongly of dance halls, calling them 'temples for pagan worship' and 'wine-flushed'. Her overall assessment was biased – 'Half-intoxicated men, half-naked girls, a riot of unbridled youth and beauty degraded to its lowest plane'[96] – but was there something in this criticism?

The discussion of dance halls in 1920s' and 1930s' Ireland was not really a debate. The Irish Bishops thought they were evil and hardly a word was said in their favour – except from Flann O'Brien who, as the author of an article lauding Dublin pubs, was not an objective source.[97] Only two themes were prominent in the discussion. The first was that the dance halls were mainly responsible for a higher illegitimacy rate during the 1920s and '30s than had existed before the First World War. This appears to be something of a red herring given that the illegitimacy rate in the Irish Republic was only 3.4 per cent of total births between 1931 and 1935, in the period leading up to the Dance Hall Act of 1935.[98] The other was that the dance halls were beginning to shape the lives of the young: introducing them to American jazz music and tempting them to travel miles from their homes and to return in darkness every week. Dance halls did not exist in Ireland before the First World War; by the start of the Second there were

1200 licensed dance halls in the south and they held approximately 5000 dances every year.[99] The interesting question is whether the dance halls were a symptom of changing lifestyles among the young between 1918 and 1939?

Youth lifestyles in the south varied greatly during the 1920s. The girls who were observed in Dublin drinking cocktails in wine bars were the daughters of professional men – lawyers, doctors, bankers, merchants and prosperous farmers. It was not clear to those who wrote about these middle-class girls whether they worked for wages or not. Nonetheless, they were affluent. 'She gives no account of her goings and comings,' one author wrote of 'The New Girl' in 1926:

> If she has not a motor car of her own, she starts forth on her treadmill bike...and scoots through the country unaccompanied....When she will return home, the Lord only knows, certainly her mother does not....The modern girl smokes like a chimney...she consumes 20 or 30 cigarettes a day, and will even do it in the public street....Her vernacular is slanguage....She addresses him (her boyfriend) as old thing, or old bean....She affects a walking stick, though she is by no means feeble of limb.[100]

She did much else besides: read sensational novels, talked incessantly about dances, theatres, cinemas, golf, tennis, and Bridge, and: 'She is a mere Hedonist.'[101] This, of course, was the Flapper lifestyle of the 1920s; but how typical it was of young wage-earning girls in the rural areas of the Irish Republic is unclear. What is clear is that the dance halls of Dublin were too expensive for girls who worked as domestic servants. A public dance in Dublin in January 1923 cost 15 shillings. A young domestic servant in the city earned between 6 shillings and 10 shillings a week.[102]

Most of the dance halls in the Republic were in rural areas and the entrance fee varied from 3d to 1s 6d. The youths and girls who attended these dances would travel on bikes or walk – a sign of their lack of affluence.[103] The newspapers that reported on them provide some details. In Galway, there were three or four dance halls in each parish. They were in the hands of businessmen rather than the clergy; they were run for profit and they admitted 'anyone'. Most of the youths and girls were thought to be 'innocent', but some males arrived in cars and had 'sinister purposes'. These were the impressions of a member of Galway County Council Homes Committee who was sent to investigate dance halls in December 1928.[104] The fact that a committee was set up to consider dance halls implies that adults knew little about them and that they were associated with youth.

Dance halls were sometimes linked with teenage deaths – but usually in a sensational way. In January 1929, six youths and girls in their teens were lost at sea travelling in a dinghy to a dance hall off Galway Bay. The bold headline in the *Irish Independent* made the connection between dance halls and death, stating: 'Three boys and three girls. Holiday party perish in sight of Homes. Had gone to attend dance.' The impression given is that the dance hall, Satan-like, lured them to their deaths. In fact, the dance had been cancelled and they were returning home in their small boat when it capsized.[105] Court cases drew much attention to dance halls. A case christened the 'Derry Road Dance Tragedy' in December 1930 gave the impression that a drunken girl who had been killed accidentally was at a dance. She had been dancing by a roadside with a group of friends and a motorist accidentally killed her.[106] Youths who appeared in court on other charges were quick to realise that linking their misdemeanours with a dance hall would deflect attention away from them and make them appear victims. In December 1930 two youths in a Dublin court were charged with stealing a car. They told the court they had been to a dance and walking along a Dublin street in the early hours of the morning 'took a car for a ride'. They claimed they wanted to go to Mass and the jury who heard the case acquitted them.[107]

Cars were linked with dance halls as twin sources of evil. Cars parked close to dance halls in rural areas meant that strangers were in the area. Some Bishops claimed they were used for soliciting young girls; others that they harboured alcohol that would be consumed during breaks from dancing. The Irish Bishops met in February 1931 to discuss, or rather denounce, cinemas, dance halls and the cars parked close to dance halls. Cardinal MacRory thought the cars were 'a great and common source of evil'. He traced the dance hall in Ireland back to the First World War when, he claimed, the British soldiers stationed in Ireland introduced it. Furthermore, he recommended that the parked cars close to dance halls should be supervised. Elderly people should watch them while the dance was being held. Other criticisms were made. One Bishop thought the girls who frequented country dance halls were too young ('mere children'). Another claimed that some were becoming pregnant and committing infanticide: 'illegitimate intercourse between the sexes . . . is surely bad enough . . . but when it is followed by wicked mothers or their friends bordering the savagery of King Herod and murdering newly-born infants to hide their shame or to save trouble you have a crime of shocking depravity'.[108]

The Dance Hall Act of 1935 did not tame the craze for dancing. It required dance hall proprietors to have their premises licensed; established rules over opening hours and supposedly reduced the number of All-Night Dances permitted each year. Smyth has called it 'draconian'; but the implementation of the Act does not support this interpretation. A government committee had been set up to investigate dance halls in 1931, the Carrigan Committee, and the Irish Bishops must have been expecting a severe curtailment of the dance hall lifestyle. Their report was never published, however, and the Act seems to have come into force in February 1935 without anyone – and certainly the Bishops – knowing anything about it. In their Lenten Pastorals (annual lectures to their congregations at the beginning of Lent) in March 1935 they were still attacking dance halls as if there had been no change. The Archbishop of Tuam, Most Reverend Dr Gilmartin, compared the 'sweet morning air' of the walk to church with the 'fetid atmosphere of the dance halls'. The Archbishop of Killaloe had heard that girls who danced at dance halls 'sometimes appeared at these dances dressed to leave nearly half the body nude'. The Bishop of Down and Connor, Most Reverend Dr Mageean, described dance halls as 'a growing menace to the community'. They had all been saying these things, however, for over ten years.[109]

The Dance Hall Act of 1935 left dance halls as purely a matter for local authorities. In practice, this meant that once a year, usually in September, the local Justice decided in court whether to issue or refuse licences for dance halls in his parish. Thus September 1935 represents the first occasion when the dance hall phenomenon could be controlled or not. Until then, in Donegal, dance halls could open until 2 a.m. before September 1935. Some restrictions were introduced in September 1935; but they could hardly be called severe. The local Judge decided that henceforth all summer dances in Donegal should end at 1 a.m. On Saturdays dance halls would close at 12 p.m. and during the following year four 'long dances', or 'All-Night' dances, could be held in each dance hall. No alcohol was to be available in the halls. Nothing was said about the age restrictions at the dance halls. Presumably, therefore, there were none.[110] Cork County Council was a bit stricter over dance hall opening hours in Cork. All dance halls had to close at 11 p.m. in the summer and 10 p.m. in the winter months and only young people of 17 or older could attend them.[111] Galway allowed its halls to open until 12 p.m. and there were no age restrictions in its halls. It made a slight concession to the Irish Bishops. Cars had to be parked 'some distance' from the halls. In certain parishes new rules were invented. In County Kildare only youths of 18 or older could attend and a local dance committee had to be established that included at least two married women. Its halls were to close at 11 p.m., except on special occasions (when they could open until 2 a.m.). Some 40 special occasions were allowed at each hall, however, which gave some scope for youths who were late night revellers. Dance halls in Kildare were even allowed to open on Sunday evenings (until 11 p.m.) after September 1935.[112]

The Dance Hall Act of 1935 was thus a fairly permissive piece of legislation and it was certainly iniquitous. The closing hours varied greatly; from 11 p.m. in Cork, for example, to 1 a.m. in Donegal and Cavan. The Act did not insist on Irish dances being a requirement. Few justices seemed concerned about the threat dance halls posed to Gaelic culture. Occasionally, they introduced arcane restrictions on entry. In County Meath youths from towns were not allowed into country halls. In Drogheda a couple seen hugging in a dance hall and reported were likely to be given a one-month prison sentence. The District Judge who introduced the rule, Judge Goff, referred in court to 'shameful embracing in public places' and told the Court 'if any such cases were proved before him he would impose the maximum penalty of one month's imprisonment'.[113]

The Irish Bishops' criticisms of dance halls were largely ignored. Before the Act many parts of the south were not covered by dance hall legislation and local clergymen in rural areas, presumably, had more say over dance halls than after 1935 when only Justices had the authority to issue or refuse licences. Apart from Judge Goff, most Justices were well disposed towards dance hall proprietors providing they sold no alcohol. Their main objection was to 'All-Night' dances; but they usually allowed some to be held during a year. Bishops, meanwhile, continued to attack dance halls in print; but hardly any were prepared to attend a court session when licences were being issued. In September 1935 a local priest appeared in court in County Mayo to protest about 'All-Night' dances. The Judge listened politely to the priest but then granted one applicant six 'All-Night' dances to 4 a.m. and also allowed dances to be held on Sunday evenings until 11 p.m. during the winter months and 12 p.m. during the summer.[114]

The Justices who issued licences were nothing like as draconian as some dance hall proprietors expected. In Waterford the local Gaelic Athletic Association (GAA) wanted to hold dances and in court its Secretary stressed that only Irish dances and old-fashioned waltzes would be part of the programme. The Judge told him they 'could dance whatever dances they wished'.[115] Other dance hall proprietors were less timid in court. One at Felthard in County Waterford told the Judge who was prepared to allow his dance hall to open from 8 p.m. to 11 p.m.: 'that would be practically useless' and the case was adjourned.[116] Occasionally, dance hall licences were refused. In County Donegal a female proprietor had built a new hall at Brunaleck and all the dances held there were Irish. A local police officer told the court that 'the trouble in the district' only occurred when the dance hall was open, and a licence was not granted.[117] On other occasions licences were refused when the halls were obviously unsafe. In County Leitrim two halls were refused licences in September 1935 for being, essentially, huts covered with corrugated iron. One was only 20 feet long and 12 feet wide and had no lavatory. The Judge gave these makeshift 'halls' short shrift, stating he would 'not degrade the court by granting licences for such places'.[118]

Conclusion

Does the detailed evidence presented in this chapter suggest any broad conclusions? The first is that youth seem to have been a lot freer in the south of Ireland during the 1920s and 1930s and the dance hall craze implies they were untouched by unemployment – a feature of youth lifestyles in Belfast during the period, if not a prominent one. The dance hall evidence is only one feature of rural youth lifestyles in the south and it may disguise another: namely, youth emigration, and the scale and nature of youth emigration during the period does need to be addressed in future research.[119] The chapter has focused on youth lifestyles in just one sphere: their leisure time. The strong impression given is that leisure time was a well defined feature of youth lifestyles in the north and the south at this period and, in the south, dance halls were obviously an escape from work. In the north this is less true in the work of the YMCAs. Work relationships are going to shape the values of the young as much as youth organisations and two groups of young workers – trade apprentices in the north and domestic servants in the south, both numerically significant in the youth labour markets in their regions – do need closer study. Both worked with adults and yet were numerically significant enough to make them feel indispensable to their employers. In my study of young wage-earners in interwar Britain, *The First Teenagers*, I discovered a trade apprentices' strike in north-west England during the 1930s. Thousands of 16- and 17-year-old lads were on strike for a wage rise and some for holidays with pay also, and they won.[120] It will be interesting if future research on youth in early twentieth-century Ireland reveals that they too were a distinct group of young workers and, like the trade apprentices of the north-west of England, received wage and employment concessions from their employers during the 1920s and 1930s.

5 Juvenile Delinquency in Northern Ireland, 1945–c.1970

One of the most distinctive features of Northern Irish society since the Second World War is its unique culture of juvenile and youth delinquency. But whilst a significant historical literature exists on juvenile delinquency in Britain over the period from 1920 to 1970, the subject is largely shrouded in mystery for Northern Ireland.[1] The following chapter represents research findings extracted from the rich archival records on juvenile and youth delinquency available in Northern Ireland; sources that have largely languished in the outhouses of the Public Record Office for Northern Ireland (PRONI) until now. Northern Ireland has produced at least two youth stereotypes over this period that make it such a fascinating case-study of youth culture within the United Kingdom of Britain and Northern Ireland created in 1922. The most notorious is the 'teenage bomber' who came to prominence (in the newspapers at any rate) during the 1970s; but had antecedents in earlier periods.[2] The second is the young Republican protesters who came to the attention of the police and military authorities in Northern Ireland during the Second World War: a small subculture of boys, all in their late teens and early twenties, who organised themselves into paramilitary units – a young republican alternative to the Boy Scouts and Boys' Brigade in a sense – and whose members were charged in the courts (and found guilty) of drilling with guns on the open spaces of Belfast; shooting at police officers and harbouring weapons in their homes. This unique band of proto-terrorists have generated a rich body of research material for the historian of Irish Republicanism to probe – and indeed the present author has written on the subject – but this group were so unique they cannot feature in a survey of British youth culture between c.1920 and 1970.[3] However, juvenile delinquency patterns in Northern Ireland, and Government and police reactions to juvenile and youth delinquency, especially during the 1950s, do present an interesting case-study of more mainstream juvenile and youth behaviour also evident in Britain.[4] The following chapter thus focuses on the decade of the 1950s in Northern Irish society; a decade that witnessed, in England, the appearance of the Teddy Boy in London during the early 1950s; the emergence of an affluent society in England and, at a policy level, the appearance of borstals administering the 'short, sharp shock' to juveniles and youths who were given custodial sentences.[5] The central questions to be explored are: how far did the Teddy Boy cult reach Northern Ireland during the 1950s? How far was Northern Ireland, as sociologists have claimed, largely insulated from the affluence of mainland Britain during the 1950s and, in effect, a society without a youth culture; at least, before the disturbing appearance of the teenage bomber in the early 1970s?

Patterns of juvenile and youth crime in Northern Ireland, 1945–*c*.1970

Juvenile delinquency has been a prominent feature of Northern Irish society since the Second World War. A whole bureaucracy was established to deal with it from the late 1940s – juvenile courts (there were 93 of these throughout Northern Ireland by 1960); a probation service; acts of Parliament addressing the problem in 1950, 1952, 1968, 1979 and 1995; and a dark regime of Training Schools, dating back to the late nineteenth century.[6] By the mid-1970s, juvenile crime – hitherto a fairly neglected subject for the Royal Ulster Constabulary (RUC), or at least one that could be safely dealt with by women constables[7] – began to be taken seriously. In the Chief Constable's official reports youths were now recognised as a distinct group of serious offenders and the number charged with terrorist acts rose yearly – from 175 in 1975, to 255 in 1976 and 267 in 1977.[8] But this was just the pinnacle of juvenile criminal endeavour. Lower down the chain were thousands charged with serious (but non-terrorist offences): 2383 juveniles alone (under-17s) were charged with serious offences in 1975 and 2187 of them were found guilty.[9]

Juvenile and youth crime is, therefore, a subject that is statistically significant in Northern Ireland and has been for over fifty years. Whereas in England juvenile crime rates peaked during and immediately after the Second World War and fell from the early 1950s, in Northern Ireland juvenile crime rose virtually every year after the War; reaching a postwar peak in 1960 when almost 4000 juveniles were charged and found guilty.[10] We can speculate about the differing experiences of policy makers in England and Northern Ireland in dealing with juvenile delinquents during the 1940s and 1950s, but these matters are not germane just yet. The patterns of juvenile and youth crime within Northern Ireland must be our starting point.

Scholars who have explored this subject have begun with the onset of the Troubles in the late 1960s and early 1970s and momentarily glanced backwards – usually to note how low juvenile crime was in Northern Ireland before *c*.1969. Professor Laurie Taylor, in a pioneering article on youth crime, argued that Northern Irish youth were well integrated into Northern

Irish society before the start of the Troubles and, seemingly, were law-abiding. There was no youth culture, either delinquent or non-delinquent, but there was no need for one. The churches and adults generally provided leisure activities. 'It was ... possible', Taylor argues, 'for many young people to find all the corporate activities they needed for leisure without going outside their own church.'[11] We also learn from Taylor that 'Irish families were close-knit'; that even youth organisations were 'quasi-religious', meaning that the Boys' Brigade, for example, provided moral training and discipline for boys who might be contemplating delinquent acts; and that adults made sure juveniles were fully involved in the parades and festivities they (adults) organised.[12]

Then the Troubles came. Youth became physically trapped on their housing estates as curfews prevented them from visiting central Belfast and in parts of the city – Roden Street, for example – they became so frustrated they destroyed property. A Residents' Association produced a pamphlet entitled, *Roden Street: Death of a Community* (1973). The title was referring to the teenage vandals who were destroying the area.[13] Meanwhile, paramilitary groups were luring young people away from churches and recruiting them into gangs – the so-called Tartan Gangs.[14] The paternalistic structure of Northern Irish society fragmented. Welfare groups, and even the police, spent less time supervising youth. It was said that juveniles who absconded from Training Schools, where they were serving sentences of usually three years, were not even pursued.[15]

But how far did the 'Troubles' era after *c*.1970 mark a watershed in juvenile and youth delinquency in Northern Ireland? Taylor candidly admitted in 1977 that the subject of youth crime had not been properly studied. On the subject of youth terrorism, for example, he wrote: 'Information on the background, characteristics and motivations of young political offenders through hard-data studies ... is almost totally lacking.'[16] He meant, presumably, that sociologists had not researched the subject; but, as will be revealed below, a rich body of archival material exists on aspects of youth culture and youth crime in pre-Troubles Northern Ireland, and it dates back to at least the 1940s. Many important questions were not raised in Taylor's article on youth crime in Northern Ireland. He gave the strong impression that juvenile and youth crime was a product of urbanisation in Northern Ireland – citing statistics on the high population density in Belfast in relation to cities of a similar size in England; the lack of open spaces and parks in Belfast; poor council house provision (only 7500 public authority houses were built in Northern Ireland in the interwar years, when 185,000 were built in Scotland and 1 million in England and Wales) and the low level of educational attainment in Northern Ireland. As late as 1961, 65 per cent of Belfast's population had left school at 14; the school-leaving age from 1924 to 1957.[17] But the history of juvenile and youth crime in Northern Ireland since the Second World War is not merely an urban phenomenon – far from it. In the late 1950s approximately 50 per cent of juvenile crime in the Province was committed outside Belfast and much of it was rural crime.[18] Furthermore, features of urban society, such as low educational attainment, also applied in rural areas – and educational standards may even have been lower in these areas. The aim of this chapter, therefore, is not to challenge Taylor's pioneering survey of youth crime in Northern Ireland; but to explore the subject historically, utilising this rich archival material that exists for the period since 1945.

Juvenile crime before the courts

A useful starting point for a discussion of juvenile and youth crime in 1950s' Northern Ireland is the work of the juvenile courts. Over the period from 1945 to c.1975 regular juvenile court sessions were held all over Northern Ireland in the 98 juvenile courts that were established to deal with the under-17s.[19] Belfast's Juvenile Court sat for a full day every week in the late 1950s – from 10 a.m. to 4 p.m., with only a half-hour break for lunch. When a *Belfast Telegraph* reporter visited the court in March 1957 he encountered whole corridors congested with juveniles waiting to appear.[20] A few were seated on benches and chairs with their parents or friends, but the seating space was hopelessly inadequate. Inside the court the reporter heard several cases. The first was a case involving nine boys, between the ages of 11 and 15, charged with stealing and receiving stolen goods. They were accused of stealing sweets, chocolate, cigarettes, money and a watch, from a number of shops and houses. One of the boys faced 9 charges of theft; another, 6 charges. A clergyman was present and testified that two of the boys were not potential criminals, but they were all found guilty. They were given various sentences and the 3 magistrates and 8 probation officers present took great care passing sentence on each. One of the boys was sent to a Training School (a pre-borstal institution with a standard sentence of three years); two others were sent to a Training School for one month; two were discharged and the rest were given fines and bound over to keep the peace.

Several more depressing cases were heard that day. A 15-year-old boy on probation had run away to Dublin and severed all contact with his probation officer. He had previous offences to be considered, including disorderly conduct inside a cinema. He was swiftly dispatched to a Training School. A third case involved a 16-year-old girl who was also on probation and had disappeared. She had been an inmate in a Home, but had escaped and for two nights had been sleeping in a local bus station. The girl was kept in custody. In a further case, a 14-year-old boy, recently discharged from a Training School, had stolen a purse containing £6 7s 6d. He was placed on probation for two years. The *Belfast Telegraph* reporter observed in court that none of the juveniles mentioned flickered when their sentences were read out. 'None', he wrote, 'showed the slightest sign of emotion on hearing the punishment.' All admitted their guilt. Most gave only one-sentence answers to explain their behaviour.

These few cases heard on a single day in a single court tell us much about juvenile crime in Northern Ireland in the late 1950s. First, the juvenile offender was often a persistent offender. Second, groups of juveniles committed certain crimes together. Third, girls who appeared in juvenile courts tended not to commit the same offences as boys. Fourth, the Training Schools and Probation system seemingly did not reform them. Finally, the criminal justice system that dealt with juveniles was extremely punitive. The juveniles were sentenced and then dispatched. There was no discussion in court of their employment circumstances, or home background. In short, the juveniles were punished rather than helped.

The earliest Juvenile Courts were established in the United States – Illinois had the first in the 1890s – but in England (and Ireland) they were introduced in 1908 under the Children Act.[21] The idea was that juveniles were to be separated from adults in court cases so that they could be reformed more easily. In Northern Ireland, from the beginning, the juvenile courts were to be held on a different day from the adult court and in a different building. The juvenile courts in fact became the principal institutions that dealt with juvenile crime in Northern Ireland for the remainder of the twentieth century; but for long periods they went unnoticed. Following the 1908 Children Act the juvenile courts were not touched by legislation for another forty odd years. In 1950 a Children and Young Persons Act noted their existence and established panels of magistrates to sit in juvenile courts. This Act also required that three magistrates should sit at every juvenile court hearing and one of these should be a woman.[22] But nothing was said in the legislation about how effectively the juvenile courts dealt with juvenile crime. A group of voluntary workers who investigated the juvenile courts situated in Northern Ireland in 1960 found there were 98 in existence throughout the Province, but only 9 Resident Magistrates were involved in juvenile court work. But they said nothing, in an official report produced on the subject, about the level of juvenile crime dealt with in these courts; the types of offences juveniles committed; or even whether juvenile crime was rising or falling.[23]

Fortunately, this voluntary group were extremely diligent and gathered a rich body of material on juvenile courts in Northern Ireland that they did not subsequently use. They in fact spent three years investigating the subject. This committee of 11 men and women (7 men; 4 women) held over 40 meetings on juvenile crime, visited several juvenile courts and produced written reports on their visits. They interviewed court officials, probation officers, senior RUC officers, senior police officers from England and youth leaders. They corresponded with the Home Office in London; and they received letters from members of the public interested in juvenile crime. The committee called itself the Child Welfare Council (CWC) and it was formed in 1953. The members included a Law Lecturer at The Queen's University of Belfast, D. G. Neill, MA, a local JP; Mrs M. I. Simpson, a solicitor; Mr F. Crilly, LLB; Mrs Maje Haughton, its chairman; and a Catholic monk, Brother Stephen Kelly. Their work generated a substantial body of material that enables us to trace, in some detail, the juvenile crime the courts dealt with and how effective the juvenile courts were in curbing juvenile crime.[24]

In the years between the end of the War in 1945 and the Child Welfare Council's intensive studies into juvenile delinquency, begun in 1953 and completed in 1960, the Northern Ireland judiciary grew increasingly anxious about juvenile crime. The Ministry of Home Affairs published statistics annually on the number of juveniles (under-16s before 1950; under-17s after this date) found guilty in court cases and these showed a progressive rise from 1635 juveniles found guilty for all offences in 1946 to 2514 in 1953, and the figures kept getting worse down to 1960 when just under 4000 juveniles were found guilty in court cases.[25] The Ministry for a long time were not unduly worried about these figures and they tended to dismiss the subject of juvenile crime as not worth discussing. In a Ministry note accompanying the juvenile crime returns for 1949 an official scribbled next to the figure of 2067 juveniles found guilty that year: 'The particulars are such that if published they should kill a lot of the ill-informed criticism of judges.' But the judges would not let the subject be dropped and eventually the Ministry of Home Affairs began to investigate juvenile crime patterns throughout Northern Ireland.

One Judge, Lord Justice Porter, followed the trend in juvenile crime very closely from the late 1940s and publicised his views in the Belfast press. He reported in March 1949 that across Northern Ireland juvenile crime had risen by over 25 per cent in a single year (1947–8). In Derry the number of juvenile court cases rose almost 500 per cent between 1947 and 1948; from 17 cases to 84. Moreover, the steepest increases were property crimes. Northern Ireland had just experienced a General Election in March 1949 and, according to Judge Porter, outbreaks of juvenile delinquency had accompanied it. At his Spring Assizes court session in Belfast, he told the court that Belfast citizens must do everything they could to 'prevent our social structure from being a breeding ground for young criminals'. It was obvious what he meant when he subsequently charged five youths with stealing jewellery worth £124.[26] In another case, he encountered a 16-year-old girl from County Donegal who had voted, illegally, in the General Election by forging her identity. She was placed on bail for two years. A 23-year-old van salesman was also charged and found guilty. He had stolen money from his employer, amounting to £244, to pay for his hobby of gambling on horses and card playing. Judge Porter asked him: 'Do you promise you will give up gambling for two years?' He replied: 'Yes, no more gambling.' He was put on bail for two years.[27]

By the early 1950s, Judge Porter was still worried about juvenile crime and was reporting his fears in the *Northern Whig* and *Belfast Telegraph*. He told the press in 1951 he had dealt that year with 'a very large number of cases' in which children and young persons were charged with housebreaking offences and stealing. They stole cigarettes, chocolate, money and lead. He reported hearing cases where juveniles had climbed onto roofs, stolen lead and subsequently sold it. (It could be sold for about £160 a ton in 1951.) Judge Porter believed parents were encouraging their juveniles to steal lead because it was so valuable. He referred in his 1951 statement to the press to 'an epidemic of lead stealing' among juveniles.[28] The subject of juvenile crime was also beginning to be studied in Belfast colleges and its University by the early 1950s. The Principal of a Law College in Belfast wrote to the Ministry of Home Affairs for juvenile crime statistics (implying that they were not readily available) and a Lecturer in Psychology at The Queen's University of Belfast wanted the Ministry to supply him with a detailed breakdown of juvenile offenders in Belfast by streets.[29] The figures that were eventually published for the late 1940s revealed that Judge Porter's concern was well founded. Over 900 boys were charged with serious offences in Northern Ireland in 1948 (the figure had risen from 691 in 1946) and delinquency among girls was rising faster than among boys (from 56 girls charged with serious offences in 1946 to 102 in 1948).[30] The offences juveniles were charged with comprised: larceny, receiving, burglary, malicious wounding, robbery with assault, sacrilege, breaking into houses and shops, entry with intent, and assault.

The first statistical picture of juvenile crime throughout Northern Ireland was published by the Ministry of Home Affairs, obviously under pressure to generate information, in 1952. It is reproduced in Table 5.1.

The figures cited make clear that the pattern of juvenile crime in the early 1950s was not merely a story of trivial misdemeanours – playing football in streets and such like. Three-quarters of juvenile crime represented crimes of intent; and the most common juvenile offences were larceny and breaking and entering – both classed as indictable offences (or serious crimes) for which the offenders charged could be tried before a jury (if they wished) and if found guilty could be sentenced to three years in a Training School.

The geographical spread of juvenile crime is the most interesting feature of the Table. Belfast, it appears, accounted for about 50 per cent of the juvenile crime committed in 1952 and well under 50 per cent in the case of some offences – larceny, receiving, malicious damage and stealing,

Table 5.1   Juvenile delinquency in Northern Ireland, 1952: by County and County Borough (found guilty)

	Belfast	L'derry	Antrim	Armagh	Down	Fermanagh	Tyrone	Total*
Larceny	220	25	54	62	83	11	32	510
Breaking/ entering	147	5	40	19	27	1	9	263
Receiving	30	2	8	12	3	–	14	74
Malicious damage	65	10	30	20	44	1	11	188
Stealing	29	4	20	39	17	2	19	132
Games in streets	168	5	12	5	12	–	4	206
Railway trespassing	60	–	–	–	–	–	–	60
Total	719	51	164	157	185	15	89	1433

*This includes some cases unaccounted for in the county figures but are recorded in the original source.
Source: Ministry of Home Affairs, Northern Ireland, File HA/10/58, PRONI.

for example. It is also interesting, and surprising, that Belfast was not the only haven for breaking and entering. About 50 per cent of all juveniles found guilty of breaking and entering were outside Belfast. Finally, there is no obvious link between juvenile crime and urban areas. Rural counties such as Antrim and Down charged numerous juveniles with larceny and breaking and entering, for example. Fermanagh, another rural county, seems to have been an exceptional case in having almost no juvenile delinquents in 1952 and their returns seem almost unbelievable, as we will discover when the picture in Fermanagh is probed in greater detail.

The pattern of juvenile crime across Northern Ireland became far clearer from the early 1950s. The Ministry of Home Affairs was largely responsible. It set about gathering information from the myriad juvenile courts in existence, and for the first time ever every juvenile court, from central Belfast to distant villages like Belleek (County Fermanagh), were required to notify the Ministry of the number of juvenile court sessions held each year and the number of children and juveniles charged.[31] The picture that emerges from these returns is of an extremely vigilant court system that pursued juveniles wherever they were observed breaking the law. There were 101 juvenile courts in Northern Ireland in the early 1950s and they all met, on average, 5 times a year. Some met far more frequently – Whiteabbey

Juvenile Court (JC), in a suburb of Belfast, met 15 times in 1946 and dealt with a constant flow of juvenile crime cases in the late 1940s: 79 in 1945, 62 in 1946 and 58 in 1948.[32] Newtownards JC, on the outskirts of Belfast, met 16 times in 1947, dealing with just 19 juveniles (14- and 15-year-olds) and 16 children (8–14-year-olds). The rural courts were as keen on pursuing juvenile crime. Greyabbey JC met 5 times in 1947 to deal with 2 juveniles and 10 children. Saintfield Juvenile Court (JC), true to its name, met 5 times to deal with a solitary juvenile and 17 children – a mere 3–4 cases per session. The juvenile courts in towns and cities were the busiest. Portadown JC met 12 times in 1947, hearing 112 juvenile cases. Enniskillen JC met 35 times between 1944 and 1948. Almost every small town or village had a juvenile delinquency problem in the late 1940s, it seems. Bangor, a coastal town in rural County Down, had a serious juvenile delinquency problem. Its juvenile court met 23 times in 1947 and 27 times in 1948. In the latter year it charged 67 juveniles and 42 children. At the other end of the juvenile crime scale was Belleek, a remote village in rural County Fermanagh. Its juvenile court heard no cases between 1944 and 1948 and it would appear Belleek had no juvenile delinquents. It was a tiny community, however, consisting of just 200 people in all. There were few juveniles living there.

Belfast JC dealt with hundreds of juvenile cases in the late 1940s. It met 53 times in 1947 and, in that year, 913 juveniles were charged. The problem was even worse than these figures suggest as the number of offences juveniles in Belfast were charged with in 1947 was 1862 – in effect, each juvenile who appeared in court was charged with two offences. The figures grew worse. In 1948, 964 juveniles were charged at Belfast JC, but the number of offences they were charged with had reached 2323 – a rise of almost 500 juvenile offences in the city in a single year and an average of almost 3 offences for every juvenile who appeared in court. Thus the problem in Belfast in the late 1940s was the growth of juvenile recidivist crime. Even during the War there was less recidivist juvenile crime in Belfast than in the late 1940s. On average, juveniles charged in 1944 committed 1–2 offences; but 2–3 offences by 1948.

What sort of crimes were juveniles charged with in Northern Ireland in the late 1940s and early 1950s? In the early 1920s juveniles were arrested for armed robbery in Belfast;[33] but the juveniles of the late 1940s were tame in comparison. There were examples of malicious behaviour; but against property rather than people. At Dervock 4 youths were charged with maliciously damaging a telegraph pole in the late '40s; but no juvenile in Dervock committed a crime against a person between 1944 and 1948. Dervock was obviously a remote place with poor public transport. A number of juveniles drove cars without being licensed to. One juvenile even stole a pony and trap. Another drove a tractor without being licensed to.

A number stole bicycles. Theft was the most common offence among juveniles of Dervock during the 1940s. Out of 48 charged between 1944 and 1948 (44 boys and just 4 girls), 11 committed theft. Few stole because they were hungry. Only 3 out of 19 charged with theft stole something edible – usually apples. Others stole bikes, trees, cigarettes, a pony and trap, a bill hook, cutlery, orange juice, timber, a chain, and money.[34]

Juveniles in Belfast had a strange propensity for stealing trees and shrubs from public parks and then selling them for up to £5 each tree. This offence was so common there were different categories of tree and shrub thieves. The first category was those juveniles who stole trees and shrubs valued at up to £1. The second was those who stole them and sold them for up to £5. Third, were those who stole trees and shrubs and were third time offenders. A fourth category were those who stole 'growing plants, fruits, vegetables, etc.' and were second time offenders.[35] In Ballymoney two youths were convicted for stealing trees in 1948; another for damaging a tree. All of the crimes involving theft of trees and shrubs were indictable crimes. But there were less serious offences dealing with damage to trees and shrubs. Two offences deemed non-indictable offences in Ballymoney's juvenile crime returns were: juveniles who destroyed trees and shrubs valued at up to 1 shilling; and, secondly, those juveniles who destroyed 'plants, fruit, vegetables etc. growing in any garden'.[36] The level of detail cited in these categories of juvenile offence indicates that offences against trees and shrubs may have been dreamed up by the members of a particular juvenile court; as a local reaction to a widespread juvenile pastime. Only Dervock and Ballymoney mention these offences in their juvenile crime returns. There was certainly a low level of tolerance in rural areas of juvenile indiscretions that were not sent to courts in urban areas. The officials at Dervock Juvenile Court seem to have relished bringing juveniles into the court for very mild offences. Of 44 juveniles charged there between 1944 and 1948, 29 were charged with theft or malicious damage; the remainder with riding bicycles without lights or on footpaths (11 juveniles), three with playing football in the street, one with driving a tractor, and one with aiding and abetting over a matter involving onions.[37]

Few juveniles in the late 1940s in Northern Ireland were charged with political crimes – though some were. The worst year was 1945 when 11 juveniles were charged with 'possessing explosives or firearms' (the number found guilty is unclear). From 1945 the figures fell to 6 in 1946, 1 in 1947, 1 in 1948 and 4 in 1949.[38] In 1949 the Lord Chief Justice for Belfast stated there was a total absence of organised and political crime 'among juveniles', but the juvenile crime statistics just cited suggest this was incorrect.[39] Also, juveniles charged with possessing explosives and firearms were not normally dealt with in juvenile courts but in the adult court; so the juvenile court statistics definitely understate the level of juvenile terrorist crime.

Exploring juvenile crime: the Child Welfare Council's Work, 1953–60

In October 1953 the Grand Jury at Belfast City Commission, the Belfast court that dealt with terrorist and other serious crimes, issued a statement requesting that a committee be set up to explore juvenile delinquency. They said that they wanted the Northern Ireland Parliament to introduce legislation on the subject. The Jury were acting on advice they had received from a local Judge, Justice Curran, who had identified yet another increase in the juvenile crime figures.[40] Meanwhile, a group of voluntary workers had already formed a study group to study juvenile delinquency. They were preparing a report on the subject for the Ministry of Home Affairs, which they published as a flimsy 20-page pamphlet in November 1953, entitled *Juvenile Delinquency: An Interim Report.*[41] The Report is of nugatory importance as it avoided any discussion of the juvenile crime statistics and concentrated on what individual members felt were the main causes of juvenile crime in Northern Ireland. (They cited comics and incompetent mothers as the two principal causes.)[42] Their discussions on the subject were more thorough – one of their meetings generated 18 pages of minutes, which were almost as long as their published report – and are a useful starting point for understanding how juvenile delinquency was approached in early 1950s' Northern Ireland.[43] This committee, it should be borne in mind, were investigating the subject for the Ministry of Home Affairs, who would be devising a policy for curbing juvenile crime.

The Child Welfare Council began with the facts. They noted that juvenile crime had risen in 1953, but they dismissed the rise as the alarmist talk of judges. 'There is nothing to be worried about,' they told each other at one of their meetings. Their chairman, a married woman (Mrs Maje Haughton), thought that only one Judge had identified an increase in the juvenile crime figures and that: 'No one misleads the public more often than the judges on this point.'[44] Their discussions continued in this refreshingly revisionist, but frequently erratic mode. They debated whether juveniles were capable of serious crimes and strongly emphasised that they were not. Juveniles found trespassing on railway lines were not guilty of a serious offence, as the law stated; and 'malicious damage' and stealing were not serious offences either. They then discussed whether there was a link between crime and religious affiliation. They believed that there was and cited examples (it is not clear whether they were referring to criminal cases or hearsay) of boys who said they liked nothing more than stoning people taking part in religious parades.[45] Children, they noted, appeared in court for vandalising churches (they cited no specific cases) and in court the parents normally sympathised with the child or juvenile if the vandalism was inflicted on a church not belonging to their denomination. (The Child

Welfare Council were very careful never to identify whether they were discussing Protestant or Catholic juveniles.) When they moved on to discuss the causes of juvenile crime their discussion became very unbalanced. A Dr Donaldson, who had written the Report on juvenile delinquency, identified 'the incompetent mother' as the main cause. He reasoned that: 'The incompetent mother problem is part of juvenile delinquency and at the same time juvenile delinquency is part of the incompetent mother,' but did not elaborate.[46] The Council's Chairman then asserted that the incompetent mother was the main cause, telling the group: 'The children are taken into care because of the incompetent mother.' She seems to have been referring here to the so-called care and protection cases that were heard in the juvenile courts, but these were not criminal cases and she did not seem to appreciate that the juvenile courts dealt with welfare cases as well as juvenile and child crime.[47]

They moved on, unconcerned about such fine distinctions. The next deliberation was over the IQs of juvenile offenders. In Northern Ireland a juvenile's IQ was never revealed in court, but in English courts it usually was.[48] No one in Northern Ireland, not even its judges, knew whether there was a strong link between low intelligence and juvenile crime. The Child Welfare Council, in one of its more constructive proposals, wanted this to be known.[49] Certain categories of juvenile and youth offender, however, as we will discover, disproved the theory. On they moved to discuss juvenile comics, which were given a whole section in their published report.[50] A Mrs Harrison began the discussion, asserting that 'so many people say that comics are a cause of juvenile delinquency'. Another member, Reverend Thomson, disagreed and pointed out that no one had studied the effects comics had on juveniles.[51] This did not stop them making a recommendation in their interim report; a very ambiguous one. 'Whether or not it can be maintained that the acts of violence and thuggery with which some (comics) abound', their report stated portentously, 'actually cause delinquency, has not been a scientific study, but we are concerned that they do not improve the child's literary taste'[52] – hardly a matter for a Ministry wishing to understand juvenile crime. The committee made its most constructive points on youth organisations, rather than juvenile crime, but they suggested that the two might be related. They had discovered that the under-12s in Northern Ireland were not allowed to join youth organisations (boys' and girls' clubs, for example). Secondly, they made an intriguing discovery. They had learned that the Boy Scouts, which taught citizenship, had no branches in central Belfast; in effect, where juvenile crime was at its highest level. The Scouts in Northern Ireland were based in villages.[53]

The Child Welfare Council's study group on juvenile delinquency held 21 meetings between July 1953 and September 1954.[54] The outcome was a Report of just 20 pages full of empty phrases used repeatedly, such as 'we feel' and 'It is our opinion that, generally speaking' and other waffle.[55] The Report was sent to all of Northern Ireland's MPs in November 1954; to local judges, magistrates, welfare authorities, education authorities, church leaders, and 200 copies were sent to the HMSO bookshop in Belfast.[56] The local newspapers ignored it and so did local judges. A child welfare journal reviewed it, and a newspaper in Philadelphia, but it seems to have received no notices in Northern Ireland.[57]

The reason is that the Child Welfare Council ignored the evidence on juvenile crime. In June 1954 they were sent figures on juvenile crime in Armagh suggesting that 180 boys there had been convicted, for theft (56 boys), breaking and entering (24 boys), receiving stolen goods (6 boys) and other offences during 1953–4 in Armagh and the committee who sent them stated: 'There has been little evidence of any downward trend in Juvenile Crime' (they introduced the capitals to emphasise their point).[58] To prove the point, they also sent the figures for 1950; when 199 juveniles were found guilty in Armagh (almost 100 for breaking and entering and larceny). The Child Welfare Council did not refer to these figures in their *Juvenile Delinquency Report*; they made no reference to Armagh and they ignored the geographical aspects of juvenile crime entirely.

The Child Welfare Council began as an independent body; but, by early 1955, it was working closely with the Ministry of Home Affairs, Northern Ireland's equivalent to the Home Office in London, responsible for domestic affairs and juvenile crime. The Committee invited the Minister of Home Affairs, Mr Hanna, to their first anniversary celebration in February 1954 and he attended. He told them: 'Your Council is one of those very happy things which brings the blue sky to the grey clouds of a Minister's work ...'[59] He noted that they were an entirely non-political body, and referred, in his address, to their work on juvenile delinquency, a subject he thought was important. He told them it was 'in my mind at all times'.[60] By 1955 the Child Welfare Council was sending the Ministry of Home Affairs detailed reports on its meetings and it was functioning as an unofficial Children's Department it seems. After its Interim Report was produced in November 1954, it continued its investigations into juvenile delinquency; and it unquestionably deepened its understanding of the subject. In the late 1950s, the Committee also began an in-depth survey of the juvenile courts. They gathered an impressive amount of material from juvenile court magistrates and other law enforcers. They established other committees besides – on children's homes and adoption, for example.[61]

The juvenile delinquency levels in Northern Ireland during the 1940s and 1950s were partly a consequence of the lack of youth clubs. The point is illustrated by two towns: Enniskillen and Omagh. In the late 1950s,

Enniskillen had no youth club and a lot of juvenile delinquents and Omagh had a youth club and hardly any juvenile delinquents.[62] The Child Welfare Council pursued this question of whether youth clubs throughout Northern Ireland attracted enough delinquents and obviously thought youth clubs were a potential cure for juvenile crime. In October 1957 the Committee invited two youth leaders to address them on the leisure time of young people. Both were from Belfast. One was a youth leader in a Catholic boys' club and it emerged that he wanted to attract juvenile delinquents. Some of his members had appeared in court. He would not admit any boy under 12. Most were between 14 and 17 and he described some of the members as 'hard-nuts'.[63] His club had 120 members in October 1957 and the club opened every night each week. This was an unusual case. The club was run by the Legion of Mary, a Catholic charity, and the club's leader visited poor children's homes to enrol boys.[64]

The other youth leader, Wing Commander J. S. Higginson, OBE, JP, was a member of the Northern Ireland Government's Youth Committee and he told the Committee, inadvertently, that he was not interested in attracting juvenile delinquents. 'Some people like to think', he told them, 'that [boys'] clubs exist *only* [my italics] for delinquents or potential delinquents.' He wanted to attract boys who were interested in educational classes and he was not interested in letting them bring their girlfriends to the clubs.[65] Both youth leaders gave the strong impression that the Northern Ireland Government was not addressing the juvenile delinquency problem through its youth organisations' policy. The Ministry of Education financed youth clubs but removed its support when the membership fell to 8 or 9 members per evening.[66] Meanwhile, there were no youth clubs of any kind in central Belfast. One youth leader thought the best way to attract delinquent boys was to open youth clubs close to the dance halls – in effect, in the city centre – to lure them away from the halls and eventually redirect them to other clubs on the outskirts of the city.[67] But the clubs would need serious financial support from the Northern Ireland Government to implement this policy. There were few buildings available in the city centre and youth clubs had to compete for them, invariably losing out to organisations that could afford to pay higher rents. The Committee heard how a Federation of Girls' Clubs had been seeking premises on the Ormeau Road in Belfast for months. When a building was found they lost it to the British Legion, who offered more money for it.[68]

Beyond Belfast, youth clubs operating in the late 1950s attracted delinquents but these were small-scale and local ventures. A boys' club in Larne recruited boys who were on probation in Ballymena.[69] In Omagh a Catholic boys' club had opened and, according to a local probation officer, had 'practically wiped out' juvenile delinquency in the town.[70] In Portadown, there were several youth clubs in the late '50s and, according to its probation officer, they attracted 'problem children'; boys, as he put it, who were 'all on the N.S.P.C.C. Inspector's list'.[71] Up to 80 boys in Portadown would attend boys' clubs every Friday in late 1957. One Church youth leader who spoke to the Child Welfare Council claimed that his club attracted: 'Teddy boys who have served prison sentences and Borstal ... and several of them have done very well.'[72] It is conceivable that such small-scale clubs could reduce juvenile crime in small towns where the annual figures for juveniles charged would be less than 100 cases and probably around 30 to 40. But the Belfast Teddy Boy seems to have escaped the net of the youth club. The reasons are not hard to fathom. A club that offered educational classes in a dingy building somewhere on the outskirts of Belfast could hardly compete for the urban youth's attention with a city-centre dance hall that held hundreds and admitted girls as well as boys. Also, Northern Ireland's youth leaders seem not to have had a collective approach to dealing with juvenile delinquency in the late 1950s. And it is revealing that the individuals who noticed that delinquent youths joined youth clubs were probation officers, not youth leaders. The youth leaders were isolated figures – some were nobly pursuing delinquents; others were unsympathetic.[73] The Government Departments that dealt with youth clubs were indifferent.

There were some juvenile delinquents in 1950s' Northern Ireland who were never touched by youth organisations – namely, those who were under 14: the schoolboy and schoolgirl delinquent. The Child Welfare Council said nothing about this group, either in their discussions or in their two reports; but they are statistically significant and their ages alarmingly young in some cases. Table 5.2 gives details of all the 'child' delinquents under 10 sent to Training Schools in Northern Ireland in the period 1950 to 1954.

The Table clearly shows there was a surprising symmetry in the number, ages and sex of child delinquents in the two religious communities of early 1950s' Northern Ireland. It is almost as if they committed crimes together; even though, once sentenced, they were sent to either Protestant or Catholic Training Schools and thus boys in the same gang would be separated for up to three years. There was also a complete absence of delinquency among girls under 10 in both communities. Just three girls in this age-group were sent to Training Schools during these years and they were all 'Education' or 'Care and protection' cases; in other words, welfare cases.[74]

The figures in Table 5.2, revealing that boys as young as 7 and 8 were committing breaking and entering offences in early 1950s' Northern Ireland, would have been disturbing reading for members of the Child Welfare Council when they were sent them – especially given the thrust of their *Juvenile Delinquency Report*. There is no record of any discussion of the

Table 5.2 Child delinquents in Northern Ireland, 1950–4

Name	Date	Age	Reason sent to Training School
Protestant boys:			
Case A	1950	10	Stealing
Case B	1950	9	Breaking, Entering and Stealing
Case C	1950	9	Breaking, Entering and Stealing
Case D	1950	9	Education Case (i.e. non-attendance)
Case E	1951	8	Breaking, Entering and Stealing
Case F	1951	9	Education Case (Educationally Sub-Normal)
Case G	1951	8	Breaking, Entering and Stealing
Case H	1951	9	Education Case
Case I	1951	9	Care and Protection
Case J	1952	8	Education Case
Case K	1952	9	Welfare Case ('Mother Unsuitable')
Case L	1953	7	Breaking, Entering and Stealing
Case M	1954	8	Malicious Damage
Case N	1954	9	Theft of a Bicycle
Catholic boys:			
Case A	1950	9	Breaking, Entering and Stealing
Case B	1951	9	Breaking, Entering and Stealing
Case C	1951	8	Malicious Damage
Case D	1951	7	Education Case
Case E	1951	9	Breaking, Entering and Stealing
Case F	1951	9	Stealing
Case G	1951	9	Malicious Damage
Case H	1951	9	Breaking, Entering and Stealing
Case I	1951	7	Breaking, Entering and Stealing
Case J	1952	8	Education Case
Case K	1953	8	'Refractory'
Case L	1953	9	Stealing

Source: Ministry of Home Affairs, File HA/13/111, Child Welfare Council File, PRONI.

Child Delinquency figures in the Council's papers, but the figures were lodged in them. Given these figures, the Child Welfare Council's claims that juvenile delinquency was not a serious matter and that local judges were alarmists seem ill-informed.

From the mid-1950s, however, the Council began to delve more deeply into the subject of juvenile delinquency. They began an investigation into school delinquency in 1957; they gathered information on the Training Schools (the ages of inmates; the record of Training Schools in England and the types of training needed in Northern Ireland) and they also discussed youth gang crime – notably, the impact of the Teddy Boy youth cult in Northern Ireland. Among the questions they wanted answers to were: why did few girls commit crime in Northern Ireland? Why was delinquency more common among children of average ability at school age than among children of below average ability? How far was the Teddy Boy a dangerous phenomenon in Northern Ireland?[75]

The Child Welfare Council found the idea that children in Northern Ireland could be agents of crime very hard to accept. Even as late as September 1956, children were only mentioned in their discussions as victims of crime or ill-treatment. They combed the local newspapers for cases of child neglect and cited them. One case discussed in September 1956 – a case of Dickensian type cruelty – involved a child in County Down who had been kept in a henhouse.[76] Others discussed included cases of child abuse.[77] But the Council's focus shifted somewhat when they read a report on delinquency in Northern Ireland schools early in 1957 – the so-called Hawnt Report, named after its author J. Stuart Hawnt, OBE, MSc, PhD, the Director of Education for Northern Ireland.[78] The Report disclosed that in 1954 over 300 school reports had been cited in criminal cases heard in the juvenile courts of Northern Ireland. The material in them gave valuable information on the academic abilities, religious background, home environments and location (by Wards, i.e. districts) of child delinquents in Belfast between the ages of 8 and 14. The study uncovered many interesting patterns.

The first was that most delinquency among under-14s was committed by primary school children – 275 cases of 337 discussed. Second, far more child delinquents attended County Primary Schools than Catholic Schools – 208 as against 129 at Catholic Schools. Third, hardly any Grammar School pupils appeared in juvenile courts in Northern Ireland – only 2 from County Grammar Schools and 3 from Catholic Grammar Schools. Fourth, most school pupils who appeared in juvenile courts in Belfast were boys (321 compared with a mere 16 girls). There were other intriguing discoveries made in the Hawnt Report. One was that the most delinquent 'Ward' in the city was St Annes (in the city centre), with 40 child delinquency cases in 1954. After this, the 'most delinquent Wards' in Belfast were East Belfast (with 32 reported cases in 1954), Shankill Ward, with 32 cases reported, and there was significantly less juvenile delinquency in the Catholic working-class district of 'the Falls' (in West Belfast), with only 21 reported cases in 1954. The most common child offences were larceny (141 cases in 1954); breaking, entering and larceny (70 cases) and breaking and entering (44 cases). A further 38 cases involved a combination of larceny, breaking and entering and malicious damage. Self-evidently, most child crime cited in this study was serious crime. Finally, most of the 337 child offenders in the Hawnt study were from homes of 'average or high income' – 160 and 121 respectively. Only 56 were from homes described as 'poor'.

The findings of this Report were very unpalatable to the Child Welfare Council and the Council called the school welfare officers who had passed on the information to the Hawnt inquiry to a meeting. The Council began by asking the school representatives why few girls committed crime in Belfast. They were told, vaguely, that girls were 'less venturesome', 'less inquisitive' and that they were kept busy in their spare time performing household duties.[79] The real issue was how the distribution of child crime in Belfast should be explained and a member of the Schools' Welfare Service provided the answer. The Wards with the highest numbers of child (i.e. boy) delinquents were St Annes, Pottinger (in East Belfast), Ormeau and Clifton. All of these districts contained warehouses. In areas of high density housing such as the Falls and Shankill Wards there were far fewer child delinquents – about half the number in Wards with warehouses.[80]

The Education officials then revealed that child crime was seasonal. At Christmas the most common offence was shoplifting. In the Autumn children raided orchards for fruit. But the level of child crime did not fluctuate greatly over a year. When the discussion began, the Child Welfare Council's members quickly introduced subjects not covered in the Hawnt Report – perhaps a sign of their quest for answers to every possible aspect of child and juvenile delinquency. When the Teddy Boy was raised, however, it is difficult to see how the school welfare officers could have said anything informative or useful.

The Teddy Boy in Northern Ireland: myth or reality?

There are glimpses of a Teddy Boy culture in the crime records for Northern Ireland during the 1950s. Earlier, it was revealed that a 15-year-old boy was found guilty in Belfast during 1957 of 'disorderly conduct inside a cinema'; which appears to suggest that he was a Teddy Boy. But Teddy Boys were not prominent in Belfast in the late 1950s. In the local press they were treated as a novelty as late as April 1957 – four years after they had appeared in London.[81] Moreover, the Belfast Teddy Boy was not thought to be a juvenile delinquent. One of the first to spot them in Belfast was a YMCA official, J. D. Hornsby. He wrote to the *Belfast Newsletter* in April 1957, reporting what he had seen. He had noticed 'youths' wearing 'draped jackets, drainpipe trousers and string ties' and thought they were not potential or actual delinquents, but boys who needed guidance – as he put it they were 'terribly in need of counsel and understanding'.[82] He was the National Secretary of the YMCA, and had observed Teddy Boys near his offices in Belfast city centre. He wanted to attract them into the YMCA and he was discussing with other church leaders how Teddy Boys could be persuaded to join youth clubs. The interesting point here is that youth leaders and church leaders had a different policy towards juveniles veering towards delinquency than the courts and the judiciary. Youth leaders, if they were not indifferent, wanted to lure juvenile delinquents into their clubs and reform them. The juvenile court system in Northern Ireland, as we have discovered in this chapter, pursued a different policy – a policy of retribution, essentially.

The Child Welfare Council, in its deliberations about juvenile and youth delinquency, discussed the Teddy Boy on several occasions; but implied that Northern Ireland had few Teddy Boys. Its Chairman, Mrs Haughton, thought they were a vicious English invention. She had heard about them from the radio. Indeed a BBC Radio programme devoted to a discussion of the Teddy Boy had distressed her and she told the rest of the Council why. 'On this programme', she reported, 'it was really made out that if one joined the Teddy Boy gangs, it would be all right.'[83] The programme had apparently portrayed Teddy Boys as non-delinquent and recommended that boys should join gangs. Mrs Haughton had contacted the BBC and complained about the programme.

Several of the people the Child Welfare Council interviewed commented on Teddy Boys. A male schoolteacher reported in 1957 that he had never seen a Teddy Boy, but his daughter had. 'My daughter was telling me', he explained, 'a little while ago, that she saw a Teddy Boy, dressed in the full costume, doing the washing for his mother.'[84] The Council were somewhat alarmed to learn from their Chairman (Mrs Haughton), in March 1957, that there were 500 Teddy Boys in Belfast and that the numbers were growing 'very rapidly'.[85]

A member of the Child Welfare Council, a Catholic monk, had actually seen Teddy Boys with his own eyes, but only in England. He gave a very negative and one-sided account of the Teddy Boy culture he had observed. It emerged that he had only seen Teddy Boys who were incarcerated in a remand home – Campsfield Detention Centre, near Oxford. When he visited in May 1954, with a Home Office official, there was much talk in England of the Teddy Boy (at this point unknown in Northern Ireland). His colleagues would have winced to hear of 'Teddy Boys' and 'Cosh Boys' in Campsfield and to hear that most of the inmates were from big cities in England – London, Liverpool and Birmingham. Complacently, he told them: 'my impression is that we have not these types in Northern Ireland'.[86] But, in truth, the Child Welfare Council were not well-informed about Northern Irish youth culture or indeed about patterns of delinquency among older youths. They never in fact studied the youth offender (the 17 to 21 age-group) and had they visited the adult courts where boys in their late teens were tried for serious offences in Northern

Ireland they would have heard cases far more frightening than those involving Teddy Boys in England.[87] It has to be said that the Council preferred to restrict their activities to innocuous juvenile crimes reported in the sedate, and largely rural, juvenile courts of Northern Ireland to the more serious crimes committed by older youths, heard in the adult courts. Thus material on the extent of Teddy Boy crime in Northern Ireland is largely absent from the juvenile and youth crime records.

The Child Welfare Council members were never really interested in exploring changes in youth culture and how far these changes altered the pattern of juvenile and youth crime. This is surprising given that one of its members, D. G. Neill, was a Social Studies Lecturer at The Queen's University of Belfast and other members sat in juvenile courts as JPs – its Chairman Mrs Haughton for example.[88] They never considered that juvenile and youth crime occurs over time and that the pattern of juvenile and youth crime might be sensitive to changes in youth culture. Given what we have already learned about them, we can also safely say they were not well-informed about youth culture – except as something alien that was imported from England. Youth culture meant, in short, the Teddy Boy – an anti-social misfit, with a ludicrous uniform strongly associated in their minds with viciousness.[89]

There are traces of youth culture in Northern Ireland during the 1950s – possibly fuelled by affluence. A probation officer from Belfast reported to the Council on 'a disturbing increase in cases of disorderly behaviour' among youths who visited dance halls and billiard halls.[90] He was referring to boys of 15 and older. He described the offence of disorder as almost unknown in Northern Ireland before the 1950s. There was some truth in this. During 1956, 23 youths in Belfast had been placed on probation for disorderly conduct and many more were fined. The local dance halls imposed no lower age limit and their proprietors were evading the licensing laws regulating dance halls by calling their premises 'dance schools' or 'clubs'.[91] The Belfast probation officer believed breaking and entering visits were planned inside the dance halls. Also, disorderly conduct was linked to other crimes – assault, for example – and both, so the Council believed, could be induced by drinking in dance halls. There were also signs of a vibrant, and possibly anti-social, youth culture in Ballymena during May 1957. Parties of Teddy Boys from Belfast had been visiting a dance hall in Ballymena. On one occasion over 100 youths were observed scuffling, but no one was charged.[92] The evidence available does not suggest that Teddy Boy crime was serious in 1950s' Northern Ireland and it was far more prominent in the courts of the Irish Republic. There, Teddy Boys were noticed sitting in the juvenile courts listening to cases, offering support to their friends.[93] The Republic's juvenile courts had also introduced a sentence to deal with the Teddy Boy problem. Those found guilty were given conditional discharges and the condition was that they would emigrate.[94]

Conclusion

It is clear from this survey of juvenile and youth crime in Northern Ireland, therefore, that juvenile delinquency was an endemic problem throughout Northern Ireland in the 1940s and the 1950s – in rural districts as well as in towns and cities. The evidence suggests that around 50 per cent of juvenile crime dealt with by the juvenile courts was committed in Belfast. There is no obvious cause of juvenile delinquency during the period, but poverty seems to have generated far less juvenile crime than acquisitiveness. The worst juvenile crime district at this period was Whiteabbey in North Belfast and it had a buoyant local economy for juveniles of both sexes. Throughout Northern Ireland, during the 1940s and the 1950s, boy delinquents far outnumbered girl delinquents and an interesting question for future research is why so few girls committed crimes of any sort in Northern Ireland. The pattern of crime among boys reveals there was a preponderance of serious crime – larceny and breaking and entering, principally – and the juvenile delinquency problem cannot be dismissed as mere mischief. One of the most interesting discoveries of this chapter is what made juvenile crime stop. There is strong evidence that England's more affluent economy during the 1950s did not curb juvenile delinquency in prosperous cities such as Birmingham.[95]

   The problem for policy makers in 1950s' Northern Ireland was how to deal with a juvenile delinquency problem that outside Belfast was fairly thinly spread, but which existed in virtually every community – rural and urban. The juvenile court system was not well-equipped to reduce juvenile delinquency, as one of the principal means of reforming juvenile criminals and reducing juvenile crime – probation – was not widely accepted.[96] In consequence, the juvenile criminal justice system in Northern Ireland during the 1940s and 1950s was largely punitive; but even in this respect it was defective because it punished the parents of juveniles found guilty of crimes rather than the juveniles. It might be argued that a three-year sentence in a Training School was not a pleasant experience for a lad of 14 or 15; but, on the other hand, a very small number of juveniles each year were sent to Training Schools. In 1959, of 3749 juveniles who appeared in juvenile courts in Northern Ireland only 154 were sent to Training Schools – less than 3 per cent.[97] So, what made juveniles in 1950s' Northern Ireland stop committing crime? The evidence considered in this chapter suggests that one of the principal influences that made a difference was a youth club. Some of Northern Ireland's youth leaders were seriously interested in reforming juvenile delinquents. This is hardly surprising since many had a Christian or broadly religious purpose. There is also clear evidence that delinquent juveniles joined youth clubs in Northern Ireland. Where a youth club that attracted juveniles with criminal records existed – as in Larne and, on a larger scale, Omagh – juvenile delinquency seems to have disappeared.[98]

6

From the Juke Box Boys to Revolting Students: Richard Hoggart and the Study of British Youth Culture

Richard Hoggart's academic career during the 1950s and 1960s coincided with the emergence of distinctive national and international youth cultures in Britain and across the world. Hoggart, first as a provincial Workers' Educational Association (WEA) tutor in the Fifties, and then as a Professor at the University of Birmingham during the 1960s, had first hand knowledge of some of the most significant youth movements and cultures to emerge in the postwar period; from the Teddy Boys of the early 1950s to the global student revolts of the late 1960s. Moreover, his work is infused with references to youth culture. These range chronologically from his vivid description of 'juke box boys' lounging in the milk bars of Northern England, and described in *The Uses of Literacy* (1957) – 'boys aged between fifteen and twenty, with drape suits, picture ties and an American slouch' – to the early identification of the teenage consumer in the *Albemarle Report* of 1960, which he co-wrote with Leslie Paul, and on into the late 1960s and beyond. He wrote about provincial youth culture in the 'Swinging' Sixties; about the student protest movements of the late 1960s and even, briefly, about Oxbridge youth under Thatcherism. It is surprising, therefore, that no cultural historian has yet appraised what Richard Hoggart has written about British Youth Culture – except Robert Colls, briefly, in his recent book *Identity of England* (2002); who pointed out that Hoggart's censorious views about youth culture are the one section of *The Uses of Literacy* in which he lost his grip on his subject.[1]

Several questions need to be posed if we are to understand, and indeed assess, Hoggart's references to Youth Culture in his work. The obvious starting point is to examine what he has written and hope this uncovers whether he felt that Youth Culture was a good thing for British society or not. The gist of what has been written by other historians is that he did not see Youth Culture as a creative force in the Fifties and Sixties.[2] But this does not mean that he disliked Youth Culture. It may simply mean that he disapproved of certain types of Youth Culture; or disapproved of culture industries that exploited Youth; the American pop industry of the late Fifties perhaps being the prime candidate.[3] Another central question in this quest to understand Richard Hoggart's views about British Youth Culture is: what were the influences that shaped Hoggart's thoughts on Youth Culture? Historians use archives as the foundation for their analysis of social movements such as Youth Culture. But no one at the time Hoggart came to national attention in the late Fifties had undertaken a detailed archival study of British Youth Culture. My own work on the interwar teenager as a consumer, published as a book entitled *The First Teenagers: The Lifestyle of Young Wage-Éarners in Interwar Britain* (1995), drew on primary historical sources such as the interwar poverty surveys of Seebohm Rowntree (an author, interestingly, who Hoggart had read by the mid-1960s[4]) and the records of Lads' and Girls' clubs; not to mention the reports and wages surveys of Government Departments such as the Ministry of Labour and the Juvenile Employment Bureaux administered by local education authorities.[5] In some ways, the concept of Youth Culture as something unique to the post-World War Two period permeated the literary journals of the 1950s and it was a deeply flawed and ahistorical vision of Youth Culture that few people at the time questioned; including Richard Hoggart.[6]

Earlier chapters of this study focused on the period between the Two World Wars when, it was argued, Youth Culture took shape not only in the form of the teenage consumer with unprecedented levels of disposable income and a new leisure world of dance halls, cinemas and holidays becoming regular features of a new youth lifestyle; but, also, Youth Culture as a concept, as an idea for young people to promote, was also pioneered during this earlier period.[7] As revealed above, Youth Culture as an idea emerged in Britain in the early 1920s in the universities and it was most prominently discussed in Cambridge, where an undergraduate named Rolf Gardiner was busy trying to establish a Youth Culture across Northern Europe. He used literature such as his pioneering cultural journal *Youth: An Expression of Progressive University Thought*, published in Cambridge from 1920 to 1924, to promote the idea of Youth Culture.[8] Gardiner had no journalists or social commentators to tell him where Youth Culture was to be found. He had learned about Youth Culture on visits to Germany where he encountered the phrase *Jugendkultur* (Youth Culture), which in that country meant youth movements.[9] But, back in Britain, he developed it in new ways; exploring what he and his friends termed 'new ways of living'.[10] The key point here is that Youth Culture in twentieth-century Britain began with upper middle-class youth who had time and income to undertake foreign travel. In its earliest guise, it was an organic movement rooted in small youth communities within universities and it developed by word of mouth, through student literature and through the international cultural exchanges organised by prime movers such as Rolf Gardiner.[11]

By the time Hoggart was writing in the late Fifties and early 1960s, Youth Culture had lost its links with the Universities and as the organic movement it started life as during the 1920s, through prime movers like Rolf Gardiner. It was now seen as closely linked with the burgeoning American pop music industry.[12]

Youth Culture is first seen in Hoggart's work in chapter 7 of *The Uses of Literacy*, which includes an account of his encounters with a group of male youths, most of them aged from 15 to 20, in a milk bar somewhere in the North of England.[13] The period in question is sometime around the mid-Fifties. He builds up, sermon-like, a critique of the entire universe of these 'Juke Box Boys' and to see how he does it we need to sample his rich prose. But before we do so, it is worth pointing out that Hoggart's observations are based solely on his own random encounters with Juke Box boys, who are presumably Teddy Boys, standing by a jukebox in a Northern milk bar. Hoggart was not peering at these youths through a window, which might have made them seem even more exotic, but sitting in the same milk bar. He was actually preparing to go and teach an Extra-Mural Class, and, possibly in work mode, he may just have been in a bad mood at the time. But his description of what he observed found its way into his classic work *The Uses of Literacy* (published in 1957) and it came over as a diatribe more suited to a nineteenth-century Presbyterian pulpit than to a detached work of social and cultural criticism.[14] He saw no good at all in the British teenager's interest in American popular music; which, of course, was chiefly heard away from parents in the milk bars and coffee bars of provincial and southern England.[15]

We have to forget, at this point, that American popular music of the mid- to late 1950s – Elvis Presley, Buddy Holly, Chuck Berry and others – gave rise eventually, in the early 1960s, to the music of the Beatles, the Rolling Stones and other home-grown and creative pop groups. In short, what had emerged by the early 1960s, indisputably, was an astonishing flowering of British popular music created, essentially, by youths in their teens and early twenties; many of whom wrote their own songs.[16] One contemporary sociologist even argued, persuasively, that pop music on Merseyside transformed potential or actual delinquent youths into creative artists.[17] The youth cults that emerged during the early 1960s, in fact, often blossomed from the dreariest London suburbs. The Mod culture is the best example. It seems to have started among a small group of fashion-conscious friends in Stoke Newington and other parts of North London around 1960.[18] It became, as is well known, a national and international youth movement that inspired pop music television programmes, the fashion industry, many youth pop groups, at the time and since; and, moreover, it enabled thousands of young males and young females to create the first geographically mobile Youth Cult in Britain – the Mod Cult – as they escaped the new suburbs of postwar London and created their own leisure worlds in coastal towns.[19]

But all of this is to look into a future that Richard Hoggart could not have foreseen in the mid-1950s. On the other hand, we could recall that Brian Epstein first discovered the Beatles performing one lunchtime in a basement cellar in Liverpool in 1961 – at a venue far less salubrious than the milk bar Richard Hoggart entered around 1956.[20] Hoggart's account is a carefully constructed, but highly distorted, glimpse of Northern youth culture in the era just before the Beatles. He begins:

> Like the cafés I described in an earlier chapter, the milk bars indicate at once, in the nastiness of their modernistic knick-knacks, their glaring showiness, an aesthetic breakdown so complete...I have in mind...the kind of milk bar – there is one in almost every northern town with more than, say, fifteen thousand inhabitants – which has become the regular evening rendezvous for some of the young men.[21]

We learn that the young men in question are 15- to 20-year-olds who attend these milk bars 'night after night', and put 'copper after copper' in the jukebox and we hear about how they react to the records – 'The young men waggle one shoulder or stare, as desperately as Humphrey Bogart, across the tubular chairs.'[22] The passage ends with a harsh judgement on the lives of Northern Teddy Boys. As Hoggart puts it: 'these are...the directionless and tamed helots of a machine-minding class'.[23] There is no mention in *The Uses of Literacy* that Richard Hoggart talked to any of these Teddy Boys, so we do not know anything specific about their family backgrounds. But, presumably, he modified his views about Teddy Boys very soon afterwards. Only a couple of years after *The Uses of Literacy* was published Hoggart encountered a Teddy Boy who was not only articulate, but had been to university and had written his autobiography, published by Faber and Faber, before he was 22: the prolific writer on teenage affairs Ray Gosling.[24] So, what was the purpose of including this brief and rather alarmist account in his pioneering and pathbreaking survey of working-class culture?

Hoggart's point, it seems, was that these working-class youths of Northern towns were not creating their own culture. They were just ciphers for American pop music and, he argued, it dulled their brains. The young men who poured their money into the jukeboxes were like zombies. They stared vacantly into space or waggled their shoulders. At this juncture, we might become curious about the types of records they listened to and what their tastes in music said about the imaginative worlds of 1950s' teenagers. Other social investigators of the time found, for example, that British youths were so inspired by the glamour of America that they wanted, as soon as was feasible, to emigrate there.[25] But Hoggart's account of the Juke Box Boys does not probe this question of why working-class youths were so fascinated by America and whether, in fact, it did give them an imaginative world not immediately apparent in the mechanical gesture of putting copper after copper into the jukebox. We also ought to bear in mind that there were no pop videos in the late 1950s; so there was still scope for youths who listened to records to imagine the worlds depicted in them. Finally, we do need to know something about the historical context, which is absent from Hoggart's description. These youths were in limbo; but it was not a limbo created by the vacuous pop world. The lives of these youths were shaped more than anything in the mid-1950s by the fractured experience of leaving school at 15, taking jobs for two to three years and then being drafted into the military services for two years to complete their National Service.[26]

Hoggart's next foray into the worlds of the young was a review of a film about Teddy Boys published in the journal *Sight and Sound* in late 1959. Richard Hoggart could be a harsh critic, especially when reviewing books; which he sometimes did for the *New Statesman* around this period.[27] But he liked Karel Reisz's documentary film about Lambeth Teds – *We are the Lambeth Boys*. His review was a characteristic piece of imaginative prose, which this time took the form of an open letter to Reisz, saying what the reviewer liked and did not care for. He began with all the film's faults. 'It (your film)', he proceeded, 'says nothing about juvenile delinquency, home relationships, personal problems or private sex-life (though all these would affect the people in the film).'[28] (The same criticism might have been levelled at the reviewer of Hoggart's *Uses of Literacy*, incidentally.) But at last, in this review, we begin to see Hoggart's views about youth culture emerging. The film was about a group of Teddy Boys who were also members of a youth club and Hoggart found them captivating. The film showed them in conversations at their work in a Post Office, apparently discussing gang warfare they were conducting with other gangs. It revealed that the boys did have an inner life, despite their boring jobs, and Hoggart found it quite heroic; referring to 'the richness, the horror and the glory, of the inner life below the drab outer level'.[29] In a later article on the same subject, published 26 years later, more details are given about the Lambeth boys of 1959. They were tough; but their songs revealed that their values were the same as those of their parents. They were proud to boast, for example, that they had good 'manners'. As one of their songs put it:

We are the Lambeth Boys,
We know our manners.
We spend our tanners.
We are respected wherever we go.[30]

There is an irony, of course, in the fact that they win respect through being good at fighting.

The Lambeth Youth Club in the film was an unusual youth club in that it was run by former pupils of Mill Hill, a boys' public school in London. Every year, the Lambeth youths had to play in a cricket match against pupils at the school, and Hoggart, whose sympathies were clearly with the working-class youths, described this match as 'a guarded, uneasy occasion on both sides, for all the attempts at heartiness'.[31] Twenty-five years after the original film was made, a follow-up film of a later generation of Lambeth boys was screened in the mid-1980s. Richard Hoggart reviewed the follow-up film and was struck by how the conversations had changed hardly at all across almost three decades. 'I heard nothing in the substance of the talk', he noted in 1985, 'which was different in kind from what it would have been like a quarter of a century ago: boys are only out for their oats; girls only want a bit of legover'.[32] Even the songs were, more or less, the same – though Hoggart noticed that the word 'manners' had disappeared from the most famous song:

Everywhere we go,
People want to know,
Who we are,
We are the Lambeth Boys.[33]

He found much evidence of continuity, however. The annual cricket match was still played in 1985 (though a new feature was the presence in the youth club team of West Indian youths).[34] The youths of Lambeth still took great care over their personal appearance. The original group always had neatly combed hair with a side parting and the boys always wore suits. By the 1980s, they still wore suits but designer suits. Their diets had barely changed at all. They had chips with everything in 1959 and in 1985; though a new dish had appeared over the intervening thirty years – chips with a side salad. In the youth club the most striking similarity with the earlier period was that the youth leader who was running the club in 1959 was still running it twenty-five years later; an example of community service that Richard Hoggart no doubt found admirable.[35]

An academic sociologist would want to know far more about what was below the surface in these two films and only touched on in Hoggart's reviews. An obvious theme for more in-depth study would be the extent of racism in a community that had witnessed a major influx of West Indians over the intervening years. 'Hardly a black face in the late '50s; now more black than white' was Hoggart's pithy summary of this complex subject.[36] But what had been revealed in interviews with the original Lambeth boys 25 years on was just how racist they had become.[37] The impulses behind this racism were not discussed by Hoggart; though he can hardly be blamed for this. A popular media magazine was not the right forum for these questions to be probed in greater detail.

If Hoggart had a thesis about the Lambeth Boys' culture across almost thirty years, from the late Fifties to the mid-1980s, it was that deference had disappeared from their vocabulary. His evidence was that words such as 'manners' and 'respect' had disappeared from their songs; which is an intriguing observation.[38] But this is a symptom of a possible change in behaviour, rather than its cause. If deference had declined, why had it declined? One possible explanation is that the youths who appeared in the first Lambeth documentary in 1959 would all have done, or be about to do, National Service. The state and authority figures were still a prominent feature of their lives, in other words, beyond school. The Lambeth youths of 1985, by contrast, would not encounter the state beyond the age of 16 unless they were arrested, became unemployed or married young – and even then they would encounter the state only fleetingly.

The next phase of Hoggart's critique of British Youth Culture is the most intriguing. In 1960 when he was a Lecturer in English Literature at Leicester University, Hoggart was asked to sit on a Committee on the Youth Service under a patrician Countess, Lady Albemarle. There is an amusing account of this Committee's work in his Autobiography.[39] After she had selected 12 people to sit on the Committee, the Countess delegated all the writing-up of the final report to just two people: Richard Hoggart and Leslie Paul, a socialist youth leader who had been involved with the Woodcraft Folk and had written a book which defined a cultural movement of the Fifties – *Angry Young Man*.[40] The research period for the interviews, the fieldwork and the production of the Report was just twelve months and all the meetings took place in the regal environment of a central London townhouse.[41] At this stage, Hoggart's own thinking on Youth and Youth Culture was still largely shaped by his instincts and observations, rather than by detailed research. As he put it, at the outset of the Albemarle Committee's work: 'I was concerned about the barren lives of many young people and glad to have a chance to look into whether some useful suggestions could be made.'[42] The tone of his statement suggests that the Committee had a rather broad remit and this is borne out by the final Report. It was not restricted to a discussion of the Youth Service, as suggested in its official title; but also included an interesting chapter, presumably written by Hoggart, on the lifestyles of 1950s' teenagers that looked in detail at their disposable incomes.[43]

The best critique of the Albemarle Report was provided by one of the beneficiaries of the Youth Service grants it made available – the intrepid and perceptive writer on teenage affairs Ray Gosling.[44] The Committee was set up by the Conservative government soon after the Labour Party had established its own Youth Commission in 1959; a gimmicky committee which had on its panel a footballer (Jimmy Hill), a Jazz band leader (Humphrey Lyttelton), a TV scriptwriter (Ted Willis); and a young pop star was asked but declined (Tommy Steele).[45] Gosling argued that the Albemarle Committee had no new ideas on Youth and in his words: 'It says nothing about teenager 1960.'[46] This was a fair criticism. The Committee certainly had no new ideas on the lifestyles of teenagers and it even used a researcher who had advised the Labour Party on teenage spending, Dr Mark Abrams.[47]

Abrams was an acute social commentator, but he was primarily a market researcher serving leisure entrepreneurs. Indeed, he worked for the largest market research organisation in London, the London Press Exchange.[48] In his work, the lives of teenagers were depicted largely in market terms. He tells you, for example, how many teenagers there were in 1959; how much they earned; and how they used their disposable incomes.[49] His observations were, essentially, superficial soundbites – 'teenage spending is on teenage goods in a distinctively teenage world' was one of his major conclusions in his pamphlet *The Teenage Consumer* (published in 1959).[50] This would have sounded wide of the mark to a teenager such as Ray Gosling in 1960. He had just dropped out of university, and was living on his wits; taking a succession of jobs in Leicester, from garage work to work promoting local bands in an attempt to simply survive.[51] Abrams was writing for business people who wished to tap the teenage market. He did not provide an in-depth account of the regional experiences of late 1950s' teenagers; an angle that was completely absent in fact from his work.[52] We learn nothing in Hoggart's published work about his views on Abrams' researches into late Fifties' teenagers. But it will be fascinating to discover if any correspondence between them has survived in the Richard Hoggart Archive (held at the University of Sheffield).

The relationship between Ray Gosling and Richard Hoggart is touched upon in the published work of both authors. Gosling was a precocious and talented writer who in the late '50s and early '60s, when he was still in his early twenties, knew far more than Hoggart and indeed any other contemporary writer about British Youth Culture. His only rival was Colin MacInnes, an Australian in his forties who lived in a squat in central London and wrote novels about teenage life around Soho and West London – *Absolute Beginners* (published in 1959) being the best known.[53] What made Gosling more interesting than MacInnes, certainly for Hoggart, was that he wanted to shape Youth Culture as well as write about it; and, secondly, his work focused on provincial experiences of Youth Culture, an angle that MacInnes, who was an archetypal Soho bohemian, simply lacked, or had no interest in acquiring.[54]

Gosling came to the attention of Hoggart in print in late 1962 when Hoggart, by this time a Professor at the University of Birmingham, and making plans to establish a Centre for Cultural Studies, found himself reviewing an incisive account of teenage life written by Gosling, a 22-year-old, and entitled *Sum Total*. It was published by the distinguished publishing house Faber and Faber.[55] At this time, Gosling's articles were appearing regularly in highbrow literary periodicals such as *Universities and Left Review*, *The New University*, an Oxford undergraduate periodical, the Marxist journal *New Left Review* and the society magazine *Queen*.[56] He was soon to become Colin MacInnes's protégé and flatmate in London.[57] At the time *Sum Total* was published, however, Gosling had recently left Leicester University after just one year (he was thrown out) and he had been living a peripatetic teenage existence, to-ing and fro-ing between London, Northampton and Leicester.[58] No doubt influenced by two celebrated American novels of the period – J. D. Salinger's *Catcher in the Rye* (1951) and Jack Kerouac's 'beat' novel *On the Road* (1957) – he tried to turn himself into a real life British teenage hero; a subversive in other words. In his review of *Sum Total*, Hoggart depicted Gosling as a romantic figure; as he put it, 'partly inspired by revolt against the nicely plotted route to security for the scholarship winner'.[59] It is interesting to speculate on whether Richard Hoggart would have said this in the late '60s when he had children at university. But his review, though mixed, ended on a positive note: '*Sum Total*, for all its bumpiness, shows that he [Gosling] has a genuine talent.'[60] We gain some insights into Hoggart's own developing views on Youth Culture from this review. Indeed, Hoggart having written no full-length articles on teenagers himself, such reviews were invaluable tools for him to clarify his own ideas.

A core theme that was emerging in Hoggart's own thoughts, here and in the review of *We Are The Lambeth Boys*, was that the forms of Youth Culture he approved of were provincial youth cultures with close ties to their parents and communities; in other words, a not fully autonomous Youth Culture was what he preferred. He praised Gosling for mentioning his 'Mum and Dad' and 'Grandma' – 'Mum and Dad never seem far away; and Grandma is always there, back in the old terrace-house.'[61] But in Gosling's case this became something of a fiction as he left his home town of Northampton after he went to university in Leicester in the late Fifties and by the early 1960s he had moved to London.[62]

Gosling and Hoggart actually met in Leicester when Gosling was, for a brief period around 1960, a youth leader – before he was sacked.[63] In fact, Gosling had secured a large grant of £12,000 to develop his Leicester Youth Club and Hoggart was a member of the Youth Club's Management Committee.[64] It is unclear from the published accounts of this episode whether Hoggart had a hand in Gosling being sacked, but he certainly hinted in his review of *Sum Total* that Gosling was a poor organiser.[65] The two still had broadly similar ideas. Gosling, like Hoggart, believed that Youth Culture should be rooted in local communities and he set about trying to attract the youths who lived close to his club in a very unsalubrious part of Leicester. He gives us some idea of what he was up against in his short pamphlet on his life as a youth club leader – *Lady Albemarle's Boys* (1961). The club's members ranged from 'the most desirable virgin of 19 to the murderer of 25, who got away with manslaughter'. On more than one occasion Gosling, who was the only full-time secretary, was badly beaten. In one management meeting he attended with Richard Hoggart he had two black eyes.[66]

It is not clear from Gosling's writings, or Hoggart's own for that matter, whether Hoggart ever visited the Leicester Youth Club that Gosling ran in the evenings. He may have disapproved if he had done. What was in the club? There was a coffee bar with a jukebox; a dance hall with a resident rock band; a television, billiard tables and magazines – all of the impedimenta associated with Americanised mass culture that Hoggart loathed.[67] But, in addition, there were quiet rooms, an office, newspapers and an information and advice centre. It is obviously worthwhile, therefore, given these tantalising details on the interiors of early 1960s' provincial youth clubs, for historians to study them – their aims and social impact – in more detail. For one thing, this youth club does reveal just how eclectic the leisure worlds of even supposedly uncultured teenagers were in the late Fifties and early Sixties, and it gives the distinct impression that both an interest in reading and in current affairs were not absent from the lives of poorly educated youths, or indeed social aspirations.

Richard Hoggart and Ray Gosling were in brief contact, therefore. But a far more significant influence in Hoggart's academic investigations of Culture was Stuart Hall. Without Stuart Hall, it is questionable whether the Centre for Contemporary Cultural Studies (CCCS) at Birmingham would ever have produced all the amazingly rich research papers, many still unpublished, on aspects of youth culture and youth subcultures stretching from the mid-1960s and on into the 1970s and beyond.[68] Hoggart himself gave no indication in his Inaugural Lecture at Birmingham that his new Centre would study youth cultures. He thought research was needed on popular fiction; the press and journals; strip cartoons; the language of advertising; public relations; and there was possibly just a hint that he was seriously interested in exploring youth cultures with his declared interest in 'popular songs and popular music in all their forms'. He may not have had in mind pop music, however, for potential research theses, as he seemed ambivalent about its value. 'It is hard to listen to a programme of pop songs...without feeling a complex mixture of attraction and repulsion', he announced in his Inaugural Lecture.[69]

Hoggart arrived at Birmingham University in 1962 and Stuart Hall, who was at this time a school teacher in London, became Hoggart's first Research Fellow in Popular Culture in 1964.[70] He was appointed to work on 'popular culture and communication'.[71] By the time he had arrived in Birmingham Stuart Hall had published several articles in literary journals about aspects of youth culture – an article on 'Student Journals', for example, in *New Left Review*; a review of Colin MacInnes's novel *Absolute Beginners* and Mark Abrams's pamphlet *The Teenage Consumer* (both published in 1959), for *Universities and Left Review*; and an article about what he called 'the politics of adolescence', in the same journal.[72] Stuart Hall was not interested in judging late Fifties' youth in Britain; but in seeking to understand how they reacted to broad cultural trends such as Americanisation. He was also interested in their reactions to cultural subjects taught in schools.[73] Hall wanted to understand why youth cults like the Teddy Boys rebelled. Was the culture of the Secondary Modern School behind this rebellion? He was interested in the impact James Dean's films *Rebel Without a Cause* and *East of Eden* had upon British youth. Later on, he became interested in the social phenomenon of Beatlemania.[74] In short, he was the prime mover in the study of youth subcultures, and Youth Culture more broadly, at Birmingham during the 1960s and several research students completed theses and research papers on aspects of youth culture: Paul Willis, for example, on Pop Songs and Youth Culture with special reference to Birmingham; John Clarke on Skinheads and Youth Culture; and Janice Winship on young women's magazines.[75] Stuart Hall himself even wrote a research paper on 'Hippies', which was subsequently published.[76]

Richard Hoggart seems to have left Stuart Hall to develop academic research on Youth at Birmingham. But there is some evidence that, by the late '60s, Hoggart himself was actively involved in this research. For instance, he gave a research paper to a Graduate seminar in 1969 on the theme: 'Reflections on the Student Movement'.[77] It is unclear whether this paper was published. It is clear from the CCCS's annual reports, however, that the student protests of the late '60s were the inspiration for several graduate dissertations at Birmingham. Some of the Centre's graduate students undertook, in 1968, an in-depth study of a Birmingham student protest. They analysed press reactions; student leaflets and student periodicals; and an official report on the protests produced by the University's Registrar.[78] It is not surprising that the University began to suspect that the CCCS was behind much of the student protest at Birmingham.[79]

Richard Hoggart's published essays on youth culture, and on student life in Britain during the 1960s, are reflective pieces mostly written after – usually several years after – the events they describe. He was interested in two central themes: the impact permissiveness was having in the universities and in the provinces; and, to a more limited extent, the causes of the student revolts of the late '60s. His most incisive essay was a short piece he wrote for *The Guardian* in 1967, exploring whether the Permissive Society had transformed provincial cities as much as 'Swinging' London. The essay is so suggestive it could provide, even now, the basis for a stimulating Ph.D. thesis.

Hoggart provides in this short essay a model of how Youth Culture, in his view, developed in British society. He argued that it was a London-centric idea and only after a time lag (unspecified) did it reach provincial towns and cities. The vehicles for the spread of this Youth Culture, he suggested, were pop programmes such as *Ready Steady Go!*, radio, magazines, fashion and records. It was a model he must have found somewhat disturbing as, at one point, he noted that teenagers in Leeds, his home town, were only interested in buying clothes sold by 'the taste leaders' in London.[80] He must have had in mind designers like Mary Quant.[81] He did not elaborate on whether these 'taste leaders' operated in other fields such as pop music and the media; but he must have been thinking also of pop stars – of the 23-year-old millionaire pop star Mick Jagger, for example; who, in July 1967, immediately after being acquitted of a drugs charge, was interviewed by the Editor of *The Times* and three senior churchmen for ITV's award-winning weekly current affairs programme *World in Action*, and was watched by several million TV viewers.[82] Jagger was surely one of the metropolitan 'taste leaders' Hoggart was alluding to; though whether Hoggart saw Jagger on *World in Action* is a moot point as he only switched on the television, according to his wife, about once every two weeks.[83]

Hoggart did not conclude in this stimulating essay that provincial cultures were finished. Instead, he offered the tantalising thesis that the 'generation gap' was most pronounced in the provinces, rather than in London, precisely because civic culture and working-class culture were so entrenched there and this alien Youth Culture was superimposed on settled communities with strong civic cultures. A researcher who wanted to pursue this Hoggart model would need to analyse whether, during the 1960s, there was a liberalisation of values in provincial towns and cities brought about by the changes in Youth Culture. It is a brilliant hypothesis. How could it be investigated? One area would be to look at how film and theatre censorship were affected by developments in Youth Culture, given that provincial Watch Committees were the bodies that issued certificates for films and licences for theatres. No one, to my knowledge, has yet investigated how provincial and civic life were affected by Youth Culture during the so-called 'Swinging' Sixties.

Hoggart's essays on student cultures of the 1960s are more personal reflections, rather than pieces suggesting new areas for social and historical research. They also contain some fascinating ideas – for example, that female students were far less liberated than male students by the spread of birth control from around 1967.[84] But in his discussion of the causes of the student protests in the late '60s he seems to have been too influenced by the work of Colin Crouch, a young Sociology student at the LSE in the late '60s; who argued that the protests at LSE were an idealistic search for new types of student community: a doubtful thesis that ignores the facts.[85]

LSE's students, 40 per cent of whom were international students in the late 1960s, were primarily interested in concrete political and indeed educational issues such as the higher fees the Labour government had imposed on international students studying in Britain.[86] Many students at LSE, it should be recalled, were from Developing Countries and there was a lot of discussion about Third World poverty at their meetings.[87] They also wanted to reform the universities and wrote cogent policy documents on how the curriculum in British universities should be refashioned.[88] They were not airy-fairy, whimsical utopians as historians such as Kenneth Morgan have suggested;[89] but social reformers, many of whom progressed from support of libertarian social causes in the 1960s to support of economic liberalism and Thatcherism during the 1980s.[90]

7 The Mod Culture in Swinging Britain, 1964–7

Few historians of Modern Britain have probed the significance and impact of the Mod culture, either in London or nationally, during the Swinging Sixties.[1] Arthur Marwick's colossal book on the 1960s, for example, devotes less than a paragraph to the Mod movement.[2] Like all the historians and sociologists who have written about the Mods, Marwick sees the movement as a product of affluence and, in its initial phase, a product of classless 'Swinging London'.[3] The Mod culture is only depicted through anecdotes, but those who recall the heady days of the 'High Sixties' Mod culture reminisce proudly about their obsession with clothes and their hedonistic lifestyle. As one apprentice printer of the time, cited in Marwick, recalled:

> Monday was Tottenham Royal, Tuesday the Lyceum, Wednesday the Scene, or maybe stay in and wash your hair, Thursday Tottenham Royal again (because it was our little hangout), then Friday night was 'Ready Steady Go' ... Then after 'Ready Steady Go' you'd go to the Scene later, Saturday and Sunday was either a party or the Tottenham Royal, then the next week you'd start again.[4]

The salient point about this Mod's experience, surely, is that though a Mod in 'Swinging London' he spent much of his week in the local environment of Tottenham rather than at Mod venues in central London. In fact, the Mod culture, it seems, largely existed on the fringes of 'Swinging London'; though this point has never been made in the literature on the Mods. Moreover, the Mods were largely excluded from much of Swinging London for two reasons: firstly, their age (most Mods were in their early to late teens, making them too young to attend the celebrated discotheques of the era – Dolly's, Annabel's, and the Ad Lib for example); and, secondly, their affluence has been greatly exaggerated. They had disposable income, as several generations of teenage consumers in Britain had done; but they could not afford to drive cars, to take foreign holidays, or to visit many of London's 'swinging' discotheques. In effect, they could not transmit their Mod culture across Britain themselves. Moreover, it should not be forgotten that the overwhelming majority of Mods lived with their parents. In other words, they could not even afford to live independently in lodgings. In this sense, their lifestyle was essentially no different from those lifestyles of interwar teenage consumers of the Northern cities such as Manchester, who visited cinemas and dance halls as habitually during the 1930s as Mods visited dance halls like The Tottenham Royal in the 1960s.[5]

The Mods are an interesting, though not unique, phenomenon. They were, essentially, teenage consumers who first surfaced in London. Largely through television and magazines, rather than through their own efforts, their culture became a national teenage craze between about 1964 and 1967. How far the Mod culture was a creative phase of youth culture is open to question. What did they create? They bought clothes extravagantly; they generated two pop groups – The Who and The Small Faces – one of which quickly fizzled out, and they are chiefly remembered for causing thousands of pounds worth of damage to shop windows and cafés at coastal resorts in the south of England during 1964 and 1965.[6] The following chapter offers a reassessment of the Mod culture of the 1960s. It will focus, initially, on the Mod movement's origins and development as a cultural movement of the young in 1960s' London. In the second half of the chapter the role of delinquency and its significance, or insignificance, in the history of the Mod culture will be addressed.

The origins and development of the Mod culture

The early years of the Mod movement, c.1960–4, are shrouded in darkness: literal and metaphorical. It has been claimed that the earliest Mods were Jewish youths from London's outer suburbs whose fathers worked in the clothing industry. They allegedly passed on an interest in clothes to their teenage sons.[7] Others claim that the first Mods were young intellectuals who visited jazz clubs in London's West End and had debates about the French philosopher Jean-Paul Sartre and modern jazz.[8] Few sources are cited in the secondary works that touch on the roots of the Mod culture, such as Jonathon Green's *All Dressed Up*. Moreover, it is not clear from any of this discussion whether a distinctive youth cult is being described, or just young people being randomly exposed to an amorphous collection of ideas as they went about their lives. Essentially, the primary sources available on the Mod movement are few and far between and, until television and the popular and quality press focused attention on the Mods, it is not clear how many people were Mods, how the movement spread and if there was a Mod lifestyle before television invented one.[9] Cathy McGowan, the 19-year-old presenter of the pop programme *Ready Steady Go!*, genuinely believed that her pop show, which was first broadcast in August 1963 and lasted until 1966, created the Mod culture.[10] Cohen has made a similar point in relation to the Mods and Rocker clashes at seaside resorts. He argued that the press gave the Mod movement a cohesiveness that did not exist in reality.[11] It is also clear from other contemporary sociological research on the Mods that only a fraction – a distinct minority – of all the youths who appeared in court for 'Mod' disturbances during 1964 and 1965 described themselves as either Mods or Rockers.[12] A sizeable minority did not know how to describe themselves. The question we need to pose, then, is: Was there a Mod culture before television and newspapers labelled young people either Mods or Rockers?

The earliest piece of evidence on the Mods is an article that appeared in a society magazine, *Town*, in September 1962.[13] This widely cited article consists of an interview with three young males from London – aged 15, 20 and 20. It is widely quoted because one of the three was Mark Feld, who a few years later changed his name to Marc Bolan and became a highly successful Glam rock pop star with the pop group T. Rex. The young Mark Feld was described as 'a Face' – a Mod name for a fashion leader in the Mod community. He is photographed wearing a dapper suit and tie, short carefully combed hair, side-parted, and wearing a waistcoat (see Figure 3). Just a few years later he had dropped his Mod image and turned himself into a twenty-year-old pop star with curly, Hippie length hair, glitter eye make-up and platform shoes. What does this article tell us about the Mod movement of early 1960s' London?

Interestingly, one of the three – Peter Sugar – described as 'definitely the leader of the group' had a Polish father who was presumably Jewish. Sugar worked in a hairdresser's, owned by his sister, and he earned £12 a week. Out of this he gave his mother 50 shillings a week (£2.50) and kept the bulk of his income, around 80 per cent of it, for his own use. He spent most of his earnings on clothes and taxis.[14]

We learn very little about the other older boy, Michael Simmonds. He also worked in a hairdresser's (in the New North Road) and we learn that he and Sugar cut each other's hair, and had done for years. Simmonds spent every Friday evening not with other Mods, however, but with his auntie. He would have a meal with her and then 'set' her hair.[15] Neither of the two older boys owned a car and they all lived a long way from central London, in Stoke Newington. A trip to central London was described as 'complicated', as the group had to arrange for a friend to drive them into the city centre and they would then abandon the driver. We do not learn how often they visited central London.[16]

Mark Feld was the youngest of the three, just 15, and the most talkative. He was still at school. Feld, like the other two, was from a working-class background. His father was a lorry driver and his mother worked on a market stall. His main interest was clothes. He claimed that he had 10 suits, 8 sports jackets, 15 pairs of trousers, 30–35 shirts, 20 pullovers, 3 leather jackets, 2 suede jackets, 5 or 6 pairs of shoes and 30 ties.[17] The interviewer, Peter Barnsley, interviewed Feld at his home and spoke to Feld's mother. She told the journalist that her 15-year-old son even ironed his own clothes. 'He irons his shirts himself. I can't do them half as well,' she remarked.[18]

Figure 3 Early Mods, 1962 (Mark Feld, alias Marc Bolan of T. Rex, in the foreground). *Source: Town*, September 1962. Reproduced courtesy of Don McCullin/Topfoto.

What baffled the interviewer was where Feld's disposable income for clothes came from as his parents were not wealthy and he only had a part-time job on a market stall.[19] The source of his income is never revealed.

Feld's interest in clothes was so obsessive that friction was created with his school peers and even with his teachers over it. What the article reveals about him is that his status at school came from his knowledge about clothes and not from conventional matters such as schoolwork or sport. He would belittle classmates whose dress sense seemed dated to him. As he put it:

> You got to be different from the other kids ... I mean you got to be two steps ahead. The stuff that half the haddocks you see around are wearing I was wearing years ago. A kid in my class came up to me in his new suit, an Italian box it was, he says 'Just look at the length of your jacket', he says. 'You're not with it', he says.
>
> 'I was wearing that style two years ago', I said.[20]

Feld certainly conforms to the Mod stereotype of being fixated with, and knowledgeable about, clothes (as his pristine appearance in the foreground of Figure 3 makes very clear). We learn that he wore Levis and rode a scooter when he was 12 (scarcely believable); that he had shopped in Paris; and that he evidently bought suits from British chain stores such as Burton's and C&A.[21] We also learn that he did not buy any of his clothes from Carnaby Street. We learn that he read books. He had been reading a biography of Beau Brummel, whom he admired because, as he put it: 'He was just like us really. You know, came up from nothing. Then he met Royalty and got to know all the big blokes and he had a lot of clothes.'[22]

Feld and his friends come over as charming and thoughtful young males from the suburbs who wanted to be rich, but were not. As Sugar, their leader, put it: 'What I want is to make money and do what I like ... Trouble is I'm lazy.'[23] It is misleading to call these young Mods affluent. What is more apparent from their conversation is that they were resourceful, and they improvised with clothes. They bought cheap goods but tried to look wealthy and sophisticated. For example, they bought pins from Woolworths for 3d which they used as tie pins. They were really cheap pins for women's hats.[24]

These early Mods did visit dance halls, but dance halls that were situated in suburbs such as Croyden and Hackney. Their leisure world was geographically a long way from the main city-centre discotheques of Swinging London.[25] Indeed, the central point about Mod culture in Britain before television programmes such as *Ready Steady Go!* transmitted news about the cult across Britain, is how rooted it was in local communities situated on the outskirts of central London. The enterprising and trend-setting 'Faces', later known as Mods, were in distant suburbs and such localised youth cultures were never going to spread rapidly across a capital city, let alone an entire country.

How did these localised cultures become a national movement? There are several ways the movement could have expanded out from its origins in London suburbs. First of all, it could have done so organically by young Mods from one district visiting other districts to attend dance halls, for example; and through such movement and activity their outfits would have been noticed further afield than where they lived. This sounds a plausible idea; especially since, from the beginning, Mods were quite mobile. A proportion of them, though by no means a majority in the early days, owned scooters. Secondly, the movement could have been transformed into a London-wide and national look through commerce and on this theme John Stephen in Carnaby Street needs to be considered. Thirdly, the Mods emerged in Britain as a British pop music industry was gradually coming into existence, following the global success of the Beatles in 1963 and 1964. Pop magazines such as *Ready Steady Go* and pop programmes such as *Ready Steady Go!* could have projected the Mod movement to a national audience. A fourth influence was the press, which will be discussed later in this chapter.

The Mod lifestyle: a product of affluence?

There is no doubt that the Mod culture of the early 1960s was lived in a subterranean world of coffee bars and basement rhythm and blues clubs such as The Marquee Club in Wardour Street.[26] This was before it was transformed by television into an amorphous youth movement in which anyone who was in their teens was referred to as either a Mod or a Rocker. John Stephen's role in the development of the Mod lifestyle deserves some credit for the development of the cult beyond London's outer suburbs. Stephen was a grocer's son from Glasgow who moved to London in the mid-1950s. He began as a clerk in a shop in Covent Garden, where he hired out military uniforms for fancy dress events and theatre work. He moved from there in the late 1950s to a men's outfitters in Newburgh Street, Soho, which was very close to Carnaby Street. At this stage, he had no knowledge of Mods or, more accurately, Modernists, as they were then known, and his clientele were mainly gay men. The shop he worked in, Vince Man's Shop, sold colourful clothes which were marketed as an alternative to wool and tweed suits and gabardine macs for men. George Melly, the bohemian jazz singer from Liverpool, was a frequent visitor. He recalled of Vince Man's Shop: 'It was the only shop where they measure your inside leg each time you buy a tie.' Sean Connery was a model for the shop.[27]

Stephen was not even aware of the teenage market for clothes at this stage. He supplemented his income from Vince's by working part-time in other men's shops in Notting Hill and Bond Street; and at night he worked as a waiter in a coffee bar in Soho. He saved £300 and then opened his first shop in Beak Street, at the southern end of Carnaby Street. His first shop was in fact just a room, on the second floor of a building. His plan was to design clothes for the men's shops he had worked for. Then, an accident occurred; which meant that he discovered the teenage market for clothes not by targeting it but by stumbling on it. One lunch-time as he was out of his shop an electric heater caught fire and the fire destroyed his workroom. Stephen's landlord kindly offered him another workroom on Carnaby Street. It had the advantage of being a ground floor room with a window; in other words, it was a shop. Stephen by this time knew Carnaby Street and when his landlord told him he would have a window where people walking by would see his clothes designs, Stephen remarked: 'Who walks by?'[28] His early customers included Cliff Richard, who wore a John Stephen pullover in one of his films, and Adam Faith. He then began to buy up other shops in the street, all of which were tiny business premises, and went into competition with himself. His window displays became well known for changing not just monthly, but even during the course of a single day. This was his sales gimmick.[29]

We can clearly see, therefore, that at the time Mark Feld and his Mod friends were being interviewed for *Town* magazine, in 1962, Stephen was still known principally as a clothes designer for celebrities – pop stars and boxers among them – and he was still seen as a designer who appealed to homosexual men. The two worlds of the Mods and John Stephen did not interact at all at this stage. Even the names of his shops suggest he was more interested in appealing to men than to young Mods by 1962. One of his shops was called 'His Clothes' and another 'Male West One'. Further down the street, imitators aiming at a similar market had emerged. Their shops carried names such as 'Adonis', 'Domino Male' and 'Gear'. It is in fact the case that there was a complete absence of shops in Carnaby Street with the name 'Mod' in the title by 1962.[30]

John Stephen was thus not the prime mover in Mod culture as he only belatedly discovered the movement and he certainly did not target his clothes exclusively at Mods even by 1964. In 1964 he owned 18 shops on Carnaby Street and only one of these had the name Mod in its title – 'Mod Male'. Others had more generic names such as 'His Clothes'. His relationship with the Mods is, in fact, quite complicated. At first, he became associated with the Mods because he sold cheap clothes that teenage clerical workers and other working-class adolescents could afford. He charged £7 to £10 for a jacket in 1964, when a male hairdresser earned about £20 a week, and £3 to £5 for a shirt. These working-class lads could not afford to shop on the King's Road and were well aware that John Stephen was at the bottom of the range of retailers in London by 1964; that is, by the period that we normally associate with Swinging London. As one Mod put it: 'While Carnaby Street's customers think nothing of spending a week's wages on a complete outfit, the class that shops on King's Road will spend that sort of money on a shirt.'[31] In other words, the Mods were aware that Stephen was serving a working-class market and was unique in Swinging London for doing so. His shops were gimmicky and appealed to the imaginations of many Mods. He decorated his shops with glossy pictures of showbusiness stars, thinking that teenagers liked to copy their idols. He made shopping for clothes an enjoyable experience and filled his shops with deafening pop music. He even attracted young Mod pop stars as customers, such as Steve Marriott of The Small Faces. Marriott recalled: 'I just loved the clothes. I used to save up all my dough and go down Carnaby Street.'[32] There is no doubt that John Stephen became synonymous with Mod fashions between 1964 and 1966. By 1966, in fact, at the age of 29, he was a millionaire and owned 24 shops in Carnaby Street.[33] He was praised in Mod magazines as the principal Mod designer. *The Mod* declared in January 1965: 'If you really want to be switched on, go to John Stephens.'[34]

But it could be argued that John Stephen was an opportunist rather than a prime mover in the Mod culture. It is hardly surprising that a man who owned 24 shops in a single street used some of his expertise to target Mods. But his primary interest, arguably, was in serving celebrities and when they deserted him he had little interest in who his customers were. When asked in 1966 who his main customers were he replied: 'They're nobody in particular. They're Mister Average.'[35] His Mod customers became disillusioned with him when he increased his prices. Even by 1965 he was receiving bad publicity in the national Mod press. *The Mod* asked: 'Why is it that a certain man who runs a shop in Carnaby Street refers to Mods as suckers?'[36] This is a highly significant piece of evidence. It suggests that Mods had become aware, by 1965, that they were being exploited by fashion designers such as John Stephen. In short, it was becoming too expensive to be a fashion-conscious Mod by 1965. Thus, from its humble origins in London suburbs around 1962 among resourceful but not particularly affluent young wage-earning lads, Mod had become a fashion label by 1965, and big business. But we have still not really discovered what was behind this transformation.

The television programme *Ready Steady Go!* is probably the key to understanding how the Mods became a national movement. It was first broadcast in August 1963 and it lasted for three years, until December 1966. One of its presenters, Cathy McGowan, claimed in an interview she gave in 1965 that her programme started the Mod movement. 'We started the Mod craze,' she pointed out. 'It all started with the idea of our show being for Young Moderns, so we just called them Mods.'[37] What actually happened is that her programme hijacked the term 'Mods' (she gained the nickname 'Queen of the Mods') and used it to describe all young people who shared an interest in pop music. But what had inspired the idea of a Mod television programme in the first place?

The programme was dreamed up by a man in his forties called Elkan Allen, who was an independent television producer. He hired three young people – Vicki Wickham, a former publisher and radio producer (who became the programme's Editor); Michael Lindsay-Hogg, who had been working in Ireland on Irish television and became the Director; and Cathy McGowan, a 19-year-old secretary from Streatham, in London, who was earning just £10 a week at the time.[38] McGowan was the main presenter and would use teen words such as 'fab' and 'smashing' with no sense of irony; in other words, she seemed to cultivate a rather witless persona. She would interview pop stars as well as introduce them. She once asked one of the Beatles, Ringo Starr, if he was 'a Mod or a Rocker'. With Liverpool wit, he replied: 'I'm a Mocker.'[39] Cathy McGowan was left speechless by this answer. So, we must be careful about accepting her dubious claim that she started the Mod culture.

It is true that the programme's presenters certainly went looking for Mods to appear as dancers in the programme. Moreover, they used a Mod group's song as one of their signature tunes – The Who's 'Anyway, Anyhow, Anywhere'; though not for the whole series. Other tunes used included Manfred Mann's '5-4-3-2-1' and Andrew Loog Oldham's instrumental tune 'Three Hundred and Sixty Five Rolling Stones'. In fact, the pop groups and singers who appeared on the programme were not necessarily ones that would have appealed to a Mod audience. For example, the Beatles appeared and the Mods loathed this group, believing they were a girls' band and their songs were too melodic.[40] It is thus more accurate to say that *Ready Steady Go!* made pop music as a whole, rather than the Mod culture, a national movement. George Melly put it well, remarking that the show 'made pop music work on a truly national scale ... sending a tremor of pubescent excitement from Land's End to John O'Groats'.[41] But, self-evidently, *Ready Steady Go!* did not reflect the Mod movement as it existed in 1963 and as it developed after 1963. The Mod culture was a largely male youth cult; and yet the studio audience of *Ready Steady Go!* were a mixed audience.[42] Also, when the Mods were seen dancing in youth clubs it was observed that they always danced alone. In the *Ready Steady Go!* studio everyone danced together.[43] A further point is that the Mods liked black music such as Tamla Motown and American Soul Music and neither of these were prominent in the *Ready Steady Go!* programme. So, Cathy McGowan's claim that *Ready Steady Go!* invented the Mod culture and was always the authentic voice of Mod culture in mid-1960s' Britain is not convincing. The programme was really a vehicle for teenage fashions and teen pop groups rather than specifically for the Mods. Undoubtedly, Cathy McGowan used the term 'Mods' to describe teenagers as a whole and thus, unwittingly, she may have turned a London term into a nationally recognised teen stereotype. But the real Mods, in practice, had a more complicated relationship to pop culture than this programme gives credit for. Also, by 1964, the Mod culture became associated with new venues such as seaside resorts and it is now necessary to explore the impulses that were behind Mod visits to the coast.

The Mods, coastal resorts and delinquency

By 1964 the geographical focus of the Mod culture in Britain had shifted from the London suburbs to coastal resorts, primarily in the south-east of England. No historian has really explored why this shift occurred. Levy suggests that the Mods of 1964 were a new generation of Mods who were more affluent and more mobile than the earliest London Mods: the ones we might call the Feld generation (the Mods of 1962, in other words). The earliest Mods, as we have discovered, were not very affluent; they used taxis or lifts from friends as their public transport and, most importantly, their culture was rooted in communities and venues that they knew. Their culture was also held together by close friendships.

The Mod culture of the seaside resorts, around 1964, was different. It was hardly a culture at all. It would be more appropriate to describe the Mod visits to seaside resorts as transitory experiences. Those who took part were, invariably, not close friends but met at the resorts. They were in unfamiliar environments, some distance from their own communities, and they were there for at most three or four days – from Friday to Monday – over Bank Holiday weekends. What fuelled the Mod invasion of seaside resorts in 1964 is not at all clear. The sociologist Bryan Wilson has suggested it was the lack of facilities such as youth clubs in the new postwar London suburbs.[44] Another factor was the end of National Service in 1962. The Mods of 1964 were the first generation of postwar youths who did not have to undertake two years of National Service, either in Britain or abroad, and in fact the state had no role in the lives of these Mods of 1964 after they left school at the age of 15.[45] It has even been suggested that the Mods of 1964 were a generation of rootless, semi-literate rejects of the state school system who rioted simply out of boredom. As Bryan Wilson put it in an article in *The Daily Telegraph* in August 1964:

> Mods and Rockers are the latest, British manifestation of the distinctive, semi-delinquent and sometimes riotous, youth culture that has been growing in the industrial societies of the world in the last decade ... their behaviour has no evident economic motivation: the participants are largely high wage-earners. But they are less articulate than the Luddites.[46]

The central questions we need to pose about the Mod culture of 1964–6 are: how affluent were these Mods?; how delinquent were they?; how far did the authorities overreact to the Mod invasions of seaside resorts?; and what role did the media play in creating the Mod culture? All of these questions can be explored through an examination of the Mod/Rocker clashes of 1964 and Government reactions to the Mods. The standard work on this subject is Stanley Cohen's book *Folk Devils and Moral Panics: The Creation of The Mods and Rockers* (1972; third edition, Routledge, 2002).

For a classic work, this study says virtually nothing about Government reactions to the Mods; but, fortunately, research has been undertaken on this question.[47]

It is useful to sketch, briefly, what is known about the Mods and Rockers of *c.*1964. The evidence historians have to draw on to determine the age-groups, family backgrounds, career profiles and economic circumstances of the Mods and Rockers who visited seaside resorts in 1964 is patchy. The newspapers that covered the Mod/Rocker clashes sometimes cited biographical information on individuals revealed in court cases; but, as we will discover, the numbers who were arrested and appeared in court comprised less than 1 per cent of all the Mods who visited coastal towns in 1964. For example, it is known that there were 1000 Mods and Rockers at Brighton over the May Bank Holiday of 1964; but only 75 were charged – less than 1 per cent.[48] At Hastings, *The Times* estimated that there were between 3000 and 5000 youths at the resort during the August Bank Holiday of 1964; but only a fraction of these were Mods and Rockers; 300, in fact, representing just 10 per cent or less of the total. Only 70 youths appeared in court at Hastings; again, less than 1 per cent of those present.[49]

Much of the scholarly discussion of the Mods and Rockers' backgrounds, from Cohen's pioneering study of press reactions to the most recent historical article, by Richard Grayson, is grounded in a single sociological survey undertaken at the time – Paul Barker and Alan Little's article in *New Society* entitled 'The Margate Offenders: a Survey'; later reprinted in a volume of influential articles from the journal *New Society*.[50] Barker and Little obtained their information through distributing a questionnaire to 44 Mods and Rockers who appeared in court at Margate on Whit Monday 1964. But they only received 34 completed questionnaires, and their observations on the social backgrounds of Mods and Rockers are based solely on those who appeared in court and were found guilty of offences.[51] The offences ranged from threatening behaviour to possessing an offensive weapon and causing bodily harm. Their sentences ranged from fines to jail sentences of three months, for 2 of the sample of 34.[52] It is obviously a dubious exercise to draw general conclusions about the typical Mod from a survey that focused exclusively on a small sample of individuals found guilty of delinquency. Moreover, as Barker and Little were well aware, their survey would not provide a broad profile of the Mod culture in 1964. As they put it: 'Ours was a survey in depth as we believe there is value in getting to know one group well. Some generalisation is possible from the results, *though it would be wrong to apply them too widely* [my italics].'[53] What did this survey uncover?

Certain facts that emerged from Barker and Little's survey were already widely known. For example, the majority of Mods and Rockers were in their teens and were single.[54] None of those charged at Margate in 1964 were fathers. The average age of those charged at Margate was 18.[55] Only 2 out of the Barker/Little sample of 34 were over 21.[56] Secondly, a majority were from London and neighbouring counties, confirming that the Mod culture even by 1964 was still essentially a southern phenomenon. Thirdly, nearly all the 34 Mods and Rockers in Barker and Little's sample were outsiders. They had travelled to Margate, a small seaside resort on the south coast, from as far away as North London and in two cases the Midlands. Thus Barker and Little's survey confirms that the Mod culture was the first truly mobile youth cult in Britain. We can see this from the geographical spread of the Barker/Little sample. Margate was over 50 miles from London but many of their sample were from London. The details are: North London (4), South London (5); East Kent (6); Medway (4); south-east suburbs (1); western suburbs (7); Midlands (2).[57]

One interesting question, only touched upon in Barker and Little's survey, is how the Mods at Margate learned about the resort. The resort was not chosen randomly. It was a planned invasion that had been discussed several months ahead. The idea had surfaced in London that there was going to be a Mod camp above Margate over the August Bank Holiday and for many London Mods it was to be the event of their year. Barker and Little spoke to one North London Mod who had heard about the camp weeks before. This Mod had learned from friends that 100 fellow Mods, none of whom he knew, were going to be in Margate over August Bank Holiday Weekend, 1964.[58]

It appears, therefore, that the Margate weekend was planned largely by word of mouth and not through young people watching the television coverage of the Clacton disturbances in March 1964 and deciding to single out another resort for the Whit weekend in May. Indeed, only 4 of the 44 charged at Margate in May 1964 had been at Clacton in March.[59] Barker and Little discovered that, in fact, Mods and Rockers hardly ever watched television. They listened to the radio; but the main reason they watched so little television was that they spent six evenings a week socialising, usually in all-male groups.[60] Neither did Mods read newspapers to learn about a Mod event.[61] It seems that there was an air of secrecy to these Mod events at coastal resorts – about which far too little is still known. In other words, the Clacton, Margate and other Mod disturbances were not part of an organised 'invasion' of coastal towns in 1964. They were in fact quite separate incidents, each one involving a fresh group of young people rather than well-known instigators of Mod riots.[62]

How affluent were the Margate Mods? It will already be evident from the discussion so far that the Mods and Rockers were geographically mobile. Many travelled to the coast over long distances; and over a single weekend went from one coastal resort to another. For example, there were cases of youths charged at Margate in May 1964 who had been at Brighton the same weekend, where there were also clashes with police.[63] But the modes of transport Mods and Rockers used to get to Margate in 1964 reveal that the majority were not affluent youths. Out of 34 in Barker and Little's sample, only 7 had a scooter or motorbike. Thirteen had used public transport to reach Margate; 12 had gone in cars. One hitched a ride.[64] We might wonder, at this point, whether the Mods were more affluent than the Rockers. It appears that there were no major differences in their incomes. The Barker/Little sample included both Mods and Rockers (14 Mods and 9 Rockers, and 12 who said they were neither). The average take-home pay of those in the sample was £11 a week. For Rockers it was slightly less – £10 a week.[65] What seems most striking from the Barker/Little survey is how similar were the backgrounds and economic circumstances of the two groups. Barker and Little tried to argue that the Rockers were more lower-class than the Mods and more likely than the Mods to be in unskilled manual jobs.[66] But what seems most evident is that both groups were poorly educated. Nearly all of the Barker/Little sample had left school at the earliest opportunity – aged 15 – and only 3 (all Mods) were receiving any kind of further training. Out of a total sample of 34 young people, only one was serving an apprenticeship.[67] Thus we can say, therefore, that the Mod culture by 1964 was very definitely a culture of consolation for youths who were receiving no further education and no work-centred training such as apprenticeships provided. These youths were possibly brought together by their lack of interest in their jobs and by the sense that they were rejects educationally – and this applied to Mods as well as Rockers.[68]

How far was the Mod culture a delinquent culture by 1964? The main Mod/Rocker clashes at coastal resorts during 1964 are summarised in Table 7.1.

Table 7.1   Mod/Rocker clashes, 1964

Date	Place	No. involved	No. arrested	No. convicted
29–30 March	Clacton	Not available	100	56
16–18 May	Brighton	1000	75	48
16–18 May	Margate	400	65	47
16–18 May	Bournemouth	Not available	Not available	54
2–3 August	Hastings	3000–5000	70	57
2–3 August	Great Yarmouth	300	31	16

Source: R. Grayson, 'Mods, Rockers and Juvenile Delinquency in 1964: the Government Response', *Contemporary British History*, Vol. 12, No. 1 (Spring 1998), p. 26.

As revealed in Table 7.1, all of the clashes took place on three Bank Holiday weekends: Easter Weekend, Whitsun Bank Holiday and the August Bank Holiday Weekend. Moreover, Mod/Rocker clashes occurred simultaneously in three different resorts over the May Bank Holiday – in Brighton, Margate and Bournemouth; and at two resorts simultaneously in August – Hastings and Great Yarmouth. The figures cited on the number of Mods and Rockers at these resorts are taken from estimates given in *The Times*. It is clear from the Table that the Mods and Rockers charged for delinquency were a tiny proportion of the total numbers of Mods and Rockers present in the resorts (less than 2 per cent), except at Margate where around 10 per cent of those present were charged and found guilty of an offence.

In Table 7.2, details are given of the estimated cost of vandalism in four of the resorts. These estimates were produced by the local authorities concerned. Most of this damage was damage to buildings, mainly shops, rather than to deckchairs. Relatively few deckchairs were broken – only 50 at Margate – and this was about the norm for a Bank Holiday weekend. But considerable vandalism was inflicted on these resorts and, of course, the figures underestimate the cost of vandalism, as much vandalism goes undetected.

What was behind these figures? Both Table 7.1 and Table 7.2 reveal that the largest number of arrests, and the worst damage, were recorded in Clacton. What drew the Mods to Clacton and what explains the high level of vandalism? Clacton poses intriguing questions for the historian of Mods to answer. First of all, it was nothing like as popular or indeed as affluent a resort as Brighton and, moreover, it was not in the south of England but on the east coast in Essex. Historically, it had been off the tourist map for all except the toughest youths from the East End of London and youths from North London suburbs. It had few facilities for young people. Easter

Table 7.2 Cost of damage at four resorts, Easter and Whitsun, 1964

Date	Place	No. of arrests	Estimated cost (£)
Easter, 1964	Clacton	97	513
Whitsun, 1964	Brighton	76	400
Whitsun, 1964	Margate	64	250
Whitsun, 1964	Bournemouth	56	100

Source: S. Cohen, *Folk Devils and Moral Panics: The Creation of the Mods and Rockers* (third edition, 2002), p. 25.

Weekend 1964 was also the coldest Bank Holiday weekend for eighty years and it was wet.[69]

What drew the Mods to such an unlovely resort is not clear. Possibly those who visited could not afford to travel further afield at Easter 1964 and were saving up their money for a visit to Brighton later in the year. What happened in Clacton? Grayson claims that police and holidaymakers were attacked by both scooter boys and youths on motorcycles. On the pavements groups of youths started scuffling with each other and throwing stones at each other. Those on motorbikes and scooters roared up and down the seafront. Windows were broken, beach huts were wrecked and one youth fired a starting pistol into the air. These were not just wildly exaggerated scenes. Altogether 100 youths appeared in court at Clacton and 56 of these were charged. The offences ranged from theft and malicious damage, to youths convicted and imprisoned for assault. In some cases, Mods had physically attacked local shopkeepers who refused to serve them in cafés.[70]

There is little evidence from eyewitnesses at this first Mod clash. The sociologist Stanley Cohen was at several later clashes, and walked up and down the seafronts interviewing people and telling them he was researching for his Ph.D. on the Mods at the University of London. But even Cohen was not at the Clacton event. One of the few eyewitnesses at Clacton was a local hotel owner, George Harnett. He blamed both the Mods and the Rockers equally, describing them as 'rude, obscene and totally irresponsible'. His comments were quoted in *The Times*.[71]

The next event, at Brighton at Whitsuntide 1964, was a very different clash. It was not between Mods and Rockers but between Mods and Beatniks. Moreover, the Beatniks actually won, according to *New Society*'s reporter Paul Barker. He mingled with the Mods along the beaches as they threw stones at both the police and the Beatniks and he recorded that the Beatniks had 'cultured voices' and were 'middle class' bohemians. The incidents reported do seem tame. Small groups of seven or eight youths would chase after each other throwing stones and then the fracas would end. All the participants were young – between 15 and 20. There were schoolchildren among the youths and there were young couples among them seen 'necking'. The scenes depicted in *New Society* suggest that the clashes were largely just stone-throwing; malevolent larking about rather than serious premeditated gang warfare.[72]

In his classic book on the Mods and Rockers, *Folk Devils and Moral Panics: The Creation of the Mods and Rockers* (1972), Stanley Cohen argues that the authorities overreacted to the Mod/Rocker clashes. He cites, for example, the harsh words the magistrate in Margate used when passing sentence on 44 youths. In the following extract from the speech, he was addressing a 22-year-old, from London, who had pleaded guilty to using threatening behaviour:

> It is not likely that the air of this town has ever been polluted by the hordes of hooligans, male and female, such as we have seen this weekend and of whom you are an example. These long-haired, mentally unstable, petty little hoodlums, these sawdust Caesars who can only find courage like rats, in hunting in packs, came to Margate with the avowed intent of interfering with the life and property of its inhabitants. Insofar as the law gives us power, this court will not fail to use the prescribed penalties. It will, perhaps, discourage you and others of your kidney who are infected with this vicious virus, that you will go to prison for three months.[73]

The magistrate in this case was Dr George Simpson and the scene is the Mod/Rocker clashes at Margate at Whitsun 1964. The magistrate had lived in Margate and practised there as a family doctor for 24 years. The night after he passed sentence on these 44 youths he walked along the seafront with his wife. The beaches were now deserted (it was Tuesday) and he strolled quietly along the beach, 'surveying the Whitsun battleground' as one newspaper put it.[74]

If we look, finally, at Government reactions to the Mods and Rockers in 1964 it appears that Cohen's thesis of an alarmist Establishment overreaction to the Mods is overstated. First of all, the Conservative government were not alarmed by the Mod clashes at all. They were highly sceptical of sensational newspaper reports on the clashes which carried such ludicrous headlines as 'The Battle of Hastings'. Cohen argues that there was an Establishment reaction to the Mods and that this 'societal' reaction was out of all proportion to the scale of delinquency involved.[75] But what is more striking is that the Conservative government, and indeed the Labour government after October 1964, were reluctant to introduce new legislation to deal specifically with the Mods.[76] The subject of the Mods and Rockers surfaced in Parliament only intermittently: sometimes through questions in the House of Commons; at other times through questions in the House of Lords. The occasions on which the Mods were discussed in Parliament are listed in Table 7.3.

The main point to stress is that, except for pursuing a new bill on drug misuse (which Henry Brooke the Home Secretary had been planning as early as February 1964, long before the first Mod/Rocker clash),[77] the Government's handling of the Mods was fairly low-key at first. It did nothing at all for at least a month after the Clacton incidents in March 1964 and, as can be seen, the issue of Mod delinquency was being brought before the Government periodically by members of the Opposition (Frank Taylor, for example) or by members of the House of Lords.

Table 7.3   Discussions of Mods and Rockers in Parliament, 1964

31 March	Drugs (Prevention of Misuse) Bill published.
8 April	House of Lords: Earl of Arran calls for the driving licence age for certain vehicles to be raised from 16 to 19 'in view of the invasion of Clacton by young motor cyclists on Easter Sunday and the consistently heavy casualty rates among the youngest age groups'.
15 April	House of Commons: Frank Taylor (Labour) tables resolution stating: 'in the light of recent regrettable events at Clacton ... for Home Department to give urgent and serious consideration to the need for young hooligans to be given such financial and physical punishment as will provide an effective deterrent'.
27 April	House of Commons: Two-hour Debate on 'Juvenile Delinquency and Hooliganism'. Mr Gurdon's Motion.
4 June	House of Commons: Statement by Home Secretary on Seaside Resorts (Hooliganism).
4 June	House of Lords: Statement by Home Secretary (read) on Hooliganism and Increased Penalties.
23 June	House of Commons: Malicious Damages Bill (Second Reading).
2 July	House of Commons: Malicious Damages Bill (Third Reading).

Source: S. Cohen, *Folk Devils and Moral Panics: The Creation of the Mods and Rockers* (1972; reprinted Oxford, 1980), p. 111.

Government inaction over Youth Culture was nothing new. No British government legislation had been introduced to deal with Teddy Boys during the 1950s. What the Conservative government did in 1964 was simply raise the level of fines for Mods and Rockers from £20 to £100, under the Malicious Damages Bill of June 1964. But these changes, it could be argued, were merely taking account of inflation between the date of the original Malicious Damages Act in 1914 and the value of money in 1964.[78] So it can be clearly seen that Cohen's thesis of a moral panic being generated by the Mod/Rocker clashes during 1964 is not borne out when we consider Government reactions to the Mods.

8

From Danny the Red to British Student Power: Labour Governments and the International Student Revolts of the 1960s*

During the 1960s the Labour Party were led by one of the most academically brilliant students of his generation – Harold Wilson. 'J. H. Wilson', as he was then known, graduated from Oxford University in 1937 with a First Class Degree in Politics, Philosophy and Economics (PPE) and gained First Class marks on all of his Finals' examination papers. Wilson was not a student radical, in his years as an undergraduate at Jesus College, Oxford (he was regarded by his contemporaries as a swot); but he did read the work of 'radical' economists such as J. M. Keynes, and his Economics tutor was astounded to discover that, just before sitting his Finals, he read the whole of Keynes' revolutionary new work *The General Theory of Employment, Interest and Money* (1936) and absorbed it.[1] During his two Labour governments of 1964–70 Harold Wilson was responsible for a period of enormous university expansion. Eight new universities were created during these years – Sussex, Kent, Warwick, Lancaster, East Anglia, Essex, York and Stirling – and 29 Polytechnics. In fact, the student population increased at a faster rate under Wilson than under any previous Prime Minister.[2] Moreover, these students were eligible for state maintenance grants as of right and these grants enabled students from working-class backgrounds to go to university. They also made it possible for more affluent middle-class students to drive cars; some driving all the way to Paris in May 1968 to offer support to the Paris students in their disputes with their universities.[3] Wilson himself regarded his greatest achievement of these years as the Open University, which he pushed through Cabinet and Parliament himself during 1965 and 1966.[4] But it was in his second period in office, from 1966 to 1970, that Wilson's Labour government was drawn into the international student revolts that had spread from the University of California, Berkeley, in the United States in 1964 to Paris, London and Northern Ireland by 1968 and 1969.[5] This chapter will be concerned with the Wilson government's handling of the international student revolts of the 1960s in two senses: first, its understanding of international student conflicts in the wider world and, second, its handling of the student demonstrations in Britain during the late 1960s, in which international students were perceived as the prime movers.[6]

Very little is known about the Labour government's views on the students of the 1960s and no monograph has yet appeared on this intriguing subject. Historians do not have much material to work from in published form. Harold Wilson, for example, does not refer to the student revolts at all in his detailed study of these years *The Labour Government, 1964–1970: A Personal Record* (1971). Two of his distinguished biographers, Ben Pimlott and Philip Zeigler, do not shed any light on this subject either. Austen Morgan's biography of Wilson has an amusing reference to Tony Benn's positive attitude towards students. Benn, who was MP for Bristol South-East in the Sixties and a junior Cabinet Minister, wanted to get to know the students at Bristol University and visited the University in June 1968. He attended lectures on revolution, black power and Vietnam, and recorded in his Diary that he found his visit an enjoyable experience. He wrote: 'I realised all of a sudden that for three and a half or four years I have done absolutely no basic thinking about politics. I have just been a departmental Minister. . . . I thought they asked a lot of important questions and I enjoyed it.'[7] About a year later, Tony Benn took part in a student 'sit-in' at a student flat in Bristol and passed on his impressions of the students he encountered to the inner cabinet at Chequers. What was said at this inner cabinet meeting is unclear; but it is clear from all the secondary sources available that Harold Wilson recorded few of his own thoughts about youth, or university students, of the late 1960s. Furthermore, Steven Fielding's recent study *Labour and Cultural Change*, volume 1 of a three-volume series on The Labour governments of 1964–1970 (2003), tends to confirm Wilson's own reticence over youth; though he is reported to have lost his temper with one long-haired 18-year-old in Bristol who heckled him, telling him: 'You're too young to know anything.'[8]

We know more about the student protesters' views of Harold Wilson. One of Wilson's biographers, for example, describes him as 'an icon of failure' among the radical students of 1968.[9] We know that, during the Grosvenor Square demonstration outside the American Embassy in March 1968, the student leader Tariq Ali scribbled a note to the Prime Minister and put it through the letterbox of Number 10 Downing Street. 'Dear Harold,' he wrote cheekily, '100,000 people came to tell you to stop supporting the Americans (in Vietnam). . . . What about it? Yours TA . . .'[10] Kenneth Morgan even makes the bold claim that the student protesters of the late Sixties forced reforms on the Labour government; most notably, the reduction of the age of consent from 21 to 18 passed in 1969 (although a government report, the Latey Report, had recommended this back in 1967).[11]

The following discussion of Labour and the International Student Revolts of the late 1960s draws on a rich vein of primary material on British student protests, and official reactions to them, held in the National Archives, London. The research programme also involves detailed archival work in other British, Irish and North American archives and research on contemporary publications, ranging from the prolix discussions in Hansard (severely truncated here) to the widespread coverage the student protests received in the national press (discussed below) and to the many often incisive articles on student power that frequently appeared in contemporary journals such as *The Spectator*, *New Statesman*, *The Listener* and others. The chapter is in two parts. In the first section, the focus is on just two months during 1968, May and June. During this two-month period the international student movement quite literally came to London. In this section, I want to explore a widely publicised event during May and June of 1968 – the visit to Britain of the charismatic and highly articulate leader of the May '68 student revolt in Paris, Daniel Cohn-Bendit (renamed by the British press of the period 'Danny the Red').[12]

This significant event of the 'British 1960s' led to an even more significant event – a major BBC TV documentary examining the International Student Revolts shown on prime-time television and eliciting much discussion in the press, in British universities and within the British political establishment.[13] Indeed, as will be discovered, the Government and the Security Services (principally the Home Office's Special Branch) were far more directly involved in this visit than any historian has so far suggested.[14] The whole visit was carefully monitored by the Home Office, and the Home Secretary at the time, James Callaghan, met Cohn-Bendit for discussions.[15] Special Branch was also closely involved, trying to monitor the threat of student revolution throughout British universities.[16] What this case-study makes possible is an exploration of the Labour government's thoughts on the student protests of the late '60s, a neglected subject, and it will enable us to reach judgements on surprisingly neglected questions such as how far the Labour Party were seeking to understand student demands (as suggested by Tony Benn's own experiences with students)? Was the Labour Party well informed about student protest movements in the wider world and indeed in Britain? Did Labour regard the whole question of student radicalism as an international or European phenomenon, somehow spreading to Britain in the late '60s? Moreover, did the Labour Party conduct its own research on how student radicalism spread from one country to another?

In the second section, the focus shifts to a more systematic analysis of the Labour Party's thinking on Youth and Student affairs in the period from *c*.1967 to 1970. It asks: how far did the Labour government of these years, and also the Government's Senior Civil Servants, see the global student protests of the late 1960s as a threat to the stability of British universities, and indeed to the stability of British society in the so-called 'Swinging Sixties'?

The International Student Revolt, May and June 1968

Student internationalism and its impact on Britain during the 1960s – both its impact in the universities and on the British Political Establishment – has not really been taken seriously by British historians. The official historian of the LSE, Ralf Dahrendorf, has described 1968 as 'a quiet year' at LSE.[17] Moreover, Colin Crouch, a third year Sociology student at LSE in May 1968, agrees. When 30,000 French students at Paris's ancient university the Sorbonne and students at the University of Nanterre in the Paris suburbs occupied these two universities for over a month; also occupied a city-centre cinema for over a month; and were involved in dramatic confrontations with the Paris police leading to five students being killed and to hundreds more being hospitalised, British universities were in a state of slumber in comparison. The clinching evidence, for Crouch, is the lack of interest British students showed in the May '68 events in Paris. When a student demonstration in support of the Paris students was held at LSE during May 1968 it was an abysmal failure. Less than a hundred students turned up in a University which had over 3000 students.[18]

These two retrospective accounts of events at LSE – one from a former Director of LSE (Dahrendorf) and the other from one of its former students (Crouch) – have led political historians examining the wider British picture in the late '60s, most notably Kenneth Morgan, to devote very little attention to the question of whether the British student protests were linked to student protests in other countries. The picture we are given in accounts such as Morgan's recent biography of James Callaghan (*Callaghan: A Life*, published in 1997) and in his earlier survey of postwar Britain, *The People's Peace*, suggests that the British authorities in 1968, from the Home Secretary down, were never seriously bothered about student protest and accordingly left the university authorities to deal with the student discontent, at LSE and elsewhere.[19]

It is clear from the archives, however, that during May and June of 1968 the subject of the international student revolt, and its possible effects on British students, was given far more serious attention in Britain than has hitherto been argued by British historians – both at Westminster and in the national press. A valuable Ph.D. thesis could be written on the sub-terranean, and intriguing, world of international student networks during 1968. Morgan, perhaps understandably in a work of synthesis, did not probe these networks in *The People's Peace* and neither did he refer to the rich material on British student protest in Government records. His account of the student 'revolts' is a 'top-down' approach to the subject which does underplay the dynamics of student revolt, especially within the British student movements of the period. An interesting question for historians to answer is how far the worlds of New Left students on the campuses of the United States, on which Doug Rossinow has written a fascinating survey entitled *The Politics of Authenticity* (1998), intersected with the worlds of radical students in Britain and Europe.[20] There is a danger of being overwhelmed by the richness of the primary sources on a single country and losing any sense of whether the students of that country travelled to other countries to preach student revolution. Rossinow, for example, has studied a single state, Texas, and has produced a monograph of almost 500 pages. Moreover, there is not a single reference in this massive study of the American New Left to the most celebrated student revolutionary beyond the United States in 1968, Daniel Cohn-Bendit.[21]

A way into the subject of student internationalism during 1968 is an exploration of reactions within Britain – from politicians, the press and from British university students – to Daniel Cohn-Bendit's visit to London in June of 1968. It is an intriguing story that has only been referred to in passing by other historians. Dahrendorf, for example, simply notes that Cohn-Bendit made 'several visits' to the LSE and leaves it at that.[22] It is quite clear from press reactions to Cohn-Bendit's visit, however, that he made a great impact in Britain, positive and negative, in the few days he was here from 11 June to 15 June 1968. Let us now explore why this event is worthy of historical study.

In mid-June 1968 when thousands of Paris students had taken over the city's ancient university, the Sorbonne, and also occupied a city-centre cinema for over a month, the BBC made a 50-minute documentary on the international student revolts. It was an ambitious and costly media event. Students were flown into London from as far afield as Japan and from Eastern Europe (Yugoslavia, for example) and, in the Western Hemisphere, from the United States and Western Europe. The BBC obviously felt this was a significant news story. They paid all the expenses – airfares, domestic travel and accommodation expenses – of the students brought to Britain to be interviewed for the programme and the programme was shown in a prime-time slot, at 9.05 p.m. on a weekday evening.[23]

Daniel Cohn-Bendit was the undisputed leader of the French student movement in Paris. He had led the original Paris student protest at Nanterre (the Sorbonne's suburban campus) over 'university conditions' (more specifically why male students were not allowed to stay in female students' rooms) and he was also involved in the student occupation of the Sorbonne and of the Odeon Cinema in Paris; a building Paris students occupied for five weeks during May and June 1968.[24] He was described, even in the liberal English press, as an anarchist. *The Observer* described him as the leader of an extremist 'anarcho-Maoist movement' at Nanterre, where he was a second-year Sociology student and aged just 23.[25] What makes Cohn-Bendit such a captivating figure for British historians to analyse is that he spoke fluent English (he was also fluent in German and his father had been German). Moreover, he was a mobile revolutionary. During May and June 1968 he found time to visit both Germany and Britain and in both countries he lectured to university students. He had great presence and spoke like a revolutionary; as if his movement was bound to succeed in the short term. For example, when he and the Paris students occupied the Odeon Theatre in Paris, expelling the owner of the theatre Jean-Louis Barrault, Cohn-Bendit told the press: 'Barrault is dead [he wasn't]. We are going to have to start again from the beginning and rethink everything.'[26] He sounded like a committed revolutionary, therefore; he travelled to different countries preaching student revolution and when he reached Britain in mid-June 1968 the British press became transfixed with him; the Labour government also became embroiled in the visit; and Parliament spent several hours debating the international student revolts, as we will discover.

It might be argued that a fracture within the international student movement was there from the beginning. We need only list the student activity around the world during May and June of 1968 to see how feeble the British student protests were in comparison with those in, for example, Columbia University in New York; at the Sorbonne in Paris and throughout Germany. The differences in scale are the most obvious point of difference. Whilst 30,000 students took part in the Paris student revolt in early May 1968, a mere 300 students occupied the University of Hull's administration building in June – around 10 per cent of the student body there.[27] The geographical spread of revolt was another point of difference between Britain and other countries. In May alone there were student protests in 27 cities across Germany. In Britain the only significant activity in that month was a student occupation at Hornsey College of Art in a suburb of North London. The third difference between Britain and elsewhere was in the spirit of the protest. The student protests in the United States and in Paris were bitter and confrontational, and the police were heavily involved. At Columbia over 900 students were arrested during a one-week-long student occupation. In Britain the protests were more sedate. The Hull occupation only lasted two days and no one was arrested. There was even an air of somnolence among British students. At Bristol University, for example, a student protest held in mid-June 1968 was advertised as a 'sleep-in'.[28]

When Cohn-Bendit arrived at Heathrow Airport around 11.30 p.m. on 11 June, there were student protests in progress in parts of Britain; though not in London. The student protesters had not, by this point, come to the attention of all Westminster's politicians; as would very soon happen. In Bristol students had set up a 'Free University' and members of the public were allowed in to attend lectures. But these lectures, given by the students, were not free at all. Each lecture cost 1 shilling to attend (12 pence).[29] There was also a Free University movement emerging in Cambridge and one of its leaders was a second-year English student at King's College, Cambridge, called Simon Hoggart. His father was the pioneering Professor of Cultural Studies at Birmingham University, Professor Richard Hoggart. Simon Hoggart would eventually become a *Guardian* TV critic.[30] In the week of Cohn-Bendit's visit members of the Free University group in Cambridge had boldly invaded a major University function in the Senate House – the installation ceremony for the New Chancellor Lord Adrian. One of the group had forced his way into the Senate House and proclaimed to all the Senior Members attending the service: 'I have an announcement to make. The Free University . . .'. But in mid-sentence he was then forcibly removed from the building and the protest was continued on the streets of Cambridge.[31]

It made a lasting impression on the dons. Some of them even wrote to the press to record their impressions.[32] Indeed when letters by eminent Cambridge scholars such as Professor G. R. Elton appeared in *The Times* the subject of student militancy had obviously become a serious issue in Britain. Elton wrote a long rebuke of the student militants of Cambridge whom he had observed 'yelling in chorus' along the pavements, as the Chancellor and senior dons processed along King's Parade to the University Church, Great St Mary's.[33] He admitted that, as *The Times* had stated in a report on the incident, there were around 100 militant students at the Senate House demonstration in June 1968 and, clearly rattled that a militant student movement had arrived in Cambridge, he described these militant students (who would have included Simon Hoggart and R. E. Rowthorn who is now a Professor of Economics at Cambridge) as 'insane' and the shouting of slogans as 'ugly'. He offered his own explanations of this student unrest in Cambridge for *Times* readers. The students, he thought, were coming under the influence of 'certain prophets' (whom he did not name) and he implied that the students were being brainwashed by these prophets. (He talked of their 'unlearned idealism' and 'unthinking admiration' for certain prophets.) Whoever these prophets were, it is obvious that they were not Cambridge tutors. So, in effect, what Elton was saying was that these militant students in Cambridge had liberated themselves from the moral and academic structures of the University. They were advocating something that had not been heard of in Cambridge before: student power.[34]

Professor Geoffrey Elton's long letter to *The Times*, printed on 12 June 1968 (Cohn-Bendit's first full day in Britain), was one among several letters published in *The Times* that brought bad publicity to Cambridge during early June 1968. Another, by Dr W. H. G. Frend of Gonville and Caius College, was even more alarmist than Elton's. It suggested that Cambridge students saw the dons as a spent force and wanted to oust them. Frend saw one banner proclaiming 'Adrian Out, Intellectuals In'. He found this declaration a grotesque insult to one of the most distinguished academics in Britain. No doubt Lord Adrian, Cambridge's new Chancellor, would have seen it as he processed along the narrow street outside King's College and the University Church.[35]

In addition to the Cambridge dons who wrote in to *The Times* about the student protest, letters from Cambridge students also appeared in the paper during June 1968. R. E. Rowthorn, a graduate student in Economics at King's College, wrote in to challenge a statement made in *The Times* by the University of Cambridge's Vice-Chancellor Lord Ashby. Ashby had suggested that students at Cambridge had no interest in sitting on university committees alongside the dons, as students at LSE had been demanding. Rowthorn dismissed this as incorrect. In two Cambridge colleges, King's and Queens', students had not only been campaigning to sit on University committees but had won this concession in one Faculty: the Faculty of Economics.[36]

How much Daniel Cohn-Bendit knew about the militant students of Cambridge in June 1968, or about the student protest at LSE in 1967, is unclear. But he did make visits to the LSE during his stay and he might have also received a warm welcome in Cambridge. At the airport he was asked by a reporter what he would do during his one-day stay in Britain. He replied, vaguely, that he might visit his mother's grave 'somewhere in Golders Green' and he wanted to visit Karl Marx's tomb in Highgate Cemetery.[37] His lack of planning is, however, quite understandable. Since late May 1968 he had been to-ing and fro-ing between France and Germany and enduring what can only be described as a disorientated and fugitive existence. At one point, in late May, he had had to dye his red hair black to disguise himself from the French police. His hair was still black when he arrived in Britain. He had also undertaken an arduous trek through woods along the German–French border near Saarbrucken and triumphantly reappeared at the Sorbonne around midnight on 29 May.[38] In short, he was a fearless and seasoned revolutionary student leader when he arrived in Britain in mid-June. He was an enigmatic speaker who spoke fluent English; he was self-assured, self-sufficient and seemingly at ease in whichever country he found himself in. When he arrived in London he had boarded a plane at Frankfurt in Germany and shortly after arriving in Britain he announced that he might seek permanent residence here as a political refugee.[39]

How much the Labour Government knew about Cohn-Bendit before he appeared in London in June 1968 is shrouded in mystery. Callaghan, Home Secretary at the time, does not mention Cohn-Bendit's visit at all in his memoirs.[40] But this may be because it proved such a humiliating episode for the Government, at least in the short term. The problem was, as we will discover, the Labour government were never consulted about the visit. The BBC had arranged the trip and Callaghan was forced to react to events at very short notice.[41] Indeed, he was reported to be irate on hearing the news that Cohn-Bendit was in London.[42] Senior Labour politicians had been following the clashes between students and police in Paris with no unanimity of response at all. There was both fear and complacency in Government ministers' speeches. For example, Denis Healey, Labour's Defence Minister, had told a group of trade unionists in Clacton during May: 'We have heard disturbing echoes from the thirties in the violence and anarchy across the Channel.'[43] Callaghan, on the other hand, dismissed any possible threat of the European student revolt reaching Britain. He told a meeting in Edinburgh during late May 1968 that 'the troubles' on the continent 'could not happen in Britain'.[44]

How far was Daniel Cohn-Bendit able to inject more purpose and dynamism into the British student protest? He faced virtually insurmountable difficulties right from the beginning. The first problem was that he was only allowed to stay in Britain for twenty-four hours and when he arrived in a breathless and dishevelled state late on 11 June 1968 his optimism about drawing British students into a wider international student movement cannot have been high. But the circumstances of his visit presented excellent potential for drawing British students into a wider international movement. There were two reasons for this. The first is that he was the most famous living student revolutionary in Europe in June 1968 and the British press were fixated with him.[45] Secondly, he had in fact been invited to Britain by the BBC, a global organisation, and he was to appear in a BBC TV programme with other international student leaders on prime-time television. In effect, if Cohn-Bendit was not able to create a global student movement himself on his tours of university campuses around Europe, the BBC might achieve this outcome for him, by bringing all its leaders together into a television studio, allowing them to talk and broadcasting what they said to several million viewers.[46] Cohn-Bendit was surely bound to succeed.

It is interesting that the quality press in Britain – *The Times*, *The Guardian*, and the *Daily Telegraph* – followed Daniel Cohn-Bendit's movements very closely throughout his stay in Britain. His photograph appeared on the front of *The Times* for three days in succession, on 12, 13 and 14 June. He appeared on *The Guardian's* front page on 12 and 13 June and on the *Daily Telegraph's* front page on 12 and 14 June. From the beginning, there was an air of mystery about him and *The Times* referred to him ominously as 'Herr Cohn-Bendit'. The paper knew that he had a German passport and gave its readers the impression that his family roots were Nazi. It also showed pictures of him with his fist raised in a salute, alongside Tariq Ali and other student radicals.[47] But all of this was far-fetched. Cohn-Bendit's father was a German Jew who fled Nazi Germany in 1933 and his mother was French. Both his parents were dead by June 1968 and so he was an orphan, along with his brother Gabriel.[48]

In his interviews with the British press, Cohn-Bendit revealed to reporters that he had a wry sense of humour and was not in any sense a sinister figure. Asked by a reporter at the airport why he was held at the immigration desk for two and a half hours, he replied: 'They think I am very dangerous, I suppose.'[49] There were all sorts of curious people at Heathrow to meet him, male and female. There were many female students dressed in mini skirts. Tariq Ali, a committed Marxist revolutionary from Pakistan who had been the President of the Oxford Union and was by 1968 a co-editor of *Black Dwarf*, a militantly leftist underground paper, was the first person Cohn-Bendit met as he walked through the airport terminal. The BBC were also there. After being photographed alongside Tariq Ali, both with clenched fists held in mid-air like the Black Power activists in the United States, Cohn-Bendit was whisked away from the airport in a chauffeur-driven car by members of the BBC.[50]

On his first night in Britain Cohn-Bendit attended a party at the offices of *Black Dwarf*. Various media celebrities of the day were there such as Kenneth Tynan, the theatre critic, who wore a kimono shirt, and Christopher Logue, a left-wing poet (described in *The Guardian* as 'the poet Laureate of the Left'). *The Times* were so interested in Cohn-Bendit they sent along one of their reporters, Richard Davy, undercover to observe him at the party. When Davy was identified the proprietor of *Black Dwarf*, Clive Goodwin, decided that a vote would have to be taken to see if the rest of the group wanted *The Times*' reporter to stay, or to be ejected. It was 2 a.m. and the guests could not be bothered to vote. Goodwin therefore decided to ask the reporter to leave and he was sent home. But Davy had enough material for an article on Cohn-Bendit, which appeared in *The Times* on 13 June.[51]

Cohn-Bendit's first full day in London, 12 June, was a hectic and important day in his stay. He was under the constant supervision of two groups of people – the student revolutionary movement of Britain headed by Tariq Ali, who in fact had ceased to be a student three years earlier, and Anthony Smith, a producer at the BBC who was making the TV programme on the international student revolt. So, for certain periods Cohn-Bendit was kept indoors at the BBC TV studios in White City. At other points during the day, he was set free to go wherever he liked. He spent several hours in dispute with the staff at the BBC. He told them he would not make the programme until his visa was extended, and he had a good argument. The other student leaders the BBC had flown in from Europe and other parts of the world were given visas for at least a week and some for two weeks. Why should his last a mere 24 hours?[52] All the press reporters and photographers who spent the day at the BBC studios – there were 100 of them – thought something dramatic would happen. Some suggested that Cohn-Bendit would be kidnapped at the BBC and held hostage until his stay was extended.[53] There was a frisson of student power at the BBC that day. While the fate of Cohn-Bendit and the fate of the BBC's programme were being decided, all the international students stood together in the BBC foyer and sang the Communist anthem 'The Internationale'.[54] This was conducted in the presence of Anthony Smith, the programme's producer, and the press reporters and Smith looked embarrassed.[55]

During the day Cohn-Bendit managed to persuade all the other international students at the BBC TV Centre to abandon the programme unless his visa was extended. This was a major embarrassment for the BBC and costly. The organisation had paid 'several' thousands to fly the students over to Britain and a programme that was supposed to be filmed at 2 p.m. on 12 June had still not been made by 7.30 p.m.[56] Cohn-Bendit, meanwhile, had gone off to meet British students and to lecture at the LSE.[57] He also visited Highgate Cemetery with Tariq Ali and other students and they stood in front of Karl Marx's tomb and sang 'The Internationale' for a second time that day.[58] Interestingly, the LSE was at the centre of the whole Cohn-Bendit saga. It was a Law Lecturer at LSE, Michael Zander, who applied to the Home Office during the day asking for Cohn-Bendit's visa to be extended.[59] Moreover, it was another LSE academic, Professor Robert McKenzie, who was to interview all the international students for the BBC TV programme.[60] Two hours before Cohn-Bendit's visa was due to expire the Home Office issued a statement to the press stating that he could stay on in Britain for a further fourteen days.[61]

The *Students in Revolt* documentary was shown on BBC1 at 9.05 p.m., a prime time, on 13 June. All the British quality press drew attention to the programme the next day. It roused *The Times'* TV critic Michael Billington to describe it as: 'Obviously...the one indispensable item on television last night'; but, rather disappointingly, he did not say what he found so indispensable in the programme.[62] In fact, he did not review it at all. It is clear from the other newspaper reports on the programme that it was not really a useful platform for Daniel Cohn-Bendit. It was too eclectic and included interviews with 11 other student revolutionaries, each representing a whole country.[63] Moreover, it seems to have done the students no favours. Indeed it was actually harmful to one student who participated, a Spanish student. Martín de Hijas, aged 23, of the University of Santiago de Compostela, was chosen for the programme because he spoke excellent English. But on his return to Spain he was arrested and charged with spreading 'illegal propaganda'.[64]

Cohn-Bendit did not impress the *Guardian*'s TV critic Stanley Reynolds, who described him as 'a trendy' and his contribution as 'unclear and vague'.[65] The appearance of the student revolutionaries was also derided by this critic, who described them all as looking like 'chubby schoolboys'.[66] This seems a somewhat sweeping and imprecise criticism. Tariq Ali, for example, was over 6 feet tall and was of slim build. Moreover, he was a young man in his late twenties who wore a thick moustache. He did not resemble a schoolboy in the slightest. If anything he looked older than a man in his late twenties.[67]

However Cohn-Bendit came over in the programme (and the reviews of his own performance were mixed), it did not stop the British press and others talking about him. After the BBC, it was the turn of the politicians and the Home Secretary, James Callaghan, was forced to answer questions on Cohn-Bendit in the House of Commons on 13 June. In fact, the Cohn-Bendit visit occupied the politicians at Westminster for several days. There were debates about him in the House of Commons and in the House of Lords and in the latter case one debate about the student protests lasted over eight hours.[68] In the House of Commons, Conservative MPs, including the Conservative leader Edward Heath, gave the impression that Cohn-Bendit was likely to foment a large-scale student rebellion while he was in London. Mr Heath wanted the Home Secretary to guarantee that 'firm action' would be taken to control Cohn-Bendit's movements.[69] Another Conservative politician, Sir Walter Bromley-Davenport (MP for Knutsford, in North-West England) thought the whole episode was irresponsible. He told the House:

> At a time when our great ally, the French people, are fighting for their very existence against a communist revolution … the BBC … bring to this country and offer payment to one of the arch-enemies of free speech and law and order.[70]

Labour politicians were silent in this debate. Given the Labour Defence Secretary's concern about events in Paris, he might have been expected to say something; but only Callaghan did speak for the Government. William Deedes, Conservative, thought the Government had 'panicked'. But there was not the slightest sense of urgency in the tone of Callaghan's response. 'I … hope that no one will exaggerate … this young man's importance,' he remarked emolliently.[71]

The House of Lords debate on Cohn-Bendit (also on 13 June) was edgier than the Commons debate. Several speakers believed he was 'a dangerous agitator' and were seriously worried about his potential to destabilise British universities. Lord Boothby wanted to know which universities Cohn-Bendit intended to visit. Lord Molson implored the Government to 'give an assurance that if this alien visitor engages in agitation in the universities, his permit...will immediately be terminated'. Several questions were tabled in both Houses on Cohn-Bendit; chiefly, on the security threat he posed. (What did Parliament think of Cohn-Bendit's threats to 'use force'? Who would pay for the extra policing? How much would it cost?, and so on.)[72]

In addition to the Parliamentary debates on Cohn-Bendit, over 30 Conservative politicians signed a petition to the Home Secretary deploring the extension of Cohn-Bendit's visa.[73] Moreover, two sharply-worded motions, both introduced by Conservatives, were put to the House on 13 June, the day after Cohn-Bendit's visa was extended. One of these is worth quoting to illustrate the passion the young Frenchman had aroused in Parliament. Sir Charles Taylor proposed the motion: 'That this House condemns the BBC for inviting a well-known foreign professional revolutionary agitator, already banned from France, to appear on one of their programmes at the expense of the British licence-holder and taxpayer.'[74]

While these debates and questions were being heard in Parliament, Daniel Cohn-Bendit was pondering his future. In France, the government had taken control of the student protest in Paris and with a vengeance. It had banned all student demonstrations in Paris for the remainder of June to prepare the population for a General Election. It had banned several extremist student organisations, including the 'March 22 Movement' which Cohn-Bendit had led. And it had deported 30 student leaders from France who had been involved in the Paris students' revolt. These deportees included 12 members of the German student group SDS. Cohn-Bendit wondered what the immediate future would hold for him if he returned to France. He told a *Times* reporter on 13 June: 'If I return to Germany or France, I believe my life would be in danger.'[75] At this point, he began to think about seeking political asylum in Britain.[76] But he had little time to think seriously about his future. There were still engagements he had to fulfil such as addressing the students at the LSE.

Cohn-Bendit's visits to the LSE during June 1968 were not successful. At a meeting there on 'Student Power' on 13 June one of the students present asked him his nationality and he refused to answer. He also told them that the French students would not cooperate with any student body that was 'anti-Communist'. Many LSE students heard him speak on 13 June. The main Lecture Hall was full and loud speakers were used to broadcast his words to students who were crammed in the corridors of the Main Building. What infuriated LSE students that day was Cohn-Bendit's decision to conduct yet another interview with the press on the LSE's premises.[77] The next day at a student meeting to launch a new revolutionary organisation at LSE, The Revolutionary Socialist Students' Federation (RSSF), the tensions between Cohn-Bendit and British student revolutionaries surfaced again. One of the organisers of this meeting, James Wickham, told a *Daily Telegraph* reporter: 'The students are fed up with the press foisting leaders like Ali, Cohn-Bendit and others on us.' He added: 'Tariq Ali only represents himself . . . Tariq Ali is not a student. He represents no student organisation. He is just someone who considers himself a revolutionary.'[78] It seems that Cohn-Bendit had been snubbed by the RSSF. He was not at the inaugural meeting at LSE. Tariq Ali was present, but sat at the back and left before the end. The next day, 15 June, as the RSSF meeting continued for a further two days, Cohn-Bendit left Britain, heading for Frankfurt.[79]

The visit Daniel Cohn-Bendit made to Britain in June 1968 divided politicians. The Home Secretary James Callaghan had warmed to him and was reassured to learn that one of the places Cohn-Bendit wanted to visit in London was Buckingham Palace. 'I could think of nothing better than that for his education,' Callaghan told MPs.[80] He was also surprised to learn from the BBC TV programme that Cohn-Bendit did not seem to know all the words of the Communist anthem 'The Internationale'. On seeing Cohn-Bendit stumble through the song, the Home Secretary made contact with Cohn-Bendit and offered to teach him all the words.[81] We have, then, a strange mood in Government circles during June 1968 about international student protest. One of the most prominent European student radicals of the period was treated not as a threat to British university life, but as a tourist. The Home Office handled the whole visit, rather than the Government as such, and the key to understanding the Home Office's decision to extend Cohn-Bendit's visa is not to be found in any Cabinet discussion of Cohn-Bendit or in the Labour Party's views of Cohn-Bendit; but most probably in the Special Branch files still unavailable to researchers. He was under constant surveillance during the week of his visit and Special Branch officers were no doubt among his closest guides.

At the other extreme from Callaghan and the Home Office, were leading Conservatives such as Edward Heath, who told the House of Commons: 'This is a matter which has caused grave concern to a large number of people.'[82] It is true that Cohn-Bendit's visit did worry the General Secretary of the National Viewers' and Listeners' Association, Mrs Mary Whitehouse. She sent a telegram to the BBC's Chairman asking why the BBC were allowing 'the foreign anarchist' to promote his ideas on the BBC.[83] But there is no evidence that large numbers of people were disturbed by Cohn-Bendit. The Editorials of all the quality newspapers were either sympathetic or at least curious; but not censorious. For example, even the *Daily Telegraph* welcomed the BBC programme on student protest, reporting: 'the nature and causes of student unrest are a matter of major public interest at the moment, and as such a proper subject for objective and balanced treatment on the air'.[84]

We are left with the impression from the newspaper coverage that the group most hostile, or indifferent, to Cohn-Bendit were his peers – British university students. There was no formal welcome for Cohn-Bendit from, for example, the National Union of Students. Nor was he invited to the launch of the Revolutionary Socialist Students' Federation at the LSE; a major snub it seems. Far more research is needed on, for example, the spread of information on the international student movement among British students during 1968 and on the so-called 'prophets' influencing the British student body – Marcuse and others. But it seems very clear from this survey that Daniel Cohn-Bendit was not one of these prophets, who allegedly inspired British student protest during the late 1960s.[85]

The Labour Government's reactions to the International Student Revolts

The Labour Government were not greatly concerned with youth affairs, even after student protests started at the London School of Economics in 1967 had spread to other universities in England, Scotland and Northern Ireland during 1968 and early 1969. In the records of central government, youth affairs were dealt with, bizarrely, by the Foreign and Commonwealth Office down to 1970. This Department (the FCO) had links with only one youth organisation; the British Youth Council, a body set up to represent British youth overseas.[86] Harold Wilson had created a 'Minister of Youth' in November 1968, in the aftermath of the anti-Vietnam demonstrations of that year in March, June and October, but the Minister in question, Mrs Judith Hart, was ridiculed in Parliament and beyond Westminster for being a Wilson gimmick. The problem was she was a Minister of Youth without Portfolio and neither she nor anyone else knew what her responsibilities were. In the House of Commons she was asked immediately after her appointment, and quite bluntly, to tell the House what she did:

> Mr Marten: ... could the Prime Minister be a little more explicit about the right honourable Lady's duties, namely, her concern with the problems of youth? What particular aspect of youth – moral, political, social – is she to be concerned with, and how old is youth before it is to get her attention?
> The Prime Minister: She is concerned with all the problems of youth, of all relevant ages.[87]

The Minister's work continued to be shrouded in mystery, however, for the remainder of the decade and as student protests developed even Labour Party members wanted to know whether she was responsible for students or not. Manny Shinwell asked Judith Hart in February 1969, after a student protest at the London School of Economics, whether she would be setting up an inquiry into student unrest. She gave an ambivalent answer. She claimed, on the one hand, that she was not responsible for student unrest (the Education Secretary Edward Short was); but she also gave the House her own explanation of the causes of the student unrest at the LSE. This was a vague statement, backed up by no evidence, noting that students at the LSE and other universities wanted 'rather more of a share in the management of various aspects of universities'.[88] She does not seem to have known very much about the LSE protest of January 1969. The LSE's students had wanted more student representation on committees some two years earlier and their dispute with the School's authorities had moved onto new territory since 1967. In January 1969 the issue at the School was gates. The students had noticed iron gates bolted to walls inside the School and thought the School had begun to look like a prison. They had decided to remove the gates with pickaxes and spanners and 30 of them ended up in Bow Street police station cells for a night, later incurring fines in court.[89] Judith Hart was possibly trying to make amends for a provocative speech Edward Short had made in the Commons the previous week when he claimed that American students were behind the protest at LSE and were wrecking, quite literally, a great educational institution.[90]

Judith Hart in fact held two posts in the Wilson government of 1966–70: Paymaster General and Minister of Youth. Her job of Minister of Youth was held in such low regard in the Cabinet that Peter Shore, her successor as Paymaster General in November 1969, refused to become Minister of Youth as well and the Education Department took over responsibility for all youth-related matters.[91] Several questions can be posed about Judith Hart's work as Minister of Youth. How much information did her Department gather on student youth? How did it gather material? Did it have a policy on youth and a view on the student protests?

Judith Hart began her work by avoiding students who were in dispute with their universities. One of her first visits was to a University Settlement in Birmingham where she sat and sipped tea and chatted with students in a hotel room. The females sat on a sofa and chairs; she sat in an armchair and the male students sat on the floor or stood. She was photographed at the meeting and the photograph appeared in a local newspaper, the *Birmingham Post*.[92] After chatting to this group of around 12 university students, Judith Hart told the press that the event was 'a most interesting and constructive meeting', giving the distinct impression that it was a very formal meeting. She later wrote back to Birmingham University and asked to be put in contact with just three of the students, though it is unclear in the Government records why she selected these three, or what was discussed at the original meeting.[93] What is evident from the official records is that Judith Hart was not instantly popular with student youth. Students who were asked to comment on the new Minister of Youth were not very kind. A 21-year-old student in Birmingham told a national newspaper

The People: 'The idea of a Minister of Youth is ridiculous.'[94] A 16-year-old student, also from the Midlands, remarked: 'If she's anything like my mum and dad, she won't do any good.'[95] A student from Dudley told *The People*: 'She's too far away. She's out of touch with the younger generation.' This student's negative judgement was quoted in another national newspaper article on the new Minister printed in the *Daily Express*.[96] When young people were asked for their suggestions on what the new Minister should focus on, an amorphous group of schoolchildren, teenagers and university students delivered a long list of policies she could pursue, including: athletic tracks instead of dance halls ('We don't all want to dance to pop music all night', the Minister was told). Another suggestion was that she should deliver better student accommodation. Schoolchildren reported that they wanted more choice over school meals, and better lessons.[97] The range of complaints makes it clear that her responsibilities were too broad and that too many different types of young people were part of her remit.

Judith Hart worked closely with civil servants and, though she denied she was responsible for student protest, the civil servants in her Department were gathering material on student youth in Britain, and beyond Britain, from very early on in the student troubles of 1968.[98] Judith Hart had a somewhat idealistic approach to youth affairs, making speeches about how 'communication' could be improved between students and their elders;[99] but this whimsical approach was far from being the Labour government's only approach to youth. Her civil servants conducted research on student protests across the world and did ask strategic questions such as whether students were a threat to British society of the late 1960s. The Government kept very detailed information on what it called 'the student movement' in Britain, as well as broad statistics on the number of students in a given year. It appears from the material in the Government records that the Wilson Government was never really worried about student protesters in Britain. But they did feel that in Northern Ireland students could create political instability (as its whole surface area was smaller than Yorkshire and only a million people lived there).[100] This prediction proved accurate and what started as a student movement at Queen's University of Belfast developed into a 'civil rights movement' of students and adults, and eventually in 1969 the O'Neill government in Northern Ireland collapsed.[101]

The Labour government felt safe knowing that the British student population was quite dispersed and that there were no colossal universities in Britain where students could present a serious law and order threat if discontent spread through a university. There was, for example, no university in Britain on the same scale as the Sorbonne in Paris, which had 160,000 students in 1968. In the whole of Britain there were only 169,000 university students in 1965.[102] Another feature of the British student body that reassured government ministers was that almost all British students

(90% in 1968) depended on state grants and, in theory, cutting student grants, or in the case of international students, raising tuition fees, was a form of control the Labour Government could exert over the student body if it felt like it. One of the issues at the London School of Economics in 1968 was that the Labour Government had raised fees for foreign students.[103] Whether this was a strategy for reducing their numbers in British universities from 1968 is a moot point, but the Labour Government never restored these fees back to their earlier level.

A third feature of the British student population that gave policy makers confidence during the years of student unrest is the absence, certainly before 1968, of professional or perpetual students in British universities. Most domestic students received a state grant for three years and then left the universities to pursue careers. It was believed that many of these students were from working-class families and valued the state's contribution to their studies. In other countries, notably the United States and West Germany, students were at liberty to retake courses and stay in the universities for an indefinite period. Some of these students migrated to Britain; such as Paul Hoch who had a PhD from an American university but began another at Bedford College in the University of London.[104] Marshall Bloom, one of the leaders of the student protest at LSE, was another of these seasoned students who lingered on in the universities into their late twenties.[105] Tariq Ali was another. He had studied in Pakistan, and then studied at Oxford in the mid-sixties, and he was still addressing student meetings in London in the late 1960s. Indeed, he led the Grosvenor Square demonstration in London in March 1968. Jim Callaghan, the Home Secretary at the time, referred to him as a 'spoilt, rich, playboy'.[106]

It is tempting to suggest that, without these affluent professional students from abroad, the student protests in London would not have developed beyond the confines of individual universities. Who would have led the British students? The international students, especially those from the United States some of whom had already participated in 'campus wars' there,[107] brought new techniques of student protest to Britain and devoted much of their time to trying to develop a student movement in Britain.[108]

British civil servants were always primarily concerned with the way British student protest was organised, and whether it posed a threat to law and order, rather than with the students' demands. From early on, the Cabinet Office believed there was no evidence that British students had links with student protesters in Europe and the United States.[109] It seemed abundantly clear to them that the student movement in Britain did not spread by design, but through students seeing their European peers on television and imitating them. Ongoing research does suggest that the protest at LSE (possibly an isolated case, but possibly not) was highly organised and carefully planned and international students were the orchestrators.[110] But the role of television, and indeed radio, in spreading knowledge does need to be studied more systematically. One British government official made the acute remark that television had turned student youth in Britain into 'instant internationalists'. At the flick of a switch, they could easily learn about the death of Che Guevara thousands of miles away in Chile, or see students demonstrating in the streets of Paris in May 1968 from their living rooms.[111] As the government civil servants mulled over the evidence from different parts of Britain, they heard nothing that would have seriously worried them. Students were probably too candid for their own good in Britain. One LSE student activist told the *Evening Standard* in May 1968: 'the movement in this country is still very weak. At the moment, things haven't got very much further than individual contacts with overseas movements.' Officials in the Cabinet Office filed this statement with their other correspondence on the student protests.[112]

The idea that American students were behind the British protests, outlined in the Commons by the Education Secretary Edward Short in January 1969, had dawned on the civil servants in the Cabinet Office as early as May 1968. They knew all about the protests at Berkeley in 1964, for example; and were aware that the phrase 'student power' was an American import first used at Berkeley. They also had the names of all the American students who were active in British universities during these years. The Cabinet Office described these American students colourfully as 'informal missionaries of student protest' and they knew that two of these 'missionaries', Eliott Isenburg and Marshall Bloom, were studying at the LSE.[113] They knew that another American activist, Michael Klein, was at Sussex; that Alan Krebbs and Joseph Berke were at Shoreditch Art College, and they were also keeping an eye on the American friends of Bertrand Russell: Ralph Schoenman, David Horovitz and Russell Stetler, who were involved with the Bertrand Russell Peace Foundation. They even recorded that the leader of the militant students at Columbia University in New York, Lewis Cole, had toured British universities in June 1968; at the time of Cohn-Bendit's visit to Britain.[114]

What made it easier for the government to track so-called student revolutionaries in Britain was that most joined extremist organisations; most notably, the Vietnam Solidarity Campaign (VSC) and the Revolutionary Socialist Students' Federation (RSSF). All the main student leaders of this period were in one or the other of these organisations. Besides the Americans, David Triesman, a student leader at Essex (now Lord Triesman), was in the Radical Students' Alliance (RSA) and so was the South African student leader at the LSE, David Adelstein.[115] The British government estimated that there were around a thousand revolutionary students in Britain in 1968 in a student population of 450,000 (which included college students as well as university students).[116] There was some concern that one of the radical student organisations, the Revolutionary Socialist Students' Federation (RSSF), advocated 'killing policemen'; but also some comfort in the fact that the membership of the NUS and the Scottish Union of Students (SUS) dwarfed that of revolutionary groups. Together these two moderate student bodies had 400,000 members in 1968.[117]

There was further comfort in the low level of student 'disturbances' in Britain and it is interesting that British civil servants never used more alarmist terms such as 'student revolt' in their communications on this subject. The government could look back over 1968 and identify just a handful of incidents involving students. There had been one death at the LSE when a porter suffered a heart attack during a surge at one meeting. Just one incident was reported from Manchester. A student demonstrator had grabbed hold of the Education Secretary. There was a single incident at Sussex University where an American diplomat had been smeared with paint, and more minor incidents elsewhere, which the Cabinet Office did not feel merited any comment other than that they occurred at Regent Street Polytechnic, Liverpool University, Leicester University, Oxford University and Hull University.[118]

By February 1969 the government was under the impression that the student protest in Britain (though not in Northern Ireland) had all but dissolved. The government kept a record of the fact that in the student elections at the LSE in February 1969 all the militant candidates were defeated.[119] A government memorandum entitled 'Student Protest, 1968–69' written in February 1969 also noted with satisfaction that the Student Union in Essex was taking responsibility for the student protest itself. The students at Essex had voted to reimburse an American diplomat whose suit had been daubed with paint. Moreover, a sit-in organised by the RSA at Essex had had to be abandoned.[120]

The behaviour of the student protesters in Britain was the prime focus of government thinking, but civil servants also discussed the influences shaping student behaviour; in particular, the intellectual influences shaping their thoughts. Two civil servants in the Cabinet Office discussed this in great detail and their exchanges were almost like an academic seminar. The influence of the American author and Berkeley academic Herbert Marcuse was probed in great depth. For example, one of the Cabinet Office's civil servants, named 'R. Jardine', went to the trouble of reading Marcuse's book *One Dimensional Man* (published in 1964), which identified students as the new revolutionary class. Jardine reported back to his colleagues that the book was incomprehensible. He described it as 'technically unreadable' and after consulting with officials in the Foreign and Commonwealth Office it was discovered that even in France none of the students who participated in the May 1968 protests in Paris had read a word of Marcuse. Daniel Cohn-Bendit, the Paris students' leader, supplied this information.[121]

As to the potential of other intellectuals or charismatic leaders to influence British students, the government were always sceptical. Jardine noted that all the heroes of British student protesters were foreign and since they were usually thousands of miles away there was no danger to the British state of these influences developing. In any case, they were emotional affinities rather than serious influences. Che Guevara, Ho Chi Minh and Fidel Castro were all mentioned in student speeches and literature, but the government felt the utterances of these foreign leaders were so vague they were laughable. Jardine noted:

> They [the students] tend to be against authority, and instead of a clear political ideology have heroes (Che Guevara, Ho Chi Minh and Fidel Castro etc.) who all tend to be foreign and far away, and whose utterances are suffused with emotion and as vague as anything out of the medieval Schoolmen.[122]

Jardine, a very donnish civil servant who thought a lot about the student protests in Britain, decided that they were not revolutionaries at all, but simply wanted to belong to a community.[123] A student activist at the LSE who wrote a Ph.D. thesis about the student revolt in Britain, Colin Crouch, reached the same conclusion.[124]

By February 1969, therefore, the Government thought the worst of the student protests in Britain was over. A government survey was undertaken the same month and 749 university students were asked if they had taken part in a student demonstration in the previous 18 months – during the highpoint of the protests. They learned that 30 per cent of the students had done, but that three-quarters were now 'satisfied with life as a student'. The civil servants rejoiced at this news. One joked: 'the general picture is not such as to cause oldies like me to turn in our graves'.[125] By April 1969, the government civil servants who dealt with youth affairs behind the scenes began to turn their thoughts to the working-class youth of the cities. They had deduced that working-class youths who committed crime were a far greater problem for society than university students. As one put it:

> I suspect that it is the non-student young who are much more important as a potential social problem.... What is ... worrying is the virtual lack of any worthwhile rapport between society and the young man who kicks your ribs in the Seven Sisters Road out of sheer boredom, or stays more peaceably at home filling up the football pools for lack of any effective encouragement to interest himself in anything else.[126]

Conclusion

More research on the government records may uncover new material on the student protest in Britain, but it seems unlikely that it will call into question my argument that at no point were civil servants or government ministers seriously worried about the student protest movements in Britain. They seem to have thought the whole subject of Youth was too frivolous for senior civil servants at Whitehall to devote time to. 'R. Jardine', who was more engaged by the subject than others, and certainly more knowledge-able than his Minister Judith Hart, told a colleague in September 1969 he never discovered what Judith Hart was supposed to do. 'We have previously discussed this question of 'youth', he stated, 'and you are aware that I find it rather difficult to pin down. Like the elephant it is easier to recognise than define, and even when identified it is far from clear how it concerns the government.'[127] After writing some interesting thoughts on the sub-ject and amassing a lot of material, he confessed that he found the whole subject too superficial – 'anything one writes on the subject tends to be of the nature of journalism rather than the more weighty prose that Whitehall is used to'.[128] We can excuse him this comment. He was not delving too deeply into his subject and only had to report on student protest, rather than delve into complex questions such as juvenile delinquency and its causes. Moreover, since he had found no disturbing evidence of a student movement in British universities, he was probably thoroughly bored with the subject.

In essence, then, it was senior civil servants within the Labour Party who were largely responsible for the Labour Government's handling of interna-tional student protest during the late 1960s. The Prime Minister, Harold Wilson, despite being an economic radical in his youth, did not regard either youth affairs or student protest movements as serious subjects wor-thy of his time – except, briefly, in relation to the youth vote and when the LSE had been forced to close for a month in January 1969.[129] Civil servants like 'R. Jardine' found that such was the Government's lack of knowledge about students and youth culture that he and colleagues had to engage in information gathering from researchers in British universi-ties who had undertaken research on student movements.[130] In September 1969, the Foreign and Commonwealth Office even sent some of their offi-cials to an international conference on 'Youth in Revolt' held in Trinidad and Tobago.[131] What these officials were interested in was how the inter-national youth revolt was affecting British Commonwealth countries, and so there was a vague sense within the Government that somewhere across its far flung Empire and Commonwealth, students might create problems for colonial governments. But closer to home the international student revolts only impinged on British political life fleetingly. Moreover, when the visit of Danny Cohn-Bendit passed without anything more threatening than the BBC's cameras and a few clenched student fists, raised in poses for the cameras, the Labour government forgot about 'student power' and focused on more pressing matters.

9

Youth Culture and Pop Culture: from Beatlemania to the Spice Girls

It is undeniable that during the 1960s British pop music emerged as a global phenomenon with domestic groups, led by the Beatles and the Rolling Stones, enjoying unprecedented commercial success; primarily in the United States but also in Europe and even in Eastern Europe.[1] It was not until the mid-1990s that any British pop group achieved comparable world record sales; and it came in the unlikely guise of five females, all in their early twenties, who had not known each other at all before an astute record producer, Simon Fuller, had the bright idea of creating a 'girl' pop group to counter all the assorted 'boy bands' that were dominating the British pop charts at the time. He called them 'The Spice Girls' and in the period between 1996 and 1998 they sold more records worldwide than any British pop group since the Beatles.[2]

Sociologists have written extensively about pop culture and its impact on youth culture; but the subject is invariably treated from, as it were, the 'top down'; far more attention is devoted to the evolution of the pop groups than to examining their impact on British youth culture.[3] John Street has written cogently on British popular music and youth culture since the 1950s, but even his work begs many questions. Like so many fellow sociologists, he assumes that popular music was the dynamo of British youth culture from the late 1950s onwards. It is almost assumed that popular music and youth culture are synonymous.[4] Thus we are told that there are various milestones in the history of postwar youth culture that can be identified neatly as: the arrival of Rock 'n' Roll music in the mid-1950s in the form of Bill Haley and his group the Comets; then, in 1963, came the emergence of the Beatles as the symbol of British youth culture for the rest of the decade; with the only other 'key figures' from the pop world influencing youth culture being the Rolling Stones, a more countercultural group than the Beatles who wrote genuinely political songs such as 'Street Fighting Man' – written for an anti-Vietnam War demonstration in 1968 led by the Oxford-educated Marxist Tariq Ali.[5]

This chapter will argue that the 1960s never really saw a monolithic youth culture come to fruition in Britain. It will emerge that, in fact, the pop world divided youth, and two powerful myths of the period will be challenged: first, the idea that the Beatles created a cohesive youth culture; and, secondly, the notion that British youth culture of the 1960s suddenly became 'classless' due to the impact of pop music.[6] The two most prominent pop groups of the period, the Beatles and the Rolling Stones, had subtly different audiences and illustrate the fractures within youth culture during the 1960s. In any case, as this study has argued in earlier chapters, the key groups that could have generated a Youth Culture were not pop groups but university students; as had happened earlier in the century.[7] In the United States it was the student body Students for a Democratic Society (SDS) that generated a truly national youth culture there; stretching from California to Texas and incorporating political campaigns, cultural contact with non-students, music, discussions, and explorations in new ways of living.[8] In a country where 50 per cent of 18-year-olds went to University, student culture became synonymous with Youth Culture and the idea of Youth Culture was given real meaning by a single political issue that affected all 18-year-olds: from 1965 onwards all young males in the United States who reached 18 had to enlist for service in the Vietnam War. In Britain there was a tiny student population in comparison to that in the United States (less than 6% of 18-year-olds even at the end of the decade went to University).[9] In addition, there was no single issue that could mobilise such large numbers as in the US. Student demonstrations at the University of California, Berkeley, for example, regularly attracted between 30,000 and 100,000 young people during 1965.[10]

It is the central argument of this book that university students are the only group who could have generated a cohesive Youth Culture in Britain; as happened, briefly, between the Two World Wars. But British students of the 1960s were not that interested in youth culture.[11] There were, in fact, real tensions between the pop world and student intellectuals; demonstrated most starkly when John Lennon became embroiled in a bitter row with the student intellectual John Hoyland about the merits of student revolution.[12] What this interview revealed was that the pop star and the student revolutionaries despised each other – and the latter especially despised the Beatles' music. At a broader social level, university students were not part of Swinging London. They were absent from the suburban dance halls of London, the basement coffee bars of Soho, and the discotheques that opened in the West End during the early – mid-1960s.[13]

Beatlemania

The relationship between the Beatles, unquestionably the most commercially successful pop group of the 1960s in Britain and the United States, and the development of British youth culture during the decade has always been somewhat nebulous. On both sides of the Atlantic the typical Beatle fan was a pre-teenage or early – mid-teen girl. As the secretary of 'the Beatles' fan club in America, Gloria Steinem, put it in 1964: the average Beatle fan was '13–17, a girl, middle-class, white, Christian, a B– student, weighed 105–140 pounds, owned a transistor radio with an earplug attachment and had Beatle photographs all over her bedroom walls'.[14] The Beatles had more 'fans', significantly more, than any other British pop group of the 1960s. Their Official Fan Club (based in London) was started in 1962. Its membership peaked at 80,000 in 1965; no doubt influenced by the fact that the group stopped performing altogether in 1966 and henceforth spent nearly all their time in recording studios. But, even despite this withdrawal from live performances, the group had far more fans than any other British group of the period. The Rolling Stones were the second most popular in terms of 'registered fans' in 1965 with just 12,000 and they were followed by the Mancunian group Herman's Hermits with just 1000 'official' fans.[15] In essence, then, the most popular groups of the 1960s had quite modest fan bases and there is an obvious dichotomy between the supposed influence of groups such as the Beatles on British youth culture, which numerically speaking embraced several million 15–25-year-olds, and the fact that not even the most globally successful group of the period could amass more than a million official fans worldwide.

Whether the Beatles had a major influence on British youth culture during the 1960s is questionable. The most visible, geographically mobile and cohesive youth cult of the period, the Mods, ubiquitous from 1964 to 1967, were never interested in the Beatles' music. They found it too melodic.[16] Moreover, given that in Britain Beatles fans were, in the main, girls of 10–14 who lost interest in pop culture at around 20 it is unlikely that the group had as much of an influence on older teenagers and those in their early-mid-twenties as the Rolling Stones, as we will discover.[17] The Beatles' main contribution to youth culture, it seems, was to generate what the *Daily Telegraph* christened 'Beatlemania'. But this was, initially, a term used to describe the reactions of a middle-aged audience to the group when they performed at a Royal Variety Performance at The Prince of Wales Theatre, London, in November 1963.[18] A far more sinister term, 'Beatlism', was coined by the journalist Paul Johnson in a widely debated article that appeared in the *New Statesman* in February 1964; the same month that the group first reached Number 1 in the American pop charts with their innocuous and tuneful single 'I Want To Hold Your Hand'.

Paul Johnson's critique of the Beatles has been described as 'one of the most scathing critiques of youth culture ever written'.[19] It was a very short article, but what so shocked readers of the *New Statesman* was its extraordinary argument that the Beatles were having an entirely negative impact on British youth.[20] He was not, contrary to the latest historian's analysis of the debate the article aroused,[21] the first to say this. Francis Newton (alias the Marxist historian Eric Hobsbawm) had dismissed the Beatles as a flash-in-the-pan in the *New Statesman* as early as November 1963: 'In 20 years' time nothing of them will survive', he predicted.[22] He even denounced them as musicians: 'What they sell is not music, but 'the sound' ... heavily accented, electronically amplified noise.'[23] He added, ramming his point home: 'Anyone can produce that sound ...'[24] In a slightly later article in the same journal, that still appeared before Johnson's critique of the Beatles, Hobsbawm proclaimed: 'The Beatles are beneath critical notice.'[25] He still felt the need to say how bad they were and how negative was their influence on youth. He began with grudging praise, arguing that the Beatles produced: 'Good tunes and clean renderings'; but he added that they also produced 'bad words'.[26] Turning to the essence of their songs, he noted that 'excitement and squalling simplicity are easily their chief credentials'. Finally, assessing their impact on youth culture, he saw nothing but harmful influence. Their audiences consisted of 'pathetic girl fans' and the whole atmosphere at their concerts was tacky ('the inevitable showbiz aura').[27]

If this sounded mean-spirited criticism of a group of working-class lads who had become the most successful pop group Britain had ever produced while still in their early twenties – and, moreover, from an historian who specialised in working-class history[28] – it was anodyne comment compared with the attack Paul Johnson launched on the Beatles and their audience in the following month, February 1964.

It is worth reflecting at this point on why the *New Statesman* in particular seemed to have a vendetta against the Beatles; for that is the obvious lesson to draw from the paper's consistent and maverick denunciations of the group from November 1963 on. It is possible that Paul Johnson, who was Deputy Editor of the paper, was orchestrating the whole anti-Beatles campaign. Johnson and the *New Statesman* were actively campaigning for the Labour Party in the forthcoming General Election.[29] What particularly angered Johnson about the Beatles was that the Conservative government had been applauding their commercial success in the United States and unashamedly cosying up to the group. The Prime Minister himself, Alec Douglas-Home, told *The Times* just a few days before Paul Johnson's scathing article appeared, that:

> If any country is in deficit with us I have only to say the Beatles are coming. ...
> Let me tell you why they have had such a success in the United States – it is because they are a band of very natural, very funny young Men.[30]

This was not just an off-the-cuff remark. Another senior Conservative, William Deedes, who was in the Cabinet (as Minister in charge of the

Government's Information Service), made a speech about the Beatles shortly after Douglas-Home's, at a meeting of Conservative City businessmen. He made the point that the Beatles were an example of youthful free enterprise that should be welcomed and nurtured by business leaders. He told them:

> They [the Beatles] herald a cultural movement among the young which may become part of the history of our time.... For those with eyes to see it, something important and heartening is happening here. The young are rejecting some of the sloppy standards of their elders ... they have discerned dimly that in a world of automation, declining craftsmanship and increased leisure, something of this kind is essential to restore the human instinct to excel at something ...[31]

Was Deedes seriously suggesting that businessmen should stop investing in traditional industries and put more money into the leisure industries? Was he asking them to invest directly in the pop world instead of into traditional apprenticeship schemes? Whatever his motives, there is no doubt that the Conservative Party were courting youth and potential entrepreneurs of youth culture in the run-up to the General Election of October 1964. Leaving nothing to chance, they even instructed all Conservative candidates to mention the Beatles in their election campaigns.[32]

It was the Conservatives' unashamed pandering to youth in early 1964 that so annoyed Paul Johnson; not the Beatles. Indeed, he began his article by listing all the Government's gimmicky activity trying to win over the youth vote. Besides their speeches, there was also a new strand of pro-youth policy in the Conservative government's programme. In late 1963, for example, the Conservative Home Secretary, Henry Brooke, had set up a Standing Committee to explore the subject of Juvenile Delinquency. Its first meeting was held in February 1964; the month Johnson's article appeared. Among the details announced to the press, were that several of its members were under 30. One was a convicted juvenile offender, and in addition there were youthful pop stars who sat alongside educationalists and legal experts at its meetings.[33]

So what did Paul Johnson say about Beatlemania? His article was, in part, an attack on the intellectuals who praised 'pop culture'. (He could not bring himself to regard pop music as culture and throughout the article placed the word in inverted commas.) This was fairly harmless and no doubt just a swipe at fellow journalists like George Melly, who wrote about pop music for serious newspapers like *The Observer*. He then turned on the Conservative Party for pandering to groups like the Beatles. And finally, and most viciously, he turned on the teenage girls who liked the Beatles and attended their concerts. Johnson was a product of a major English public school and Magdalen College, Oxford, where he read History. His attack on Beatles fans came over, in the words of one critic, as 'almost nasty'. It was certainly snobbish. He wrote:

> What a bottomless chasm of vacuity they reveal! The huge faces, bloated with cheap confectionery and smeared with chain-store make-up, the open, sagging mouths and glazed eyes, the hands mindlessly drumming in time to the music, the broken stiletto heels, the shoddy, stereotyped, 'with-it' clothes.

There was more in this vein. He continued:

> Those who flock round the Beatles, who scream themselves into hysteria, whose vacant faces flicker over the t.v. screen, are the least fortunate of their generation, the dull, the idle, the failures ... their existence, in such numbers, far from being a cause for ministerial congratulation, is a fearful indictment of our educational system, which in 10 years of schooling can scarcely raise them to literacy.

Undoubtedly, as Henry Fairlie pointed out in *The Spectator*, Johnson's analysis of Beatlemania was 'rather exaggerated'.[34] But behind Paul Johnson's verbose language was a serious point. The Beatles were not, as William Deedes had argued, at the forefront of a cultural movement of the young. They were young capitalists who, far from developing a youth culture, were exploiting youth culture by promoting fan worship, mindless screaming and nothing more than a passive teenage consumer. Of course, what Johnson overlooked was the teenage girl's romanticism. She was not being exploited by a commercial machine. She was using the pop music of groups like the Beatles to learn about the adult world. As one female Beatle fan from Liverpool put it: 'Any pop music was the route to adulthood. It was one way to feel grown-up and go through grown-up feelings – feelings like being passionately in love with people one's never met.'[35] This was Lizzie Bowden, a Beatles fan in 1963 who moved on from teen worship of the Beatles to become an Oxford graduate; thus demonstrating that not all teenage Beatles fans were educationally subnormal. Moreover, the Beatles themselves were far from dim. Three of the four had attended grammar schools in Liverpool – George Harrison, Paul McCartney and John Lennon – and Lennon had moved on to art school.[36]

Johnson's article provoked a national debate on the Beatles that was conducted in several current affairs journals, both left-leaning and conservative. Undoubtedly, the Beatles divided the middle-classes. There were over 200 letters sent to the *New Statesman* alone in the wake of the Johnson article and around a third (66) supported his attack on the Beatles and their negative impact on the young. One reader agreed wholeheartedly:

> Sir, Congratulations to Paul Johnson on his realistic appraisal of Beatlism. A pity more left-wing writers didn't express such views. The fatuous remarks of Mr Deedes are hardly surprising. After all, the Tory Party has an interest in keeping idiots idiotic.[37]

This writer thought that the Beatles were unashamed capitalists who had no real interest in working-class youth, except as a market for their records. As he put it: 'these four lads earn 6,250,000 a year, while thousands of other young Merseysiders go straight from school to the dole queue'.[38] This was a salient point. Although the Beatles had emerged from Liverpool, where many of the early Sixties' Beat groups had begun as juvenile gangs,[39] they had ceased to be a Liverpool pop group by early 1964. George Melly made the acute observation that when their film 'A Hard Day's Night' was premièred in Liverpool in May 1964, and the group were asked to appear at the official opening, they all immediately returned to London the same evening.[40] In truth, the Beatles seem to have alienated 'Liverpudlians' as their careers developed. By the late 1960s, the Beatles had reinvented themselves as hippies. They grew their hair long, took LSD and made dreamy albums such as their magnum opus '*Sergeant Pepper's Lonely Hearts Club Band*' (1967). But the city they were reared in never embraced hippie culture. It remained a working-class city and, moreover, a city that saw prolonged strike action in 1966, with the national dockworkers' strike. Even female workers in the city who were employed in the motor car industry at Halewood undertook strike action a year later, in 1967, demanding 'equal pay' (the year '*Sergeant Pepper*' was released). The Beatles wrote songs about Liverpool in the late '60s – 'Penny Lane' and 'Strawberry Fields Forever', for example, both released in 1967. But these were songs about the Liverpool of their childhood, not the industrial city of the late '60s experiencing industrial strike action and the beginning of its economic decline.[41]

There were others in February 1964 who sensed that the Beatles' influence on youth was as negative as Johnson had suggested. One contributor to the *New Statesman* debate was David Holbrook, a Fellow of King's College, Cambridge. He was especially interested in the impact pop music in general had on teenagers. Holbrook was an English don who had studied under F. R. Leavis and, like his mentor, saw nothing praiseworthy in mass culture. In the Beatles he saw nothing but a corrupting influence on youth. In February 1964, still very early in the so-called 'Permissive' decade, Holbrook did not have much material on which to base his argument; but it is worth briefly considering the ideas he raised, as they were taken seriously at the time. He had two hypotheses about the Beatles. The first was that their lyrics were promoting an interest in sex among young girls. He believed that the Beatles' song 'Twist and Shout' had a sexual meaning. He saw in these words the cruder message 'copulate and cry out'. He believed the whole dance craze The Twist was nothing more than a manifestation of the flaunting of sexual prowess. He argued that the wriggling of the pelvis could only mean one thing: it was mimicking masturbation.[42] He had many theories about the significance of pop stars' gestures. He wondered why the Beatles shook their heads and then decided they were imitating 'people possessed by sexual ecstasy approaching orgasm'. He described the Beatles' whole stage act – four young men dressed in sharp suits standing, playing guitars and at the end of a song shaking their heads – as nothing more than 'a masturbation fantasy'. He could not find anything positive to say about the Beatles at all. 'As entertainment . . . they hardly count. As culture, there is nothing there except the expression of manic vitality – there is not even talent.' Having dismissed the group as talentless and nothing more than a sexualised act, he next analysed their impact on teenage audiences. Echoing Paul Johnson, he reiterated that the Beatles did not promote creativity in their audiences (as schoolwork would do). He thought the Beatles' lyrics were puerile: 'She Loves You Yeah Yeah Yeah' was not going to inspire young people to think. Holbrook put it more cogently: '[The Beatles' lyrics were] a closed circuit which leads to no fresh discoveries – about themselves, or about human nature or the nature of the world'.[43] Clearly, he seems to have wanted the Beatles to be educationalists rather than entertainers. He did, however, want to learn more about Beatlemania from other people and he invited teachers, and 'Beatlemaniacs', to write to him in Cambridge with their own experiences of a cultural phenomenon that perplexed him.[44]

Only a week later a letter from a teacher at a secondary modern school appeared in the *New Statesman*, reporting some 'disturbing' effects of Beatlemania on 13-year-old boys. The author was at pains to point out that they were bright secondary school boys – and were all in the top-stream at the school. He then disclosed to *New Statesman* readers how they had succumbed to Beatlemania. Two of the boys had had radical Beatle haircuts, and now sported Beatle 'mops'. Even worse, they had taken to walking about the school 'hand in hand'. The teacher had glimpsed a group of his other boys listening to the Beatles on a transistor radio in a classroom and 'with a terrifying dead blankness on their faces, moving their pelvises rhythmically in time with each other'.[45]

This was an interesting contribution to the Beatle debate because it revealed something that had not been noticed by other critics. Teenage boys were also fans of the Beatles. But whether it confirmed Holbrook's theories about the Beatles promoting the sexualisation of youth is less certain. Holbrook went on to write extensively about the corrupting effects of pop music, turning his gaze from the Beatles onto the Rolling Stones as the innocent teen songs of the early Beatles gave way to the more sexually explicit lyrics of the late sixties' Stones. What must he have thought as he heard dissolute 24-year-old Mick Jagger singing about not caring to see a 15-year-old's ID, on an album released in 1968?[46]

No consensus has emerged on whether the Beatles did shape youth culture during the 1960s, but the evidence cited above suggests it is highly unlikely for several reasons. First, in both Britain and the United States they appealed primarily to girls between 10 and 14, and did not have the same kudos with youth cults such as the Mods or middle-class youths in the universities.[47] Second, from very early in their careers the Beatles became so phenomenally successful that their appeal was universal rather than to youth. They appeared on the Ed Sullivan show in the US in February 1964; and on the Morecambe and Wise Christmas show in Britain in December 1963. They even appeared in pantomime with Rolf Harris and Cilla Black over Christmas and the New Year 1963–4. In effect, they were family enter-tainment, rather than at the cutting edge of youth culture and, to reinforce the point, they even wrote a catchy song about growing old ('When I'm 64'). As John Muncie has argued: 'The Beatles were safe. The cutting edge of youth culture was to be found elsewhere'.[48] This does seem to have been the case. For the Beatles to have reflected youth culture they would, pre-sumably, have needed to be in contact with young people. But they stopped touring in 1966 and what seems most striking is how detached they were from youth culture by the late 1960s. One of the more telling comments on Beatlemania, their main contribution to youth culture, was made by John Lennon. He was by this time, the late '60s, living in a stately home, Tittenhurst Park in Twickenham, Surrey, and one day he noticed a group of Beatles fans outside his house. He told a reporter:

> They treat my house like a b——y holiday camp, sitting in the grounds with flasks of tea and sandwiches and thinking that they have come to a Beatle National Park.[49]

Pop Culture in Swinging London

Below the elevated level of the Beatles and their phenomenal global success (they earned £6.25 million a year by February 1964[50]) we can see from contemporary accounts that there were significant fractures within youth culture, even in the capital city, by the mid-1960s. There were two youth cultures in 'Swinging' London: first, the working-class youth cultures of the suburban dance halls, which were barely touched by the 'Swinging' discotheques of the city centre; and, second, the world of upper-class and upper middle-class debutantes – a world of exclusive nightclubs such as The Scotch, Sibylla's and Annabel's in the West End, where young fashion designers and debutantes mingled with pop stars like Brian Jones of the Rolling Stones (see Figure 4). Jane Wilson, a feisty middle-class Oxford graduate in her mid-twenties, visited several suburban dance halls of 'Swinging' London for the cultural journal *London Life*. She discov-ered that working-class youth culture in mid-'60s London was rooted in the suburbs and these youths simply could not afford to visit West End

Figure 4   Youth Culture in 'Swinging' London: Brian Jones of the Rolling Stones leaves Sibylla's Nightclub, 1966.
Source: *London Life*, 2 July 1966.

discotheques.[51] The discotheques of the West End were so exclusive some, such as Annabel's and Sibylla's, the latter part-funded by Beatle George Harrison, only admitted 'members'. They had to pay an annual subscription of roughly £5 and then a nightly entrance fee of £1. Working-class young Londoners were largely restricted to suburban dance halls like The Orchid Ballroom in Purley, where the entrance fee was a princely 3 shillings during the week (8 shillings at weekends); there was little pressure on space (The Orchid would hold around 8000 ravers) and there was 'continuous pop music from 7.30 pm to 11 pm'.[52] Jane Wilson visited The Orchid Ballroom, Purley, in December 1965 and found its clientele consisted entirely of working-class young people. Soon after she arrived she was accosted by a youth, who pulled one of her earrings from her ear and told her: 'It's a very hard area round here darling'.[53] There was visible evidence that this was the case. The Ballroom employed 30 'bouncers' who wore dinner jackets and were called 'supervisors'. Wilson noticed that the décor of the hall looked plush and gave the impression of affluence (there were automatic doors, for example, and palm trees); but on closer inspection she discovered that the palm trees were plastic. It did not seem to bother the clientele that the affluence was fake. 'Everyone walks about', Wilson observed, 'in a happy daze of dreams-of-affluence-fulfilled.'[54]

She then moved on to a dance hall in Tottenham called 'The Royal'. There was a shop in this dance hall, which sold 'Steady Rings' for 25 shillings and musical cigarette boxes with pop-up ballerinas inside. This hall also had a veneer of opulence and had christened its female lavatories 'The Palace of Beauty'. Wilson discovered, as she entered them, that there were 55 mirrors and dressing tables, Regency period striped wallpaper and a machine selling perfume. What she found slightly disconcerting was the youthfulness of the clientele. She encountered girls as young as 13 and at weekends, she learned, there was a dance held on Saturday afternoons for 7–12-year-olds. She deduced that anyone older than 12 was allowed to visit the dance hall in the evenings. On the night Wilson visited, hardly anyone was dancing and, invariably, young girls danced together. Many of the clientele talked and stared at each other.[55]

Her next visit was to the Starlite Ballroom in Greenford (West London), which targeted Mods. The poster in the hall notified the clientele that: 'Friday Nite is Rave Nite – Wear All Your Mod Gear'. Some of the young dancers on the pop programme '*Ready Steady Go!*' would visit this club on Fridays after the show. But it was hardly a centre of Swinging London. In fact, the hall was used as a bingo hall and social club for most of the week and was only a dance hall for a couple of evenings.[56] Still, the attraction of this dance hall was that live bands played regularly. Its regulars were a group called the Birds, whose guitarist was called Ron Wood (who later joined the Rolling Stones). Indeed, the group tried to imitate the Rolling Stones' sound. As Jane Wilson was told by one of the regulars who saw them: 'Mick Jagger should have taken out a b———y patent.' This dance hall was in the same mould as the others Jane Wilson visited. There was a veneer of mock affluence with sofas, abstract murals, and shiny black surfaces everywhere. But despite the décor it was, essentially, a place for teenagers. There was even a 'Teen Bar', serving 'cider' to teenagers, which was in fact apple juice![57]

At the Tiger's Head Dance Hall in Catford, Jane Wilson had to resist the advances of a youth who implored her: 'Come here darlin'. I know stork from butter.' But she was feisty enough to handle herself. She even danced with a young carpenter from Islington who 'shouted . . . in my ear from a range of one and a half inches'. After he had moved her around the dance floor 'in ever decreasing circles', he cheerily admitted that he was a poor dancer. Jane Wilson found that the atmosphere in the dance halls she visited was never menacing, but the teenagers were boisterous. At the Tiger's Head they were served drinks in bottles and if the bins were full they would smash the empty bottles and grind the glass into the ground.[58]

These dance halls were where most of the pop groups of Swinging London would play. At the Tiger's Head in Catford the entrance fee for a live band was just 5 shillings; and there were so many pop groups that some would be turned away by the management. The manager at the Tiger's Head, Catford, complained that there were too many pop groups in his area of London. He told Jane Wilson: 'There's so many groups it's getting ridiculous. And most of them are no use at all. We've had three in already this evening looking for work.'[59] Several of the suburban dance halls would have two bands performing in a single evening. For example, the Starlite Ballroom at Greenford had 'The Birds' and 'The Sons of Fred' on the evening Jane Wilson visited the venue.[60]

Jane Wilson's final visit was to a dance hall in Wimbledon, the Wimbledon Palais de Dance, in a suburb of south-west London. It had a resident DJ (Ed Stewart), who had a mid-Atlantic accent, wore a beard and horn-rimmed glasses and was dressed in a sawn-off dressing gown with belt. Jane Wilson visited on a Saturday night, when local groups would mime to their latest records as the DJ played them from his turntable. At a certain point in the evening, games were played. Boys sat on chairs with bibs round their necks, while girls would force crisps and bottles of 'Seven Up' down their throats. The girls were then ushered to the stage where they entered a competition to blow up and pop a balloon and the winner won a record – Manfred Mann's latest LP.[61] There were bouncers at this venue, as at dance halls elsewhere in the London suburbs. The head 'steward' at the Wimbledon dance hall was a Scot who claimed he usually only had to issue warnings to boisterous youths; but a regular contradicted him: 'No you don't mate – you give 'em one'; adding 'Jock here is very rough on the punch-up lads. He's been up here for years and he's worth a bob or two to the Palais I can tell you.'[62] When Jane Wilson chatted with girls of 16 and 17, she discovered that dance halls like the Wimbledon Palais de Danse and Streatham Locarno were the only dance halls that the girls could afford to visit. They never attended discotheques in the West End. As one girl told her: 'the West End ... clubs are too small and too dear. This place is "with-it" and so's the Streatham Locarno. We go there Tuesdays.'[63]

Even the Mods, the archetypal Swinging London youth cult, were not actually part of Swinging London at all, except at weekends.[64] There is a powerful Swinging London image of Mods spending their Saturdays shopping and posing in Carnaby Street; but it is a somewhat exaggerated image. Carnaby Street was actually a very short and narrow street. It covered a distance of just 150 yards and its whole length could be covered in a few minutes. It was also hidden and so was not really a choice venue to pose in. Jane Wilson visited it and found that, logistically, it was not a good place for a youth culture that wanted to be seen. 'Once you've been the length in your purple and yellow striped Mongolian lamb coat – that's it. Everybody has taken note, and if you hang about thereafter the proper air of nonchalance is lost.'[65] The Mods were, basically, outsiders in Swinging London. They spent most evenings in the suburbs, no doubt attending the dance halls Jane Wilson visited. They had 9-to-5 jobs and they lived with their parents. The suburban dance halls closed at 11 p.m. on weekdays. There were, it is true, some Mod venues in the West End of London – The Marquee, Tiles and a Mod café called 'Chips with Everything'. But the Mods did not attend West End discotheques. Their venues were hidden away in basements. Symbolically, there was a Mod club beneath Annabelle's nightclub in the West End; but it only served soft drinks, as Mod clubs invariably did.[66]

George Melly described the London discotheques as 'the wombs of Swinging London';[67] but this leaves a very misleading impression. All the London discotheques during the 1960s (they were introduced from France in 1962) were exclusive establishments that almost seemed designed to exclude youth culture. There were 10 London discotheques listed in *London Life* in the mid-sixties (1965) and they all charged a subscription as well as an entrance fee. The Scotch in St James' charged a membership fee of over £5 (5 guineas). In addition, there was a nightly entrance charge of 10 shillings to members and 15 shillings to their guests. The In-Place was a 'members only' discotheque and members had to be invited to become members. The Ad-Lib in Leicester Square charged over £5 for membership (5 guineas) and a nightly entrance fee of 25 shillings. Dolly's in Jermyn Street had a membership fee of 5 guineas and an entrance fee of 25 shillings. Sibylla's in Swallow Street, part-owned by the Beatles, had a membership fee of 7 guineas, and charged 30 shillings for a meal and 12s 6d for a drink.[68] Clearly, these prices were far higher than those of the dance halls in the suburbs, and the whole tone was different. People were only given access to these discotheques either if they were members or knew members. Who attended these discotheques?

A typical London discotheque attender was Lucy Bartlett, aged 24, an upper middle-class girl who lived with her parents – though in a separate flat – in St John's Wood. (Her father Sir Basil Bartlett was a writer.) Lucy had left school at 16 and then attended Chelsea School of Art and subsequently the Royal College of Art. She had no job, but instead received an allowance from her parents (of £400 a year). She told *London Life* in 1966 that she regularly visited discotheques in central London – Dolly's, the Scotch, Annabel's. She shopped at the boutiques in King's Road (an area the Mods never visited owing to the high prices charged for clothes) and she would spend, on average, £15 a week on clothes. She would pay 1 guinea to have her hair cut at Vidal Sassoon's.[69] Lucy Bartlett was one of the set known as the 'Chelsea Girls'. They all lived close to the city centre nightlife. Some had office jobs and to earn extra income did freelance work – modelling, waitressing, or clothes-designing. The typical Chelsea girl drove a car – a mini – and lived in a flat. They liked pop music, but also high culture. Lucy Bartlett regularly visited the Tate Gallery, for example. This world was very different from the suburban lifestyles of working-class youth of the period. None of them owned cars. Indeed, some Mods maintained that they only bought scooters because they could not afford cars or motorbikes. Nationally, the 17–24 age-group in Britain in 1965 comprised 15% of the population; but only 5% of them owned cars (which included second-hand cars as well as new ones). A new Mini Cooper cost £590 in 1964 and this was way beyond the pockets of most 15–24-year-olds. The average salary among this age-group was around £1000 a year in 1965. Even a modest Mini would therefore cost them over half their annual wage.[70]

How far did the pop music of the 1960s break down class barriers? It is probably a mistake to regard pop music of this, or any other, era as an egalitarian force in youth culture. Two of the most celebrated pop groups of the late 1960s, the Rolling Stones and the Pink Floyd, were both deeply middle-class pop groups and in the case of the former its two principal songwriters, Mick Jagger and Keith Richards, were far more interested in cultivating a middle-class audience and indeed endearing themselves to the bohemian upper middle-classes of 'Swinging' London than with reflecting the leisure worlds of working-class teenagers.[71] In the Beatles' songs there were all sorts of working-class characters – men from 'the motor trade'; aunties and uncles with memorable proletarian names like 'Vera, Chuck and Dave'; barbers; and, of course, John Lennon went on to write an autobiographical song called 'Working-Class Hero'. But the Rolling Stones sang about girls who were from St John's Wood and Knightsbridge ('Play With Fire'); about Elizabethan aristocrats ('Lady Jane' – about Lady Jane Grey, Jagger enunciating every word in cut-glass upper-class diction), and, in some of their most celebrated songs of the 1960s, they tried to reflect the angst of disaffected students (in 'Street Fighting Man', for example, about student protest in 1968, and 'You Can't Always Get What You Want', which refers to student demonstrations). They sang about sexually liberated bohemian youth ('Satisfaction'), or about political events that assumed quite detailed knowledge of international affairs ('Sympathy for the Devil'). Moreover, in Mick Jagger the Rolling Stones had a singer and leader who was the perfect representative of a Home Counties' bourgeois youth – a suburban middle-class upbringing (father a Physical Education Lecturer); educated at Dartford Grammar School where he gained 7 'O' levels and 2

'A' levels and, subsequently, a student at one of England's most prestigious universities, the London School of Economics.[72]

In June and July of 1967, as we will shortly discover, Mick Jagger emerged triumphantly as a charismatic, articulate, thoughtful and even intellectual youth whose image with the middle-classes of the Home Counties was transformed from fear and contempt to undoubted respect. He even agreed to be grilled on television for 30 minutes by senior Establishment figures. They included the Editor of *The Times*, and two senior theologians, representing the Catholic Church and the Church of England. He won universal admiration for his courteous manners, thoughtful and penetrating answers and, as became clear in the interview, his innate cultural conservatism.[73] In essence, the events of June and July 1967 made Mick Jagger, a 23-year-old pop star, and acquitted drug user, the youngest member of the British cultural establishment – and, coincidentally, a far less popular figure among his peers within British youth culture.

Pink Floyd emerged from the university city of Cambridge in the mid-1960s where its two founding members, Syd Barrett and Roger Waters, were school friends. Barrett, the chief songwriter, was the son of a Lecturer in Pathology at Cambridge University and the family lived in a 'large, detached ivy-clad house [which] stood back from the road'.[74] Waters was brought up by his mother, a schoolteacher. Both boys attended a public school in Cambridge (the Perse School for Boys), along with the later member and now leader of the Pink Floyd, David Gilmour. The rest of the original line-up made the Pink Floyd probably the most socially privileged British pop group in history. Nick Mason, an Architecture student, whose parents lived in a stately home in Hampstead (his father was a documentary film maker), was recruited when Roger Waters, also studying Architecture, formed the group in London in late 1964. He also recruited Rick Wright, a public-school-educated Londoner and another Architecture student; and his old friend Syd Barrett, who became the principal songwriter, lead singer and guitarist and, in December 1964 when they began playing concerts together, was studying Art at Camberwell School of Art.[75]

Cambridge was an unlikely place for a pop group to emerge during the 1960s and especially a countercultural pop group like Pink Floyd. It was a small and ancient university town, with a population of just 80,000 people, where new ideas about music, art, politics, culture and religion invariably emerged, and remained, within the cloistered setting of the university.[76] But pop culture in Cambridge did not emanate from the university. It was a fusion of 'Town' and 'Gown' and the Pink Floyd are a prime example. Although the Cambridge members of the group, Barrett and Waters (and later Gilmour), were all from privileged middle-class families, none of them attended Cambridge University. Yet they belonged to a subculture that included university students, local poets and local musicians.[77]

How one of the most innovative and revered pop groups of the 1960s took shape in a genteel city like Cambridge, with no history of pop culture before the early 1960s, is a fascinating challenge for a graduate history student to undertake a dissertation on; but, so far, the details are still sketchy. One historian has claimed that there were 'well over a hundred' pop groups in Cambridge by 1962.[78] No one else has corroborated or questioned this figure. Nor do we know what types of music these groups played. Were they beat groups playing pop? Did they include folk groups and skiffle groups and rhythm and blues groups? We do not know. We do know that the 16-year-old Syd Barrett was a member of one of these groups – and played electric guitar in 'Geoff Mott and the Mottoes'.[79] His musical heroes, at this stage, were Bo Diddley, the black blues guitarist; and, perhaps more surprisingly in the light of his later antipathy towards commercial pop music, the Beatles.[80] While the maturing songwriter Syd Barrett was simply not interested in releasing his songs as pop singles (for example, he was reluctant to let the band release two of his songs which became major hits for the group in 1967 – 'Arnold Layne' and 'See Emily Play', the latter reaching Number 6 in the Hit Parade), the teenage Barrett bought the anodyne Beatles' debut single 'Love Me Do'.[81] Moreover, he was devastated when the Beatles performed in Cambridge in 1963, and he was forced to attend an interview in London for a place at Art College on the same day.[82]

Barrett's teenage years were spent performing in a cellar coffee bar beneath the Anchor pub in Cambridge. He was a classic beatnik. He read Jack Kerouac's *On the Road*, wore skin-tight jeans and attended poetry evenings, where he learned about young poets like Arthur Rimbaud, the French symbolist, and the Cambridge poet Rupert Brooke.[83] Most of Barrett's friends were middle-class youths. Some were studying at Cambridge University (including their first manager Peter Jenner) and, collectively, they became known among their peers as 'tea heads' for avoiding pubs and only frequenting coffee bars (see Figure 5 for other Cambridge and student youth celebrities of the 1960s).[84] One of Barrett's closest friends in the mid-sixties was Mick Rock. He was studying French and German Literature at Cambridge and recalled of their mutual interest in poetry:

> I was at Cambridge studying French and German Literature . . . Being on the Left Bank of Paris doing drugs and writing wild poetry – that seemed to me what life was about. It was not about having lots of money. I was steeped in all that kind of mythology about the poets and the painters and the artists. And Syd [Barrett] became that kind of mythological figure for me – 'the divine light'.[85]

Barrett's trajectory between 1962, when he joined his first pop group in Cambridge, and 1968, when he left the Pink Floyd after writing most of the

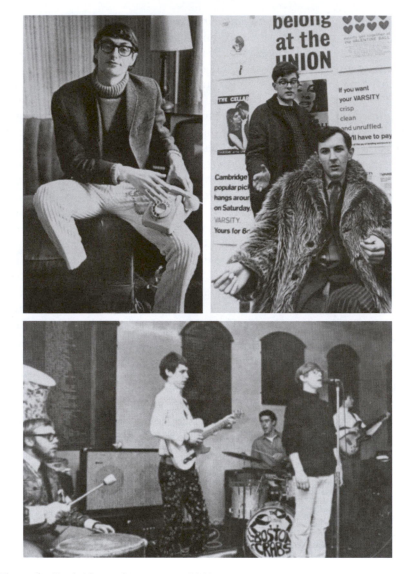

Figure 5   Cambridge student pop stars, 1966.
Source: *London Life*, 16 April 1966.

songs on their first two albums and their only singles hits of the Sixties, is not really a central aspect of 1960s' youth culture – except, perhaps, on the margins of student youth culture. The band played several gigs at university campuses during the Barrett years, for example, as well as being a resident group at the UFO club in London – a centre of the London 'Underground', which stood for 'Unlimited Freak Out'.[86] It could possibly be argued, with more research, that the Pink Floyd represent the countercultural aspects of 1960s' youth culture well. They were middle-class, uncompromisingly anti-commercial, they took drugs, they were student pop stars, they were promiscuous, and they produced both enchanting and barmy pop songs (one of Barrett's songs was about his bicycle). Unquestionably, if fleetingly, a gifted songwriter, Syd Barrett's most notable contribution to youth culture was to inspire the pop icon of the early 1970s – David Bowie.[87] But the early Pink Floyd hardly qualify as pop stars of the 1960s, with just two 'hits'. They were formed in 1964; had two hit singles in 1967 and were forced to sack their leader in 1968. They hardly benefited from youth culture at all. In 1965 they could only command a fee of £15 for a concert in London. After they had paid for their equipment and paid their manager, each member received just 25 shillings.[88]

Youth Culture and the British Establishment: The Rolling Stones drugs trial, 1967

The trial of two members of the Rolling Stones, Mick Jagger and Keith Richards, along with their friend 29-year-old Robert Fraser, an old Etonian, former Guardsman, and owner of an art gallery in London's West End, has been seen by historians and biographers as perhaps the most celebrated example of 'a generation gap' fracturing relations between youth and their elders in the Britain of the 1960s.[89] Contemporary newspapers, predictably, portrayed it as a 'conflict of generations' and academic sociologists such as Bryan Wilson agreed.[90] But when probed in more detail, using the primary sources available, it emerges that the trial aroused far more interest among the progressive middle-classes than among the young. Moreover, when the young were asked about the trial what they revealed in their statements was that there were fractures within contemporary youth culture – and these fractures were along class lines rather than between different age groups. As to Marianne Faithfull's retrospective claim that an 'Establishment' conspiracy, led by MI5, was attempting, from early 1967 onwards, to destroy the Rolling Stones – on the grounds that they were a 'decadent' pop group – it is clear that the 'official' evidence released so far suggests this is somewhat farfetched.[91]

The details of the Trial are well known. In February 1967 the *News of the World* printed a story claiming that 'Mick Jagger' of the Rolling Stones had confessed to being a drug user. (It was actually Brian Jones, the group's guitarist, who had supplied the information and passed himself off as Mick Jagger. He would also face a separate trial for drugs in May

1967.)[92] At this point, Mick Jagger, reclining in his bed with Marianne Faithfull and assiduously reading all the Sunday papers of that February day, leapt up and began to panic.[93] Jagger then issued a libel claim against the newspaper and a week later a police raid on Keith Richards' 5-bedroomed Tudor cottage, 'Redlands', in the Sussex village of West Wittering, led to the arrest of three members of the house party going on there – Jagger, whose coat pocket contained 4 amphetamine tablets that actually belonged to Marianne Faithfull; Richards, who as owner of the house was charged with allowing cannabis resin to be smoked on his property; and Robert Fraser, a cultured, Old Etonian Art Dealer who was found in possession of 24 heroin tablets. It was the most celebrated 'pop' trial of the 1960s and the only example of two supposed leaders of youth culture being sent to prison; at least for a few days, until the sentences were overturned on appeal on 31 July 1967.

The press coverage of the trial focused much attention on the opulent lifestyles of the two youth pop stars in the dock. Richards, it emerged, not only owned a large Tudor cottage in Sussex but also employed a manservant called Mohammed and his house was full of exotic furnishings – 'Would you mind stepping off that Moroccan cushion, because you're ruining the tapestries', he instructed a female police officer as she searched his house during the police raid.[94] Mick Jagger, the 'mild-mannered middle-class boy' from Dartford, as Marianne Faithfull has described him, seemed throughout the proceedings to be parading his undoubted wealth. When he was released on bail from Brixton Prison in late June, his blue chauffeur-driven Bentley collected him and then drove on to Wormwood Scrubs to collect his fellow band member Keith Richards.[95] There was much talk in the tabloids about the outfits Jagger and Richards wore during the three-day trial. 'Every day of the trial', Faithfull recalled, 'we were treated to a full fashion report in the press of what the two dandies in the dock were wearing'. She claims it was the only time she ever saw Keith Richards wearing a suit. Jagger, on the day he was finally acquitted, 31 July 1967, wore a white smock at the press conference immediately afterwards.[96]

What were the themes of the Trial? Was it an 'Establishment' conspiracy to contain youth culture? The Government files on the trial throw some light on this question. Three files were generated on the Mick Jagger/Keith Richards Drug Trial and they reveal a complete absence of interest in the threat posed to society by youth role models like the two Rolling Stones.[97] Both pop stars were only 23 at the time; but what was noted in the official files was that their fans were significantly younger – mere teenagers – if the evidence of those who attended the court hearings was representative. Thus, cuttings from *The Times* were kept; containing reports that girls tried to pull locks of hair from 'long-haired' Mick Jagger at the first court hearing in May 1967.[98] Other newspaper reports held in Government files of the case contain material that was hardly alarming to a Government Minister such as the Home Secretary – if he ever saw the files. One report noted that the crowd of 600 at Chichester comprised 'mini-skirted girls', children in school uniforms and 'middle-aged people'. Moreover, their reactions to the two young pop stars were distinctly mixed. Some screamed; some booed.[99] A cutting from a local newspaper, filed in the Metropolitan Police's records of the trial, reinforced the point that the Rolling Stones' fans were young, female and boisterous; but not a threat to anyone. All that could be observed outside the court were 'hundreds of screaming teenagers'.[100]

The details of the arrests do not support Marianne Faithfull's claim of a Government conspiracy orchestrated by MI5. In fact, it was the local police force of West Sussex Constabulary who undertook the raid on Richards' house party. The Metropolitan Police were not involved, except in giving evidence at the trial (about the effects of cannabis smoking).[101] The official Government files clearly indicate that the 'Government' – which, in reality, meant the Metropolitan Police, as no Government department produced any documentation on the Mick Jagger/Keith Richards Drug Trial of 1967 – were seemingly more interested in the trivia of the trial than its impact upon youth culture. For example, the Metropolitan Police pursued William Rees-Mogg, the new Editor of *The Times*, more zealously than they pursued either Jagger or Richards. One of *The Times*' photographers, allegedly, had taken a photograph of the trial 'within the precincts of the court'; which was illegal. The Metropolitan Police were considering bringing a case against *The Times*. Rees-Mogg himself was worried that he might be brought to trial and, through a solicitor, claimed that he was not 'on duty' on the night of the court case in Chichester. In the end, the Director of Public Prosecutions decided not to pursue the case against *The Times*; but it is not inconceivable that Rees-Mogg himself might so easily have been charged during the Mick Jagger/Keith Richards Trial and not just the two young pop stars and their friend.[102]

The *New Statesman* argued that the trial had exposed a generational fracture in British society. Its Editor proclaimed:

> it is clear from the strong feelings generated by the Rolling Stones affair that . . . we must recognise the existence of a deep division of thought and outlook, reflected in behaviour, between generations. . . . Pop singers and judges have emerged as symbols of colliding force and mass; each is identified with attitudes neither understood nor respected by the other.[103]

This does seem far too simplistic, however. What the trial had actually revealed was that most of the Fleet Street journalists who wrote about the trial supported Jagger and Richards; most famously the middle-aged, practising Catholic Editor of *The Times*, William Rees-Mogg;[104] but also *The*

Observer ('a show trial'); *The Sunday Times* ('unjustly severe') and that other organ of middle-aged Middle England *The Sunday Express*. It pronounced the original 3-month prison sentence imposed on Jagger 'monstrously out of all proportion to the offence he committed'.[105] Readers of the national newspapers were even more vociferous in support of the two young pop stars. The historian Robert Skidelsky, a Fellow of Nuffield College, Oxford in 1967, defended the two Stones in *The Guardian*, on the grounds that their privacy had been invaded and that far worse private indiscretions had not reached court; Lloyd George's adultery, for example.[106] An elderly reader from County Donegal, Ireland, wrote in to *The Daily Mail* in support of the two young pop stars, remarking: 'I am elderly and apt to recoil from pop, yet feel that the Rolling Stones were savagely dealt with.'[107] There was also support for the two pop stars among married women. A Mrs J. Smith from Birmingham asserted in *The Daily Mail*: 'This is not justice but a witch hunt' and a Mrs Smith from Kent supported young Jagger unequivocally in the same paper, stating: 'Jagger has been made the whipping boy for the sins (real or imaginary) of the whole pop scene'.[108]

One theme not explored in the press coverage of the trial was the relationship between the Rolling Stones and youth culture. During the trial an intriguing National Opinion Poll was conducted. Almost 2000 young voters (21–34-year-olds) were asked about the prison sentences imposed on Jagger and Richards (Jagger was originally given a 3-month prison sentence: Richards, a 12-month sentence). The age-groups polled were Jagger and Richards' peers. But the results would have alarmed them. Eighty-five per cent of those asked thought the sentences were either 'about right' or 'not severe enough'. Moreover, there was a strong class component to the voting. Among working-class voters in the 21–34 age-group, a majority, 56 per cent, thought that the sentences were 'not severe enough'. Among lower middle-class voters only a minority, 45 per cent, thought the sentences 'not severe enough'; and among upper middle-class voters only around a third (34 per cent) wanted the two pop stars to be given longer prison sentences. In effect, support for the two Rolling Stones was significantly higher among middle-class youth than among working-class youth.[109]

What did the trial reveal about Mick Jagger and Keith Richards' views about youth culture? It unquestionably revealed that they were detached from it. Richards described in great detail in court what it was like to be a pop star and he did not praise the band's youthful following. From 1963 onwards, he had experienced a complete lack of privacy. He was asked by the QC Michael Havers if he needed protection against fans. He replied: 'Oh, yes. I need an army.' He claimed he had been 'strangled' by one fan and had clothes stolen.[110] But his friend and bandleader Jagger gave the most revealing interviews on the Rolling Stones' relationship to youth culture. The first was an impromptu press meeting immediately after his acquittal. One journalist at the meeting asked him if he agreed with the Judge in the case that he 'was the idol of a large number of the young'. Jagger cowered and replied defensively: 'I've been given that responsibility ... pushed into the limelight.' He then denied that he was a spokesperson for youth at all: 'I don't propagate religious views, such as some pop stars do (presumably referring here to John Lennon's bold claim made in 1966 that the Beatles were bigger than Jesus Christ). He added: 'I don't propagate drug views, such as some pop stars do ...'[111]

In an extended interview Jagger then conducted with senior Establishment figures on the front lawn of a country house in Essex (the home of the Lord Lieutenant of Essex Sir John Ruggles-Brice – see Figure 6), Jagger admitted he knew nothing about youth culture. When asked the question 'What do the young people in this country really think'? he replied: 'I didn't think my knowledge was enough to start pontificating on the subject.'[112] He did not see himself, in any sense, as a spokesperson for youth, but purely as a musician. Asked how he wished to be understood by older people he replied: 'For my music. Just for playing music.'[113] As this 30-minute interview developed, it emerged that Jagger was really speaking as a libertarian who happened to be young rather than as a leader of youth culture. He complimented the older generation for its bravery in the Second World War and for surviving the Depression of the 1930s. 'Our parents', he told his inquisitors, 'went through two World Wars and a Depression. We've had none of that ... I'm sure you do your best'.[114] He admired his elders. He was in no sense an anti-adult youth rebel. Indeed, he came over to William Rees-Mogg as an extremely conservative pop star. As Rees-Mogg recalled years later: 'I thought he was one of nature's conservatives' and his views about personal responsibility were 'pure John Stuart Mill'.[115] He had no interest in empowering young people by, for example, campaigning for 18-year-olds to be given the vote (Jagger thought the vote would be wasted on 18–21-year-olds).[116] Instead, he revealed that he was largely preoccupied with his own liberty. He was asked whether drugs were 'a crime against society' and gave the classic libertarian's answer: 'It's a crime against a law. I can't see it's any more a crime against Society than jumping out of a window.'[117] His middle-aged interviewers, who all had 'clipped Oxbridge accents', found Jagger beguiling and could not trump him at all. 'So, who won?', George Melly asked. He added: 'Jagger, in my view, although largely because the opposition seemed to be sympathetic'.[118]

Mick Jagger's interview on '*World in Action*' has been described by one of his biographers as 'a kind of generational summit' and, less augustly, by George Melly as 'like a lost scene from Lewis Carroll'.[119] His inquisitors – William Rees-Mogg, the Editor of *The Times*; Father Thomas Corbishley, a Jesuit priest; Lord Stow Hill, a Labour politician and former Home

Figure 6 Mick Jagger meets members of the Establishment, 1967.
Source: Unknown

Secretary; and John Robinson, the Bishop of Woolwich– all wore suits and looked hot and crumpled as they sat in the sun. But Jagger, who arrived by helicopter, wore an open-necked smock and looked comfortable in the heat.[120] It is farfetched to see the programme as anything other than a brilliant idea dreamed up by '*World in Action*'s young producer; a 22-year-old recent Oxford graduate called John Birt.[121] It was his idea to call the programme 'Drugs, the Establishment and Mick Jagger' and it was only his determination that resulted in the programme being made.[122] Initially, Jagger was reluctant to appear and Birt had to cajole Jagger's staff to pass on his home telephone number so that he could plead with Jagger to appear.[123] He was unable to persuade any member of Wilson's Labour government to appear on the programme and so was forced to use, as his token politician, Lord Stow Hill (a 'former' Home Secretary in the Wilson Government of 1964–6).[124]

The ongoing Jagger drugs trial did not make things easy for Birt, who nervously attended Jagger's appeal hearing on 31 July not knowing whether the programme would be made or not.[125] If Jagger was sent back to prison, the programme – due to be screened the very next day, on 1 August – would have to be jettisoned. In the end, the programme was made, and screened at 9.30 p.m. on 1 August, and it was only Birt's youthful optimism that brought it to the screen. It was shown in a peak-time slot and around 30 million people watched Jagger expound his views on youth culture, British justice and the older generation.[126]

Pop stars of the 1960s were marketed as spokespersons for youth culture and no one more prominently than Mick Jagger. Stephen Jessel of *The Times* told *Times* readers: 'He is the symbol of the young generation, and the epitome of part of it ... he is in the vanguard of a movement of young people that transcends class barriers ...'[127] Some British historians of the period, most notably Arthur Marwick, argue that the pop culture of the 1960s and its youth culture were 'classless'. Kenneth Morgan, meanwhile, sees the 1960s as witnessing an abrupt transition from the 'somewhat staid palais de danse' of the 1950s to the new youth venues – the 'informal, hectic and garish discos'.[128] Both of these views of the 1960s are questionable. There was, as this chapter has demonstrated, certainly no cohesive and classless pop culture during the 1960s; at least in Britain. There were, in fact, two youth worlds even in 'Swinging London'. Firstly, there was the world of working-class teenagers; who continued to spend their leisure time in the venues that their parents and grandparents had used in the 1950s and right back to the 1930s. The 'palais de danse' were still the main meeting places for suburban working-class youth of 1960s' London, who simply could not afford to attend the 'Swinging' discotheques of London's West End. Secondly, there was a middle-class and upper middle-class youth subculture, centred on the West End discotheques, restaurants and shopping districts of West London. Thirdly, the most celebrated youth icons of the period – among them Mick Jagger and Keith Richards – were not in reality representatives of youth culture in any meaningful sense. They were physically and mentally detached from the teenagers who bought pop records – Jagger lived in a flat in Cheyne Walk, Chelsea; whilst Richards lived deep in the Sussex countryside. Moreover, their celebrated drug trial of 1967 does not demonstrate that the two had a close affinity with their teenage following. Their statements to the press, and the interview Jagger gave to members of 'The Establishment' in July 1967, reveal that these two young pop stars hardly ever thought about youth culture.

An American historian Robert Pattison has argued that the Rolling Stones' strongest cultural affinities were not with British teenagers but with bohemian literary figures of the eighteenth and nineteenth centuries.[129] There is something in this; after all, Marianne Faithfull, who lived with Mick Jagger for three years between 1967 and 1970, once said that to understand his sensibility one had to immerse oneself in the Romantic literary movements of the eighteenth century.[130] Keith Richards was even photographed by the celebrated Stones' photographer Annie Leibovitz in 1972, re-enacting the death scene of the young Romantic poet Henry Chatterton (who took arsenic in 1770 and died at just seventeen).[131] It therefore seems entirely in keeping with their literary sensibilities that when Jagger and Richards' drug trial was over in July 1967, the Rolling Stones began work on a promotional film for their new single 'We Love You' – a thank-you message to their fans (which pop critics thought was modelled too closely on the Beatles' single of the summer of 1967 'All You Need Is Love'). The subject of the Stones' film is highly revealing – a re-enactment of the Oscar Wilde Homosexuality Trial of 1895. Jagger played Oscar Wilde; who, of course, spent two years in Reading Jail after he lost the case. Keith Richards played the aristocratic Marquess of Queensberry; and Jagger's then girlfriend Marianne Faithfull played Lord Alfred Douglas. The single did not re-establish the Rolling Stones as serious rivals to the Beatles. The pop fans, in fact, saw through it and it only reached Number 8 in the Hit Parade. The band had to wait another year before they were at the top of the pop charts again with 'Jumpin' Jack Flash'.[132] It was a difficult life being a young pop star in late 1960s' Britain.

Postscript: the Spice Girls phenomenon

'Everyone, however remote from youth culture, has heard of them,' pronounced Philip Norman, biographer of the Beatles, in the *Sunday Times Magazine*. They were, he went on, 'role models for their generation'. Seventeen million copies of their records had been sold. They had had Number 1 singles in over 30 countries and they had made a film, glorifying 'a day in the life of the band'.[133] It is easy to assume that Norman was writing in the early 1960s and was describing the Beatles; but he was actually writing these words in September 1997 and was describing the most successful British pop group, commercially, since the Beatles – the Spice Girls. Though a fleeting pop phenomenon – they had their first Number 1 single in Britain in July 1996 and the original line-up disbanded in 1998 – this group of five, feisty, early twenty-something females achieved far wider commercial success than any British pop group since the Beatles. Moreover, they achieved something none of the British teen pop stars of the late '50s and early '60s did (including Cliff Richard and Tommy Steele); or indeed any of the 'Britpop' artists of the 1990s (Oasis, Blur, Pulp). They had Number 1 singles in the United States, as well as in Britain.[134] But what is their role in the history of British youth culture?

The Spice Girls were five ordinary-looking girls drifting through stage and acting schools in London in the early 1990s. David Baddiel likened them, derisively, to 'somebody you might see in Tesco's and think, "Oh, she's very attractive – for someone who works in Tesco's'.[135] Unlike the other pop groups discussed in this chapter – the Beatles, the Pink Floyd and the Rolling Stones – who emerged from friendships established between band members in school, the Spice Girls were a manufactured pop group. In February 1994 each of the five (none of whom knew each other at this point) replied to an advertisement placed in the theatre magazine *The Stage* for a girl pop group. They were selected from 400 entrants and two of them were only recruited belatedly, in May 1994, when two original members of the group dropped out.[136] They were not blessed with musical ability. None of the five could play a musical instrument. None of them wrote pop songs. None had any professional training as a singer and none had learned to dance. They were chosen by a record producer for their 'all-round ability and personality'.[137] The idea was a good one: to produce a girl group that could displace the ubiquitous 'boy bands' of the era – Take That, Boyzone, East 17 and others – in the hearts of the young females who bought pop records.[138]

The band hardly blazed a trail at the beginning. They were formed in May 1994 and did not secure a recording contract until May 1995. Their first hit single, 'Wannabe', was released a year later in July 1996.[139] From the beginning, they were marketed as a 'girl' group – somewhat misleadingly as the youngest, Emma Bunton, was 20 at the time 'Wannabe' was in the charts and the eldest, Geri Halliwell, was 24. Moreover, the concept used to market them – 'Girl Power' – was also somewhat misleading, given that all their hit singles were written by four male songwriters: Richard Stannard and Matthew Rowbottom ('Wannabe', '2 Become 1', 'Mama', 'Spice Up Your Life', 'Viva Forever') and Paul Wilson and Andy Watkins ('Who Do You Think You Are?', 'Stop', 'Too Much').[140] But commercially, for two years, they were unbeatable. 'Wannabe' reached Number 1 in 22 countries and was Virgin's biggest-selling single for 13 years. It sold over a million copies in Britain and 22 million worldwide. Indeed, in terms of singles' sales, the Spice Girls were the most successful British group since the Beatles. Their first five singles reached Number 1 in the British pop charts. Eight of their nine singles went to Number 1 and both their albums did so. 'Wannabe' was a Number 1 in the United States and the most successful British debut single in America since the Beatles.[141]

But these raw statistics say nothing about their cultural significance. In America they were never taken seriously as a cultural phenomenon as the Beatles and the Rolling Stones were. The serious American music magazine *Rolling Stone*, founded in the mid-1960s to acknowledge the intellectual and cultural weight of the Rolling Stones, dismissed the Spice Girls as: 'attractive young things ... brought together by a manager with a marketing concept'.[142] In Britain the serious broadsheet press patronised them. Simon Sebag Montefiore, a Cambridge-educated historian of Russian High Culture, mocked their dress-sense and general appearance in the Christmas issue of *The Spectator* for 1996: 'A Spice Girl may have the thighs and hot pants of a feeble hussy, but she possesses the heart and soul of a Tory country squire,' he wrote sardonically.[143] Kathy Acker, cultural critic for *The Guardian*, described them sniffily as: 'not from the educated classes';[144] and there were many other examples of metropolitan snobbism, such as Emma Forest's observation in *The Independent* that: 'No matter how glossy the tunes, the girls always look like they have hangovers' and her caustic comment referring to their cheap make-up: 'You can tell that their make-up is Maybelline rather than Yves Saint Laurent.'[145]

The Spice Girls were really young female entrepreneurs rather than pop stars. They endorsed all sorts of merchandise – Spice Girl trainers, dolls, keyrings, cameras, pillows, blankets, body spray, hats, calendars, mugs and a video game entitled 'Spice World: The Game'.[146] Within weeks of having their first hit record, they had written a Guide Book for their fans called *Girl Power*.[147] The idea for the book came from the oldest and most articulate member of the group, Geri Halliwell. By no means a bimbo (she was educated at Watford Grammar in North London), and possessing a caustic wit (she described the laddish Mancunian pop group Oasis as 'The Spice Girls in drag'), Geri Halliwell was the obvious brains of the group and from the beginning played a central role in the shaping of the group's image. Indeed, she claims she even came up with the name for the Spice Girls.[148] Precisely what 'Girl Power' meant has been probed at a somewhat abstract level by cultural studies' academics, and one recent academic essay on the Spice Girls describes it thus: 'Like the capitalist feminism of mainstream women's magazines that it reworks and revisions, girl power ultimately de-historises feminist politics.'[149] Geri Halliwell defined it far more cogently as: 'It's like feminism – but you don't have to burn your bra.'[150]

Whether Geri Halliwell was well informed about feminism, however, is a moot point; as she had a slippery grasp of British politics. Undoubtedly, as Sebag Montefiore discovered, Halliwell was politically a Conservative. She described Margaret Thatcher, memorably, as 'the first Spice Girl'; but she told another interviewer that she admired Margaret Thatcher because 'she was the first woman ever in the government'.[151] It seems that the safest way to examine what 'Girl Power' meant is to consider what the Spice Girls meant by the term.

It was quite an elastic concept, and had to be as their audience and record buyers ranged from pre-teens to sexually-active young women in their late teens and early twenties. The concept began as a marketing strategy; a catchy phrase which may have meant nothing, but might have the desired effect of weaning female record buyers from loyalty to the commercially very successful 'boy bands' of the mid-1990s. These groups had such a grip on the charts in 1996 that when the Spice Girls' first single reached Number 1 it replaced a song by former Take That singer Gary Barlow and kept another song by a former Take That singer, Robbie Williams, at Number 2.[152] Moreover, the Spice Girls' trumping of the 'boy bands' was a decisive moment in mid-1990s' pop history. Their first single remained at Number 1 for seven weeks.[153] It seems doubtful, as some cultural studies' scholars have suggested, that the Spice Girls were incipient feminists wanting to create more gender equality in society. Indeed, their manual *Girl Power* sets out a series of contradictory statements on 'Girl Power' rather than a coherent feminist ideology. Thus, members of the group define 'Girl Power', vaguely, as 'The future is female', 'Girls should follow their destiny etc.'[154] But what this Spice Girls manifesto does reveal is the differences in outlook within the group. One member, 'Mel B', who was from Leeds in Yorkshire, thought 'Girl Power' basically meant advocating anti-social behaviour. 'If you want to stand up and say Aaaargh then do it,' she informed the Spice Girl reader; adding: 'You decide the kind of life you want to lead.'[155] In an earlier generation, this spontaneous shrieking would have been called Situationism.

Geri Halliwell, the book reveals, was not interested in promoting such a vacuous and imprecise term as 'Girl Power'. What she wanted to promote was social equality. Young people of both sexes, she argues, should aspire to have proper careers. She gives the rather farfetched example of a boy of 16 going to his School Careers Officer and saying he wanted to be an astronaut. Geri Halliwell assumed he would be told to stop being stupid. But her advice was for the Careers Officer as much as the boy: 'The Careers Officer should say: "OK, then. First, you'll have to learn about astrophysics".'[156] Geri Halliwell seems to be saying here that all young people, regardless of their gender, need dreams. It is interesting that she sees further education as the best way of achieving something, for the school leaver, and not pop music. We can sense, from the example she gives, that she was going to leave pop music behind (she left the group in 1998). In fact, she went on to work as an Ambassador for the United Nations.[157]

It is doubtful that the Spice Girls have shaped British youth culture in any meaningful sense. How could they have done so? They lasted about eighteen months in their original 5-member form and by late 1997, just one year after their breakthrough single, they were touring and singing to 7- and 8-year-olds accompanied by their parents – both in the United States and in Britain.[158] It must have been the case that parents, rather than teenagers, were responsible for the Spice Girls' phenomenal global success commercially. They bought much of the merchandise and the concert tickets, and accompanied pre-teenage girls to the concerts.[159] As their prime following by the end of 1997 was among pre-teenage girls, it could be argued that the group's image was not exactly wholesome. A middle-aged mother might be alarmed at a 12-year-old daughter listening to 'Wannabe', which instructs a boyfriend on what to do if he wants to be a lover; or at having to explain to her daughter what the phrase 'Zig-a-zig-ahh' meant. It was assumed in the music press to be a reference to sex; but the teen magazine *Smash Hits* could only bring itself to admit that it had something to do with 'a cigar'.[160] At least one of the group had worked in the adult entertainment industry before becoming a young pop star; Geri Halliwell had been a glamour model.[161] Their songs were infused with sexual references. Indeed, Emma Bunton ('Baby Spice') claimed in an interview in the *New Musical Express* that they always tried to include sexual references in their songs.[162]

It appears, finally, that the legacy of the Spice Girls, a phenomenally successful pop group – even when compared with the most successful pop groups of the 1960s such as the Beatles and the Rolling Stones[163] – seems uncertain. A BBC Radio 5 Live Programme celebrating ten years of the Spice Girls, due to be broadcast in July 2006 (ten years after 'Wannabe' reached Number 1 in the British charts), had to be abandoned due to lack of interest in the group. Few people know that the first word of 'Wannabe', the song they will be most remembered for, is an Anglo-Saxon word that appeared in the medieval poem Beowulf – 'Yo'. But, apart from this song with its catchy lyrics, the group's music was highly derivative. One of the most melodic of the group's hit singles was the ballad '2 Become One'; which sounded uncannily like the Bee-Gees' song 'How Deep is your Love?' and still reached Number 1. For a few seconds in the chorus of '2 Become One', even a person over thirty can appreciate the appeal of the Spice Girls; as the song, so reminiscent of the sublime Bee-Gees' ballad from the film 'Saturday Night Fever', transports you back to the dark glamour of the late Seventies' disco. It has a magical tune; but to describe it as wholly original and sublime would be overstating the case. Perhaps more than anything, the Spice Girls reveal that there are, essentially, two types of pop group – manufactured pop groups and organic pop groups and the former (The Monkees, the Archies and the Spice Girls being among the most successful) are always forgotten; or merely treated with indifference, years later.[164] Who cared, for example, when the Monkees, a very successful American pop group of the 1960s unashamedly modelled on the Beatles, split up? Who even knows when the Monkees split up? But everyone who has followed pop music since the 1960s remembers when the organic pop groups split up – the Beatles, most famously, in 1970; the original Pink Floyd with Syd Barrett in 1968, and the Rolling Stones seemingly never.

Conclusions

The chronological focus, and content, of this study point towards a fundamental revision of what historians ought to study when writing about youth culture. In the 1960s it became fashionable for middle-aged politicians like the late William Deedes, then a Conservative Cabinet Minister, and for middle-class 'with it' journalists and academics – from George Melly to the conservative sociologist Bryan Wilson – to write about the 'new' youth culture that they observed in Britain and linked with the 'rise' of the teenager; the emerging pop world of 'Swinging London'; and the student revolutionaries creating havoc in British, European and American universities. But these authorities on the 'new' youth culture were not historians and they have misled both historians and sociologists into thinking that youth culture is a product of the 1950s and 1960s.[1]

It did not help that the founders of Cultural Studies, Professor Richard Hoggart, Stuart Hall, and others, were not historians either and they too perpetrated an ahistorical approach to youth cultures and youth subcultures that skewed the subject towards the analysis of working-class youth and narrowly conceived concepts such as the 'resistance' of working-class youth to control – using cults like the Skinheads and Mods as prime examples.[2] Much of this research is so devoid of serious scholarly analysis as not to merit detailed engagement with. Moreover, the idea that modern youth culture is what goes on in girls' bedrooms is interesting; but hardly has a bearing on how youth culture has evolved across a whole century in Britain; and, in any case, this micro-sociological analysis of youth culture never engages with the idea that youth culture might have a longer and, frankly, more glorious history.[3] Even the perceptive Richard Hoggart's thoughts on youth culture are, as Chapter 6 demonstrated, impressionistic, superficial and based on a flawed understanding of the roots of youth culture in British society; a development which emerged in his own lifetime and which as a pioneering Professor of Cultural Studies at Birmingham University he ought to have devoted some time to tracing before offering his thoughts on it – both in print and before Government Committees.[4]

This book has shown that the pioneers of youth culture in Britain were not teenagers, or Beatles fans, or Teddy Boys; but a small group of university students in the early 1920s led by the charismatic, articulate, and hyperactive youth enthusiast Rolf Gardiner; a student at St John's College, Cambridge, from 1921 to 1924. Indeed, Chapter 2 suggested that Cambridge, more than any other British university over the twentieth century, has been the crucible of youth culture as a body of ideas and as something that mattered. It is true that this early expression of youth culture was shaped by elite youth; but the crucial point is that these elite youths were not elitists and through various means they sought to develop their version of youth culture, or new 'ways of living' as they envisaged it, both across Britain and across Europe and further afield.

Admittedly, there is then a hiatus in the story of British youth culture which leaves the period from the late 1930s down to the early 1950s, the era of the Teddy Boy, a void. In some ways, it was the long gap in the visibility of youth culture between the 1930s and the early 1950s – from the era of student youth cultures in the 1920s and of teenage consumers in the towns and cities during the 1920s and 1930s to the appearance of the Teddy Boy in 1953 – that produced a form of collective amnesia in British society after the Second World War. When the teenage culture of late 1950s' London began to be noticed, by critics like Colin MacInnes and George Melly, it was a full twenty years since anything like it had been seen on Britain's streets; and in the era of 'austerity' and rationing that survived in Britain until well into the 1950s people simply forgot about the earlier generations of youth who had been the 'first teenagers' and, in the universities, the pioneers of youth culture as a way of life. Moreover, these myths of the novelty of 'postwar youth' still survive in the works of reputable historians.[5]

There is thus no linear history of youth culture in twentieth-century Britain; but it is clear from this survey that its roots lie in the 1920s and not in the 1950s or the 1960s. Gender historians will argue with the central implication of this work: that the history of youth culture in twentieth-century Britain has been largely shaped by male youth – though the Flapper cult of interwar Britain is a notable example of a female youth cult that spread organically via dance halls, cinema, retail outlets, and magazines to all classes of female youth. But, as argued in Chapter 3, the Flapper cult was primarily a culture of aspiration rather than an expression of youth culture as a distinctive culture exclusively for young people under, say, 25. Flapperdom was all about looking youthful rather than belonging to a particular age-group and it did not have the inner coherence structured by age that the student youth culture of the 1920s had.

This work has revealed that historical and sociological analysis of youth culture during the 1960s is based on a false premise: that pop culture was an expression of youth culture. This is a gross oversimplification and, as Chapters 7, 8 and 9 sought to argue, several aspects of the youth culture of the 1960s need to be rethought. First, the Mods were not products of affluent, 'Swinging London'; but were marginal to the world of 'Swinging London'. Second, the Beatles were not in any meaningful sense a reflection of youth culture during the 1960s. Their appeal was chiefly to pre-teenage girls. Third, the 1960s were not an era of classless youth cultures in Britain. On the contrary, class cultures survived and were clearly visible to contemporaries who looked hard for them; even in the quintessential classless and 'swinging' city, London.[6] Fourth, the evidence available suggests that working-class youth were alienated by the representations of youth culture made in speeches by middle-class pop stars like Mick Jagger; and, to working-class youth in Liverpool, the Beatles' dalliance with hippie values in the late 1960s was too much to bear.[7]

This study has concentrated on reviewing a mass of new and unexploited primary and secondary material on the history of youth culture, asking new questions and advancing new arguments on the history of youth culture. It now seems clear that central to that history are the youths of the middle-classes, who have hitherto been neglected in existing historical work on the subject.[8] So, historians who wish to take this story further will need to read not only the rich archival collections available in universities on the roots of British youth culture but also the novels that these creative student youths published; their essays and reflections in student periodicals; and what they discussed in their student debates, minutes of which survive for debating societies such as the Cambridge Union and Oxford Union.

If this study has one overall conclusion it is that youth culture developed in Britain over the course of the twentieth century by organic means – through word-of-mouth, domestic and foreign travel, cultural contact between elite youths and working-class communities, Mods observing each other and their outfits in suburban dance halls, countercultural youth pop groups like the Pink Floyd learning their repertoire in the basement of a Cambridge pub, and so on. Youth culture, in other words, is not merely an offshoot of mass culture – the cinema, the dance hall, teenage magazines like *Jackie* and *Just Seventeen*. Its inner life lies in places that we might least expect to find it – in universities situated in medieval cities, in prosaic postwar suburbs like Streatham in London and in the basement cellars of provincial cities like Cambridge.

Appendix

Rolf Gardiner: Chronology of His Early Life and Youth Activities, 1902–34

1902:	Born in London: son of Alan Henderson Gardiner, Egyptologist, and Hedwig (née von Rosen)
1913–1916:	West Downs Preparatory School, Hampshire
1916–1918:	Rugby, boys' public school
1918–1921:	Bedales, progressive, co-educational school, Wiltshire
1921–1924:	Read Modern Languages at St John's College, Cambridge; Editor of *Youth: an Expression of Progressive University Thought* (1923–4)
1922 (September):	Organised an English Folk Dance Tour to Germany.
1923 (August):	Attended a North European Youth Assembly at Hellerau (near Dresden), Germany.
1924 (June):	Established the Cambridge Morris with Arthur Heffer, a Cambridge bookseller, and toured the Cotswolds; establishes contact with German Youth Movements ('Bunde').
1925:	Becomes 'Gleemaster' of Hargrave's Kibbo Kift Kindred and its European Representative; resigns July 1925.
1926:	'Travelling Morrice' tour to Europe, visits Germany and the Baltic States (June and July); German singers visit Britain and tour southern England (September and October); attends a North European Youth Leaders' Conference in Germany (October); organises a 'Midwinter' hike from Somerset to London (December).
1927:	Folk song and dance tour to Graz, Austria (January); organises a work camp in Hermannsburg, Germany (Easter); folk dance tour to Holland with English and German singers and dancers (August); a German Youth Group visit England and go on an expedition to Northumberland (September); visits Holland to teach folk dance (October); moves to Gore Farm, Dorset (November).
1928:	Attends music festival in Graz (February); attends a work camp with 'peasants', workers and students in Lowenberg,

	Silesia, Germany (March); 'Travelling Morrice' tour to Germany (June and July); organises a tour of England for a group of German singers (der Deutscher Singkries) (October).
1929:	Attends music festival in Graz (February); a work camp in Lowenberg, Germany (March); organises a folk dance school in Sedburgh, Yorkshire (Whitsun); attends a 'Festival of Baltic Youth' at Tallin in Estonia (June); teaches at a Summer School for English and Germans in Ostmark, Germany (August); begins teaching folk dance at the Musikheim, a College for the Arts in Eastern Germany (October).
1930:	Attends work camps in Germany at Lowenberg (February) and Frankfurt on the Oder, Eastern Germany (April); organises a folk dance school at Sedburgh, Yorkshire (June); organises a tour for German singers and English dancers to Ostmark (August); begins to plan a Baltic tour to Estonia, Finland and Sweden (September and October).
1931:	Visits the Musikheim to teach folk dance and attend a work camp for a German Youth Movement (the Deutsche Freischar) (January–March); organises an 'Easter Reunion' at the Musikheim for English dancers and players and German singers; teaches folk dance at Sedburgh, Yorkshire (June); attends a 'Nordic' folk dance festival with the English Folk Dance Society (EFDS) in Copenhagen (July); organises a German singers and English dancers tour of Yorkshire (August and September); organises an Anglo-German production of Shakespeare's *A Midsummer Night's Dream* at the Musikheim, Eastern Germany (October).
1932:	Organises the first English work camp at Cleveland, Yorkshire (April); organises his first 'Baltic Tour' with English singers to Denmark, Finland, Estonia, and Sweden (August and September).
1932 (September):	RG marries Marabel Hodgkin, daughter of Stanley Hodgkin, a Quaker manufacturer from Reading, and Florence Hodgkin, a devout Quaker and author of cookery books, including *Hints to Marabel* (1934); a cookery and advice book written specifically for her daughter shortly after her daughter's marriage. The marriage service was at Southwark Cathedral, London; miners from the north-east of England attended the wedding.
1933:	Moves to Springhead, a farm in Fontmell, Dorset (September); organises a 'Midwinter' work camp at Springhead (December).

1934:   Establishes the Springhead Ring, a group of 50 of RG's friends, to promote 'the social arts'; organises a Harvest Camp at Gore Farm (August and September); the Gardiners produce a play, 'St George', a 'masque', and perform it at Iwerne Minster, Dorset (September); organises a work camp at Springhead (December).

Source: Rolf Gardiner Papers, Cambridge University Library.

Appendix

2 Tables

Table A1. YMCA membership in Ireland, 1920–1

Branch	Membership	Members who served in the First World War
Northern Ireland:		
Belfast (Wellington Place)	350	350
Mountpottinger (East Belfast)	108	55
Ballymena	59	25
Bessbrook	10	1
Enniskillen	35	35
Londonderry	283	109
Omagh	67	35
Mid-Ireland:		
Dublin	199	250
Dublin (Ringsend)	20	50
Dublin (Rathmines)	55	20
Ballinasloe	20	26
Carlow	7	10
Dundalk	20	25
Moneygall	34	8
South Ireland:		
Cork	98	58
Ennis	8	4
Listowel	14	19
Tralee	20	8
Waterford	236	50

Source: Returns of Local YMCA Associations, D3788/2/1, P.R.O.N.I.

Table A2.   YMCA membership in Ireland, 1935*

Branch	Boys under 14	14–18	18+	Girls	Total
Balleymoney	–	4	46	–	50
Banbridge	–	1	33	–	34
Belfast (East)	60	50	200	50	310
Belfast (City)	125	230	1550	–	1905
Belfast (Shankill Road)	82	90	200	35	372
Carrickfergus	–	–	125	18	125
Enniskillen	10	18	68	–	96
Londonderry	–	108	371	22	479
Omagh	–	10	71	–	81
Bessbrook	8	23	20	–	51
Cork	10	35	201	–	246
Dublin (Rathmines)	–	3	40	–	43
Balbriggan	–	–	23	–	23
Carlow	–	4	28	3	32
Clara	–	–	30	–	30
Ennis	–	–	12	–	12
New Ross	–	2	27	–	29
Kilkenny	16	–	64	–	80
Sligo	–	35	45	–	80

* The Figures are as documented in the original membership lists. Some totals do not add up as in some figures the data on 'girls' has not been included.
Source: Survey of Local Associations, 1935 (for King George's Jubilee Trust), YMCA Papers, D3788/2/2, P.R.O.N.I.

Table A3.   Mountpottinger (East Belfast) YMCA membership, 1921–7

Year	Emigrated	Deceased	Total membership
1921	1	4	100
1922	–	–	
1923	4	2	
1924	1	1	
1925	2	–	
1926	1	–	
1927	–	1	84
Total 'Lost'	**9**	**8**	

Source: Mountpottinger YMCA, Members' and Associates' Subscription Register, 1921–1927, D3788/4/4/2, P.R.O.N.I.

Table A4.   Mountpottinger (East Belfast) YMCA, 1921–7: Destination of young emigrants

Name/Age	Destination	Year
David Coulter 18+	Canada	1924
R. W. Charlesson 18+	Whitehead	1925
John Hipkins 18+	USA	1927
H. Hunter 18+	Dublin	1926
Jas H. Latta 21+	London	1925
S. Jardine u18	Dublin	1925
N. G. Leeper 18+	–	1926

(Continued)

Table A4.   (*Continued*)

Name/Age	Destination	Year
E. Monday 21+	England	1926
R. Morrison 18+	America	1925
R. J. Murphy u18	USA	1925
D. Mackenzie 21+	Glasgow	1927
E. Rainey 18+	England	1925
W. Tollens 18+	Bangor (County Down)	1922
S. A. Wilson 18+	Canada	1922

Source: Mountpottinger YMCA, Members' and Associates' Subscription Register, 1921–1927, D3788/4/4/2, P.R.O.N.I.

Table A5.   Juvenile crime in Northern Ireland, 1946–69*

Year	Number found guilty (all offences)
1946	1635
1947	1683
1948	2081
1949	2067
1950	2407
1951	2645
1952	2717
1953	2514
1954	2799

(Continued)

Table A5. (*Continued*)

Year	Number found guilty (all offences)
1955	2948
1956	3407
1957	2908
1958	3757
1959	3749
1960	3778
1961	3664
1962	3252
1963	3412
1964	2355
1965	2512
1966	2382
1967	2372
1968	2414
1969	2101

* 'Juveniles' denotes under-17s from 1950; under-16s before that date.
Source: Reports on the Administration of Home Office Services, 1952–71.

Appendix

3 Students in British Universities, 1964–8

1964	138,700
1965	169,500
1966	184,800
1967	199,300
1968	203,000

Source: National Archives, Kew, CAB 151/67.

Appendix

Chronology of the British and International Student Revolt, May and June 1968

Late April/EarlyMay

Student occupation at Columbia University, New York, 993 students arrested.

May

7–12   Revolt of 30,000 Paris students.

13   Student occupation of the Sorbonne begins. Lasts over a month.

23/24   LSE student 'sit-in' in sympathy with French students, 150 participate.

28–   Student occupation at Hornsey College of Art, North London (continues throughout June).

June

7   A 'Free University' demonstration in Cambridge.

11   Daniel Cohn-Bendit, the French student leader, arrives in Britain.

11–13   Student occupation at Hull University, 300 students participated.

12   Filming for BBC TV programme '*Students in Revolt*', 12 international student leaders interviewed at BBC TV Centre, White City, London. Daniel Cohn-Bendit participates.

13   Debate in Parliament (House of Commons) about Cohn-Bendit's visit, 33 Conservative MPs sign a motion 'deploring' Cohn-Bendit's visit to Britain.

13   Daniel Cohn-Bendit visits LSE for a 'teach-in' on 'Student Power'.

        BBC TV Programme '*Students in Revolt*' shown on BBC1 at 9.05 p.m. Lasts 50 minutes.

14   Launch of Revolutionary Socialist Students' Federation (RSSF) at LSE. Cohn-Bendit not present.

15   Daniel Cohn-Bendit leaves Britain for Frankfurt.

15–16	Committee of Vice-Chancellors and Principals (CVCP) Meeting at Downing College, Cambridge, to discuss Student Protest.
17	Bristol University student 'sleep-in'.
19	House of Lords Debate on Student Unrest.

Sources: The Times, The Daily Telegraph, The Guardian, The Observer.

Notes

Notes to the Preface

1. The Last Poets, 'The Revolution Will Not Be Televised' (1968). I owe this reference to my friend Professor Paul Remley of the University of Washington, USA.
2. A. J. P. Taylor, *A Personal History* (London, 1983), ch. vii; for Taylor's Manchester essay see idem., *Essays in English History* (London, 1976), ch. 31. The quotation is on p. 307.
3. See Chapter 9.
4. Dominic Sandbrook, *Never Had It So Good: A History of Britain from Suez to the Beatles* (London, 2005), pp. 475, 675–8, briefly discusses Beatlemania; and an earlier study by two sociologists, S. Hall and P. Whannel, *The Popular Arts* (London, 1964), touches on the subject. But contemporary periodicals such as the *New Statesman*, *The Spectator* and *The Listener* debated the Beatles' positive and negative impact on teenagers far more extensively. See below, Chapter 9 for the contemporary debate on the cultural impact of the Beatles.
5. My earlier monograph *The First Teenagers: The Lifestyle of Young Wage-earners in Interwar Britain* (London, 1995), based on extensive archival research for the interwar years, explored the burgeoning youth culture of industrial cities such as Manchester – and thus is, technically speaking, a study of youth culture *well* before the Beatles. Selina Todd's recent study *Young Women, Work, and Family in England, 1918–1950* (Oxford, 2005), a meticulously researched exploration of young wage-earning women between the Wars, largely focuses on their work environment and familial relationships, but see ch. 7 on 'Leisure and Courtship'. Dominic Sandbrook, *Never Had it So Good,* ch. 12 is very incisive and entertaining on 'The Teenage Consumer', though it contains no original archival research. B. Osgerby, *Youth in Britain since 1945* (Oxford, 1998), lacks the intellectual bite of Sandbrook's study and is often superficial; Adrian Horn, 'Juke Boxes and Youth Culture in Britain, 1945–1960', Ph.D. thesis, University of Lancaster (2004), is both original and scholarly, though, as yet, unpublished.
6. See Chapter 1.
7. K. Götsch-Trevelyan, *Unharboured Heaths* (London, 1934). For further discussion of Kathleen Trevelyan see Chapter 2 below.

Notes to the Introduction

1. T. Parsons, 'Age and Sex in the Social Structure of the United States' (1942), reprinted in his *Essays in Sociological Theory* (New York, 1954),

pp. 89–103. For Parsons, youth culture meant 'having a good time: often in the company of the opposite sex' (p. 92). His discussion was restricted to American college and high school students. Wilson's essays on youth culture originally appeared in an array of newspapers and popular weeklies, including *The Daily Telegraph* (August 1964), *The Guardian* (November 1964), *The Observer* (March 1967), *The Spectator* (April and September 1966) and *New Society* (February 1966). For him, the term meant Mods and Rockers, university students, hippies, juvenile delinquency and the Age of Majority. The essays are reprinted in B. Wilson, *The Youth Culture and the Universities* (London, 1970).

2. See Chapter 6.
3. Ibid.
4. H. Butterfield, *The Discontinuities between the Generations in History: Their Effect on the Transmission of Political Experience* (Cambridge, 1971).
5. J. H. Plumb, 'Secular Heretics', in his *In the Light of History* (London, 1972), Pt. II, ch. 1. The sociologist Bryan Wilson was also fascinated by American Hippies and spent a year at the University of California, Berkeley, in 1966–7, during which he wrote an article for *The Observer* on the Hippie culture; reprinted in Wilson, *Youth Culture and the Universities*, ch. 13. The author is currently undertaking new research on 'Cambridge Historians and the Swinging Sixties'.
6. See, for example, P. Abrams, 'Rites de Passage: the Conflict of Generations in Industrial Society', *Journal of Contemporary History*, Vol. 5, No. 1 (1970), pp. 175–90.
7. *Spectator*, 7 February 1969, p. 172; 14 February 1969, p. 208. Brogan was shocked by the free mixing of the sexes at Cambridge by the late 1960s, recording: 'I am mildly shocked when I see young women entering Trinity College Cambridge at eleven o'clock at night ... ways of life which were not open to me forty years ago.'
8. For Elton's and other Cambridge reactions to youth culture and student protest during the 1960s, see below, Chapter 8.
9. Between 1961 and 1971 the number of British households with a television set rose from 75 per cent to 91 per cent and, during the 1960s, a typical household spent 20 hours a week watching television. See M. Donnelly, *Sixties Britain: Culture, Society and Politics* (London, 2005), p. 77.
10. For the best contemporary study of Beatlemania, see M. Braun, *'Love Me Do!': The Beatles' Progress* (1964; reprinted London, 1995). See also D. Sandbrook, *Never Had it So Good: A History of Britain from Suez to the Beatles* (London, 2005), pp. 475–7, 675–7, and see below, Chapter 9.
11. D. Sandbrook, *White Heat: A History of Britain in the Swinging Sixties* (London, 2006), pp. 215–16.
12. Sandbrook, *Never Had it So Good*, p. 676.
13. See Chapter 7.
14. See Chapter 7.
15. For a discussion of the Beatles and British youth culture, see Chapter 9.
16. See Chapter 8.
17. See Chapter 8.

18. Personal information from a former LSE Professor.
19. See *The Times*, 1 August 1967, p. 6 and for a discussion of the Mick Jagger drug trial of 1967, see below, Chapter 9.
20. On the period 1900–39, see especially the work of Elizabeth Roberts, Andrew Davies and more recently Selina Todd. The latter particularly takes issue with the thesis developed in the present author's monograph *The First Teenagers: The Lifestyle of Young Wage-earners in Interwar Britain* (London, 1995), that a homogeneous, commercialised youth culture had emerged in British cities such as Manchester and London by the late 1930s. See especially, S. Todd, 'Young Women, Work and Leisure in Interwar England', *Historical Journal*, Vol. 48, No. 3 (September 2005), pp. 789–809. For a new angle on this debate, the Flapper cult of interwar Britain, see below, Chapter 3. For a more recent challenge to my earlier thesis of interwar youth as 'the first teenagers', see B. Beaven, *Leisure, Citizenship and Working-Class Men in Britain, 1850–1945* (Manchester, 2005), ch. 5, who argues that Late Victorian and Edwardian youths enjoyed very similar lifestyles to interwar 'teenagers' – 'Substitute the cinema for the music hall, and in the late nineteenth century you have a broadly similar male youth leisure profile' (p. 176). This is not really convincing as there was no unemployment benefit system before 1911 to shield young male workers from having to support their families during periods of economic depression; meaning that their disposable incomes in the earlier period would have been significantly lower than in the interwar period. Also, the leisure supply between the Wars was far more directed towards young wage-earners than in the earlier period and the thousands of dance halls that opened after 1919 (see Chapter 3) are clear evidence of a far more youth-orientated leisure world than the Victorian and Edwardian era of music halls. Finally, the real wage improvements for adult males, and for juveniles, between 1918 and 1939 are beyond dispute and helped fuel the emergence of a modern teenage lifestyle only after 1918. See J. Stevenson, *British Society, 1914–45* (1984; reprinted Middlesex, 1986), ch. 4; S. G. Jones, *Workers at Play: A Social and Economic History of Leisure, 1918–1939* (London, 1986), and Fowler, *First Teenagers*, ch. 4 and Appendix, Table 4.3, p. 182 on young male workers' vastly improved wage rates between 1906 and 1935. For historians who stress the uniqueness of youth culture during the 1950s and 1960s, see especially A. Marwick, *The Sixties: Cultural Revolution in Britain, France, Italy and the United States, c.1958–c.1974* (Oxford, 1998), Pt II, ch. 3, and B. Osgerby, *Youth in Britain since 1945* (Oxford, 1998).
21. See, in addition to the authors cited in note 20, the work of John Springhall on British youth movements of the early twentieth century, Stephen Humphries and Victor Bailey on juvenile and youth delinquency, Claire Langhamer on young women's leisure and courtship, and Penny Tinkler on young females and cigarette smoking.
22. See Chapter 2.
23. See Chapter 3.
24. See Chapter 7.
25. See Chapter 2.

26. The phrase was coined by Rolf Gardiner, a pioneering figure in early twentieth-century British youth culture. See below, Chapter 2.
27. For an exploration of class, region, income and changes in work patterns as influences on the Flapper cult of interwar Britain see below, Chapter 3.
28. One fascinating aspect of youth creativity during the period 1920–70 not dealt with systematically in this study, and one on which further historical research is needed, is the undergraduate novel. A spate of these novels appeared in the early 1930s and they have never been used by historians to shed light on the preoccupations of student youth during the 1930s. See, for example, I. McCartney, *Break of Day* (London, 1932), a novel about student life in Cambridge.
29. For the best introductory survey of British youth movements of the period, see J. Springhall, *Youth, Empire and Society: British Youth Movements, 1883–1940* (London, 1977). For the fortunes of the lads' and girls' club movement, as well as more conventional uniformed movements, with young wage-earners of the interwar years, see Fowler, *First Teenagers*, ch. 6.
30. See Chapter 9.
31. The writer J. B. Priestley was one of these Ex-Service students. He went to Cambridge in 1919 and recalled: 'by the time I went up to Cambridge in the Michaelmas Term of 1919, I was a man not an overgrown boy, already in my twenty-sixth year and a battered old soldier. I wanted to get on with my life and not clown around with lads newly released from school and given their first chequebooks.' See *New Society*, 26 November 1965, p. 823; for a fuller discussion see below, Chapter 2.
32. See below, especially Chapters 2–5, 7–8.
33. A. Marwick, 'Youth in Britain, 1920–1960: Detachment and Commitment', *Journal of Contemporary History*, Vol. 5, No. 1 (1970), p. 37.
34. See Chapters 3, 4, 6 and 7.
35. For an investigation of the 'secret world' of premarital sex before the 1960s, see S. Humphries, *A Secret World of Sex: Forbidden Fruit: The British Experience, 1900–1950* (London, 1988).
36. John Lennon's comment in a radio interview, not authenticated.
37. See Chapter 6.
38. Ibid.
39. See, for example, Osgerby, *Youth in Britain since 1945*, p. 42; P. Hewitt (ed.), *The Sharper Word: A Mod Anthology* (London, 1999), pp. 107–11. A. Sinfield, *Literature, Politics, and Culture in Postwar Britain* (Berkeley and Los Angeles, 1989), pp. 169–71, discusses MacInnes's teenager novel *Absolute Beginners*.
40. Colin MacInnes was born in South Kensington on 20 August 1914. His father, a Scot, was a professional singer and his mother, Angela Thirkell, a novelist. He described himself as 'an "English", London-born, Australian-reared Scot'. MacInnes's first essays on teenagers and pop music were published in 1957 and 1958 when he was in his early forties. For biographical details and a useful discussion, see T. Gould, *Inside Outsider: The Life and Times of Colin MacInnes* (London, 1983), pp. 15, 126–8, 138.

41. T. Gould (ed.), *Absolute MacInnes: The Best of Colin MacInnes* (London, 1985), pp. 10–13; Gould, *Inside Outsider*, ch. 3.
42. See C. MacInnes, 'Out of the Way', *New Society*, 3 January 1963, p. 21: 'The figures ... in *Absolute Beginners* are all emblematic ... never to be found intact in actual life.'
43. He did, however, use newspaper reports of attacks on black youths that appeared in the late '50s, as material for his novel *Absolute Beginners*. See Gould, *Inside Outsider*, pp. 134–5.
44. Sandbrook, *Never Had It So Good*, p. 324: 'the narrator (an unnamed sixteen-year-old) is not merely implausible but also downright irritating ... and the whole thing comes over as a relatively feeble pastiche of *The Catcher in the Rye*'.
45. MacInnes's weekly column 'Out of the Way' appeared in *New Society*'s first issue on 4 October 1962 (p. 19) and ran continuously throughout the 1960s and on into the 1970s. He also wrote many incisive articles on cultural topics for other periodicals.
46. See M. Abrams, *The Teenage Consumer* (London, 1959); M. Abrams, *Teenage Consumer Spending in 1959* (London, 1961).
47. Abrams's market research approach to complex social and cultural trends was subjected to a rigorous and damning attack by the late historian Raphael Samuel. See, R. Samuel, 'Dr Abrams and the End of Politics', *New Left Review*, 5 (September–October 1960), pp. 2–9.
48. See especially, Fowler, *First Teenagers*, ch. 4, and Osgerby, *Youth in Britain since 1945*, pp. 24–6.
49. Much of the sociological work on youth subcultures has focused, in any case, on post-1960s developments, which are not the focus of this study. For an introduction to the work of the cultural studies researchers based at Birmingham University, see S. Hall and T. Jefferson (eds), *Resistance Through Rituals: Youth Subcultures in Postwar Britain* (London, 1976).
50. A. Davies, *Leisure, Gender and Poverty: Working-Class Culture in Salford and Manchester, 1900–1939* (Buckingham, 1992), ch. 4; S. Todd, *Young Women, Work and Family in England, 1918–1950* (Oxford, 2005), especially chs 2 and 7; S. Todd, 'Young Women, Work and Leisure', *Historical Journal, passim*; C. Langhamer, *Women's Leisure in England, 1920–60* (Manchester, 2000), ch. 3.
51. See below, Chapter 2.
52. Fowler, *First Teenagers*, chs 4 and 5; Sandbrook, *Never Had It So Good*, ch. 12; Osgerby, *Youth in Britain since 1945*, ch. 4.
53. See below, Chapter 5.
54. On urban gangs see, in addition to Pearson's and Humphries' work, A. Davies, 'Street Gangs, Crime and Policing in Glasgow during the 1930s: the case of the Beehive Boys', *Social History*, Vol. 23, No. 3 (October 1998), pp. 251–67. On the Mod culture of the 1960s, see below, Chapter 7.
55. On the idea of the student protests of the 1960s as an attempt to create new communities, see C. Crouch, *The Student Revolt* (London, 1970), and see below, Chapter 8.

56. For discussion of these points, see below, Chapter 7.

57. See, for example, I. McCartney, *Break of Day* (1932), on student life in interwar Cambridge.

58. See Chapter 2.

59. See Chapter 4.

60. See Chapter 2.

61. But see Marwick, *The Sixties*, which utilises student periodicals; though not for Britain.

62. P. Jephcott, *Girls Growing Up* (London, 1942); P. Jephcott, *Rising Twenty: Notes on some Ordinary Girls* (London, 1948); P. Jephcott, *Some Young People* (London, 1954); F. Zweig, *The Student in the Age of Anxiety: A Survey of Oxford and Manchester Students* (London, 1963).

63. See below, Chapters 2 and 9.

64. Of all the historical works cited above, only Osgerby discusses middle-class youth. See Osgerby, *Youth in Britain since 1945*, ch. 7. This chapter comprises a conventional, thought-provoking, but media-driven and cursory analysis of post war countercultures beginning with the Beats (mostly focusing on the United States), and touching on the Hippies (mostly on the US Hippies), student protest (in less than two pages), the 'Underground' movement of late '60s London, the Oz Trial etc. and ending, strangely, with a discussion of football hooliganism in the 1970s and 1980s.

65. For Cambridge's role in youth culture during the period covered by this survey, see below, Chapters 2 and 9.

66. See Chapter 2. pp. 37, 41. The huge influx of working-class, Ex-Service students into British universities in 1919 is totally neglected in R. McKibbin, *Classes and Cultures: England, 1918–1951* (Oxford, 1998). He discusses the 'Fisher Act', but overlooks this key aspect of it. See ibid., pp. 206–9.

67. See below, Chapter 2.

68. See Osgerby, *Youth in Britain since 1945*, for a wide-ranging discussion of post-World War Two youth cults such as the Teenager and Teddy Boy; J. Street, 'Youth Culture and the Emergence of Popular Music', in T. Gourvish and A. O'Day (eds), *Britain since 1945* (London, 1991), ch. 14; J. Street, 'Youth Culture', in P. Johnson (ed.), *Twentieth-Century Britain: Economic, Social and Cultural Change* (London, 1994), ch. 26.

69. For the middle-class students who developed youth culture in Britain during the 1920s see below, Chapter 2; for middle-class pop groups of the 1960s see below, Chapter 9. For the information on 'Keane', see the website www.keaneshaped.co.uk/faq/.

70. A. J. P. Taylor, *A Personal History* (London, 1983), chs VII–VIII, for his Manchester years (1930–8).

71. H. R. Trevor-Roper, *Archbishop Laud* (1940; reprinted London, 1965): H. R. Trevor-Roper, *The Last Days of Hitler* (1947; reprinted London, 1995).

72. The author is currently undertaking research on the Cambridge Garden House riot of 1970 for a wider project on 'Cambridge Historians and the Swinging Sixties'.
73. On the King and Country debate of 1933, see M. Ceadel, 'The "King and Country" Debate, 1933: Student Politics, Pacifism and the Dictators', *Historical Journal*, Vol. 22, No. 2 (1979), pp. 397–422.
74. For details of Artur Axmann, see Trevor-Roper, *Last Days of Hitler*, p. 220; I. Kershaw, *Hitler, 1936–45: Nemesis* (London, 2000), pp. 812–13.
75. For a pioneering study of European youth cultures which explores the cultural movements of youth, and especially the role of university students in developing youth culture in mainland Europe, see A. Schildt and D. Siegfried (eds), *Between Marx and Coca-Cola: Youth Cultures in Changing European Societies, 1960–1980* (Oxford, 2006). For Rolf Gardiner's important role as a prime mover in the development of youth culture in Britain, and beyond Britain, between the Wars, see below, Chapter 2.

Notes to Chapter 1: Edwardian Cults of Youth, c.1900–1914

1. S. Brigden, 'Youth and the English Reformation', *Past and Present*, 95 (May 1982), pp. 36–67.
2. S. R. Smith, 'The London Apprentices as Seventeenth-Century Adolescents', *Past and Present*, 61 (November 1973), pp. 149–61.
3. Brigden, 'Youth and the English Reformation', p. 37.
4. S. E. Morison, *Harvard College in the Seventeenth Century, Part II* (Cambridge, MA, 1936), pp. 446–7.
5. M. J. Childs, *Labour's Apprentices: Working-Class Lads in Late Victorian and Edwardian England* (London, 1992), ch. 6. He stops short, however, of arguing that there was a youth culture and does not consider female youth at all. See ibid., p. 134.
6. Cited in H. Hendrick, *Images of Youth: Age, Class, and the Male Youth Problem, 1880–1920* (Oxford, 1990), p. 121.
7. The best historical treatment of this medley of Edwardian diatribes is H. Hendrick's, *Images of Youth*, especially chs 3 and 5.
8. For biographical details on Charles (C. E. B.) Russell, see David Fowler, *The First Teenagers: The Lifestyle of Young Wage-earners in Interwar Britain* (London, 1995), p. 118, and V. Bailey, *Delinquency and Citizenship: Reclaiming the Young Offender, 1914–1948* (Oxford, 1987), pp. 10–11, 329.
9. A. Freeman, *Boy Life and Labour: The Manufacture of Inefficiency* (London, 1914), pp. iv–xi.
10. Ibid.
11. Ibid.
12. Ibid., pp. 110–11.
13. Ibid., pp. 116–17.
14. Ibid., p. 117.
15. Ibid.

16. Ibid., pp. 111–12.
17. Ibid., p. iii.
18. Ibid., pp. 154–6.
19. Ibid., p. 156.
20. Ibid.
21. Ibid.
22. Ibid., pp. 158–9.
23. Ibid., p. 154.
24. Ibid., p. 155.
25. Ibid., pp. 112–14.
26. Ibid., p. 155.
27. Ibid., p. 113.
28. Ibid., p. 141.
29. Ibid., p. 157.
30. Ibid., pp. 199–205.
31. On the myths about 'blind-alley work' and a detailed discussion of the labour market behaviour of juveniles in interwar Britain see Fowler, *First Teenagers*, ch. 1. On the Edwardian debate see Hendrick, *Images of Youth*, pp. 58–64, and Childs, *Labour's Apprentices*, ch. 3.
32. Freeman, *Boy Life and Labour*, pp. 204–5.
33. Ibid., pp. 169–70.
34. Fowler, *First Teenagers*, ch. 1 and Table 3.4, Appendix, p. 179.
35. For details of Cyril Jackson's survey see Hendrick, *Images of Youth*, pp. 55–6; Freeman, *Boy Life and Labour*, p. 203.
36. Ibid., p. 204.
37. Ibid.
38. Ibid., p. 76.
39. Ibid., pp. 110–19.
40. Ibid., p. 113.
41. Ibid., p. 112.
42. Ibid., p. 110.
43. Ibid., pp. 212–23.
44. Ibid., pp. 217–18.
45. Ibid., p. 222.
46. Ibid., pp. 110–19; Brigden, 'Youth and the English Reformation', pp. 43–51.
47. Freeman, *Boy Life and Labour*, pp. 110–19.
48. Brigden, 'Youth and the English Reformation', pp. 49, 55–8.
49. Freeman, *Boy Life and Labour*, ch. VII; Brigden, 'Youth and the English Reformation', p. 49.
50. For the lives of young wage-earners between the Wars, see Fowler, *First Teenagers*, ch. 4. On the disorientating effects of National Service on Glasgow youths in the 1950s see T. Ferguson and J. Cunnison, *In Their Early Twenties: A Study of Glasgow Youth* (Oxford, 1956), pp. 31–2.
51. Brigden, 'Youth and the English Reformation', p. 49; Smith, 'Apprentices as Seventeenth-Century Adolescents', p. 149.

52. M. N. Keynes, *The Problem of Boy Labour in Cambridge* (Cambridge, 1911), pp. 8–9.

53. Ibid., p. 20.

54. Ibid., pp. 4–5, 8.

55. Ibid., p. 7.

56. J. Mortimer-Granville, *Youth. Its Care and Culture: An Outline of Principles for Parents and Guardians* (London, 1880).

57. Ibid., p. 74.

58. Ibid., pp. 95–6.

59. Ibid., pp. 96–7.

60. Ibid., p. 121.

61. Ibid., p. 123.

62. Ibid., pp. 95–6, 99.

63. See E. Pethick-Lawrence, *My Part in a Changing World* (London, 1938), ch. IV, for her years at the West London Mission. The author, a prominent suffragette before the First World War, was also a youth worker at the West London Mission during the 1890s. She claimed it was for factory girls 'of the roughest class' and there is some evidence to support this. A number of members had vandalised the club's furniture in the 1890s (ibid., p. 73). Her husband was Frederick William Pethick-Lawrence, a Labour politician, suffragist and Financial Secretary to the Treasury in the Labour Government of 1929–31. The club's founder was Mrs Price Hughes, an admirer of Mazzini and the Young Italy movement, and a socialist. She ran the club for over fifty years, from 1887 to 1937 (ibid., p. 72).

64. Ibid., pp. 79, 84.

65. Ibid., pp. 80–1.

66. Ibid., pp. 81–2.

67. Ibid., pp. 84–5.

68. F. Kidson and M. Neal, *English Folk Song and Dance* (Cambridge, 1915), pp. 168–9.

69. Ibid., pp. 162–3.

70. Ibid., p. 163.

71. Ibid.; Pethick-Lawrence, *Changing World*, pp. 135–6.

72. Ibid., pp. 138–9.

73. Ibid., pp. 135–6, 138–9.

74. Ibid., p. 136.

75. Ibid., p. 139.

76. See below, Chapter 2.

77. See Federation of Working Girls' Clubs, London, *A Handbook in Club Work* (London, 1921), p. 78. There were many working girls' clubs outside London. The *Handbook* lists clubs operating in Birmingham, Bradford, Bristol, Brighton, Glasgow, Hampshire, Hull, Kidderminster, Leeds, Liverpool, Manchester, Middlesbrough, Nottingham, and Sheffield (ibid., pp. 27–8).

78. Ibid.

79. See below, Chapter 2.
80. D. Reynolds (ed.), *Christ's: A Cambridge College over Five Centuries* (London, 2004), Introduction (pp. ix–xvi).
81. Front cover of an issue of the *Daily Telegraph*, June 2006.
82. On Rupert Brooke, see especially P. Delany, *The Neo-Pagans: Friendship and Love in the Rupert Brooke Circle* (London, 1987). Jon Savage's discussion of Brooke in *Teen Age: The Creation of Youth Culture* (London, 2007), pp. 108–12, draws heavily on Delany.
83. See N. G. Annan, 'The Intellectual Aristocracy', in J. H. Plumb (ed.), *Studies in Social History: A Tribute to G. M. Trevelyan* (London, 1955), ch. VIII.
84. Ibid., pp. 262, 264, 284.
85. Details of the Trevelyan family tree are in Annan, 'Intellectual Aristocracy', p. 259.
86. See D. Cannadine, *G. M. Trevelyan: A Life in History* (London, 1992).
87. For biographical details of Rupert Brooke see Delany, *Neo-Pagans*, ch. I; on his years as a student at King's College, Cambridge, see Delany, *Neo-Pagans*, chs I–III; C. Hassall, *Rupert Brooke: A Biography* (London, 1964), chs IV and V. On Oscar Browning see I. Anstruther, *Oscar Browning: A Biography* (London, 1983).
88. On the homosexual ethos of King's in the Edwardian period see Delany, *Neo-Pagans*, pp. 17–18. On D. H. Lawrence's visit to Cambridge in 1915, see www.britannia.com.
89. Delany, *Neo-Pagans*, p. 39.
90. Ibid., p. 241, note 20. For a history of the Cambridge Apostles see W. C. Lubenow, *The Cambridge Apostles, 1820–1914: Liberalism, Imagination, and Friendship in British Intellectual and Professional Life* (Cambridge, 1998).
91. Delaney, *Neo-Pagans*, pp. 31–4.
92. See Delany, *Neo-Pagans*, photographs between pp. 174 and 175.
93. On Edward Carpenter, see Delany, *Neo-Pagans*, pp. 9–13, 39–40. On Abbotsholme, see ibid., pp. 12–13. Abbotsholme opened in 1889. Reddie, a bachelor, became its Headmaster. The school specialised in promoting cooperation rather than competition and it taught practical subjects like country pursuits as well as academic subjects. Every member of the school had to wear a simple uniform of Norfolk jacket made from grey tweed; knee breeches, thick socks and strong boots. It was a single-sex, boys' school for boys of 11 to 18 and its chapel and grounds had many statues of naked boys. Reddie openly gave the boys lessons in sex education. Moreover, in the summer they had compulsory nude bathing in the local river. Hardly surprisingly, many parents withdrew their boys from the school because of rumours about what went on there. Indeed, when Reddie retired in 1923 there were only three pupils still at the school. One of the boys withdrawn was Lytton Strachey, though he was removed on health grounds.
94. Delany, *Neo-Pagans*, p. 40.

95. Ibid., pp. 42, 50–1.
96. For a discussion of the production see Delany, *Neo-Pagans*, pp. 43–7; F. Spalding, *Gwen Raverat: Friends, Family, and Affections* (London, 2001), ch. 9.
97. Delany, *Neo-Pagans*, p. 43.
98. Ibid., p. 45.
99. Ibid.
100. See below, Chapter 2.
101. On Rolf Gardiner see below, Chapter 2. On Rosamond Lehmann at Cambridge see S. Hastings, *Rosamond Lehmann* (London, 2002), ch. 3. On Cambridge's role in the Swinging Sixties see below, Chapter 9.

Notes to Chapter 2: Rolf Gardiner, Cambridge and the Birth of Youth Culture between the Two World Wars

* I presented an earlier version of this chapter to the Modern British History Research Seminar at the University of Oxford in May 2004. I am grateful to Dr John Davis of Queen's College, Oxford, and Dr Ross McKibbin of St John's College, Oxford, for providing me with this opportunity, and to the participants for their comments.

1. The following chapter draws on Rolf Gardiner's extensive archive held in Cambridge University Library. The papers have been held there since 1990, but few historians have used them. The author is preparing a full-scale, scholarly biography of Gardiner provisionally entitled *The Youth Apostle: A Biography of Rolf Gardiner*. The best introduction to the life of Rolf Gardiner is Andrew Best's edited volume, A. Best (ed.), *Water Springing from the Ground: An Anthology of the Writings of Rolf Gardiner* (Shaftesbury, Dorset, 1972). Several historians have written about Rolf Gardiner. Until very recently, the historical literature largely focused on his role in the development of a proto-fascist movement in Britain during the 1930s. See especially R. Griffiths, *Fellow Travellers of the Right: British Enthusiasts for Nazi Germany, 1933–39* (Oxford, 1980), *passim*; G. Boyes, *The Imagined Village: Culture, Ideology and the Folk Revival* (Manchester, 1993), ch. 7; D. Matless, *Landscape and Englishness* (London, 1998), passim; A. Bramwell, *Ecology in the 20th Century: A History* (Yale, 1989), *passim*; T. Harrod, *The Crafts in Britain in the 20th Century* (Yale, 1999), pp. 160–2; P. Wright, *The Village that Died for England: The Strange Story of Tyneham* (London, 1995), chs 12 and 13. For a new emphasis on his pioneering ideas on agriculture see R. J. Moore-Colyer, 'Back to Basics: Rolf Gardiner, H. J. Massingham and "A Kinship in Husbandry" ', *Rural History*, Vol. 12, No. 1 (2001), pp. 85–108; R. J. Moore-Colyer, 'Rolf Gardiner, English Patriot and the Council for the Church and Countryside', *Agricultural History Review*, vol. 49 (2001), pp. 187–209. For Rolf Gardiner's ideas on youth movements see R. Moore-Colyer, 'A Northern Federation? Henry Rolf Gardiner

and British and European Youth', *Paedagogica Historica*, Vol. 39, No. 3 (June 2003), pp. 305–24, and especially M. Chase, 'North Sea and Baltic: Historical Conceptions in the Youth Movement and the Transfer of Ideas from Germany to England in the 1920s and 1930s', in S. Berger, P. Lambert und P. Schumann (eds), *Historikerdialoge: Geschichte, Mythos und Gedachtnis im deutsch-britischen kulturellen Austausch 1750–2000* (Vandenhoeck and Ruprecht, 2002), pp. 309–30. I am grateful to Malcolm Chase of the University of Leeds for sending me a copy of this chapter.

2. See D. Fowler, *The First Teenagers: The Lifestyle of Young Wage-earners in Interwar Britain* (London, 1995), for a revisionist interpretation. For studies that emphasise the 'uniqueness' of the post-1945 period in the development of youth culture in Britain see especially A. Marwick, *The Sixties: Cultural Revolution in Britain, France, Italy and the United States c.1958–c.1974* (Oxford, 1998); B. Osgerby, *Youth in Britain since 1945* (London, 1998).

3. See especially, Griffiths, *Fellow Travellers of the Right*; Boyes, *The Imagined Village*, ch. 7; Matless, *Landscape and Englishness, passim*; and, more recently, D. Stone, *Responses to Nazism in Britain, 1933–1939* (Basingstoke, 2003).

4. Copies of *Youth: An Expression of Progressive University Thought* (1920–4) are held in Cambridge University Library at T200.b.2. The British Library also holds copies.

5. On Harold Acton and Brian Howard see M. Green, *Children of the Sun: A Narrative of Decadence in England After 1918* (1976; reprinted London, 1992).

6. Rolf Gardiner to Arthur Heffer, 1 April 1931, Rolf Gardiner Papers, Cambridge University Library (CUL), J3/7.

7. *The Eagle: College Magazine* (St John's College, Cambridge), Vol. LXV, No. 278 (June 1972), p. 65.

8. Rolf Gardiner Diary, Vol. 7, Part 7, January–February 1923, CUL.

9. Rolf Gardiner's correspondence with Arthur Heffer is at J3/7, CUL. The longest letter is the last from RG to AH, dated 1 April 1931. Heffer died at just 31 in 1931, shortly after Rolf Gardiner had written to him with his reflections on their youth movements of the Twenties.

10. Arthur Heffer to Rolf Gardiner, October/November 1925. Heffer wrote candidly: 'I wish to God that Lawrence (who is a great man) had never been born – he's ruined your prose, and you think in terms of D.H.L. all the time.'

11. See especially Shama's scholarly, but ostentatiously written book, *Landscape and Memory* (London, 1995).

12. Rolf Gardiner published a large number of articles and reviews during his Cambridge years and these cover literature, folk dance, youth movements, and religion. Many of his early articles are in A5/1: Press Articles etc. 1922–1923 and A5/2: Press Articles etc. 1923–1930. He wrote several essays on German youth movements. See especially, R. Gardiner, 'German Youth Movements', *Youth*, March 1923,

pp. 202–3; R. Gardiner, 'Young Germany', *The Gownsman*, 24 November 1923; R. Gardiner, 'The Revolt of Youth in Germany', *The Nation*, 1924 – copies of which are in A5/1, CUL. He later published an article on German youth movements in *The Times Literary Supplement*. See Rolf Gardiner, 'The Outlook of Young Germany', *Times Literary Supplement*, 18 April 1929, A5/2. Rolf Gardiner also gave talks on German youth movements at Cambridge; for example, at St John's College, Cambridge, in November 1923 he spoke for over an hour and to 'a large crowd'. This talk was very well received. The *Cambridge Gownsman* described it as 'a vigorous address'. See *Cambridge Gownsman*, 3 November 1923, p. 9, and also p. 11 under 'College Notes'. It is important to stress that his publications files in the CUL are not comprehensive, and seemingly dramatically underrecord his prodigious journalism in his early twenties. As he put it himself: 'Heaven knows what happens to my articles . . .' A5/1: Press Articles etc. 1922–1923.

13. A. L. Rowse, *Politics and the Younger Generation* (London, 1931), ch. 1. Rowse argued that Germany had a youth culture in 1931, which was being developed by middle-class youths who were intensely nationalistic; but Britain did not have one. He thought youth culture was a good thing, noting: 'It is . . . essential to form our own outlook, to build up our own fabric of experience, to construct a system of thought, so that those coming after may have something to look to' (p. 25). He seems to have been unaware that Rolf Gardiner was devoting all his energies to developing youth communities in Britain and in Germany. Nor does he refer to Gardiner or his pioneering journal *Youth*.

14. T. Winslow and F. P. Davidson (eds), *American Youth: An Enforced Reconnaissance* (Harvard, 1940), Foreword. Roosevelt wrote of Rolf Gardiner's contribution to the volume: 'The essay by the Young Briton indicates remarkable foresight and an indomitable spirit in England' (p. xi). The subject of Rolf Gardiner's essay ('The Battle Dress Generation Must Win the Peace', pp. 207–10) was work camps for the young unemployed; a subject Eleanor Roosevelt was directly involved with in the United States. See, for example, R. A. Reiman, *The New Deal and American Youth: Ideas and Ideals in a Depression Decade* (Georgia, 1992).

15. See Catalogue of the Rolf Gardiner Papers, prepared by Kathleen Cann, CUL.

16. F. Trentmann, 'Henry Rolf Gardiner (1902–1971)', in B. Harrison (ed.), *Oxford Dictionary of National Biography* (*ODNB*), Vol. 21 (Oxford, 2004), pp. 427–9.

17. Rolf Gardiner's ideas on youth movements are explored in Chase, 'North Sea and Baltic: Historical Conceptions in the Youth Movement'. Moore-Colyer's article 'A Northern Federation? Henry Rolf Gardiner and British and European Youth' only discusses Rolf Gardiner and the Kibbo Kift Kindred. His recent articles on Rolf Gardiner's rural affairs suggest that Gardiner had progressive views on agriculture during the 1930s. See Moore-Colyer, 'Back to Basics: Gardiner, Massingham and "Husbandry" '; Moore-Colyer, 'Rolf Gardiner, the Church and Countryside'.

18. Moore-Colyer describes Rolf Gardiner as 'one of the most original thinkers among the interwar ruralists'. This is likely to mislead historians who do not know Gardiner's metropolitan origins. The central point about his profile during the 1930s is that he had reinvented himself as a 'ruralist'. A weakness of Moore-Colyer's work is that he draws too uncritically on Gardiner's autobiographical writings, which are highly distorted and historically inaccurate. Describing Gardiner as a 'ruralist' is as narrowly conceived as describing Sir Edward Grey, the British Foreign Secretary in 1914, as a fly fisherman. See Moore-Colyer, 'Rolf Gardiner, the Church and Countryside', p. 187. Chase, meanwhile, argues that Rolf Gardiner's cultural roots were German as 'most of his early childhood was spent in Berlin'. See M. Chase, 'Rolf Gardiner: an Interwar, Cross-Cultural Case Study' in B. J. Hake and S. Marriott (eds), *Adult Education between Cultures* (Leeds, 1992), p. 226. This, again, is misleading. His father, an eminent English Egyptologist, held a post in the Kaiser Friedrich Museum in Berlin before the First World War, but Gardiner was educated by nannies and subsequently at schools in England. He never attended a school in Berlin. See above, pp. 34–7. for his schooling.

19. On his parents' house in Holland Park see R. Gardiner, *North Sea and Baltic: An Autobiographical Record of the Younger Generation in 1926–32* (typescript, 1969), ch. 1, CUL, A2/10/3. The typescript is not paginated.

20. Ibid.; Rolf Gardiner Diary, Vol. 7, Part 7, January–February 1923. Rolf Gardiner was a voracious reader of English novels at Cambridge, even those by writers he could not abide such as Virginia Woolf. After reading *Jacob's Room* in early 1923, he described her in his diary as 'a Cambridge intellectualist' and her book as 'a mere trick'. He described Cambridge thinkers as 'metallic' after hearing R. B. Braithwaite, a Cambridge don, describe Cambridge philosophers as 'metallists'. Rolf Gardiner did not clarify what he meant by the term 'metallic', but he seems to have dismissed a large number of Cambridge minds for having this vice; among them J. M. Keynes, Lowes Dickinson (both Fellows of King's College), E. M. Forster, I. A. Richards and Bertrand Russell. Patrick Wright suggests that H. J. Massingham, the rural writer, also used the term in articles he wrote for the periodical *New Age*. Gardiner was an avid reader of *New Age* in the early Twenties so he may have stolen the term from Massingham. Massingham was referring to agricultural machinery made from metal and used the term 'metallic' to mean modern, or technologically advanced. Gardiner seems to have used 'metallist' and 'metallic' to mean 'brainy'.

21. *The Times*, 8 November 1902; photographs in Rolf Gardiner Papers, 'Miscellaneous Family Papers', B5/2, CUL.

22. For his nanny's reports on his progress at school see 'K.B.' (Kathleen Boileau) to Mrs Gardiner, 13 October 1912; 'K.B.' to Mrs Gardiner, 22 February 1914, B5/2, CUL.

23. Rolf Gardiner's letters to his parents from West Downs are full of references to the Scouts. See B3/2/1–19: Letters to Parents from West

Downs, Winchester, 1913; B3/3/1–33: Letters to Parents, 1914. For his parents' concern over his lack of work see RG to Parents, 11 October 1914, in B3/3/, and for the centrality of scouting to the West Downs curriculum see RG to Parents, n.d. October 1914?, B3/3. On his Scout-leader Roland Phillips, see RG to Parents, 27 February 1916; RG to Parents, 16 July 1916, B3/5: 'It is very sad', he wrote in his letter of 16 July 1916, on hearing of the death of his teacher.

24. On RG's war work scrubbing floors at Euston Station see Roland Phillips to RG, 24 May 1916, C1/1/1–13: West Downs letters, 1916–1922, CUL. Phillips told him the work was valuable: 'It is the scout who is not ashamed to scrub a floor that one day will rule an Empire.' Gardiner, however, never showed the slightest interest in the Empire; though he did want Britain to defeat Germany in the War. See Rolf Gardiner, Diary, 13 April 1918: 'Latest news better tonight. Allies regain lost ground'. RG, Diary, Vol. 2, 1918 (April–June), CUL.

25. 'K.B.' (Kathleen Boileau) to Mrs Gardiner, 13 October 1912, B5/2.

26. Rolf Gardiner to Parents, 14 November 1915, B3/4.

27. On being chastised for having an Austrian mother see Rolf Gardiner to Parents, 15 November 1914, B3/3; on telling his parents to 'Be Prepared' see RG to Parents, 5 November 1912, B3/1, and RG to Parents, n.d. October/November 1913?, B3/2, and for the same advice to his nanny see RG to 'Kathleen' (Boileau), 3 September 1914, B3/3; for further Scout references, see B3/1 *passim* and B3/3 *passim*; on the Boy Scouts and Empire see Rolf Gardiner to 'Kathleen' (Boileau), 3 September 1914, B3/3.

28. RG to Parents, 8 February 1917, B3/6.

29. RG to Mother, 18 March 1918, B3/8. For his new interest in horti-culture see RG to Parents, 13 May 1917, B3/6; 20 May 1917, B3/6; on driving in a Morgan sports car, RG to Parents, 7 September 1917, B3/6; on his new hobby of life-drawing see RG to Parents, 28 October 1917, B3/6. RG was doing farmwork in aid of the War effort in 1918. He worked alongside some German prisoners on the farm at Rugby and was employed as an interpreter. See RG to 'Uncle Balfour' (Gardiner), 15 April 1918, B3/8.

30. For his comments on G. K. Chesterton's *Short History of the English People* see RG to Parents, 24 February 1918, B3/8. On his interest in Finland, see RG to Parents, 12 May 1918, B3/8. On his interest in European affairs, see RG to Parents, 10 February 1918, B3/8.

31. On the relaxed ethos of Bedales see RG to his Parents, B3/9/1–39: 1919, *passim*. The school was so relaxed it let Rolf Gardiner take several lessons when his teacher was absent. He gave a series of lectures on Guilds, Economics, French History 'from the beginning', Cromwell and the English Civil War, and the French Revolution. RG to Father, 30 May 1920, B3/10. On the lack of discipline and absence of competition between pupils see RG to Parents, 31 October 1920, B3/10. On the freedom for male and female pupils see Rolf Gardiner, *David's Sling*,

Book I. For his 'English' essays see the file C1/7/3: 'English Essays, 1919'.

32. See the essay on 'Modern Drama', dated 10 October 1919, C1/7/3.

33. Ibid. The essay is not paginated.

34. RG to Parents, 9 February 1919, B3/9.

35. Fisher's figures are corroborated by the Board of Education's official statistics on the Ex-Servicemen's scheme. See *Report of the Board of Education, 1919–1920* (London, 1921), Cmd. 1451, p. 82. In total, 27,643 Ex-Service students entered British universities in 1919 and they all received state grants for fees and maintenance amounting to £225 a year. Cambridge took more of them than any other university, absorbing 1,726 ex-soldiers in 1919; closely followed by Oxford, which took in 1,519. Only one other British university took more than a thousand (Liverpool), and Manchester, another major provincial university, took just 705. For the numbers in individual universities see ibid., Table, p. 83. Ross McKibbin fails to mention the Ex-Servicemen's scheme in his chapter on 'Education' in *Classes and Cultures: England, 1918–1951* (Oxford, 1998), but it had a major demographic effect on the universities, especially Oxford and Cambridge, quite apart from the cultural effect on the student body. For Fisher's comments see H. A. L. Fisher, *An Unfinished Autobiography* (1940), p. 114. On the influx of Ex-Service students into Cambridge University, most from working-class backgrounds, see 'Report by Universities on the Ex-Servicemen's Higher Education Scheme, 1920 (National Archives, Kew, ED 47/16). See especially the suggestive evidence cited by various Cambridge colleges. For example, the Senior Tutor at Trinity Hall reported that the vast majority of Ex-Service students there were from working-class backgrounds and 'created a fusion of types . . . a decided benefit to college life'; the Provost of King's College recorded that several Ex-Service students there were 'from very humble circumstances'; and at Fitzwilliam Hall, Cambridge, where almost half its undergraduates at Easter 1920 were Ex-Service students (110 out of 256 students), the college tutor reported that 'many [were] from homes which would not be ordinarily thought of in this connection'. He even claimed, intriguingly, that the Ex-Service students scheme had brought to Cambridge students from regions of Britain that had never previously sent students to the university. (Sadly, he did not identify these regions).

36. RG to Parents, 14 December 1919, B3/9.

37. His Oxford interview in late 1919 is recalled in his unpublished autobiographical work 'Wisdom and Action in Northern Europe: a Chronicle of Youth' (1944), p. 16. The details of where he was placed in the Brackenbury Scholarship competition are in R. Gardiner, *David's Sling: a Young Man's Prelude, 1918–1925*, his unpublished autobiographical novel (started in 1924 and completed in 1967), Book I, p. 26. He was one of four Bedales pupils (all male) to try for Oxford in 1919 and all failed to win places. See RG to Parents, 11 October 1919, B3/9.

38. Rolf Gardiner's subsequent folk dance tours to Europe were meticulously planned months in advance, but his period of travel between leaving Bedales and starting at Cambridge was purely experimental and unplanned. Early in January 1921, he sat in his bedroom in Holland Park, West London, closed his eyes and whirled a pencil round a map of Europe, sticking it into the map and finding it had lodged in Carinthia (in Austria). He ran down to his father's study, told his father he needed to borrow £35 for a nine-month trip to Europe and he left London the same month for Vienna. He 'slummed it' through Austria, Northern Italy and Germany, claiming he was so hungry at one point he had to tear off material from his Oxford bags and sell it for food. See Wright, *Village that Died for England*, p. 179. Two notable features of this early trip to Europe are, firstly, that he witnessed the postwar depression in Austria, which subsequently moved him to send books and clothing to impoverished Austrian students when he was at Cambridge (see Diary, Vol. 7, Pt 2, March–May 1922, mentioning that he was sending 13 of his own books to impoverished Viennese students); and, secondly, that he saw Italian peasants for the first time, whose costumes, dances and culture intrigued him and inspired some of his later writing. On the details of this nine-month gap period see R. Gardiner, 'Wisdom and Action', ch. 2. On his vagueness about which subject to study at university see RG to Father, 9 March 1921; 16 March 1921, B3/11. Gardiner's relations with his father at this point were very strained and two intermediaries wrote to his father suggesting that unless Rolf was given an allowance and total freedom he might decide not to go to Cambridge. See R. E. Roper to Mr Gardiner, 19 May 1921; Camilla (Coventry?) to Mr Alan Gardiner, May 1921, B3/11. Even after arriving at Cambridge in October 1921, he had still not decided which subject to read for his Degree. He told his parents in October 1921: 'I shall decide after a long talk with Rivers (a tutor) at tea tomorrow', RG to Parents, October 1921, B3/11.

39. For the striking clothes he wore at Cambridge see R. Gardiner, *David's Sling*, Book II, p. 121. He draws an interesting distinction between those who dressed smartly, such as himself, and the 'unwashed' bohemian students from London who he never identified with: *David's Sling*, Book I, p. 3. Rolf Gardiner was very proud of his physique; so proud he made sketches of his torso in his notebooks. He always rose early, at about 7 a.m., and did various physical exercises before breakfast. He liked horse-riding at weekends and evening swims in the River Cam. One evening in November 1921, he went swimming in the Cam with a female student. For an amusing account of this incident see *David's Sling*, Book II, p. 129.

40. On Orage see W. Martin, *The New Age Under Orage: Chapters in English Cultural History* (Manchester, 1967).

41. There is some correspondence between John Middleton Murry and Rolf Gardiner in the Rolf Gardiner papers. Middleton Murry made the initial approach, writing to Gardiner to congratulate him on *Youth* and asking to become a subscriber. Middleton Murry was in his mid-thirties at the time

and an established Literary Editor for *The Adelphi*. See John Middleton Murry, to RG, 14 June 1923, C2/4. Gardiner later visited Middleton Murry, who lived in a cottage in the countryside. They discussed D. H. Lawrence, and Gardiner, in a fit of romantic agony, declined a bed for the night; preferring to sleep outside in a field. See R. Gardiner, *David's Sling*, Book III, pp. 270–2.

42. Rolf Gardiner used the phrase *Jugendkultur* (Youth Culture) in an article he published on 'Young Europe' in *The Healthy Life* (April 1925), pp. 332–41, in A5/1: Press Articles, 1922–1923. The phrase was also used in articles published in his periodical *Youth*. For RG's own ideas on 'youth culture' see Rolf Gardiner, Diary, Vol. 7, Part 10, August–September 1923, CUL.

43. See above, note 12.

44. See Rolf Gardiner Diary, Vol. 7, Pt 10, August–September 1923, CUL, for the following details.

45. *Cambridge Gownsman*, 18 October 1924, p. 26. A year earlier the paper had referred to him in glowing terms as 'the magnetic Editor of *Youth*', *Cambridge Gownsman*, 20 October 1923, p. 8. On Keynes' favourable reaction to *Youth* see his letter to RG in C2/4: Youth magazine: correspondence, 1923–1924. Several established literary editors wrote to endorse the paper, including John Middleton Murry, Editor of *The Adelphi*, and T. S. Eliot, the poet and Editor of *The Criterion*. For details see C2/4, CUL. For the correspondence between RG and Edward Dent see J3/6, CUL.

46. For personal correspondence between RG and several of these Cambridge friends see file J/3.

47. Cited in M. Drakeford, *Social Movements and their Supporters: The Green Shirts in England* (London, 1997), pp. 67–8. The quotation is also cited in J. Craven, 'Redskins in Epping Forest: John Hargrave, the Kibbo Kift and the Woodcraft Experience', unpublished Ph.D. thesis, University of London, 1999, p. 205. On British and German youth movements of the Twenties See: M. J. Mertens, 'Early Twentieth Century Youth Movements, Nature and Community in Britain and Germany', unpublished Ph.D. thesis, University of Birmingham, 2000.

48. For details see RG to Margaret Gardiner (his sister), 7 November 1921, Add. 8932, in Rolf Gardiner Papers, CUL.

49. For R. A. Butler's Cambridge years, see Rab Butler Papers, Trinity College, Cambridge, files C6, C13, C15 and D48. The political biographer Anthony Howard refers to these files in his biography, *Rab: The Life of R. A. Butler* (London, 1987), but he does not do justice to this huge amount of rich material documenting Butler's Cambridge years as a whole. See Howard, *Rab*, pp. 21–2. He has nothing to say, for example, about the development of youth consciousness in the Universities after the First World War, so his discussion is somewhat superficial.

50. We know surprisingly little about The Heretics or The Socratics, two intriguing Cambridge societies. The first is only briefly mentioned in C. N. L. Brooke, *A History of the University of Cambridge*, Vol. IV,

1870–1990 (Cambridge, 1993), p. 126, and The Socratics not at all. T. A. B. Howarth, *Cambridge Between Two Wars* (London, 1978), pp. 50–3, discusses The Heretics, but not The Socratics. The Heretics was started before the First World War and began holding meetings from about 1912. It was a University Society and its first President was C. K. Ogden of Magdalene College, a Philosophy don. Ogden was still President when Rolf Gardiner joined the society in 1921. Far less is known about The Socratics. Both societies admitted females from the beginning. See The Heretics Printed Programmes, 1912–1923, Cambridge Papers Collection, 4510, Rare Books Room, CUL; 'The Socratics' in Cambridge Papers, J8057, Rare Books Room, CUL. The reports on The Heretics give details of its members. Rolf Gardiner joined The Heretics in his First Term at St John's and was made a member of the committee from the beginning. Several Cambridge dons were members of The Heretics including G. G. Coulton, Edward Dent, G. Lowes Dickinson, Eileen Power and J. M. Keynes. The Heretics' programme focused heavily on cultural themes in 1922, with talks on: Modern French Literature, Chinese Poetry, Zen Buddhism, Jazz, Travel in India, China and Europe, and 'German Drama'. Rolf Gardiner gave a talk to The Heretics at the end of his First Year. His theme was: 'Art as Communal Recreation'. See RG Diary, Vol. 7, Pt 3, May–June 1922. The Socratics specialised in educational topics, and in February 1920 it heard a talk on 'Co-Education' by J. H. Badley, the Headmaster of Bedales School, where Rolf Gardiner was a pupil.

51. Ibid.
52. On Coulton see his autobiography, *Fourscore Years: An Autobiography* (Cambridge, 1943), and S. Campion, *Father: A Portrait of G. G. Coulton* (London, 1948). Coulton's anti-Catholicism is mentioned in Howarth, *Cambridge Between Two Wars*, p. 50. In personal correspondence between the author and Professor Christopher Brooke of Gonville and Caius College, Cambridge, Professor Brooke recalled hearing Coulton lecture on 'Religion'; and described the lecture as 'a pathetic diatribe against the Catholic Church'.
53. Maurice Dobb to RG, 19 May 1922; 25 December 1921, C2/1: Cambridge, 1920–1925, CUL. Dobb frequently wrote to RG from 'The 1917 Club' in central London. See, for example, MD to RG, 18 October 1922. Another friend, Edward Davison, remarked on the seediness of the club and described it as 'a thieves' kitchen'. See Edward Davison to RG, 1 January 1921, C2/1.
54. He found his contemporaries at St John's very uninspiring, reporting to his parents after just a few days at Cambridge: 'I have never seen ... such a gloomy number, as we first year men I mean ... look down the middle table at Hall and see lugubrious Scotchmen and uncomfortable-looking Indians, Japs and what nots mixed with the usual public school dullness – not a single bright intelligent or adorable face!', RG to Parents, October 1921, B3/11. Admittedly, this was in his first few days at the University and he had not settled in. He wrote more charitably

in his next letter, but still remarked on how unsophisticated his contemporaries were and definitely felt superior to them. See RG to Parents, 10 October 1921, B3/11. One of his friends later criticised him for not mixing with students at his own college. See RG Diary, Vol. 7, Pt 6, November–December 1922, CUL.

55. Gardiner, *David's Sling*, Book II, pp. 121, 127, 130.
56. The St John's Debating Society was revived after the War by an Ex-Service student called Captain A. B. Dumas. See St John's College, Cambridge, Debating Society, *Minutes*, 1918–1922, St John's College, Cambridge, Library. See the minutes for the Lent Term 1918. Ex-Service students comprised a third of the audience at college debates in 1918.
57. See above, note 35, for details.
58. *New Cambridge*, 15 October 1921, p. 1. The *New Cambridge* clearly despised the Ex-Service students, describing them as 'a great mass of War-Undergraduates' (ibid.).
59. St John's Debating Society, *Minutes*.
60. *Youth*, No. 1 (May 1920), p. 2; No. 2 (November 1920), p. 21. The article on 'The Conduct of the Coal Industry' is in ibid., pp. 32–6.
61. *Youth*, No. 1 (May 1920), p. 5.
62. Ibid., pp. 1–2.
63. Rolf Gardiner took over the Editorship of *Youth* in June 1923 and predicted in his first issue as Editor, with characteristic self-assurance, that it would become 'the most significant journal of our time'. See *Youth*, No. 10 (June 1923), p. 216. He began publicising youth movements through its pages in the previous issue. See R. Gardiner, 'German Youth Movements', in *Youth*, No. 9 (March 1923), pp. 202–3. In his first issue as Editor, he published an article on the German cult of nakedness (See Figure 1). In his numerous contributions to *Youth*, he developed his ideas about youth culture. See especially, *Youth*, *Special Supplement*, December 1923, pp. 1–2: '. . . the German Youth Movement, one of the most portentous crusades of history, [is] an attempt of a minority, a single generation, to build up and maintain *a new culture* [my italics], within the chaos and disrupting ruins of the old'.
64. Harold Sandon to RG, 24 June 1923, in C2/4: Youth magazine: correspondence etc. 1923–1924, CUL.
65. Dr Stanton Coit to RG, 22 June 1923, C2/4.
66. Geoffrey Whitworth to RG, 14 June 1923; *The Criterion*, n.d. 1923?, C2/4.
67. RG to John Hargrave, 7 May 1923, C6/1; *The Times*, 30 October 1924, C2/4.
68. On the distribution of *Youth* see RG's correspondence with Moya Jowitt, who ran the KKK's office in central London; especially MJ to RG, 23 October 1923; 24 January 1924; 7 February 1924; 6 March 1924; 2 September 1924; 3 September 1924, C6/2. On the global sales of *Youth* see RG to Father, 22 January 1924, B3/14. He definitely sold copies abroad. He had sold 34 copies in New York alone by February 1924. See The National Student Forum (New York) to RG, 28 February

1924, C5/4. Joseph Shipley of New York reported that he would send copies of *Youth* to American colleges and to young writers throughout the United States. See Joseph Shipley to RG, 27 October 1923. The paper was also known about in India. An Indian correspondent from Madras, for example, wrote to the paper in 1923. See G. S. Arundale to RG, 15 November 1923, C5/4.

69. RG to 'Stephen', 2 April 1924, C2/4.

70. Ibid.

71. Ibid.; RG to Father, 22 January 1924, B3/14.

72. Theodore Besterman, Federation of British Youth, 29 April 1925, C5/2. Gardiner warned Besterman not to start a journal with the title *Youth* and threatened legal action against him if he did.

73. RG to Mother, 26 May 1924, B3/14.

74. G. Stedman Jones, 'The Meaning of the Student Revolt' in A. Cockburn and R. Blackburn (eds), *Student Power: Problems, Diagnosis, Action* (Harmondsworth, Middlesex, 1969), pp. 25–56 (especially pp. 41–3).

75. B. Harrison, 'College Life, 1918–1939' in B. Harrison (ed.), *The History of the University of Oxford, Vol. VIII: The Twentieth Century* (Oxford, 1994), ch. 4.

76. On university youth during the General Strike see Harrison (ed.), *History of the University of Oxford*, pp. 100, 391, 524. At Brasenose College, Oxford, there were *c.*120 students in 1926 and only 8 did not volunteer their services to the Government in the General Strike (p. 524). On Cambridge students in the General Strike see C. N. L. Brooke, *A History of the University of Cambridge, Vol. IV, 1870–1990* (Cambridge, 1993), pp. 520–1: 'the instinctive response of great numbers of students was to support the government, not the strikers . . .' (p. 520).

77. See Chapter 8.

78. M. Green, *Children of the Sun: A Narrative of Decadence in England After 1918* (1977; reprinted London, 1992).

79. For brief biographical details on John Hargrave (1894–1982) see Rolf Gardiner Catalogue, CUL. Gardiner first made contact with Hargrave in April 1923 when Gardiner was 20 and Hargrave was 29. See JH to RG, 1 May 1923; 4 June 1923, C6/1. For the origins of the Kibbo Kift see John Hargrave, *A Short History of the Kibbo Kift* (typescript, 1924), C6/1.

80. Hargrave, *Short History of the Kibbo Kift*, p. 2.

81. Craven thesis, p. 137.

82. Few of Rolf Gardiner's letters to John Hargrave are in the Rolf Gardiner Papers. The first is dated 15 July 1924, but they had been corresponding for over a year by this date. JH to RG, 1 May 1923, alludes to RG's first letter in April. See C6/1.

83. JH to RG, 8 February 1924, C6/1.

84. Ibid.

85. On the correspondence that went to Gardiner's parents' house addressed to 'Rolf the Ranger' see C6/3: RG's correspondence with KKK members, 1923–1926; especially Anon. to RG, n.d. 1925? For JH's letters to RG, again many sent to his parents' house, see C6/1. Hargrave was

a cultural philistine and it is surprising that RG cooperated with him at all; though his main reason, as argued above, was to use the KKK to establish contacts for his own cultural movements. RG brought an appreciation of English plays and of English culture to the KKK. JH was only interested in bewitching people with his arcane language and Back-to-Nature ideas. Gardiner put on Mummers' Plays at the KKK's annual events and introduced its members to Morris dances. Moreover, he recommended the only books mentioned in the KKK's records, apart from Hargrave's manuals; namely, J. G. Frazer's *The Golden Bough* and Jane Harrison's *Ancient Art and Ritual*. See John Hargrave, 'Notes for Mummers, Gleemen and Minstrels of the Kibbo Kift' (n.d., 1924?). Hargrave had received only a basic education and had left school at 12. He had little interest in culture and drama and liked Kin members to act out their own 'plays' rather than perform Shakespeare. JH to RG, 6 November 1924, C6/1. Nor did he like educated people. He refused to allow RG's friend Austin Lee, a student at Trinity College, Cambridge, to become a member on the vague grounds that 'he is not the right type'. JH to RG, 22 November 1924, C6/1.

86. JH to RG, 14 August 1924, C6/1.
87. JH to RG, 20 August 1924, C6/1.
88. RG to Parents, 26 November 1922, B3/12.
89. Rolf Gardiner, 'Oberammergau', *The Saturday Review*, 13 May 1922, pp. 485–7, A5/1.
90. Ibid., p. 486.
91. See RG to Parents, 7 November 1920, B3/10. The poem is printed in Rolf Gardiner, *The Second Coming* (1920).
92. RG to JH, 1 November 1924, C6/1. Rolf Gardiner's relations with the German Youth Movements of the interwar years will be dealt with in greater detail in D. Fowler, *The Youth Apostle: A Biography of Rolf Gardiner* (forthcoming).
93. RG to JH, 1 November 1924, C6/1.
94. J. Hargrave, *The Confession of the Kibbo Kift* (London, 1927), p. 91.
95. Rolf Gardiner, *David's Sling*, Book III, p. 267; RG to JH, 13 June 1925, C6/1.
96. Hargrave, *Confession of the Kibbo Kift*, p. 96. Hargrave was even planning to admit pensioners to the Kibbo Kift movement; a 'Kin Reserve' as he put it (ibid., note).
97. Ibid., pp. 96, 40. Hargrave thought youth lacked maturity and should not have any role in determining the policies of the Kibbo Kift (p. 40).
98. JH to RG, 18 October 1923, C6/1. On Mary Neal and Mrs Pethick-Lawrence see above, Chapter 1.
99. See above, note 1.
100. See especially D/2: Files on Folk Dance, 1922–*c*.1930, for the breadth of his European cultural contacts during the 1920s.
101. For a record of the 1922 folk dance tour see D2/1: Book of the English Folk Dancers' Tour in Germany, 1922. This is a scrapbook containing much of the correspondence generated by the tour and includes musical

programmes. See especially the poster Rolf Gardiner produced advertising the tour, 'English Folk Dancers: Tour in Germany, September 1922'. Rolf Gardiner tried to attract interest through the promise of a 'delightful and very inexpensive holiday'; but the cost to each member was £10 for a two-week event, making it beyond the pockets of all but the middle-class youth of the period. Arthur Marwick wrote a pioneering article on youth in twentieth-century Britain, published in the era of the student revolts of the late 1960s. He discussed, albeit briefly, student youth in Britain between the Wars. See A. Marwick, 'Youth in Britain, 1920–1960: Detachment and Commitment', *Journal of Contemporary History*, Vol. 5, No. 1 (1970), pp. 37–51.

102. The correspondence generated by the tour is in D2/1, including letters from Cecil Sharp to RG.

103. 'JSW' of Bedales School to RG, 5 July 1922, D2/1.

104. Winifred Shuldhamshaw to RG, 29 April 1922, D2/1.

105. Cecil Sharp to RG, 9 July 1922, D2/1.

106. See Book of the English Folk Dancers' Tour, p. 12; on the orchestra see 'Bill' to RG, 30 November 1922, D2/1.

107. See 'The English Folk Music Company, *Programme of Dance and Song*, Cologne, 3 September 1922', D2/1. The name adopted for the folk dance tour was slightly mischievous; not very different from 'The English Folk Dance Society', Cecil Sharp's London group. Rolf Gardiner was shrewd enough to know that hardly anyone would know the difference between the two groups in England, let alone in Germany, and thus Germans who attended the concerts would think they were seeing England's official folk dance society perform.

108. Kenneth Spence to RG, 14 July 1922, D2/2: Dance Tour, 1922: Correspondence.

109. See D2/2 for this correspondence.

110. See *Programme of Dance and Song*, Cologne, D2/1.

111. For several press reviews of the Frankfurt and Dresden concerts see D2/1. For RG's comment: 'We have blazed a trail' see 'Last Circular With Financial Statement', 1922, D2/1. For the quotation cited in the text see Sarah Waites to RG, September 1922, D2/2.

112. Rolf Gardiner, 'English Folk Dance and Song', *Cologne Post*, 31 August 1922, D2/1.

113. For the tour's finances see 'Last Circular with Financial Statement', 1922, D2/2. Despite the hyperinflation they encountered, the tour was not a financial disaster. After the tour had ended each member was asked to send a further £3 to Rolf Gardiner to balance the books. See 'Bill' to RG, 30 November 1922, D2/2.

114. Claire Vintcombe to RG, October 1922. In a provisional list of participants sent to Cecil Sharp, only 2 of the 6 female dancers were students. Both were at Oxford and were probably secured through Arthur Heffer, Rolf Gardiner's friend at Oxford, who was also on the tour. A further two females were based in Manchester; one was from Plymouth and one from Edinburgh. No personal details are given on the male dancers other than

their names; suggesting they were all friends of Gardiner's and probably students at either Cambridge or Oxford. See RG to Cecil Sharp, 10 July 1922, MK/4/46–50, Vaughan Williams Memorial Library, Cecil Sharp House, London.

115. 'Malini' (Mrs Pethick-Lawrence) to RG, 20 November 1925, C3/1. Mrs Pethick-Lawrence, a celebrated pre-War suffragette, heaped praise on Rolf Gardiner, telling him that he inspired her and that he was a leader of 'a Community of Youth'. See also Mary Neal to RG, 19 September 1922, C3/1. The English Folk Dance Society, however, never forgave Rolf Gardiner for defying Cecil Sharp. See Kenworthy Schofield to RG, June/July 1924, C3/1. He wanted Gardiner to 'apologise' to the EFDS for going on tour with 'a set of irresponsible people'. By this time, of course, Cecil Sharp was dead.

116. Edward Dent to RG, n.d. 1922?, D2/1.

117. Edward Dent (1876–1957) knew Rupert Brooke in Cambridge before the First World War and saw Gardiner as another inspirational youth. For his correspondence with RG see J3/6. On Cambridge as 'the intellectual leader of all that is best in English life', ED to RG, 28 November 1931. For Gardiner's criticisms of Dent's Little Englandism see ED to RG, 23 November 1931; and 28 November 1931. Gardiner had described Dent's Cambridge propaganda work abroad as 'in bad taste'.

118. To give Dent credit, he saw music as a way of improving relations between England and Germany and was sensitive to the types of English music German audiences would respond to. He thought they preferred 'Old Music' (Purcell, for example) to Vaughan Williams and advised Gardiner against using Vaughan Williams for folk dances as, he felt, Vaughan Williams lacked 'excitement'; whereas Purcell had 'rhythm'. ED to RG, 8 April 1926. On Dent's high reputation with the *Daily Telegraph*, see ED to RG, 26 March 1926. On Dent's propaganda work for Gardiner in Trinity College, Cambridge, see ED to RG, 23 November 1931.

119. On RG's refusal to cooperate with Dent in Cambridge, see ED to RG, 28 November 1931. The two stopped corresponding for five years after November 1931. For more on Rolf Gardiner's relationship with Edward Dent see the author's forthcoming biography, *The Youth Apostle*.

120. W.H. Auden to RG, 4 March 1932; David Ayerst to RG, 4 December 1931, D3/6: Yorkshire Festival Tour, 1932: Correspondence.

121. See D3/6 for the musical backgrounds of participants, and lack of musical backgrounds. On Virginia (Gina) Coit see several letters about her experiences in South Wales and Germany, in D3/6. See also her letters to RG in J3/4.

122. For details see D3/6.

123. Jack Saunders of Stowe School to RG, 18 September 1931, D3/6.

124. Rolf Gardiner was speaking in Hull to the Lord Mayor of the city. See Log of the Yorkshire Festival Tour, 15 August–15 September 1931, pp. 93–4, D4/9.

125. The tensions between the young Britons and young Germans were referred to in the official Log of the Tour (written by a female English

participant, Phyllis M. Thomas). See especially pp. 6, 9 and 72–3. At one point, the English group left the Germans and Phyllis Thomas reported: 'we were feeling highly excited and pleased with ourselves; (a) we were going to the parish of a friend ... (b) we were going alone without the Germans' (pp. 72–3). See the press reports of the tour, including descriptions of the musical performances, in A5/14: Yorkshire Festival Tour, 1931: Newspaper Cuttings.

126. For the factory visits in Leeds and York see Log of the Tour, pp. 67–8, 90. For Christopher Scaife's summary see ibid., pp. 96–7.

127. *Leeds Mercury*, 14 August 1931, A5/14.

128. *The Times*, 9 July 1931, A5/14.

129. Log of the Tour, p. 89.

130. Marabel Hodgkin to RG, 22 September 1931, D3/6.

131. *Leeds Mercury*, 14 August 1931, A5/14.

132. *The North Eastern Daily Gazette*, 21 August 1931, A5/14.

133. For the outfits see *York Gazette*, 21 August 1931, A5/14. For details of the English and German performances see *Durham County Advertiser*, 28 August 1931, describing a performance at Durham Cathedral; a mixture of early Church music (sung by the Germans) and folk dances performed by the English.

134. For the separate performances at Middlesbrough Town Hall see Log of the Tour, pp. 16–17, D4/9.

135. Ibid., *passim.*

136. *Yorkshire Post*, 24 August 1931, A5/14.

137. For the inaccurate reporting of his status as a 'student' see *Leeds Mercury*, 22 July 1931; 14 August 1931.

138. He explored the idea of youth communities in two publications around the time of the Yorkshire Tour. See Rolf Gardiner, *In Northern Europe 1930* (London, 1930), and Rolf Gardiner, *Reconstruction in Silesia* (London, 1930?).

139. For a study of youth consumers between the Wars see D. Fowler, *The First Teenagers: The Lifestyle of Young Wage-earners in Interwar Britain* (London, 1995). See also below, Chapter 3.

Notes to Chapter 3: The Flapper Cult in Interwar Britain: Media Invention or the Spark that Ignited Girl Power?

1. On the American flapper see K. A. Yellis, 'Prosperity's Child: Some Thoughts on the Flapper', *American Quarterly*, Vol. 21, No. 1 (Spring 1969), pp. 44–64; A. J. Latham, *Posing a Threat: Flappers, Chorus Girls and other Brazen Performers of the American 1920s* (New Hampshire, USA, 2000); E. Stevenson, *Babbitts and Bohemians: From the Great War to the Great Depression* (1967; reprinted London, 1998), ch. IX. On the Fitgeralds' essays on the flapper see J. Savage, *Teenage: The Creation of Youth 1875–1945* (London, 2007), pp. 201–3. The best account of American

youth in the 1920s is still P. Fass, *The Damned and the Beautiful: American Youth in the 1920s* (Oxford, 1977; reprinted in paperback 1979).

2. For Clara Bow and Colleen Moore see Savage, *Teenage*, pp. 205, 227–8. On Louise Brooks see M. Rosen, *Popcorn Venus: Women, Movies and the American Dream* (New York, 1973), ch. 5.

3. See D. Fowler, *The First Teenagers: The Lifestyle of Young Wage-earners in Interwar Britain* (London, 1995), p. 103.

4. Savage, *Teenage*, p. 228.

5. Rosen, *Popcorn Venus*, ch. 5.

6. Savage, *Teenage*, p. 205.

7. Ibid., pp. 203–5.

8. Cited in Savage, *Teenage*, p. 228.

9. *Daily Express*, 18 April 1927, p. 7.

10. S. Zdatny (ed.), *Hairstyles and Fashion: A Hairdresser's History of Paris, 1910–1920* (Oxford, 1999), pp. 33–4; S. Zdatny, 'The Mode "A la Garconne" and the Meaning of Hair', unpublished paper delivered at the Social History Conference, Roehampton Institute, London, January 1993.

11. See R. Graves and A. Hodge, *The Long Weekend: A Social History of Great Britain, 1918–1939* (1940; reprinted London, 1995), pp. 43–4; D. Beddoe, *Back to Home and Duty: Women Between the Wars, 1918–1939* (London, 1989), pp. 22–4; A. Woollacott, *On Her Their Lives Depend: Munitions Workers in the Great War* (London, 1994), pp. 4, 143–4. Surprisingly, Selina Todd's meticulous monograph on young women between the Wars, *Young Women, Work, and Family in England, 1918–1950* (Oxford, 2005), entirely ignores the Flapper cult of inter-war England. Claire Langhamer's *Women's Leisure in England, 1920–60* (Manchester, 2000) has a solitary reference to 'a great number of flappers' in a Manchester café in 1925 (p. 53).

12. S. Rowbotham, *A Century of Women: The History of Women in Britain and the United States* (London, 1997), p. 120.

13. In addition to Rowbotham, two other historians argue that the flapper was a press and, more specifically, a *Daily Mail* creation. See A. Bingham, ' "Stop the Flapper Vote Folly": Lord Rothermere, the *Daily Mail*, and the Equalisation of the Franchise, 1927–1928', *Twentieth Century British History*, Vol. 13, No. 1 (2002), pp. 17–37; C. Horwood, *Keeping Up Appearances: Fashion and Class Between the Wars* (Stroud, Gloucs, 2005), p. 142.

14. The classic British flapper novel, set in London, is M. Arlen, *The Green Hat: A Romance for a Few People* (London, 1924); but a series of other flapper novels appeared, such as W. D. Newton, *Phillip and the Flappers* (London, 1918), E. Graye, *The Fascinating Flapper* (London, 1926), A. E. James, *Her Majesty the Flapper* (London, 1912), H. Tuite, *The Southdown Flapper* (London, 1926), and B. Morgan, *The Flapper's Daughter* (London, 1935). On flapper memoirs see Anon., *Meditations of a Flapper By One* (London, 1922), N. Shute, *We Mixed our Drinks: The Story of a Generation* (London, 1945), R. Cutforth, *Later than we Thought: A*

Portrait of the Thirties (London, 1976). For a working-class memoir see E. M. Horton, *Youth on the Prow: A Flapper's View of the Life and Events during the Years 1921–1932* (Oxford, 1994). On historians, see above, notes 11 and 12.

15. On college flappers and the pervasiveness of Flapper culture in US universities during the 1920s see M. A. Lowe, *Looking Good: College Women and Body Image, 1875–1930* (Baltimore, MD: 2003), ch. 5.

16. See below, pp. 68–9.

17. C. Buckley and H. Fawcett, *Fashioning the Feminine: Representation and Women's Fashion from the Fin de Siècle to the Present* (London, 2002), pp. 88–9, 115–16.

18. Ibid., pp. 87–91, briefly discusses working-class flappers in Northern England.

19. Beddoe, *Back to Home and Duty*, p. 23.

20. See *Oxford English Dictionary*, Second Edition, Vol. V (Oxford, 1989), p. 1008.

21. Ibid.

22. See B. Melman, *Women and the Popular Imagination in the Twenties* (London, 1988), pp. 27–30 for the best discussion of the etymology of the term.

23. Woollacott, *On Her Their Lives Depend*, p. 143 hints at this.

24. Bingham, 'Stop the Flapper Vote Folly'; A. Bingham, *Gender, Modernity and the Popular Press in Interwar Britain* (Oxford, 2004), pp. 135–9.

25. Ibid., pp. 137–8. On visual images of the flapper in the press of the period see below, pp. 65–6.

26. Anne-Marie Sohn claims that, in fact, 1 million copies of Margueritte's novel were sold and that between 12 and 25 per cent of the French population read it. See A. Sohn, 'Between the Wars in France and England' in F. Thebaud (ed.), *A History of Women in the West, Vol. V* (London, 1994), p. 93. See also Zdatny, 'Meaning of Hair', for the cultural impact of Margueritte's novel.

27. Zdatny, 'Meaning of Hair', p. 7.

28. Savage, *Teenage*, p. 209. On American college flappers see also, Lowe, *Looking Good*.

29. Savage, *Teenage*, p. 209.

30. Ibid.

31. Savage, *Teenage*, discusses the college film *The Plastic Age*, pp. 209–10. Lowe, *Looking Good*, argues that college students in the US shaped youth culture during the 1920s (ch. 5).

32. Savage, *Teenage*, pp. 209–10, 227–8.

33. Ibid., p. 209.

34. In the mid-1920s there were 29,275 students studying at English universities (20,899 males, 8376 females). Oxford and Cambridge students comprised around one-third of the total: Cambridge (5203), Oxford (4353). The largest student population was at London University (8797), followed by Cambridge (5203) and Oxford (4353). The other universities

ranged in size from Manchester (1748 students) to Reading (558). For the figures, see C. L. Mowat, *Britain Between the Wars, 1918–1940* (1955; reprinted London, 1968), p. 210. On the Asquith Commission into Oxford and Cambridge see C. Dyhouse, *Students: A Gendered History* (London, 2006), pp. 83–4.

35. Lowe, *Looking Good*, ch. 5.
36. R. McKibbin, *Classes and Cultures: England, 1918–1951* (Oxford, 1998), p. 248.
37. See above, Chapter 2.
38. See Chapter 2; Mowat, *Britain Between the Wars*, p. 210.
39. Ibid.
40. *Cambridge Gownsman*, 17 November 1923, pp. i, 8–9, 18.
41. *Cambridge Gownsman*, 26 November 1927, p. 20. For photographs of flapper students see *Cambridge Gownsman*, 27 October 1923, pp. 15, 17.
42. *Cambridge Gownsman*, 25 October 1924, p. 9.
43. See above, Chapter 2.
44. A thorough analysis of Rolf Gardiner's diaries held in Cambridge University Library, Manuscripts Room, has revealed no references to the cinema or flappers.
45. The film is mentioned in Beddoe, *Back to Home and Duty*, p. 44.
46. See notes 1 and 10 above, for references.
47. *The Times*, 5 February 1920, p. 9.
48. Ibid.
49. *Daily Mail*, 5 February 1920, p. 7; *Manchester Evening News*, 5 February 1920, p. 4.
50. *The Times*, 13 September 1920, p. 4.
51. See *The Times*, 6 October 1919, p. 7; 4 November 1919, p. 40; 3 June 1920, p. 12; 9 July 1920, p. 14; 27 January 1926, p. 17.
52. *The Times*, 23 June 1922, p. 16.
53. *The Times*, 9 February 1924, p. 7; 26 February 1924, p. 22; 28 November 1924, p. 7.
54. In the press the flapper became synonymous with the 'flapper vote' in 1927. See *The Times*, 3 May 1927, p. 18.
55. See especially the cartoon of Stanley Baldwin and a flapper in a park, *Daily Express*, 26 April 1927, p. 2. On one occasion, Baldwin as Prime Minister unveiled a statue of the suffragette leader Emmeline Pankhurst. As two of his biographers put it: 'Whatever may be said of the Conservatives' late conversion to her cause, Baldwin's own conviction is unquestioned.' See K. Middlemas and J. Barnes, *Baldwin: A Biography* (London, 1969), p. 468. On Baldwin's liking for the novels of Mary Webb see P. Williamson, *Stanley Baldwin: Conservative Leadership and National Values* (Cambridge, 1999), p. 244. Baldwin used the word 'flapper' in a speech to the Conservative Women's Association at the Albert Hall, London, in May 1928. See Melman, *Women and the Popular Imagination*, p. 29. Baldwin's depiction in the press as the Prime Minister who enfranchised 'flappers' may just have been bad timing. His Conservative Government

announced that it would enfranchise young women in April 1927. Clara Bow's film *It* was released in London the same month. See *Daily Mail*, 14 April 1927, p. 17.

56. See note 14 above, for details.

57. *Daily Express*, 14 April 1927, Front page; 26 April 1927, p. 2. Baumer's *Punch* cartoon is reproduced in E. Wilson, *Adorned in Dreams: Fashion and Modernity* (London, 1985), p. 121.

58. *The Times*, 25 May 1923, p. 9.

59. A. Thorpe, *Britain in the Era of Two World Wars, 1914–1945* (London, 1994), p. 64.

60. Fowler, *First Teenagers*, ch. 3; Todd, *Young Women, Work, and Family*, ch. 4.

61. Todd, *Young Women, Work, and Family*, Table 6, p. 129; on the Juvenile Employment Bureaux see Fowler, *First Teenagers*, pp. 29–35, 77–9.

62. *Daily Mail*, 20 April 1927, p. 9.

63. Shute, *We Mixed our Drinks*, pp. 9, 15.

64. Ibid., p. 26.

65. For an informative discussion of the Bright Young Things see Savage, *Teenage*, ch. 17.

66. Savage implies that they were significant in the history of British youth culture ('the first British youth culture to be defined in aspirational terms'); but this ignores the flappers, who appeared slightly earlier, and it overstates the social impact of the Bright Young Things beyond London. See Savage, *Teenage*, p. 248. For a more convincing assessment see J. Montgomery, *The Twenties* (London, 1957; reprinted 1970), p. 202.

67. Savage, *Teenage*, p. 248: 'The Bright Young people were no . . . exemplars of social inclusion.'

68. On Acton and Howard see Martin Green's brilliant study, *Children of the Sun: A Narrative of Decadence in England after 1918* (1976; reprinted London, 1992).

69. Shute, *We Mixed our Drinks*, p. 27.

70. Ibid., p. 15.

71. Ibid., ch. V.

72. Sally Alexander argues that the cinema was the main medium for projecting the flapper image; but as she does not discuss the dance halls it seems questionable. See S. Alexander, 'Becoming a Woman in London in the 1920s and 1930s', in M. Schiach (ed.), *Feminism and Cultural Studies* (Oxford, 1999), ch. 10 (especially pp. 218–19).

73. On the phenomenal growth of dance halls and dance hall culture after 1918 see J. Nott, *Music for the People: Popular Music and Dance in Interwar Britain* (Oxford, 2002), pp. 153–4. On Hammersmith Palais see H. Wyndham, *Nights in London: Where Mayfair makes Merry* (London, 1926), pp. 60–1. On the patrons of interwar dance halls see Fowler, *First Teenagers*, pp. 103–4.

74. Wyndham, *Nights in London*, pp. 53–63, for an evocative description of Hammersmith Palais.

75. Ibid., pp. 60–2.

76. Ibid., p. 63.
77. Ibid., pp. 53, 60.
78. Ibid., p. 54.
79. Ibid., pp. 60–1.
80. Ibid., pp. 60–3.
81. W. L. George, *A London Mosaic* (London, 1921), p. 71.
82. Ibid., p. 72.
83. Ibid., pp. 77, 79.
84. V. Macclure, *How to be Happy in London* (London, 1926), pp. 105–6.
85. H. Llewellyn Smith et al. (eds), *The New Survey of London Life and Labour*, Vol. VIII (London, 1934), p. 307.
86. Ibid., pp. 302–3.
87. Macclure goes further, suggesting that the youths and girls who attended the Hammersmith Palais for just 2s 6d could also afford boat trips up the River Thames in the summer months. See Macclure, *How to be Happy in London*, pp. 105, 164.
88. George, *London Mosaic*, pp. 71–2.
89. *Manchester Evening News*, 4 May 1925, p. 7.
90. Buckley and Fawcett, *Fashioning the Feminine*, p. 88, fig. 4.1.
91. Ibid., p. 89, fig. 4.2.
92. A. de la Haye, 'The Dissemination of Design from Haute Couture to Fashionable ready-to-wear during the 1920s', *Textile History*, Vol. 24, No. 1 (Spring 1993), p. 43.
93. Ibid., pp. 40–2.
94. P. Tinkler, 'Red Tips for Hot Lips: Advertising Cigarettes for Young Women in Britain, 1920–70', *Women's History Review*, Vol. 10, No. 2 (2001), p. 250.
95. P. Tinkler, 'Rebellion, Modernity and Romance: Smoking as a Gendered Practice in Popular Young Women's Magazines, Britain 1918–1939', *Women's Studies International Forum*, Vol. 24, No. 1 (2001), pp. 117–19.
96. Reprinted in Buckley and Fawcett, *Fashioning the Feminine*, p. 90.
97. See Savage's discussion of London night clubs of the 1920s, which mentions cocaine use, but does not link it with the flappers: Savage, *Teenage*, pp. 244–5.
98. P. Horn, *Women in the 1920s* (Stroud, 1995), p. 183. Horn points out that there were far more dance halls than cinemas in Britain by the mid-1920s: 11,000 as against 3500 cinemas.

Notes to Chapter 4: Youth Culture in Early Twentieth-Century Ireland

1. R. Fraser et al., *1968: A Student Generation in Revolt* (London, 1988), p. 205. In her autobiography, *The Price of My Soul* (London, 1969), she makes no reference to student movements in Britain or elsewhere.
2. R. F. Foster, *Modern Ireland, 1688–1988* (London, 1988), p. 587.

3. See, for example, T. Brown, *Ireland: A Social and Cultural History* (London, 1981); Foster, *Modern Ireland*; and A. Jackson, *Ireland, 1688–1998: Politics and War* (Oxford, 1999). Sociologists have been the pioneers in this field. See, especially, D. Bell, *Acts of Union: Youth Culture and Sectarianism in Northern Ireland* (London, 1990), a study of contemporary youth cultures in Derry.

4. On the Public Dance Hall Act of 1935 see J. Smyth, 'Dancing, Depravity and All That Jazz: the Public Dance Halls Act of 1935', *History Ireland*, Vol. 1, No. 2 (Summer 1993), pp. 51–4.

5. 'The Newsboys' Club', *Belfast Newsletter*, 20 October 1931, p. 8. All newspapers cited in this chapter are held at Belfast Central Library.

6. *The Irish News and Belfast Morning News*, 20 October 1926, p. 7.

7. See *Belfast Newsletter*, 25 October 1926, p. 8; 26 October 1926, p. 5; 28 October 1926, p. 11; *Northern Whig*, 23 October 1926, p. 8; 25 October 1926, pp. 5, 8; 26 October 1926, p. 9; 27 October 1926, p. 9; 28 October 1926, p. 11; 1 November 1926, p. 5. For a series of articles on local youth during 1926 see *Northern Whig*, 16 October 1926, p. 6; 19 October 1926, p. 6; 20 October 1926, p. 6; 25 October 1926, p. 8; 1 November 1926, p. 5.

8. See D.M.J., 'Dr. Harry Miller: An Inspired Personality', *Northern Whig*, 23 October 1926, p. 8.

9. Ibid.

10. *Northern Whig*, 25 October 1926, p. 5; 20 October 1926, p. 1.

11. *Northern Whig*, 20 October 1926, p. 1.

12. See above, note 7.

13. See W.A., 'Ulster's Youth', *Northern Whig*, 20 October 1926, p. 6.

14. W.A., 'Youth and the Corporation', *Northern Whig*, 19 October 1926, p. 6.

15. On the 'Lost Generation' of the Twenties in England see Martin Green's brilliant study, *Children of the Sun: A Narrative of Decadence in England since 1918* (1976; reprinted London, 1992), and for the same phenomenon in the United States see Paula Fass, *The Damned and the Beautiful: American Youth in the 1920s* (Oxford, 1977).

16. See Appendix 2, Table A1.

17. See Appendix 2, Table A2.

18. The Northern Ireland YMCA's records are held at the Public Record Office of Northern Ireland, Belfast (hereafter P.R.O.N.I.) See the Northern Ireland District YMCA, Executive Committee Minutes (hereafter Y.M.C.A., Minutes), 21 July 1922–11 February 1969, D3788/1/6, P.R.O.N.I. See Y.M.C.A., Minutes, 27 March 1924. Wright was aged 65 when he retired as National Secretary of the Irish YMCAs in March 1924. He had been National Secretary since January 1901. Some of his colleagues on the Executive Committee were also in their sixties, it seems. Several had been placed on the Irish YMCA's 'Pensions List'.

19. See Y.M.C.A., Minutes, 27 March 1924; 24 November, 1924; *The YMCA in Ireland* (Belfast, 1925), p. 7.

20. See Cork YMCA, *Annual Report*, 1919–20, front cover.

21. Irish Union of YMCAs, *Annual Report*, 1925, p. 8.
22. Londonderry YMCA, *Prospectus*, 1925–26, pp. 2, 23; Londonderry YMCA, *Syllabus*, 1930–31, p. 21.
23. *The YMCA in Ireland: Work in Wartime* (Belfast, 1917), pp. 7–8; *Y.M.: The British Empire Y.M.C.A. Weekly: Organ of the Y.M.C.A. in Great Britain and Ireland*, 12 May 1916, p. 431. The YMCA huts in France were 'within two or three miles of the firing-line'.
24. See Appendix 2, Table A1, for the following statistics.
25. Y.M.C.A., Minutes, 21 July 1922.
26. Ibid.; Y.M.C.A., Minutes, 14 May 1919.
27. Y.M.C.A., Minutes, 20 October 1921; 21 July 1921; 27 October 1922.
28. Y.M.C.A., Minutes, 17 December 1920.
29. Y.M.C.A., Minutes, 22 March 1921.
30. Y.M.C.A., Minutes, 29 April 1921.
31. Y.M.C.A., Minutes, 22 September 1920.
32. Y.M.C.A., Minutes, 27 October 1920.
33. Y.M.C.A., Minutes, 29 April 1921.
34. Y.M.C.A., Minutes, 31 March 1920.
35. See Mountpottinger YMCA, Belfast (also known as East Belfast YMCA), Minute Book, 1920–1923, D3788/4/1/4, P.R.O.N.I., 12 August 1920.
36. Mountpottinger YMCA, Minutes, 23 September 1920.
37. Mountpottinger YMCA, Minutes, 10 February 1921.
38. Mountpottinger YMCA, Minutes, 10 March 1921.
39. Mountpottinger YMCA, Minutes, 8 September 1921; 11 November 1921.
40. Mountpottinger YMCA, Minutes, 9 March 1922; 16 May 1922. Mountpottinger's troubles were even discussed in the Northern Ireland Parliament in July 1922. See Y.M.C.A., Minutes, 21 July 1922.
41. See Ballymena YMCA, newspaper cutting, n.d. 1921?; Ballymena YMCA, letter to Belfast YMCA, 10 December 1920, File on Local Associations, *c*.1920–1935, D3788/2/2, P.R.O.N.I.
42. Letter from Banbridge YMCA to Belfast YMCA, 13 May 1921, Local Associations File.
43. Strabane YMCA (County Tyrone), details from Local Associations File; Enniskillen YMCA, Programme for 1924–1925, Local Associations File.
44. See, for example, a letter from its First Secretary, n.d. December 1930?, Bessbrook YMCA, Minute Book, April 1930–January 1935, D3858/A/9, P.R.O.N.I.
45. See newspaper report, un-named and undated, in Bessbrook YMCA, Minutes, December 1930.
46. Bessbrook YMCA, Minutes, 7 June 1926.
47. Bessbrook YMCA, Minutes, 26 November 1928; 4 February 1929; 30 December 1929; 3 March 1930; 21 December 1931. One talk in November 1927 was on the macabre theme: 'The Valley of Dry Bones as is found in the 37th of Ezekiel'. See Bessbrook YMCA, Minutes, 28 November 1927.

48. Y.M.C.A., Minutes, 31 July 1923.
49. Mountpottinger YMCA, Minutes, 18 January 1923; 15 February 1923.
50. Mountpottinger YMCA, Minutes, 15 February 1923; 6 September 1923.
51. Mountpottinger YMCA, Minutes, 11 October 1923.
52. Ibid.
53. See Appendix 2, Table A3.
54. See, especially, *Belfast Newsletter*, 9 January 1922, p. 5; 12 January 1922, p. 5; 3 April 1922; 20 April 1922, p. 5; 21 April 1922, p. 5; 26 May 1922, p. 7; 27 May 1922, p. 5. Not all the youths mentioned in these press reports were victims. A group of youths brandishing revolvers raided a shop in Belfast city centre in January 1922. See *Belfast Newsletter*, 5 January 1922, p. 5. Two days later a Belfast police inspector told a Belfast court 7000 youths in the city owned revolvers. See *Belfast Newsletter*, 7 January 1922, p. 7.
55. Mountpottinger YMCA, Members' and Associates' Subscription Register, 1921–1927, D3788/4/4/2, P.R.O.N.I.
56. See typed account of the YMCA's history in D3788/2/2, Local Associations File, P.R.O.N.I. It was included in a High Court case involving the YMCA in the Irish Republic during 1942.
57. Ibid.
58. *The YMCA in Ireland* (Belfast, 1925), p. 13. The Cork YMCA Secretary, George Bird, was offered the post at a salary of £300 per annum, but refused it. He was offered it again at a higher salary of £400 in 1927, but refused again. See Y.M.C.A., Minutes, 27 March 1924; 24 November 1924; 13 May 1927; 28 July 1927.
59. *The YMCA in Ireland*, p. 13.
60. See Cork YMCA File, 1925–1945, D3788/3/14, P.R.O.N.I.
61. *The YMCA in Ireland: Work in Wartime* (Belfast, 1917), p. 5.
62. Ibid., pp. 7–8.
63. Ibid., p. 8.
64. Ibid.
65. *The Red Triangle in Ireland* (Belfast, 1920), pp. 9, 12.
66. Ibid., p. 12.
67. Ibid.; Y.M.C.A., Minutes, 7 December 1923.
68. See Local YMCA Associations File, D3788/2/1, P.R.O.N.I.
69. See letter from George Williams of 'Bessbrook' to Belfast YMCA, 3 October 1910; 1909; n.d., YMCA, Local Associations File, *c*.1920–1935, D3788/2/2, P.R.O.N.I.
70. Letter from Cork YMCA (County Kerry) to Belfast YMCA, 9 October 1909, Local Associations File, D3788/2/2, P.R.O.N.I.
71. There were donations from Belfast retailers, printers, a ginger ale manufacturer, and the East Downshire Steamship Company (of County Down). See YMCA, Local Associations File, D3788/2/2, P.R.O.N.I., *passim*.
72. See letter from J. Ellis of 'Cannes' to Belfast YMCA, n.d., 1918?; letter from J. S. Fry, chocolate manufacturer of Bristol, to Belfast YMCA, 23

February 1923; Letter from Cadbury Brothers of Birmingham to Belfast YMCA, 10 March 1921., YMCA, Local Associations File, D3788/2/2, P.R.O.N.I.

73. Returns of Local YMCA Associations, D3788/2/1, P.R.O.N.I.

74. Ibid.; *Ballymena Observer*, 6 April 1923.

75. See Shankill YMCA Annual Survey, 1931, Returns of Local YMCA Associations, D3788/2/1, P.R.O.N.I.

76. See Mountpottinger YMCA, Annual Survey, 1929; Banbridge YMCA, Annual Survey, 1929, Returns of Local YMCA. Associations, D3788/2/1, P.R.O.N.I.

77. Cloughjordan YMCA, Annual Survey, 1929, Returns of Local YMCA Associations, D3788/2/1, P.R.O.N.I.

78. See City of Belfast YMCA, Annual Survey, 1929, Returns of Local YMCA Associations, D3788/2/1, P.R.O.N.I.

79. Y.M.C.A., Minutes, 27 October 1922; Irish Union of YMCAs, *Annual Report*, 1926, p. 13, YMCA Publications File, *c*.1917–*c*.1981, D3788/1/9, P.R.O.N.I.

80. *The YMCA in Ireland*, p. 12.

81. At Shankill Road YMCA, situated in a very poor area of Belfast where men and youths were said to be 'addicted to drink and gambling', the leaders had great difficulty trying to extract even the subscription fee from the members who simply refused to pay. See Y.M.C.A., Minutes, 16 July 1919; 31 March 1920; Shankill YMCA, *Annual Survey*, 1929. The club's leader recorded in the 1929 survey: 'Marked increase of gambling amongst youths and boys. Difficulty in obtaining fees from many . . . using club.' See Returns of Local YMCA Associations, D3788/2/1, P.R.O.N.I. On the early school-leaving age, see Census of Population of Northern Ireland, 1926, *General Report*, Part IV, Table 13. Of 24,481 15-year-olds in Northern Ireland in 1926, only 6880 were in full-time education – approximately, 25 per cent of the age-group.

82. See 'Memorandum on Instructional Camp for Unemployed Workers between the ages of 18 and 20', n.d. July 1923?, CAB 9C/31/1 Juvenile Training Centre and Employment Exchange, P.R.O.N.I.

83. On the benefit levels for juveniles and a discussion of juvenile unemployment in interwar Britain see D. Fowler, *The First Teenagers: The Lifestyle of Young Wage-earners in Interwar Britain* (London, 1995), ch. 3.

84. 'Memorandum on Instructional Camp', p. 3.

85. See 'Cabinet Conclusions', Proposed Juvenile Training Centre and Employment Exchange, 4 February 1929, CAB 9C/31/1, P.R.O.N.I.

86. Belfast Juvenile Advisory Committee, 'Memorandum on Proposed Juvenile Centre', January 1929, p. 1, CAB 9C/31/1, P.R.O.N.I.

87. Ibid. There were 34,295 16- and 17-year-olds in the workforce in Northern Ireland in 1926. The Belfast centre was the only centre in existence in the Province in 1929. Its 330 unemployed juveniles therefore represented just 1 per cent of the labour force among 16- and 17-year-olds. For the figures see Belfast Juvenile Advisory Committee, 'Memorandum',

p. 1; Census of Population of Northern Ireland 1926, *General Report*, Part IV, Table 16.

88. Belfast Juvenile Advisory Committee, 'Memorandum', p. 1.
89. See Government of Northern Ireland, 'The Instruction of Unemployed Juveniles', Cmd 193 (Belfast, 1938), p. 8. See also, letter from L. Allen (the Superintendent of the Belfast Juvenile Instruction Centre) to the Cabinet Secretariat, 18 May 1942; Belfast Juvenile Instruction Centre, n.d. May 1942?, CAB 9C/31/1, P.R.O.N.I.
90. See Government of Northern Ireland, *Parliamentary Debates, House of Commons*, Vol. 15, No. 50, 24 October 1933, col. 2483.
91. Ibid., cols 2483–502.
92. Arthur E. Clery, 'Votes for Youth', *Studies*, Vol. IV, No. 14 (June 1915), pp. 279–85.
93. Ibid., pp. 283–4.
94. See K. H. Connell, 'Peasant Marriage in Ireland: its Structure and Development since the Famine', *Economic History Review*, Second Series, Vol. XIV, No. 3 (1962), p. 502. See also K. H. Connell, 'Catholicism and Marriage in the Century after the Famine' in K. H. Connell, *Irish Peasant Society: Four Historical Essays* (Oxford, 1968; reprinted Blackrock, 1996), ch. 4.
95. Eithne, 'The Saving of Girls', *Irish Monthly*, Vol. 53 (January 1925), p. 127.
96. Eithne, 'Where are you going to, my pretty maid?', *Irish Monthly*, Vol. 54 (August 1925), p. 460.
97. Flann O'Brien, 'The Dance Halls', *The Bell*, Vol. 1, No. 5 (February 1941), pp. 44–52. For his lively essay on Dublin public houses see his, 'The Trade in Dublin', *The Bell*, Vol. 1, No. 2, (November 1940), pp. 6–15.
98. See D. Dempsey, 'Facts and Figures about Eire's Population', *Irish Monthly*, Vol. 67 (1939), p. 533.
99. O'Brien, 'Dance Halls', p. 44.
100. Senex, 'The New Girl', *Irish Monthly*, Vol. 54 (1926), pp. 739–40.
101. Ibid., p. 740.
102. *Irish Independent*, 25 February 1922, p. 4; 27 January, 1923.
103. O'Brien, 'Dance Halls', p. 49; E. M. Wells, 'The Dance-Board', *The Bell*, Vol. 1, No. 3, (December 1940), pp. 77–80. The author was a young female from Liverpool visiting County Kilkenny on holiday. She visited a local dance with a local youth and they cycled 'for what seemed hours to me'. They arrived at the scene, a field, saw dozens of bikes stacked against hedges and were admitted to the dance, for 4d. The dance floor was a wooden board (hence the title of her essay) of about 10 feet–12 feet square and around fifty couples were dancing on it. The music was provided by two old men; one playing a violin and the other a concertina.
104. *Irish Independent*, 7 December 1928, p. 7.
105. *Irish Independent*, 16 January 1929, p. 7.
106. *Irish Independent*, 6 December 1930, p. 10.
107. *Irish Independent*, 13 December 1930, p. 6.

108. *Irish Independent*, 16 February 1931, pp. 7–8.
109. On the Carrigan Committee and the Irish Bishops' anxieties over dance halls see D. Keogh, *The Vatican, the Bishops and Irish Politics, 1919–39* (Cambridge, 1986), pp. 163–6, 205–7; J. Smyth, 'The Public Dance Halls Act', *History Ireland*, 1993, p. 54; *Irish Independent*, 4 March 1935, pp. 6–7. For a scholarly study that touches on the subject of dance halls during this period see J. H. Whyte, *Church and State in Modern Ireland* (Dublin, 1971).
110. *Irish Independent*, 6 September 1935, p. 11.
111. Ibid.
112. *Irish Independent*, 7 September 1935, p. 11.
113. *Irish Independent*, 6 September 1935, p. 11; 9 September 1935, p. 5; 11 September 1935, p. 12.
114. *Irish Independent*, 11 September 1935, p. 12; 13 September 1935, p. 6.
115. *Irish Independent*, 14 September 1935, p. 11.
116. Ibid.
117. *Irish Independent*, 14 September 1935, p. 11.
118. *Irish Independent*, 16 September 1935, p. 7.
119. Juvenile and youth emigration from Ireland in the early years of the century was statistically significant. See, for example, the *Irish Catholic Directory and Almanac*, 1920, pp. xxix–xxxix. In 1911 the 15–24 age-group comprised 59.2 per cent (204,824) of all emigrants from Ireland.
120. See D. Fowler, *The First Teenagers: The Lifestyle of Young Wage-earners in Interwar Britain* (London, 1995), ch. 2.

Notes to Chapter 5: Juvenile Delinquency in Northern Ireland, 1945–*c.*1970

1. There is a growing historical literature on juvenile delinquency in postwar Britain. See especially A. Wills, 'Delinquency, Masculinity and Citizenship in England, 1950–1970', *Past and Present*, No. 187 (May 2005), pp. 157–85; V. Bailey, *Delinquency and Citizenship: Reclaiming the Young Offender, 1914–1948* (Oxford, 1987); P. Rock and S. Cohen, 'The Teddy Boy' in V. Bogdanor and R. Skidelsky (eds), *The Age of Affluence, 1951–1964* (London, 1970); J. Davis, *Youth and the Condition of Britain: Images of Adolescent Conflict* (London, 1990), ch. 7; D. Sandbrook, *Never Had It So Good: A History of Britain from Suez to The Beatles* (London, 2005), ch. 12. On the Mod culture, see below, Chapter 7. The only historical literature touching on the subject for Northern Ireland is S. O'Connell, 'From Toad of Toad Hall to the "Death Drivers" of Belfast: an Exploratory History of Joyriding', *British Journal of Criminology*, 46 (2006), pp. 455–69, which is an innovative and interesting account of 210 joyriding cases reported in Belfast newspapers between the 1930s and the 1950s.
2. See *Belfast Newsletter*, 6 August 1976; *Belfast Telegraph*, 1 March 1976; *Belfast Telegraph*, 8 October 1976; *Belfast Telegraph*, 2 November 1976. For an analysis of youth crime and youth culture during the Northern

Ireland Troubles see the pioneering survey, L. Taylor and S. Nelson, 'Young People and Civil Conflict in Northern Ireland' in *Conference on Young People in Northern Ireland: Three Papers* (Belfast, 1977). For the antecedents of the teenage bomber of the early 1970s, see D. Fowler, *Patterns of Juvenile and Youth Crime in Northern Ireland, 1945–2000* (Northern Ireland Office, Research Report, Belfast, 2001), ch. 2.

3. For an exploration of youth crime in Northern Ireland since the Second World War see Fowler, *Patterns of Juvenile and Youth Crime in Northern Ireland, passim.*

4. On the delinquent youth cultures of 1950s' England, see especially Wills, 'Delinquency, Masculinity and Citizenship in England'; Rock and Cohen, 'The Teddy Boy'; Sandbrook, *Never Had It So Good*, pp. 415–20, on the Teddy Boy cult in England and in British films of the 1950s; Davis, *Youth and the Condition of Britain*, ch. 7 on 'Teds' and 'Teenagers'. For a classic contemporary study, featuring much discussion of Teddy Boys, see T. R. Fyvel, *The Insecure Offenders: Rebellious Youth in the Welfare State* (1961; Harmondsworth, 1963).

5. On the emergence of Detention Centres and the 'short, sharp shock' approach to juvenile and youth delinquency see V. Bailey, *Delinquency and Citizenship: Reclaiming the Young Offender, 1914–1948* (Oxford, 1987), ch. 10; Wills, 'Delinquency, Masculinity and Citizenship'; on female delinquency see P. Cox, *Gender, Justice and Welfare: Bad Girls in Britain, 1900–1950* (Basingstoke, 2003).

6. Fowler, *Patterns of Juvenile and Youth Crime in Northern Ireland*, Introduction.

7. Ibid., pp. 118–24.

8. RUC, *Chief Constable's Report*, 1976, p. 3 and 1977, p. 3.

9. RUC, *Chief Constable's Report*, 1975, Appendix 1, Table 6.

10. See below, Appendix, Table A5, for the juvenile crime statistics for Northern Ireland during this period. For the English figures see M. Grunhut, *Juvenile Offenders Before the Courts* (Oxford, 1956), Table III, p. 11.

11. Taylor and Nelson, 'Young People and Civil Conflict in Northern Ireland', p. 6.

12. Ibid.

13. Ibid., p. 7.

14. Ibid., p. 8. On youth gangs active in Northern Ireland during the early 1970s see also M. Fraser, *Children in Conflict* (London, 1973); S. Jenvey, 'Sons and Haters: Ulster Youth in Conflict', *New Society*, 20 July 1972.

15. Taylor and Nelson, 'Young People and Civil Conflict', p. 8.

16. Ibid., p. 14.

17. Ibid., pp. 3–6.

18. See below, pp. 98–9, 101.

19. There were actually 100 juvenile courts in existence in Northern Ireland in 1960, but 2 – Portadown and Dungannon – were closed. See Government of Northern Ireland, *The Operation of Juvenile Courts in*

Northern Ireland: A Report by the Northern Ireland Child Welfare Council (Belfast, 1960), p. 15. See Appendix B in the Report, where they are all listed.

20. See *Belfast Telegraph*, 28 March 1957, for the following details.
21. See M. Grunhut, *Juvenile Offenders Before the Courts* (Oxford, 1956), p. 2; Government of Northern Ireland, *Juvenile Courts*, p. 7.
22. Government of Northern Ireland, *Juvenile Courts*, p. 7.
23. Ibid., *passim*.
24. The Child Welfare Council (CWC) published only two reports on juvenile crime in Northern Ireland: *Juvenile Delinquency* (Belfast, 1954) and *The Operation of Juvenile Courts in Northern Ireland* (Belfast, 1960). Both were short and flimsy documents, but they disguise a considerable amount of research undertaken. The members of the Child Welfare Council are cited in CWC, *Juvenile Courts*, p. 3.
25. See below, Appendix, Table A5.
26. See HA/10/58, 'Juvenile Crime Statistics, *c*.1949–1959', P.R.O.N.I. See the Ministry's 'Memorandum on Lord Justice Porter's Remarks about Juvenile Delinquency', March 1949. Lord Justice Porter's comments were also reported in *Belfast Newsletter*, 5 March 1949; 21 March 1949.
27. *Belfast Newsletter*, 21 March 1949.
28. *Belfast Telegraph*, 16 October 1951; *Northern Whig*, 17 October 1951.
29. See John Renshaw, Principal, Shaftesbury House Tutorial College, Belfast, to Ministry of Home Affairs (MHA), 6 November 1951; George Seth, Department of Psychology, The Queen's University of Belfast, to MHA, 26 September 1952. See also the series of talks Professor J. L. J. Edwards of the School of Law at Queen's University gave for BBC Radio during 1954. One broadcast on 17 June 1954 was entitled 'The Young Criminal'. The typescript is in HA/10/58, P.R.O.N.I. The Federation of Soroptimist Clubs of Great Britain and Ireland were also researching juvenile crime in the early 1950s. They wrote to the MHA in December 1951, requesting figures for a report into juvenile delinquency they were presenting at an international conference in Copenhagen. See The Federation of Soroptimist Clubs of Great Britain and Ireland to MHA, 10 December 1951.
30. See HA/10/58, 'Juvenile Crime Statistics' File.
31. The Ministry began collecting juvenile crime statistics when it was considering a probation service for the whole of Northern Ireland. See MHA, 'Memorandum on Juvenile Courts', 19 April 1949, HA/10/58, P.R.O.N.I. See also MHA letter to 'Juvenile Courts in Northern Ireland', 23 February 1949.
32. See HA/10/58 for all the returns submitted and for the following statistics.
33. See the cases reported in the *Belfast Newsletter* during March and April 1922. For similar behaviour during the Second World War see Fowler, *Patterns of Juvenile and Youth Crime in Northern Ireland*, ch. 2.
34. See HA/10/58 for the details.

35. The various categories are identified in Petty Sessions District of Bally-money, 'Juvenile Court Sessions, 1944–1948', Typed Report, n.d. 1948?, HA/10/58.
36. Ibid.
37. The Dervock return was submitted with the Ballymoney figures.
38. The 'Explosives and Firearms' cases are cited in the Ministry's figures for 'Non-Indictable' between 1939 and 1948.
39. *Belfast Newsletter*, 21 March 1949.
40. *Northern Whig*, 21 October 1953.
41. See the Child Welfare Council's letter to the *Northern Whig*, dated 21 October 1953: printed in *Northern Whig*, 22 October 1953, and *Belfast Newsletter*, 22 October 1953.
42. Child Welfare Council, *Juvenile Delinquency: An Interim Report* (Belfast, 1954).
43. For the discussion of the Juvenile Delinquency report see CWC, Minutes, 29 June 1954, HA/13/111, P.R.O.N.I.
44. CWC, Minutes, 29 June 1954, p. 1.
45. Ibid., pp. 2, 4.
46. Ibid., p. 5.
47. Ibid. The Child Welfare Council's 'Chairman' was a woman; Mrs Maje Haughton, a local JP.
48. See, for example, Basil Henriques' discussion in B. L. Q. Henriques, *The Indiscretions of a Magistrate: Thoughts on the Work of the Juvenile Court* (London, 1951), pp. 90–3, 131–2. The author was a juvenile magistrate in East London and had done this work for almost 25 years. The information on a juvenile's IQ came from Headteachers and was passed on to the Juvenile Court, in the form of a written report, by Children's Officers working for the local authorities. Northern Ireland did not have Children's Officers working for the juvenile courts at this period.
49. CWC, Minutes, 29 June 1954, p. 8.
50. CWC, *Juvenile Delinquency*, p. 11.
51. CWC, Minutes, 29 June 1954, p. 9.
52. Ibid. See also CWC, *Juvenile Delinquency*, p. 11.
53. CWC, Minutes, 29 June 1954, pp. 14–15.
54. See CWC, 'Notes on the Work of the Child Welfare Council', July 1953–July 1954, September 1954, HA/13/112, P.R.O.N.I.
55. The surprising fact is that the Council discussed every section of the *Juvenile Delinquency Report* at their meeting on 29 June 1954 and were happy to include such vacuous phrases in their report. See CWC, Minutes, 29 June 1954, p. 12.
56. CWC to MHA, 3 February 1955, HA/13/112, P.R.O.N.I.
57. See CWC, Minutes, 20 January 1955; 21 April 1955.
58. See Armagh County Welfare Committee, Report of the Children's Sub-Committee, June 1954, HA/13/111, P.R.O.N.I.
59. CWC, Minutes, 5 February 1954, HA/13/111, P.R.O.N.I.
60. Ibid.

61. For the CWC's work during 1955 see HA/13/112, P.R.O.N.I. See especially CWC, 'Draft Final Report (to the MHA)', January 1956.
62. See the revealing discussion in CWC, Minutes, 11 March 1958. The story can also be tracked in the court records for Omagh and Enniskillen. See Petty Sessions, Juvenile Court Order Books, HA1/49/AA/1–3, P.R.O.N.I.
63. CWC, Minutes, 22 October 1957.
64. Ibid.
65. CWC, Minutes, 22 November 1957.
66. CWC, Minutes, 22 October 1957.
67. Ibid. See the comments of Mr Jeffery of the Churches Youth Welfare Council.
68. Ibid.
69. CWC, Minutes, 11 March 1958.
70. Ibid.
71. CWC, Minutes, 20 October 1957.
72. CWC, Minutes, 22 October 1957.
73. The Child Welfare Council were disappointed that the Belfast youth leaders they interviewed were not interested in attracting juvenile delinquents to their clubs. Mrs Harrison: 'I think it is a great pity if the Youth Committee feel that their clubs are not for juvenile delinquents.' Mrs Haughton (Chairman): 'I don't say that you should make every youth club into a rehabilitation centre for delinquents but in a district where there are children getting into trouble I feel the youth leaders have a duty to them ...' CWC, Minutes, 14 January 1958.
74. See 'List of Children under 10 sent to Training Schools, 1950–1954', HA/13/111, P.R.O.N.I.
75. Members of the Council seem to have discovered the 'Teddy boy' on visits to juvenile courts in England during 1956. See above, p. 110.
76. CWC, Minutes, 25 September 1956.
77. Ibid.
78. The Hawnt Report was never published. A copy is lodged in the Child Welfare Council's papers. See 'Report on the Juvenile Court', n.d. 1957?, HA/13/113, P.R.O.N.I., for the following statistics.
79. CWC, Minutes, 15 February 1957.
80. Ibid. In effect, the city centre and districts closest to the city centre had significantly higher levels of juvenile delinquency than residential areas on the outskirts.
81. For the emergence of Teddy Boys in England see Rock and Cohen, 'The Teddy Boy'.
82. See *Belfast Newsletter*, 15 April 1957.
83. See CWC, Minutes, 15 February 1957.
84. Ibid. For details of Mrs Haughton's complaint to the BBC, see CWC, Minutes, 15 March 1957.
85. CWC, Minutes, 15 March 1957, HA/13/113, P.R.O.N.I.
86. CWC, Minutes, 17 June 1954.

87. See Fowler, *Patterns of Juvenile and Youth Crime in Northern Ireland*, ch. 3.
88. See CWC, 'Typed Report, 1958–1959', n.d. 1959?, HA/13/136, P.R.O.N.I.
89. The CWC discussed the Teddy Boy on several occasions at their meetings; always in a reproving way. They never discussed girls' involvement in youth culture or other themes in the lives of the young.
90. CWC, Minutes, 27 November 1956.
91. Ibid.
92. See CWC, 'Visit to Ballymena Juvenile Court', 1 May 1957, HA/13/136, P.R.O.N.I.
93. See J. O'Connor, 'The Juvenile Offender', *Studies*, Vol. LII, No. 52 (1963), p. 87.
94. Ibid., p. 89.
95. See Birmingham City Police to CWC, Belfast, n.d. April 1958?, HA/13/114, P.R.O.N.I.
96. For a more detailed discussion of the probation system in Northern Ireland during the 1950s, see Fowler, *Patterns of Juvenile and Youth Crime in Northern Ireland*, ch. 1.
97. MHA, Annual Report, 1959, HA/8/685, P.R.O.N.I.
98. See above, note 62.

Notes to Chapter 6: From the Juke Box Boys to Revolting Students: Richard Hoggart and the Study of British Youth Culture

1. See R. Colls, *Identity of England* (Oxford, 2002), p. 190. Dominic Sandbrook's *Never Had It So Good: A History of Britain from Suez to The Beatles* (London, 2005) discusses Hoggart, but not his work on youth. For a recent article on Hoggart's discussion of milk bars in *The Uses of Literacy* see J. Moran, 'Milk Bars, Starbucks and the Uses of Literacy', *Cultural Studies*, Vol. 20, No. 6 (November 2006), pp. 552–73. For a new interpretation of the postwar history of British Youth Culture see below, chs 7–9. See also B. Osgerby, *Youth in Britain since 1945* (Oxford, 1998); on the global student revolts see especially A. Marwick, *The Sixties: Cultural Revolution in Britain, France, Italy and the United States, c.1958–c.1974* (Oxford, 1998), ch. 12.
2. Colls, *Identity of England*, p. 190; Moran, 'Milk Bars', pp. 552–9.
3. See R. Hoggart, *The Uses of Literacy: Aspects of Working-Class Life with Special Reference to Publications and Entertainments* (London, 1957), pp. 203–5, for his critique of American influences shaping provincial youth cultures.
4. Cited in R. Hoggart, *Higher Education and Cultural Change: A Teacher's View* (The 44th Earl Grey Memorial Lecture, Newcastle, 1965), p. 4.
5. D. Fowler, *The First Teenagers: The Lifestyle of Young Wage-earners in Interwar Britain* (London, 1995).

6. For contemporary comment on 'the birth of the teenager' post-1945 see, most famously, Mark Abrams' pamphlet *The Teenage Consumer* (London, 1959). The supposed novelty of postwar teenage lifestyles permeates contemporary political and literary journals such as *Universities and Left Review, Socialist Register, New Left Review, New Statesman and Society* and also political discourse as well. See, for example, Ministry of Education, *The Youth Service in England and Wales,* Report of the Committee Appointed by the Minister of Education in November 1958, Cmnd 929 (London, 1960), ch. 2. Some historians have also perpetuated this myth. See, for example, Osgerby, *Youth in Britain since 1945, passim*; and more recently, Peter Hennessy, *Having It So Good: Britain in the Fifties* (London, 2006), pp. 19, 491–2.

7. See above, Chapters 2 and 3. The author is also preparing a full-scale biography of Rolf Gardiner, which focuses on his central role in interwar Youth Culture and European Youth Movements of the period, *The Youth Apostle: A Biography of Rolf Gardiner* (forthcoming, 2008).

8. Copies of *Youth: An Expression of Progressive University Thought* are held in the Periodicals Section of Cambridge University Library and in the British Library at St Pancras.

9. See above, Chapter 2.

10. For more discussion of Gardiner's novel ideas on Youth Culture see above, Chapter 2.

11. Ibid.

12. For an incisive contemporary essay linking the British teenage culture of the late 1950s with American pop music see Ray Gosling, 'Dream Boy', *New Left Review*, 3 (May–June 1960), pp. 33–4. For an exploration of the subject by an historian see Sandbrook, *Never Had It So Good,* ch. 13.

13. Hoggart, *Uses of Literacy,* pp. 203–5. Hoggart does not provide details in *The Uses of Literacy* of the milk bar he visited. Years later, however, he revealed that he had encountered the juke box boys 'several times' in a milk bar in Goole, as he prepared to take his evening classes. He was, at the time, an Extra-Mural Tutor in English at the University of Hull and Goole was close to Hull. See R. Hoggart, *Between Two Worlds: Essays* (London, 2001), p. 308.

14. For the historian Robert Colls' own critical assessment, see above, note 1; for Nicholas Tredell's rigorous questioning of Hoggart on this section of *The Uses of Literacy* see Hoggart, *Between Two Worlds,* pp. 308–9. Hoggart's views on the youths who frequented milk bars were alarmist, even at the time. For more favourable discussion of milk bars as valuable 'public spaces' for youths to meet see T. R. Fyvel, *The Insecure Offenders: Rebellious Youth and the Welfare State* (London, 1963), pp. 67–9; and for George Melly's retrospective reflections of London milk bars see G. Melly, *Revolt into Style: The Pop Arts in the '50s and '60s* (1970; reprinted Oxford, 1989), p. 48. Pearl Jephcott, in a contemporary survey of Nottingham youth, noted that milk bars were valuable meeting places for youths and girls; especially on Sundays in 'the dead hour between Sunday dinner

and the five o'clock picture queue'. Pearl Jephcott, *Some Young People* (London, 1954), p. 34.

15. On the role of jukeboxes in postwar British youth culture see A. Horn, 'Juke Boxes and British Youth Culture, 1945–1960', unpublished PhD thesis, University of Lancaster, 2004.

16. For the pioneering study of 1960s' youth pop groups as creative artists see George Melly, *Revolt into Style,* much of it based on his pop reviews in the *New Statesman and Society.* On the Beatles as songwriters see Wilfrid Mellers, *Twilight of the Gods: The Beatles in Retrospect* (London, 1973) and the brilliant study by the late Ian MacDonald, *Revolution in the Head: The Beatles Records and the Sixties* (London, 1994).

17. C. Fletcher, 'Beat and Gangs on Merseyside', *New Society,* 20 February 1964, pp. 11–14.

18. 'Faces Without Shadows: Young Men who Live for Clothes and Pleasure', *Town,* Vol. 3, No. 9 (1962), pp. 48–53.

19. For an elaboration of these points see below, Chapter 7. On the Mods, see also J. Green, *All Dressed Up: The Sixties and the Counterculture* (1998), ch. 5; Osgerby, *Youth in Britain,* pp. 41–7 is somewhat superficial.

20. Sandbrook describes Epstein's first encounter with the Beatles in *Never Had It So Good,* p. 465. He describes the venue (the Cavern) as 'damp' and 'dingy'. The meeting took place in November 1961.

21. Hoggart, *Uses of Literacy,* p. 203.

22. Ibid., p. 204.

23. Ibid., p. 205.

24. For Gosling's first autobiographical memoir see R. Gosling, *Sum Total* (London, 1962). See also his later work *Personal Copy: A Memoir of the Sixties* (London, 1980).

25. See the personal testimony of the 19-year-old youth interviewed in B. S. Rowntree and G. R. Lavers, *English Life and Leisure: A Social Study* (London, 1951): 'This country's no good. It's finished. I'd like to go to America' (p. 249).

26. For the disorientating effects of National Service among Glasgow youths see T. Ferguson and J. Cunnison, *In their Early Twenties: A Study of Glasgow Youth* (Oxford, 1956), pp. 31–2.

27. He described a biography of Lord Thompson, a Fleet Street newspaper editor, he reviewed for the *New Statesman* as 'a totally inconsiderable biography in any serious meaning of the term'. See *New Statesman,* 29 October 1965, p. 648.

28. R. Hoggart, 'We Are The Lambeth Boys', *Sight and Sound,* Vol. 28, No. 3 (Summer–Autumn 1959), p. 164.

29. Ibid., p. 165.

30. R. Hoggart, 'Lambeth Boys', *Sight and Sound,* Vol. 54, No. 2 (Spring 1985), p. 107.

31. Ibid., p. 108.

32. Ibid., p. 106.

33. Ibid., p. 107.

34. Ibid., p. 108.

35. Ibid.
36. Ibid., p. 106.
37. Ibid.
38. Ibid., pp. 106–7.
39. R. Hoggart, *An Imagined Life: Life and Times, 1959–1991* (Oxford, 1992), pp. 19–21.
40. See Leslie Paul, *Angry Young Man* (London, 1951).
41. Hoggart, *Imagined Life*, p. 21.
42. Ibid., p. 19.
43. Ministry of Education, *Youth Service in England and Wales*, ch. 2.
44. See R. Gosling, *Lady Albemarle's Boys* (Fabian Pamphlet, 1961).
45. These details have been extracted from the Youth Commission Papers held in the Labour Party Archives, Manchester. On this Commission see also C. Ellis, 'The Younger Generation: The Labour Party and the 1959 Youth Commission', *Journal of British Studies*, Vol. 41, No. 2 (April 2002), pp. 199–231. Its membership is discussed on pp. 207 and 208. The theme of the postwar Labour Party and Youth Culture is discussed in S. Fielding, *Labour and Cultural Change* (Manchester, 2003), ch. 7, though he does not mention its Youth Commission survey.
46. Gosling, *Lady Albemarle's Boys*, p. 15.
47. *Youth Service in England and Wales*, ch. 2.
48. For Abrams see D. Fowler, *The First Teenagers: The Lifestyle of Young Wage-earners in Interwar Britain* (London, 1995), ch. 4.
49. Ibid.
50. Discussed in Fowler, *First Teenagers*, ch. 4.
51. Gosling, *Personal Copy*, pp. 61–7.
52. Fowler, *First Teenagers*, ch. 4.
53. For a useful portrait of Colin MacInnes see Gosling, *Personal Copy*, pp. 71–7. See also T. Gould, *Inside Outsider: The Life and Times of Colin MacInnes* (1993).
54. Gosling notes that MacInnes abhorred provincialism and castigated him for being from the provinces. Gosling, *Personal Copy*, p. 93.
55. R. Hoggart, Review of R. Gosling, *Sum Total* (1962), *New Statesman*, November 1962, p. 788. Ray Gosling, like Hoggart, was from a working-class background. His father was a car mechanic. He was born in Northampton in 1939. See R. Gosling, *Personal Copy*, for his family background.
56. Brief details of Gosling's publications at this period are given in *The New University*, October 1960.
57. Gosling lived with MacInnes in London from 1962 to 1964. He implies in his later memoir that the two had a homosexual relationship. See Gosling, *Personal Copy*, pp. 71–2.
58. Gosling, *Personal Copy*, for details.
59. Hoggart, *New Statesman*, p. 788.
60. Ibid. Hoggart's review was slightly patronising. He referred to Gosling as 'the only talking teenager'; revealing a touch of envy, it seems, that Gosling was in such great demand as a writer on youth affairs,

when Hoggart was only contributing occasional book reviews to literary journals.

61. Ibid.
62. See note 57 above.
63. The following episode is recounted in Gosling, *Personal Copy*, pp. 61–7.
64. Ibid. See also Gosling, *Lady Albemarle's Boys*, p. 23, for details of the grant.
65. Hoggart, *New Statesman*, p. 788. Hoggart was Chairman of the Trustees of the Leicester Youth Club Gosling ran, so he must have known that Gosling was dismissed. See Gosling, *Personal Copy*, p. 62.
66. Gosling, *Lady Albemarle's Boys*, p. 26. His two black eyes are mentioned in Gosling, *Personal Copy*, p. 66.
67. Gosling, *Lady Albemarle's Boys*, p. 26.
68. A rich collection of the Birmingham CCCS's unpublished research reports on youth is held in the Periodicals Section, Cambridge University Library at L200.b.301.
69. R. Hoggart, 'Schools of English and Contemporary Society', Inaugural Lecture, University of Birmingham, reprinted in R. Hoggart, *Speaking to Each Other: Essays*, Vol. 2 (Middlesex, 1970), p. 242.
70. Hoggart, *Imagined Life*, p. 90.
71. G. Cannon, 'Popular Culture and Society', *New Statesman*, 17 October 1963, p. 22. Details of Stuart Hall's status as a school teacher are in S. Hall, 'Politics of Adolescence?', *Universities and Left Review*, 6 (Spring 1959), p. 2.
72. See S. Hall, 'Student Journals', *New Left Review*, 7 (January–February 1961), pp. 50–1; S. Hall, 'Absolute Beginnings', Review of Colin MacInnes and Mark Abrams, *Universities and Left Review*, Autumn 1959, pp. 17–25; Hall, 'Politics of Adolescence?', pp. 2–4.
73. For these points see his interesting review article 'Absolute Beginnings'.
74. Ibid. See also S. Hall and P. Whannell, *The Popular Arts* (London, 1964), p. 312 (on Beatlemania).
75. Details are given in University of Birmingham, Centre for Contemporary Cultural Studies (CCCS), *Annual Reports*, held in Cambridge University Library, L200.b.214.
76. S. Hall, 'Hippies: an American Moment' (University of Birmingham, CCCS Stencilled Paper, 1968) reprinted in J. Nagel (ed.), *Student Power* (1969).
77. University of Birmingham, Centre for Contemporary Cultural Studies, *Annual Report*, 1968–1969, p. 15.
78. Ibid., p. 19.
79. On this see Hoggart, *Imagined Life*, ch. 5.
80. R. Hoggart, 'Proper Ferdinands?' in *The Permissive Society: The Guardian Inquiry* (London, 1969), p. 78. This essay was reprinted under a different title, 'Images of the Provinces', in Hoggart, *Speaking to Each Other: Essays* (1970). The citations are from the original version.
81. Discussed in Hoggart, *The Permissive Society: Guardian Inquiry*, on pp. 18–25 (but not mentioned by name in Hoggart's piece).

82. See below, Chapter 9.

83. Sandbrook, *Never Had It So Good*, p. 368.

84. Hoggart, *Imagined Life*, ch. 5. See also R. Hoggart, 'The Student Movement and Its Effects in the Universities' in S. Armstrong (ed.), *Decade of Change*, Society for Research into Higher Education, Annual Conference Papers (Surrey, 1979), pp. 3–10; R. Hoggart, *Higher Education and Cultural Change: A Teacher's View*, 44th Earl Grey Memorial Lecture, University of Newcastle (Newcastle, 1965).

85. The author is currently working on Student Protest Movements of the 1960s, from archives. Hoggart's own reading on student protest, and even on student cultures, was slight. He had not read Ferdynand Zweig's survey of students at Manchester and Oxford published as *The Student in the Age of Anxiety* (1963) by the time of the Earl Grey Lecture in 1965. He cites Crouch's work in his essay 'The Student Movement and Its Effects in the Universities' published in 1979; but by this date there was a wealth of other scholarly work on the student protests of the late '60s besides Crouch's *The Student Revolt* (published in 1970). See, for example, H. Kidd, *The Trouble at LSE* (Oxford, 1969) and T. Blackstone et al., *Students in Conflict: LSE in 1967* (London, 1970). Nowhere in his 1979 article does Hoggart mention his own son Simon's involvement with a student protest movement at Cambridge in the late 1960s, the 'Free University' movement. For a discussion of student protest in these years, see below, Chapter 8.

86. See below, Chapter 8.

87. Ibid.

88. See, for example, D. Adelstein's pamphlet, *Teach Yourself Student Power* (1968), and Adelstein's essay in A. Cockburn and R. Blackburn (eds), *Student Power: Problems, Diagnosis, Action* (Harmondsworth, 1969), which also contains an insightful essay on 'The Meaning of the Student Revolt' by Gareth Stedman Jones; then a Research Fellow at Oxford University.

89. K. Morgan, *The People's Peace: British History, 1945–1990* (Oxford, 1990), pp. 292–8, 354–5.

90. On the links between 1960s' student libertarians and Thatcherism see R. Cockett, 'The New Right and the 1960s: the Dialectics of Liberation' in G. Andrews et al. (eds), *New Left, New Right and Beyond: Taking the Sixties Seriously* (1999), pp. 85–105.

Notes to Chapter 7: The Mod Culture in Swinging Britain, 1964–7

1. D. Sandbrook, *White Heat: A History of Britain in the Swinging Sixties* (London, 2006), contains only scattered references to the Mod cult; see especially pp. 196–200. B. Osgerby, *Youth in Britain since 1945* (London, 1998), pp. 41–5, is a bit superficial on the Mods and sometimes erroneous (see note 5 below). J. Green, *All Dressed Up: The Sixties and the Counterculture* (1998; reprinted London, 1999), ch. 5, gives a flavour of the Mod culture.

2. A. Marwick, *The Sixties: Cultural Revolution in Britain, France, Italy and the United States, c.1958–c.1974* (Oxford, 1998), pp. 77–8, 560.
3. Ibid., p. 77; Sandbrook, *White Heat*, p. 234; Green, *All Dressed Up*, pp. 44–5; S. Cohen, *Folk Devils and Moral Panics: The Creation of the Mods and Rockers* (1972; reprinted Oxford, 1980), p. 201.
4. Cited in Marwick, *The Sixties*, p. 78.
5. In a recent essay on postwar youth, Bill Osgerby argues that the Mods visited 'London nightclubs' like The Scene and the Flamingo; but this is erroneous. These venues were non-licensed youth music clubs, which only served soft drinks. See B. Osgerby, ' "Seized by Change, Liberated by Affluence": Youth Consumption and Cultural Change in Postwar Britain' in H. van Nierop (ed.), *Twentieth Century Mass Society in Britain and the Netherlands* (Oxford, 2006), p. 183. For the absence of alcohol in the clubs, see Green, *All Dressed Up*, pp. 42–3. Given that the Mods were actually attending some of the same dance halls as their interwar equivalents, the Streatham Locarno for example, the continuities in British youth culture between the 1930s and the mid-1960s seem clear. On the teenage consumers of interwar Britain see D. Fowler, *The First Teenagers: The Lifestyle of Young Wage-earners in Interwar Britain* (London, 1995), ch. 4.
6. On the Mods and delinquency, see below, pp. 309–24.
7. Green, *All Dressed Up*, p. 41; T. Rawlings, *Mod: A Very British Phenomenon* (London, 2000), p. 49; R. Barnes, *Mods!* (London, 1991), p. 8.
8. Green, *All Dressed Up*, p. 41.
9. Green asserts that by 1965 there were 'around half-a-million Mods' in Britain, but does not cite his source. See Green, *All Dressed Up*, p. 45.
10. McGowan claimed in October 1965: 'We started the Mod craze. It all started with the idea of our show being for Young Moderns, so we just called them Mods.' See K. Wohlgemuth, 'Teen interview from October 1965', www.readysteadyball.co.uk, p. 1.
11. Cohen, *Folk Devils and Moral Panics*, p. 34.
12. Two sociologists, Paul Barker and Alan Little, interviewed 44 of those arrested at Margate in 1964 and found that 14 described themselves as Mods, 9 as Rockers and the rest as neither. See P. Barker and A. Little, 'The Margate Offenders: a Survey', *New Society*, 30 July 1964, p. 8.
13. See 'Faces Without Shadows: Young Men Who Live For Clothes and Pleasure', *Town*, Vol. 3, No. 9 (September 1962), pp. 48–53, for the following details.
14. Ibid., p. 50.
15. Ibid.
16. Ibid.
17. Ibid.
18. Ibid.
19. Ibid.
20. Ibid., pp. 50–1.
21. Ibid., p. 51.
22. Ibid.

23. Ibid.
24. Ibid.
25. Ibid.
26. Green, *All Dressed Up*, pp. 42–3. See also T. Wolfe, 'The Noonday Underground' in T. Wolfe, *The Mid-Atlantic Man and other New Breeds in England and America* (London, 1968), pp. 99–112.
27. On John Stephen see S. Levy, *Ready, Steady, Go!: Swinging London and the Invention of Cool* (London, 2002), pp. 116–17; Green, *All Dressed Up*, p. 44.
28. Levy, *Ready, Steady, Go!*, p. 117.
29. Ibid., pp. 117–18; Green, *All Dressed Up*, p. 44.
30. For details of John Stephen's shops see Levy, *Ready, Steady, Go!*, p. 118.
31. Ibid., pp. 124–5.
32. Cited in K. Badman and T. Rawlings, *Quite Naturally the Small Faces* (London, 1997), p. 150. On the ambience of a John Stephen shop see N. Cohn, 'Carnaby Street' in P. Hewitt (ed.), *The Sharper Word: A Mod Anthology* (London, 2002), p. 35.
33. *Daily Mirror*, 15 June 1966, p. 3.
34. *The Mod*, January 1965, p. 7.
35. Cited in Levy, *Ready, Steady, Go!*, p. 225.
36. Cited in *The Mod*, August 1965, p. 6.
37. See note 10 above.
38. For the following details see Levy, *Ready, Steady, Go!*, p. 127.
39. Author's recollection of seeing an episode of *Ready Steady Go!* (*RSG*) during the 1980s.
40. Marwick, *The Sixties*, p. 77.
41. G. Melly, *Revolt into Style: The Pop Arts in the '50s and '60s* (1970; reprinted Oxford, 1989), p. 188.
42. Green, *All Dressed Up*, ch. 5 on Mods as a male youth cult; see photographic images of *RSG* programmes in various issues of *The Mod*.
43. See, for example, reports of Mod dances and *RSG* programmes in various issues of *The Mod*.
44. B. Wilson, *The Youth Culture and the Universities* (London, 1970).
45. Osgerby makes this point. See Osgerby, *Youth in Britain since 1945*, pp. 19–20.
46. B. Wilson, *The Youth Culture and the Universities* (London, 1970), p. 86. The quotation is from an essay originally published in the *Daily Telegraph* in 1964, and reproduced as ch. 6.
47. R. Grayson, 'Mods, Rockers and Juvenile Delinquency in 1964: the Government Response', *Contemporary British History*, Vol. 12, No. 1 (Spring 1998), pp. 19–47.
48. Ibid., p. 26.
49. Ibid.
50. Cohen, *Folk Devils and Moral Panics*, p. 35, refers to the Barker and Little essay as 'the Barker–Little sample', thus converting a lightly researched and impressionistic essay into a major academic source; Grayson, 'Mods, Rockers and Juvenile Delinquency in 1964', pp. 24–5. I have used the

reprinted version of the Barker and Little article: P. Barker, 'The Margate Offenders: a Survey (1964)' reprinted in T. Raison (ed.), *Youth in New Society* (London, 1966), pp. 115–27.

51. Barker, 'The Margate Offenders: a Survey (1964)' reprinted in Raison (ed.), *Youth in New Society*, pp. 115, 117.
52. Ibid., p. 116.
53. Ibid., p. 115.
54. For a contemporary survey that includes interviews with Mods see C. Hamblett and J. Deverson, *Generation X* (London, 1964).
55. Barker, 'The Margate Offenders', pp. 116, 118.
56. Ibid., p. 116.
57. Ibid., p. 120.
58. Ibid., pp. 119–20.
59. Ibid., p. 119.
60. Ibid., p. 120.
61. Ibid., p. 119.
62. Ibid.
63. Ibid.; Grayson, 'Mods, Rockers and Juvenile Delinquency in 1964', p. 26, Table 1.
64. Barker, 'The Margate Offenders', p. 122.
65. Ibid., p. 122.
66. Ibid.
67. Ibid., pp. 122, 125.
68. Ibid., p. 125.
69. Green, *All Dressed Up*, p. 46; Cohen, *Folk Devils and Moral Panics*, p. 29.
70. Grayson, 'Mods, Rockers and Juvenile Delinquency in 1964', pp. 25–6.
71. On Cohen's research methods and 'fieldwork' for his study, conducted between Easter 1964 and September 1966, see Cohen, *Folk Devils and Moral Panics*, Appendix, pp. 205–10. George Harnett, a local hotelier, is quoted in *The Times*, 31 March 1964, p. 10, cited in Grayson, 'Mods, Rockers and Juvenile Delinquency in 1964', pp. 26–7.
72. See P. Barker, 'Brighton Battleground', *New Society*, 21 May 1964, pp. 9–10.
73. Cited in Green, *All Dressed Up*, p. 41.
74. Sandbrook, *White Heat*, p. 199.
75. Cohen, *Folk Devils and Moral Panics*, pp. 32–6.
76. Grayson, 'Mods, Rockers and Juvenile Delinquency in 1964', pp. 28–36, 39–42.
77. Ibid., p. 28.
78. Ibid., p. 33.

Notes to Chapter 8: From Danny the Red to British Student Power: Labour Governments and the International Student Revolts of the 1960s

* I would like to thank the participants at the 'Labour and the Wider World' Conference, held in Cambridge in July 2004, for commenting

on an earlier version of this chapter. I would also like to thank Dr Alan Sked of the London School of Economics for the opportunity to present the paper at the Departmental Research Seminar, International History Department, at LSE in February 2006. Finally, I wish to thank Dr Alastair Reid of Girton College, Cambridge, for his comments.

1. B. Pimlott, *Harold Wilson* (London, 1992), p. 59.
2. Ibid., p. 513; A. Marwick, *The Sixties: Cultural Revolution in Britain, France, Italy and the United States, c.1958–c.1974* (Oxford, 1998), p. 555.
3. See Marwick, *The Sixties*, for the most comprehensive survey of student life in 1960s' Britain. Information on British students travelling to Paris in May 1968 was supplied by my former colleague at The Queen's University of Belfast, Mr Peter Blair (a student at LSE at the time).
4. Marwick, *The Sixties*, p. 555; K. Morgan, *The People's Peace: British History since 1945* (1990; second edition, Oxford, 1999), pp. 240–1.
5. There is a huge secondary literature on '1968', but for background see W. J. Rorabaugh, *Berkeley at War: The 1960s* (Oxford, 1989); Marwick, *The Sixties*, ch. 12; C. Fink et al. (eds), *1968: The World Transformed* (Cambridge, 1998); and R. Fraser, *1968: A Student Generation in Revolt* (New York, 1988).
6. See below, pp. 155–7, 162–3.
7. Cited in A. Morgan, *Harold Wilson* (London, 1992), pp. 336–7.
8. Benn's involvement in the Bristol University students' 'sit-in' is mentioned in Morgan, *Wilson*, p. 337; Wilson quotation cited in S. Fielding, *Labour and Cultural Change* (Manchester, 2003), p. 228 n. 52.
9. Morgan, *Wilson*, p. 336.
10. T. Ali, *Street Fighting Years: An Autobiography of the Sixties* (1987), pp. 227–8.
11. Morgan, *People's Peace*, p. 297.
12. This was the most commonly-used nickname he was given in the British press of the period. Even the broadsheets adopted the term. See, for example, *Daily Telegraph*, 15 June 1968, p. 13. *The Times*, meanwhile, preferred the more threatening term 'Herr Cohn-Bendit'; a reference to the fact that he was part-German. See *The Times*, 29 May 1968, p. 1; 12 June 1968, p. 1. For other references to 'Danny the Red' see *Daily Mail*, 13 June 1968, p. 1; *The Observer*, 12 May 1968, p. 1. *The London Evening Standard* ran a cartoon of Cohn-Bendit, known in France as 'Danny le Rouge', mistaken by a BBC TV producer for Danny La Rue, a popular television drag artiste at the time. See *Evening Standard*, 13 June 1968, p. 6.
13. See below, pp. 154–6.
14. On Special Branch involvement see note 16, below. Marwick's immensely rich and learned survey, *The Sixties*, entirely overlooks Cohn-Bendit's visit to Britain in June 1968, as do Kenneth Morgan in *The People's Peace* and Steven Fielding in *Labour and Cultural Change*. None of the Wilson biographers mention it either. Fielding is the only other historian,

it appears, who has examined the Labour government's files on the student protests. For his rather brief, but cogent, discussion of student protests in Britain see his *Labour and Cultural Change*, pp. 177–80.

15. Callaghan was severely criticised in the Commons debate on Cohn-Bendit for extending his 24-hour visa (see above, pp. 156), and told Parliament he had warmed to the young Frenchman after meeting him. But later in the year, in October, when Cohn-Bendit applied to visit Britain again Callaghan refused to allow him back into the country. The proposed visit just happened to coincide with a large anti-Vietnam demonstration through London and Callaghan felt it was not safe to allow Cohn-Bendit to join this protest. See J. Callaghan, *Time and Chance* (London, 1987), p. 259.

16. It is very clear from Government records that Special Branch monitored student protest in Britain during the late '60s, but exactly how, where, when and with what results are not easy to determine. It was claimed in the press that Special Branch officers accompanied Daniel Cohn-Bendit to the BBC TV studios during his visit to Britain; see *Daily Mail*, 13 June 1968, p. 1. There are also in existence Special Branch reports on 'student militancy' covering these years; but, frustratingly, they have been 'Temporarily retained by the Department [i.e. the Home Office]'. See National Archives Kew, HO 325/127 (hereafter HO etc.). Several foreign students studying in London claimed that Special Branch tried to recruit them to spy on radical students at British universities. See *Daily Express*, 19 June 1968, p. 9.

17. R. Dahrendorf, *LSE: A History of the London School of Economics and Political Science, 1895–1995* (Oxford, 1995), p. 456.

18. C. Crouch, *The Student Revolt* (London, 1970), p. 109.

19. Morgan summarises the impact of student protest in Britain in 1968 thus in *The People's Peace*: 'The student revolts of the 1968 period had been transient affairs, with only a limited impact beyond the narrow, cloistered confines of the universities' (pp. 354–5).

20. D. Rossinow, *The Politics of Authenticity: Liberalism, Christianity and the New Left in America* (New York, 1998).

21. Ibid. This is an immensely scholarly book that deals in detail with the travels American students undertook to preach social revolution (mostly across America); but he does not deal at all with the large numbers of American students who travelled to Britain and Europe to study and therefore with the cultural networks between British and American campuses.

22. Dahrendorf, *LSE*, p. 456.

23. The programme was discussed in all the leading national newspapers – The *Times*, *The Guardian*, The *Daily Telegraph*, The *Daily Mail*, The *Daily Express* and The *Daily Mirror*, to name all of those consulted. It was a TV discussion chaired by a Professor of Politics at the London School of Economics, Professor Robert McKenzie. See *The Times*, 12 June 1968, p. 1; 13 June 1968, pp. 10, 16, for the details given in the text. Michael Billington, TV critic for *The Times*, reported enthusiastically on 14 June

1968: 'Obviously ... the one indispensable item on television last night' (referring to *Students in Revolt*). See *The Times*, 14 June 1968, p. 7.

24. See *The Sunday Times*, 26 May 1968, pp. 1, 7, for the background to the Paris students' revolt, which includes details of Cohn-Bendit's confrontation with the French Minister for Youth, François Missoffe (who had written a book on French Youth) during the Minister's visit to Nanterre. Cohn-Bendit was a second-year student studying Sociology at Nanterre. As the Minister stepped from his car, Cohn-Bendit addressed him thus: 'M. Missoffe, I have read your book. I don't altogether agree with you on some points.' He went on: 'There is nothing in it, from beginning to end, about the sexual problems of French youth.' The Minister tried a put-down: 'I remember when I was young. In my day ... it was better to go to the swimming pool to solve these problems.' Events quickly overtook the Minister, however, who was eventually forced to resign, while Cohn-Bendit became the spokesman for the entire Paris student body of over 30,000 students.

25. *The Sunday Times*, 26 May 1968, pp. 7–8; *The Observer*, 12 May 1968, p. 1; 19 May 1968, p. 2.

26. Two of *The Observer*'s reporters, Patrick Seale and Maureen McConville, heard Cohn-Bendit give speeches in Paris during May of 1968 and praised him highly as 'a born leader, a mob orator of real talent'. *The Observer*, 19 May 1968, p. 2. Dr Robert Boyce of the Department of International History at LSE, who also heard Cohn-Bendit speak in Paris during May 1968, confirmed that he was a gifted speaker and a real intellectual. (Information from Dr Robert Boyce of LSE, February 2006.) For Cohn-Bendit's fluent command of several languages see *The Times*, 29 May 1968, p. 1. For his peripatetic existence during May 1968 see *Daily Telegraph*, 25 May 1968, p. 22. For Cohn-Bendit's speech at the Odeon Cinema in Paris see *Daily Telegraph*, 27 May 1968, p. 10.

27. The following details are taken from an analysis of the British newspaper coverage of the student protests during May and June 1968. The newspapers consulted were: *The Times*, *The Guardian*, *The Daily Telegraph*, *The Daily Mail*, *The Daily Express*, *The Daily Mirror*, *The Sunday Times*, *The Sunday Telegraph* and *The London Evening Standard*.

28. The event took place on 17 June 1968.

29. Around 100 students at Bristol launched the 'Free University', out of a student population of 2000 – a tiny proportion (5% of the total). See *The Times*, 11 June 1968, p. 10.

30. The Free University Movement in Cambridge, Simon Hoggart's role and his father, Richard Hoggart's, reactions to student protest movements of the late 1960s are discussed at greater length in Chapter 6.

31. There is a good discussion of the Cambridge protest in *The Times*, 7 June 1968, p. 3.

32. *The Times*, 12 June 1968, p. 11 (Elton); 10 June 1968, p. 9 (Frend); 13 June 1968, p. 11 (response from a Fellow of Darwin College, Cambridge); 12 June 1968, p. 11 (response from an Oxford don at Hertford College, Oxford).

33. See *The Times*, 12 June 1968, p. 11, for the following details.

34. The concept of 'student power' was widely publicised in Britain with the publication of a collection of essays by radical students in 1969. See A. Cockburn and R. Blackburn (eds), *Student Power: Problems, Diagnosis, Action* (Harmondsworth, 1969).

35. *The Times*, 7 June 1968, p. 3; 10 June 1968, p. 9.

36. *The Times*, 3 June 1968, p. 7. In his letter to *The Times*, Rowthorn described the Cambridge students' demands as 'student power'; a full year before the publication of the Penguin volume *Student Power*. For Lord Ashby's views of Cambridge students see *The Times*, 30 May 1968, p. 2.

37. *The Times*, 12 June 1968, p. 1.

38. Ibid.; *Daily Telegraph*, 25 May 1968, p. 22; 30 May 1968, p. 27.

39. *The Times*, 13 June 1968, p. 1.

40. Callaghan, *Time and Chance*.

41. *The Times*, 13 June 1968, p. 10.

42. *The Daily Mail* reported that 'in private Mr Callaghan, Home Secretary, is seething'; the reason being that the BBC had not told him about the visit. See *Daily Mail*, 14 June 1968, p. 2.

43. *The Times*, 28 May 1968, p. 1.

44. Ibid.

45. All the broadsheets carried profiles of Cohn-Bendit during May and June 1968, but see especially the series of articles in *The Times* by Richard Davy, published in late May 1968.

46. The idea for the *Students in Revolt* programme seems to have been dreamed up by its colourful and 'with-it' Producer Anthony Smith, who, as well as being a BBC Producer, was also a 'balloonist' and a zoologist. On the day of the broadcast, it was noticed that he wore an exotic shirt. See *The Guardian*, 13 June 1968, p. 20. For biographical details see *The Times*, 13 June 1968, p. 10. For Smith's own account of the experience see *The Listener*, 20 June 1968, pp. 806–7.

47. See *The Times*, 29 May 1968, p. 1; 12 June 1968, p. 1; 13 June 1968, p. 1.

48. Throughout, *The Times*'s coverage of Cohn-Bendit was portentous; hinting at the fact that he might be a very dangerous subversive indeed. For example, on 29 May it reported his comment to an English reporter: 'The Wilson Government is not doing too well in England, is it? Perhaps you will have a revolutionary movement there ... very soon.' *The Times*, 29 May 1968, p. 1. The paper's sinister use of the phrase 'Herr Cohn-Bendit' to scare its readers has been noted above. Some of its readers did not like this criminalising of Cohn-Bendit, and among these was the Oxford Philosophy don Iris Murdoch: 'Sir,' she wrote in to the paper, 'Danny Cohn-Bendit is not a criminal, and what he has to say, whether we agree with it or not, is interesting and important.' Iris Murdoch, Letter, *The Times*, 18 June 1968, p. 9. Interestingly, it was *The Daily Telegraph* that revealed Cohn-Bendit to be the son of a German Jew. See *Daily Telegraph*, 25 May 1968, p. 22. *The Times* neglected to mention

that, though holding a German passport, he had spent most of his life in France and the fact that his father was a German Jew. See *The Times*, 29 May 1968, p. 1.

49. *The Times*, 12 June 1968, p. 1.
50. Ibid.; *Daily Telegraph*, 12 June 1968, p. 1; *The Guardian*, 12 June 1968, p. 1.
51. For Richard Davy's detailed description of the party see *The Times*, 13 June 1968, p. 10. For the guests see *The Guardian*, 13 June 1968, p. 10.
52. *The Times*, 13 June 1968, p. 10.
53. Ibid.
54. Ibid.
55. Ibid.
56. Ibid.; *The Guardian*, 13 June 1968, p. 20.
57. *The Times*, 13 June 1968, p. 10.
58. Ibid. During the trip to Highgate Cemetery Cohn-Bendit and his fellow students were accidentally locked in the cemetery – not with any malicious intent it seems. See *The Guardian*, 13 June 1968, p. 20.
59. *Evening Standard*, 13 June 1968, p. 1.
60. See note 23, above.
61. Until the Special Branch and Home Office papers on Cohn-Bendit's visit are released, we will not know the precise facts. The pressure to allow him to stay was exerted on the Home Office by Anthony Smith of the BBC; the National Council for Civil Liberties were also involved in the discussions with the Home Office, along with two senior Labour MPs Lord Brockway and Eric Lubbock. Smith conducted his part of the discussions by 'phone; Dr Zander of LSE attended the Home Office in person on behalf of Cohn-Bendit. James Callaghan, the Home Secretary, made the final decision just before Cohn-Bendit's visa was about to expire. See *Evening Standard*, 13 June 1968, p. 1.
62. *The Times*, 14 June 1968, p. 7.
63. *The Times*, 13 June 1968, p. 10, on the participants and their countries. For comments on the student discussion see *Daily Telegraph*, 14 June 1968, p. 36; *Guardian*, 14 June 1968, p. 10. Apparently, the BBC's Chairman of Governors had a meeting with the BBC's Director General Sir Hugh Greene about Cohn-Bendit on 13 June, before the programme was shown. Greene had watched the programme himself and 'approved it'. The BBC then issued a statement to the press defending their decision to show it. See *Daily Mail*, 14 June 1968, p. 1.
64. *Daily Telegraph*, 24 June 1968, p. 15.
65. *The Guardian*, 14 June 1968, p. 10.
66. Ibid. The *Evening Standard*'s television critic Milton Shulman was no more charitable to the students; describing them as 'a bunch of fairly intelligent, fairly young people talking in confused and sometimes incomprehensible terms about the kind of society they think they want to live in' (*Evening Standard*, 14 June 1968, p. 6). Somewhat overstating his case, he called Cohn-Bendit 'this chubby, left-wing ogre' (*Evening Standard*,

19 June 1968, p. 5). A television viewer who wrote in to *The Daily Mail* about the programme agreed. Cohn-Bendit reminded her of the TV comedian Benny Hill: 'He looks too much like Benny Hill to be taken seriously.' See *Daily Mail*, 17 June 1968, p. 4 (letter from Mrs Mary Colliesin of London).

67. Tariq Ali was not technically a student at all in 1968, but a journalist. He was 24, but his serious demeanour and thick moustache made him look much older. Another of the 'students' who appeared on the programme had a Ph.D., Dr Krippendorf of Germany. For one TV critic, the Japanese student also looked mature beyond his years: 'If still a student Mr Ishii from Japan must, to judge from appearances, have started his academic career in the reign of the Emperor Meiji.' See *The Listener*, 20 June 1968, p. 814.

68. See *The Times*, 20 June 1968, pp. 3, 8, for a summary of the House of Lords debate (which took place on 19 June from 2.30 p.m. to 10.20 p.m.).

69. Reported in *The Times*, 14 June 1968, p. 6.

70. Ibid.

71. *House of Commons Debates*, Fifth Series, Vol. 766, Session 1967–68, June 1968, cols 438–9.

72. *House of Lords Debates*, Fifth series, Vol. CCXCIII, 1967–68, cols 215–28; *House of Commons Debates*, 1967–68, cols 104–5.

73. *The Guardian*, 15 June 1968, p. 3.

74. *The Guardian*, 13 June 1968, p. 1.

75. *The Times*, 13 June 1968, p. 1

76. Reported in *The Times*, 13 June 1968, p. 1.

77. *The Times*, 14 June 1968, p. 1; *Daily Telegraph*, 15 June 1968, p. 13.

78. *Daily Telegraph*, 15 June 1968, p. 13.

79. Ibid.; *Daily Telegraph*, 17 June 1968, p. 13.

80. *The Times*, 14 June 1968, p. 6.

81. Ibid.

82. Ibid.

83. *The Times*, 13 June 1968, p. 10.

84. *Daily Telegraph*, Editorial, 13 June 1968, p. 18.

85. See above, pp. 163–4, for an assessment of Herbert Marcuse's impact on British students of the late 1960s.

86. CAB151/67, Notes on 'Youth', Office of the Minister without Portfolio, 3 February 1970.

87. CAB151/67, Extract from House of Commons Debates, 21 November 1968, cols 1526–7.

88. CAB151/66, Extract from House of Commons Debates, 10 February 1969, cols 856–7.

89. The best discussion of the LSE 'Troubles', 1967–9, is in H. Kidd, *The Trouble at LSE, 1966–1967* (Oxford, 1969), *passim*, and Dahrendorf, *LSE*.

90. Short's speech on LSE students, delivered on 29 January 1969 in the House of Commons, was a provocative account of the subversive

influence of foreign students in British universities of the period. It is mentioned in Fielding, *Labour and Cultural Change*, pp. 179–80. Short was pointing the finger, largely, at the American students studying at LSE. The Home Office, meanwhile, were investigating whether they could expel foreign students involved in the LSE dispute from Britain: 'we will examine individually those aliens against whom the LSE have obtained an injunction in the High Court'. See HO325/126, Note on Students at LSE, 31 January 1969. Not all of these 'aliens' who had been banned from LSE were Americans; indeed not even a majority were. Thirteen students were banned from using LSE after the 'Gates' incident. Of these, 6 were British students, 3 were Americans, 2 were South Africans, 1 was an Australian and 1 was Italian. HO325/126, Notes on Student Leaders in 1968–1969, n.d. 1969? Altogether, 35 students at LSE were arrested in January 1969 over the 'Gates' incident and the Government's statistics make clear that only 3 were American. The vast majority were British. See HO325/126, Metropolitan Police to Home Office, 21 March 1969. In effect, therefore, Edward Short was not only exaggerating the disruptive role of American and 'alien' students at LSE; he was seriously distorting it.

91. The Prime Minister seems to have abolished the post of Minister for Youth in November 1969. See CAB151/67, R. Jardine to 'Minister without Portfolio', 3 November 1969.

92. CAB151/67, Extract from *Birmingham Post* (n.d., October 1968?); Judith Hart to Birmingham Settlement, 23 October 1968.

93. Ibid.

94. The following quotations are from newspaper extracts, all presumably November 1968, in CAB151/67.

95. Ibid.

96. *The Daily Express and Star*, 7 November 1968 (no page reference).

97. CAB151/67, Newspaper Extracts, November 1968.

98. Much of the material is in the following files: CAB151/66; CAB151/67; FCO68/128; HO325/46; HO325/126; HO325/ 128; HO325/129; CO1045/858.

99. CAB151/67, Office of the Minister without Portfolio, Notes on Youth, 3 February 1970.

100. The statistics on student numbers are in CAB151/67. Senior civil servants' reflections on the scale and nature of student protest in Britain are dispersed across the files cited in note 98. Separate files were kept on student protest in Northern Ireland; and in the Irish Republic. See HO325/48, HO221/146, CJ3/30, CJ3/41, CJ4/33 on Northern Ireland; FCO33/1198 on the Irish Republic.

101. On the Northern Irish political situation in 1969 see the brilliant discussion in J. J. Lee, *Ireland, 1912–1985: Politics and Society* (Cambridge, 1989), ch. 6.

102. See CAB151/66, Student Protest in 1968, typed report, October 1968, pp. 1–3, for the Government figures. See also Appendix 3, below.

103. CAB151/66, Student Protest in 1968, p. 3.

104. CAB151/66, Student Protest in 1968, pp. 3–5; Dahrendorf, *LSE*, *passim*.
105. On Marshall Bloom see Kidd, *Trouble at LSE, passim*, but especially pp. 121–2. Bloom, a graduate of Amherst College in the United States, was a Graduate student at LSE and had been an active member of the 'New Left' in the United States before moving to Britain. On returning to the United States in 1969, he committed suicide. This is not mentioned in Crouch, *Student Revolt*, but is discussed in T. Gitlin, *The Sixties: Years of Hope, Days of Rage* (New York, 1993).
106. The comment was made on BBC Radio 4 during Cohn-Bendit's visit to Britain in June 1968. It is mentioned in *The Times*, 17 June 1968, and in Fielding, *Labour and Cultural Change*, p. 179 n. 87.
107. See note 105, above.
108. The author is currently undertaking further research on the cultural networks of British students and foreign students studying in Britain during the late 1960s.
109. CAB151/66, Student Protest in 1968, pp. 3–5.
110. See note 108 above.
111. FCO68/128, The Pattern of Unrest: Youth in Revolt, An International Report, 1969, p. 3.
112. CAB151/66, Extract from *Evening Standard*, 8 May 1968, cited in Student Protest in 1968, p. 5.
113. Ibid., pp. 5–6.
114. Ibid., p. 6.
115. Ibid., p. 10.
116. Ibid.
117. Ibid., pp. 10–11.
118. Ibid., p.11.
119. CAB151/66, Student Protest in 1968–1969, February 1969, pp. 12–13.
120. Ibid.
121. CAB151/66, Note by R. Jardine, Student Protest, 10 April 1969; Student Protest in 1968, p. 4; FCO68/128, Student Protest, 1968–1969, September 1969, p. 4.
122. CAB151/66, R. Jardine to Mr Isserlis, Student Protest, 10 April 1969.
123. Ibid.; FCO68/128, Student Protest, 1968–1969, p. 4.
124. Crouch, *Student Revolt*, ch. 6.
125. CAB151/66, University Students, April 1969; A. R. Isserlis to Paymaster General, 2 June 1969.
126. CAB151/66, A. R. Isserlis to Paymaster General, 17 April 1969.
127. FCO68/128, R. Jardine, Paymaster General's Office to the FCO, 15 September 1969.
128. Ibid.
129. On the Labour Cabinet's discussions of youth votes see PREM13/2076; on Harold Wilson's response to the closure of LSE see PREM13/2787. It was only a short comment to his Education Secretary, Edward Short.

130. HO325/128 Prime Minister's Meeting with Vice Chancellors of Universities, 15 April 1970.
131. FCO68/128 Parliamentary Conference, Trinidad and Tobago, 1969: Youth in Revolt.

Notes to Chapter 9: Youth Culture and Pop Culture: from Beatlemania to the Spice Girls

1. On the Beatles' impact beyond Britain see especially D. Sandbrook, *Never Had It So Good: A History of Britain from Suez to the Beatles* (London, 2005), ch. 19; Dr Sandbrook, *White Heat: Britain in the Swinging Sixties* (London, 2006), pp. 102–8. On the impact of the Beatles and other British groups in the US see A. Marwick, *The Sixties: Cultural Revolution in Britain, France, Italy and the United States, c.1958–c.1974* (Oxford, 1998), ch. 10. The British Embassy in Prague, Czechoslovakia, reported to the British Government that 'Beatlemania' had reached Czechoslovakia by May 1964. See British Embassy, Prague, Czechoslovakia, to Foreign Office, London, 13 May 1964, National Archives, FO371/177493.
2. See below, pp. 191–2.
3. See especially Simon Reynolds' study of post-punk pop groups, *Rip It Up and Start Again: Post-Punk 1978–84* (London, 2005), and Jon Savage's classic work on the Sex Pistols, *England's Dreaming: Sex Pistols and Punk Rock* (1991; second edition, London, 2001). There is no comparable study of pop and its social impact for the 1960s, other than the opinionated and unreliable G. Melly, *Revolt into Style: The Pop Arts in the 50s and 60s* (1970; reprinted, Oxford, 1989).
4. J. Street, 'Youth Culture and the Emergence of Popular Music' in T. Gourvish and A. O'Day (eds), *Britain since 1945* (London, 1991), ch. 14; J. Street, 'Youth Culture' in P. Johnson (ed.), *Twentieth-Century Britain: Economic, Social and Cultural Change* (London, 1994), ch. 26.
5. Street, 'Youth Culture and Emergence of Popular Music', pp. 306–11, 314.
6. For the idea that the Beatles were somehow creating a cohesive youth culture during the 1960s see Street, 'Youth Culture and Emergence of Popular Music', p. 311. For the argument that British youth culture of the 1960s was 'classless'; or, rather, involved the mingling of youth from different social backgrounds at, for example, the art schools of Swinging London and other youth venues, see Marwick, *The Sixties*, especially pp. 55–80.
7. See Chapter 2.
8. American youth culture of the 1960s has been probed in far more detail than British youth culture of the period. For two fascinating and scholarly works see W. J. Rorabaugh, *Berkeley at War: The 1960s* (New York, 1989); D. Rossinow, *The Politics of Authenticity: Liberalism, Christianity, and the New Left in America* (New York, 1998).

9. On the Draft and American student reactions to it, see Marwick, *The Sixties*, pp. 536–46. On the numbers in higher education in Britain during the 1960s see A. H. Halsey (ed.), *Twentieth-Century British Social Trends* (London, 2000), Tables 6.1 and 6.3. Just 4 per cent of 18-year-olds in Britain went to university in 1962; which had only marginally risen to 7 per cent by 1972.

10. Marwick, *The Sixties*, pp. 542–3.

11. See Chapter 8.

12. A heated correspondence between the two was conducted in the 'Underground' journal *Black Dwarf*, edited by the revolutionary Marxist Tariq Ali, during 1968. The paper had just given The Beatles' single 'Revolution' (written by Lennon) a bad review; their pop critic describing it as 'intelligent Establishment propaganda'. Lennon had made the mistake of criticising the Communist leader of China, Chairman Mao. *Black Dwarf* hit back; claiming that Mao had 'the biggest fan club in the world'. John Hoyland then wrote a piece directed at John Lennon, with the grand title: 'An Open Letter to John Lennon', which criticised Lennon's song for being 'no more revolutionary than Mrs. Dale's Diary'. Hoyland went further, saying that he found the Rolling Stones more 'authentic' than the Beatles because two members of the group had been to prison. Lennon struck back with an angry letter to John Hoyland. 'Tell me of one successful revolution', he railed; 'Who f——d up Communism, Christianity, Capitalism, Buddhism … etc.? Sick heads, and nothing else.' But it was Lennon who eventually revised his views on revolution. When he moved to New York in 1970, he began wearing a Chairman Mao badge and another revolutionary symbol – a black beret. See *Black Dwarf*, 15 October 1968, p. 8; 27 October 1968, p. 6; 10 January 1969, p. 3; I. Macdonald, *Revolution in the Head: The Beatles' Records and the Sixties* (London, 1994), p. 237.

13. See Chapters 7 and 8.

14. Cited in J. Makela, *John Lennon Remembered: Cultural History of a Rock Star* (New York, 2004), p. 250 n. 15.

15. The figures are cited in B. Dawbarn, 'Fan Clubs', *Melody Maker*, 19 June 1965, p. 8.

16. Marwick, *The Sixties*, p. 77.

17. See below, pp. 183–90.

18. *The Daily Telegraph* coined the phrase 'The Beatle Mania' after this performance. The commotion as the group sang 'Twist and Shout' was created by middle-aged, middle-class people. See *Daily Telegraph*, 5 November 1963, cited in D. Holloway (ed.), *The Sixties: A Chronicle of the Decade* (London, 1992), p. 69. The *Daily Mirror* first used the phrase the very next day. See Sandbrook, *Never Had It So Good*, p. 675, note 13. J. Lawton, *1963: Five Hundred Days: History as Melodrama* (London, 1992), pp. 109–10, suggests wrongly that the *Daily Mirror* coined the term and gets the venue of the Beatles' concert wrong as well.

19. Lawton, *1963*, p. 114.

20. P. Johnson, 'The Menace of Beatlism', *New Statesman*, 28 February 1964, pp. 326–7.
21. D. Sandbrook, *Never Had It So Good*, pp. 677–8.
22. F. Newton (Eric Hobsbawm), 'Beatles and Before', *New Statesman*, 8 November 1963, p. 673.
23. Ibid.
24. Ibid.
25. F. Newton, 'Beats and Beatles', *New Statesman*, 17 January 1964, p. 82.
26. Ibid.
27. Ibid.
28. Hobsbawm also taught at Birkbeck College, London, which specialised in adult education for those who had jobs. His article on working-class living standards during the Industrial Revolution had appeared in the *Economic History Review* in 1957–8 and a further article on the same subject in 1963–4. See, for example, E. J. Hobsbawm, 'The British Standard of Living, 1790–1850', *Economic History Review*, 2nd series, vol. 10 (1957–8).
29. H. Fairlie, 'Beatles and Babies', *The Spectator*, 6 March 1964, p. 300.
30. *The Times*, 17 February 1964, cited in Lawton, 1963, p. 115.
31. P. Johnson, 'Menace of Beatlism', p. 326.
32. Ibid.
33. Ibid., pp. 326–7. For a brief account of the Committee's work see M. Jarvis, *Conservative Governments, Morality and Social Change in Affluent Britain, 1957–64* (Manchester, 2005), pp. 38–40. The Committee was set up in September 1963. There were 40 Committee members, of whom 6 were under 30.
34. Fairlie, 'Beatles and Babies', p. 300.
35. Cited in Lawton, 1963, p. 113.
36. P. Norman, *Shout!: The True Story of The Beatles* (London, 1981), pp. 9, 15, 36, 39–40.
37. *New Statesman*, 6 March 1964, p. 364. For the debate on 'Beatlism' see, in addition to *New Statesman*, 6 March 1964; *New Statesman*, 13 March 1964; 20 March 1964; *The Spectator*, 6 March 1964.
38. *New Statesman*, 6 March 1964, p. 364.
39. C. Fletcher, 'Beat and Gangs on Merseyside', *New Society*, 20 February 1964, pp. 11–14.
40. Melly, *Revolt into Style*, p. 78.
41. On Liverpool during the 1960s and the city's aversion to hippie culture, see J. Murden, 'Psychedelic Liverpool?' in C. Grunenberg and J. Harris (eds), *Summer of Love: Psychedelic Art, Social Crisis and Counterculture in the 1960s* (Liverpool, 2005), ch. 13.
42. D. Holbrook, Letter, *New Statesman*, 13 March 1964, pp. 397–8.
43. Ibid., p. 398.
44. Ibid.
45. *New Statesman*, 20 March 1964, p. 448.
46. See especially D. Holbrook, *Creativity and Popular Culture* (London, 1994). For the song about a fifteen-year-old see 'Stray Cat Blues' on

'Beggar's Banquet', released in 1968. The song was, naturally, never released as a single.

47. On the teen, and indeed pre-teen, following of the Beatles in Britain see Melly, *Revolt into Style*, pp. 73–7. Melly recalled how even his step-daughter (aged 3) sat transfixed when the Beatles came on television. 'Every time she heard "the Beakles" on record, or saw them on television, she would become rigid as though hypnotised. We could hear her having imaginary conversations with them all over the house too' (p. 76). On the frosty reception the Beatles received among student radicals in London, and the warm reception given to the more 'authentic' Rolling Stones, see above, note 12.

48. Sandbrook, *Never Had It So Good*, p. 679; Marwick, *The Sixties*, p. 457; J. Muncie, 'The Beatles and the Spectacle of Youth' in I. Inglis (ed.), *The Beatles, Popular Music and Society: A Thousand Voices* (London, 2000), p. 45. The Beatles appeared on the Ed Sullivan show in the US on 9 February 1964 and the programme was watched by a record-breaking family audience of 73 million people (Marwick, *The Sixties*, p. 457).

49. Cited in Makela, *John Lennon Remembered*, p. 87.

50. Johnson, 'Menace of Beatlism', pp. 326–7.

51. On the exclusivity of central London discotheques see *London Life*, 9–15 October 1965, p. 14, which gives membership rates and entrance charges; *London Life*, 2 July 1966, p. 5 – a photograph of Brian Jones of the Rolling Stones leaving Sibylla's in Swallow Street, Piccadilly, and about to enter his chauffeur-driven Rolls Royce (see Figure 4, p. 175). The paper described Sibylla's as 'London's most civilised discotheque, where they take great pains to keep the customer in a state of elegant satisfaction ...'. On the suburban dance halls patronised by working-class youth see J. Wilson, 'Not Much Bottle at the Beat Ball', *London Life*, 27 November–3 December 1965, pp. 35–7.

52. Ibid., p. 36.

53. Ibid.

54. Ibid.

55. Ibid.

56. Ibid.

57. Ibid.

58. Ibid., pp. 36–37.

59. Ibid., p. 37.

60. Ibid., p. 36.

61. Ibid., p. 37.

62. Ibid., pp. 36–37.

63. Ibid., p. 37.

64. See Chapter 7.

65. J. Wilson, 'Teenagers' in L. Deighton, *Len Deighton's London Dossier* (Harmondsworth, 1967), p. 26.

66. Details of the Mod culture as a marginal aspect of Swinging London can be found in Wilson, 'Teenagers', *passim*; and in various issues of *London*

Life for 1964–1966; and it is touched upon in Marwick, *The Sixties*, pp. 77–8.

67. Melly, *Revolt into Style*, p. 66.
68. See various issues of *London Life*, October 1965.
69. Details in Jack Wilson, 'Girls Like Lucy', *London Life*, 8–14 January 1966, pp. 26–33.
70. For details of car ownership among 15–25-year-olds in Britain see *London Life*'s 'Which Car Leads Inquiry?', *London Life*, 23–9 October 1965, pp. 35–42.
71. See below, pp. 186–7.
72. Jagger himself described his upbringing as 'very bourgeois, very middle class'. See *The Times*, 1 August 1967, p. 8; for his family background and education see the biographies by P. Norman, *The Stones* (London, 1984); C. Andersen, *Jagger Unauthorised* (London, 1993); C. Schofield, *Jagger* (London, 1983); Marwick, *The Sixties*, p. 74; K. Morgan, *The People's Peace: British History 1945–1990* (Oxford, 1990; reprinted 1992), p. 261 (which states, incorrectly, that Jagger was 'a graduate of the London School of Economics', when in fact he left before taking his degree).
73. See below, pp. 187–9.
74. See J. Palacios, *Lost in the Woods: Syd Barrett and the Pink Floyd* (London, 1998), pp. 7–8; N. Schaffner, *Saucerful of Secrets: The Pink Floyd Odyssey* (New York, 1991), pp. 22–3; M. Watkinson and P. Anderson, *Crazy Diamond: Syd Barrett and the Dawn of Pink Floyd* (London, 1993), pp. 13–15.
75. Schaffner, *Saucerful of Secrets*, pp. 22–3; Watkinson and Anderson, *Crazy Diamond*, pp. 14–15.
76. Palacios, *Lost in the Woods*, p. 7.
77. Ibid., pp. 17–22; Schaffner, *Saucerful of Secrets*, p. 27.
78. Schaffner, *Saucerful of Secrets*, p. 18.
79. Ibid.
80. The most comprehensive treatment of Syd Barrett's early life in Cambridge, and his musical influences, is in Palacios, *Lost in the Woods*, ch. 1.
81. Ibid., p. 17.
82. Ibid.
83. Ibid., pp. 19–20.
84. Ibid., pp. 21–2.
85. Cited in Schaffner, *Saucerful of Secrets*, p. 27.
86. Ibid., pp. 27–8; Palacios, *Lost in the Woods*, ch. 2.
87. This is not documented. For example, Osgerby's recent survey of 'Youth Culture' from the 1950s down to the late 1990s treats the two entirely separately. See B. Osgerby, 'Youth Culture' in P. Addison and H. Jones (eds), *A Companion to Contemporary Britain, 1939–2000* (Oxford, 2005), ch. 8. Nonetheless, in several interviews, David Bowie has acknowledged Barrett as one of his mentors and he recently (December 2006) performed a cover of Barrett's song 'Arnold Layne' with the latest incarnation of the Pink Floyd.

88. Palacios, *Lost in the Woods*, p. 55.
89. Sandbrook, *White Heat*, pp. 516–19, 522–6; Norman, *The Stones*, p. 209; Schofield, *Jagger*, p. 134.
90. *The Observer*, 2 July 1967, cited in Schofield, *Jagger*, p. 134; B. Wilson, 'The War of the Generations' in his *The Youth Culture and the Universities* (London, 1970), ch. 6.
91. M. Faithfull, *Faithfull* (London, 1994), pp. 97, 101, 107.
92. Sandbrook's account of the Trial in *White Heat* is the most comprehensive. On Brian Jones, see M. Faithfull, *Faithfull*, pp. 100–1.
93. Faithfull, *Faithfull*, pp. 100–1.
94. Cited in A. E. Hotchner, *Blown Away: The Rolling Stones and the Death of the Sixties* (London, 1990), p. 254.
95. Faithfull, *Faithfull*, p. 98; *Daily Mail*, 1 July 1967, p. 1.
96. Faithfull, *Faithfull*, p. 115; Norman, *The Stones*, p. 212. Jagger was photographed wearing the smock in *The Times* on 1 August. He also wore it at his interview for *World in Action* immediately afterwards (see Figure 5, p. 188).
97. For the following details see National Archives, DPP2/4831, MEPO2/10964, MEPO2/11079.
98. MEPO2/10964, extract from *The Times*, 11 May 1967.
99. Ibid.
100. MEPO2/10964, extract from *The Evening News and Star*, 10 May 1967.
101. MEPO2/11079, Statement by West Sussex Constabulary re. Michael Philip Jagger and Keith Richards, 5 June 1967; Detective Inspector Lynch (New Scotland Yard) to MEPO, 15 June 1967.
102. MEPO2/10964, Times Newspapers Ltd to Scotland Yard, 11 July 1967; 15 July 1967; Metropolitan Police, Statement re. 'Photographs within the precincts of a court', 22 September 1967.
103. *New Statesman*, 7 July 1967, p. 1.
104. Rees-Mogg wrote the celebrated Editorial 'Who Breaks a Butterfly on a Wheel', about the Mick Jagger Trial, which appeared in *The Times* on 1 July 1967, p. 11.
105. *Observer*, 2 July 1967, p. 6; *Sunday Times*, 2 July 1967, p. 10; *Sunday Express*, 2 July 1967, p. 12.
106. *Guardian*, 5 July 1967, p. 8.
107. *Daily Mail*, 5 July 1967, p. 6.
108. Ibid.
109. *Daily Mail*, 14 July 1967, pp. 1–2.
110. *The Times*, 30 June 1967, p. 2.
111. Norman, *The Stones*, p. 212.
112. Ibid., pp. 212–13.
113. Ibid., p. 213.
114. Ibid., p. 214.
115. Cited in R. Cockett, 'The New Right and the Dialectics of Liberation' in G. Andrews et al. (eds), *New Left, New Right and Beyond: Taking the Sixties Seriously* (London, 1999), p. 92.
116. S. Jessel, 'Mr Mick Jagger Speaks His Mind', *The Times*, 1 August 1967, p. 8.

117. Norman, *The Stones*, p. 214.
118. *Observer*, 6 August 1967, p. 16.
119. C. Andersen, *Jagger Unauthorised*, p. 151; *Observer*, 6 August 1967, p. 16.
120. Norman, *The Stones*, pp. 212–14.
121. For Birt as the instigator of the interview see J. Birt, *The Harder Path: The Autobiography* (London, 2002), pp. 86–90.
122. Norman, *The Stones*, pp. 209–10: Birt, *The Harder Path*.
123. Birt, *The Harder Path*, p. 87.
124. Ibid., p. 89.
125. Norman, *The Stones*, p. 211.
126. Birt's account of the press coverage of the trial is not entirely accurate. He claimed in his autobiography that: 'The newspapers the next day brimmed with coverage of the interview' (p. 90); but this is a gross over-statement. It was mentioned, in a couple of sentences, in *The Times* (the newspaper that had the greatest interest in Mick Jagger's drug trial) and was largely ignored by the rest of the Fleet Street press.
127. S. Jessel, 'Mr Mick Jagger Speaks His Mind', *The Times*, 1 August 1967, p. 8.
128. In his last article on 1960s' youth culture the late Arthur Marwick implies that a classless youth culture had emerged in Britain by the late 1960s (he refers to 'the essential unity of youth culture', for example, and to the fact that it now embraced 'teenagers' and 'university students', who were 'more and more the dominating constituent'). See A. Marwick, 'Youth Culture and the Cultural Revolution of the Long Sixties', in A. Schildt and D. Siegfried (eds), *Between Marx and Coca-Cola: Youth Cultures in Changing European Societies, 1960–1980* (Oxford, 2006), p. 45. This seems erroneous in the British context; where, as argued above, university students of the 1960s were not by and large interested in youth culture and they were certainly not the major beneficiaries of pop culture. Morgan also implies that a classless youth culture had come into existence during the 1960s; but without probing the subject in any depth. See Morgan, *People's Peace*, pp. 207–8, 256. His point about the discotheques replacing the old 'palais de danse' as the meeting places of youth is asserted rather than demonstrated (see p. 256).
129. R. Pattison, *The Triumph of Vulgarity: Rock Music in the Mirror of Romanticism* (Oxford, 1987), pp. 84, 119, 151–153.
130. Cited in various interviews Marianne Faithfull has given since her split with Jagger in 1970.
131. Pattison, *Triumph of Vulgarity*, pp. 152–3.
132. Schofield, *Jagger*, p. 142; S. Barnard, *The Rolling Stones: Street Fighting Years* (London, 1993), p. 134.
133. P. Norman, 'Spice Lolly', *Sunday Times Magazine*, 21 September 1997, cited in Muncie, 'Beatles and the Spectacle of Youth', p. 51.
134. The details of their recording career can be found on the Spice Girls' website www.spicegirls.com.
135. Cited in J. Davies, 'It's Like Feminism, but You Don't Have to Burn Your Bra: Girl Power and the Spice Girls' Breakthrough

1996–7' in A. Blake (ed.), *Living Through Pop* (London, 1999), p. 166.

136. E. E. Leach, 'Vicars of Wannabe: Authenticity and the Spice Girls', *Popular Music*, Vol. 20, No. 2 (May 2001), p. 148. Details about the two original members who left can be found at www.spicegirls.com.

137. Leach, 'Vicars of Wannabe', p. 148.

138. Davies, 'Girl Power and the Spice Girls' Breakthrough', p. 161.

139. See A. L. Golden, *The Spice Girls* (New York, 1997), p. 212, and for other details of the group's evolution and recording career see their website www.spicegirls.com.

140. Leach, 'Vicars of Wannabe', p. 164 n. 4.

141. P. Lester, *Spice Girls* (London, 1997), p. 36. For their record sales and comparisons with the Beatles see www.spicegirls.com.

142. Cited in K. Acker, 'All Girls Together', *Weekend Guardian*, 3 May 1997, p. 12.

143. S. Sebag Montefiore, 'Spice Girls Back Sceptics on Europe', *Spectator*, 14–21 December 1996, p. 17.

144. Acker, 'All Girls Together', p. 12.

145. E. Forest, 'Cheers', *Independent Tabloid*, 25 October 1996, p. 2.

146. For details see www.spicegirls.com.

147. The Spice Girls, *Girl Power* (London, 1996).

148. Lester, *Spice Girls*, pp. 12, 29, 36–7; S. Whiteley, *Women and Popular Music: Sexuality, Identity and Subjectivity* (London, 2000), p. 218.

149. Davies, 'Girl Power and the Spice Girls' Breakthrough', p. 168.

150. Ibid.

151. Sebag Montefiore, 'Spice Girls Back Sceptics', pp. 14, 16; Lester, *Spice Girls*, p. 29.

152. Whiteley, *Women and Popular Music*, p. 215.

153. Ibid.

154. Spice Girls, *Girl Power*, p. 5.

155. Ibid., p. 19.

156. Ibid., p. 72.

157. See the Spice Girls' website for details of Halliwell's subsequent career.

158. P. Norman, 'Gone But Not Forgotten', *The Sunday Times News Review*, 21 June 1998, pp. 1–2.

159. Ibid., p. 2. Philip Norman toured the United States with the Spice Girls and described the experience as 'a children's crusade'. Parents would always attend the concerts with their children.

160. The lyrics of 'Wannabe' are printed as an Appendix in Leach, 'Vicars of Wannabe', pp. 162–3. The sexual innuendo of Spice Girls' lyrics is explored in Emma Bunton's interview in *New Musical Express*, 18 October 2003, p. 12. On the sexual innuendo of the phrase 'zig-a-zig-ahh', see Davies, 'Girl Power and the Spice Girls' Breakthrough', pp. 162–3. The song 'Wannabe' contained even more explicit phrases such as: 'Do you still like it in your face'; see *New Musical Express*, 18 October 2003, p. 12.

161. See www.spicegirls.com.

162. See note 160.
163. Philip Norman, who wrote an acclaimed biography of the Beatles, argued in 1998 that: 'Spicemania was as potent a force as Beatlemania ever was.' See *Sunday Times News Review*, 21 June 1998, pp. 1–2.
164. A Spice Girls' Reunion concert in Toronto reached only page 13 of the *Daily Telegraph* as this book was going to press. See *Daily Telegraph*, 4 December 2007, p. 13.

Notes to Conclusions

1. For the earliest accounts of youth culture as a product of the 1950s and 1960s, see especially C. MacInnes, *England, Half English* (New York, 1961) – for reprints of his early articles on teenagers; C. Booker, *The Neophiliacs: The Revolution in English Life in the Fifties and Sixties* (1969; reprinted London, 1992); G. Melly, *Revolt into Style: The Pop Arts in the 50s and 60s* (1970; reprinted Oxford, 1989); and B. Wilson, *The Youth Culture and the Universities* (London, 1970). For more recent studies along the same lines see A. Marwick, *The Sixties: Cultural Revolution in Britain, France, Italy and the United States, c.1958–c.1974* (Oxford, 1998), Pt II, ch. 3; J. Street, 'Youth Culture and the Emergence of Popular Music' in T. Gourvish and A. O'Day (eds), *Britain since 1945* (London, 1991), ch. 14; J. Street, 'Youth Culture' in P. Johnson (ed.), *Twentieth Century Britain: Economic, Social and Cultural Change* (London, 1994), ch. 26. Osgerby is more circumspect and acknowledges the interwar roots of consumer youth cultures of the 1950s and 1960s. See B. Osgerby, 'Youth Culture' in P. Addison and H. Jones (eds), *A Companion to Contemporary Britain, 1939–2000* (Oxford, 2005), ch. 8.
2. See especially S. Hall and T. Jefferson (eds), *Resistance Through Rituals: Youth Subcultures in Postwar Britain* (London, 1976); P. E. Willis, *Learning to Labour: How Working Class Kids Get Working Class Jobs* (1977; reprinted Basingstoke, 1981), and S. Humphries, *Hooligans or Rebels?: An Oral History of Working-Class Childhood and Youth* (Oxford, 1981).
3. A. McRobbie in M. Shiach (ed.), *Feminism and Cultural Studies* (Oxford, 1999), ch. 3.
4. See above Chapter 6.
5. See, for example, Peter Hennessy's widely acclaimed recent history of the 1950s, *Having It So Good: Britain in the Fifties* (London, 2006) which, on the subject of youth culture, is clichéd and sometimes erroneous. He notes 'the first stirrings of affluence' only among 1950s' teenagers and implies that British youth culture only 'burst upon the scene with Bill Haley and Elvis Presley in the mid-1950s' (see pp. 19, 491–2).
6. For further discussion of these points see Chapter 9.
7. See above, Chapter 9.
8. For the only historical survey of British youth culture that deals with middle-class youth see B. Osgerby, *Youth in Britain since 1945* (Oxford, 1998), ch. 7.

Bibliography

Primary sources

(a) Archival material

Cambridge

Cambridge University Library, Manuscripts Department
Rolf Gardiner Papers
Proctor's Records re. Garden House Riot, 1970

Cambridge University Library, Rare Books Department
Cambridge Gownsman
Cambridge Opinion: student periodical, 1960s
Granta
The Heretics' Printed Programmes, 1912–23, in Cambridge Papers Collection, 4510
New Cambridge
'The Socratics' in Cambridge Papers Collection, J8057
Varsity

King's College, Cambridge, Modern Records Centre
Edward J. Dent Papers
Edmund Leach Papers
Rosamond Lehmann Papers
Correspondence re. *Cambridge Opinion*: student periodical, 1960s

St John's College, Cambridge, Archives
Rolf Gardiner: Personal File
The Eagle: College Magazine (St John's College Cambridge)
St John's College Cambridge, Debating Society, *Minutes*, 1918–22

Trinity College, Cambridge, Archives
R. A. Butler Papers

London

King's College, London, Liddell Hart Military Records Centre
Arthur Bryant Papers

National Archives, Kew
CAB151/66   Student Protests, 1967–1969
CAB151/67   General Papers on Youth, 1968–1969
CAB151/73   Youth Enquiry, 1968–1970
CO1045/858   Student Protests, 1966

DPP2/4831	Mick Jagger Drug Trial, 1967
ED47	Board of Education: Scheme for the Higher Education of ex-Servicemen, Papers, 1918–1925
ED54/406	Advice to LEAs re. student sit-ins
ED124/257	Delinquency and Youth, 1963–1968
ED188/263	Student Protests, 1968
ED188/340	Student Unrest at LSE, 1969
FCO68/128	Parliamentary Conference, Trinidad and Tobago, 1969: Youth in Revolt
FCO371/177534	Youth in Revolt: Reports and Discussions, 1969
FO371/177493	Beatlemania, 1964
HO325/26	London School of Economics, 1969
HO325/46	Demonstrations, 1969–1970
HO325/89	Youth Protest: Trafalgar Square, 1968
HO325/126	Student Unrest: LSE, 1969–1970
HO325/128	Prime Minister's Meeting with Vice-Chancellors of Universities, 15 April 1970
HO325/129	Student Unrest: Prime Minister's Meeting with Vice-Chancellors, April 1970
HO325/141	Anti-Vietnam Demonstrations: Reports from Security Services and Metropolitan Police, 1968–1969: Closed
MEPO2/11079	Mick Jagger Drug Trial, 1967
MEPO2/10964	Mick Jagger/Keith Richards Drug Trial, 1967
MEPO2/11473	Assaults on police officers during student unrest at LSE, January 1969
MEPO31/1	Mick Jagger Court Case, 1969–1970
PREM13/2076	Voting Age, 1967–1968: Elections
PREM13/2787	Edward Short on Student Protests, 1969
PREM13/3172	Reduction of Voting Age to 18: Conference, 1968–1970

Vaughan Williams Memorial Library, Cecil Sharp House
Rolf Gardiner's Correspondence with Cecil Sharp

Manchester

Labour Party Archives
Youth Commission Papers, 1959

Northern Ireland

Belfast Central Library, Newspaper Library
Belfast Newsletter
Belfast Telegraph
Irish Independent
Northern Whig
The Irish News and Belfast Morning News

Public Record Office of Northern Ireland (PRONI), Belfast

CAB/9B/255/1 'Notes of a Meeting of the Board of Education (Northern Ireland) Committee held in Belfast, 7 October 1941'

CAB 9C/31/1 Juvenile Training Centre and Employment Exchange, 1920s

HA1/34AC/1–5 Londonderry Juvenile Court Order Book, 1950–1959

HA1/49/AA/1–3 Petty Sessions, Juvenile Court Order Books

HA/8/685 Ministry of Home Affairs, *Annual Report*, 1959

HA/8/774 Juvenile Delinquency Handbook prepared by the Northern Ireland Council of Social Welfare, 1946–1956

HA/8/873 Juvenile Delinquency File, 1941–1945

HA/8/985 Departmental Committee on Juvenile Delinquency, Minutes, 1941–

HA/8/1087 Ministry of Home Affairs, File on the White Paper, 1948

HA/8/1248 File on 'Alleged Drug Addiction among Young Persons, 1952'

HA/9/2/157 Ministry of Home Affairs, 'Notes on Probation', 10 March 1948

HA/9/2/158 Northern Ireland Probation Service, Report for the Year 1950

HA/9/2/159 Ministry of Home Affairs (MHA), 'Notes on Probation', June 1951

HA/9/2/278 Malone Training School: Church Attendance File, 1946–1956

HA/9/2/300 Malone Training School: Visiting Committee, Reports, 1951–1952

HA/9/2/699 Malone Training School: Letters of Appreciation from Former Inmates, 1938–1939

HA/9/2/706 Malone Training School: Escapes, 1949–1954

HA/10/38 St Patrick's Reformatory and Industrial School, Inspections, 1923–1955

HA10/44 Whiteabbey Remand Home for Protestant Girls, Northern Ireland, 1950s

HA/10/58 'Juvenile Crime Statistics, c.1949–1959'

HA/13/111 Child Welfare Council, Minutes, June 1954–

HA/13/112 Child Welfare Council, 'Notes on the Work of the Child Welfare Council', July 1953–July 1954, September 1954

HA/13/113 'Report on the Juvenile Court', n.d. 1957?

HA/13/114 Child Welfare Council Papers, 1958

HA/13/136 Child Welfare Council, Juvenile Delinquency Study Group Papers, 1950s

HA/13/137 Child Welfare Council, Juvenile Delinquency Study Group Papers, 1950s

HA/13/146   Children's Homes and Training Schools Committee (CHTSC),
            Minutes and Reports, 1950s and 1960s
HA/13/154   File on the Children and Young Persons Act, 1950

Records of Northern Ireland YMCAs

Royal Ulster Constabulary, Police Museum, Belfast
Correspondence re. Police Juvenile Liaison Schemes, 1940s–1980s
County Crime Registers, 1922–1945
Inspector General, Royal Ulster Constabulary, Correspondence, 1940s
'Notes on a Women's Police Conference, held at Belfast Law Courts, 1 April 1942'
Royal Ulster Constabulary, Juvenile Liaison Scheme Reports, 1970s

(b) Printed sources

Parliamentary Papers
Census of Population of Northern Ireland, 1926, *General Report* (Belfast, 1926)
Government of Northern Ireland, *Parliamentary Debates, House of Commons*,
    Vol. 15, No. 50 (1933)
Government of Northern Ireland, 'The Instruction of Unemployed Juveniles',
    Cmd 193 (Belfast, 1938)
Government of Northern Ireland, 'The Protection and Welfare of the Young and
    the Treatment of the Young Offender', Cmd 264, 1948
Government of Northern Ireland, *Children and Young Persons Act (Northern
    Ireland)* 1950
House of Commons Debates
House of Lords Debates
Ministry of Education, *The Youth Service in England and Wales*, Report of the
    Committee Appointed by the Minister of Education in November 1958, Cmnd
    929 (London, 1960)
Northern Ireland Parliament, *House of Commons Debates*
Report of the Board of Education, 1919–1920 (London, 1921), Cmd 1451

Reports
Child Welfare Council (Northern Ireland), *Juvenile Delinquency* (Belfast, 1954)
Child Welfare Council (Northern Ireland), *The Operation of Juvenile Courts in
    Northern Ireland* (Belfast, 1960)
Government of Northern Ireland, *Juvenile Delinquency: Interim Report by the
    Northern Ireland Child Welfare Council* (Belfast, 1954)
Government of Northern Ireland, *The Operation of Juvenile Courts in Northern
    Ireland: a Report by the Northern Ireland Child Welfare Council* (Belfast, 1960)
Kennedy, H.P., QC, *Report of a Public Inquiry into the Proposed Permanent Use
    of Lisnevin School, Newtownards, as a Training School/Remand Home Under
    the Children and Young Persons Act (Northern Ireland) 1968 (Lisnevin Report)*
    (Belfast, 1979)
*Legislation and Services for Children and Young Persons in Northern Ireland: A
    Consultative Document* (Belfast, 1977)

Report of the Children and Young Persons Review Group (Black Report) (Belfast, 1979)

Royal Ulster Constabulary (RUC), *Chief Constable's Annual Reports*, 1970–2000

Newspapers, Journals, and Magazines
Black Dwarf
Cambridge Review
London Life
New Cambridge
New Left Review
New Society
Rave
Socialist Register
The Adelphi
The Cambridge Gownsman
The Daily Express
The Daily Mail
The Daily Mirror
The Daily Telegraph
The Guardian
The Healthy Life
The Irish Catholic Directory and Almanac
The Listener
The London Evening Standard
The Manchester Evening News
The Mod
The Nation
The New Age
The New Musical Express
The New Statesman
The New University
The Observer
The Spectator
The Sunday Express
The Sunday Times
The Times
The Times Educational Supplement
The Times Literary Supplement
Town
Universities and Left Review
Varsity
Youth: an Expression of Progressive University Thought (1920–1924)

Contemporary publications (books and articles, including novels)

Abrams, M., *The Teenage Consumer* (London, 1959).
Abrams, M., *Teenage Consumer Spending in 1959* (London, 1961).

Abrams, P., 'Rites de Passage: the Conflict of Generations in Industrial Society', *Journal of Contemporary History*, Vol. 5, No. 1 (1970), pp. 175–90.

Adelstein, D., *Teach Yourself Student Power* (London, 1968).

Annan, N. G., 'The Intellectual Aristocracy' in J. H. Plumb (ed.), *Studies in Social History: A Tribute to G. M. Trevelyan* (London, 1955), ch. VIII.

Anon., *Meditations of a Flapper By One* (London, 1922).

Arlen, M., *The Green Hat: A Romance for a Few People* (London, 1924).

Barker, P., 'Brighton Battleground', *New Society*, 21 May 1964, pp. 9–10.

Barker, P., 'The Margate Offenders: A Survey (1964)' reprinted in T. Raison (ed.), *Youth in New Society* (London, 1966), pp. 115–27.

Barker, P. and Little, A., 'The Margate Offenders: A Survey', *New Society*, 30 July 1964, pp. 6–10.

Bowley, R., 'The Cost of Living of Girls Professionally Employed in the County of London', *Economic Journal*, Vol. XLIV (1934), pp. 328–34.

Braun, M., *'Love Me Do!': The Beatles' Progress* (1964; reprinted London, 1995).

Campion, S., *Father: A Portrait of G. G. Coulton* (London, 1948).

Cannon, G., 'Popular Culture and Society', *New Statesman*, 17 October 1963, p. 22.

Clery, A. E., 'Votes for Youth', *Studies*, Vol. IV, No. 14 (June 1915), pp. 279–85.

Cockburn, A. and Blackburn, R. (eds), *Student Power: Problems, Diagnosis, Action* (Harmondsworth, 1969).

Coulton, G. G., *Fourscore Years: An Autobiography* (Cambridge, 1943).

Dawbarn, B., 'Fan Clubs', *Melody Maker*, 19 June 1965, p. 8.

Dempsey, D., 'Facts and Figures about Eire's Population', *Irish Monthly*, Vol. 67 (1939), pp. 529–35.

Devlin, B., *The Price of My Soul* (London, 1969).

Eithne, 'The Saving of Girls', *Irish Monthly*, Vol. 53 (January 1925), pp. 127–32.

Eithne, 'Where are you going to, my pretty maid?', *Irish Monthly*, Vol. 54 (August 1925), pp. 404–9.

'Faces without Shadows: Young Men who Live for Clothes and Pleasure', *Town*, Vol. 3, No. 9 (1962), pp. 48–53.

Fairlie, H., 'Beatles and Babies', *Spectator*, 6 March 1964, p. 300.

Federation of Working Girls' Clubs, London, *A Handbook in Club Work* (London, 1921).

Ferguson, T. and Cunnison, J., *In their Early Twenties: A Study of Glasgow Youth* (Oxford, 1956).

Fisher, H. A. L., *An Unfinished Autobiography* (London, 1940).

Fletcher, C., 'Beat and Gangs on Merseyside', *New Society*, 20 February 1964, pp. 11–14.

Freeman, A., *Boy Life and Labour: The Manufacture of Inefficiency* (London, 1914).

Fyvel, T. R., *The Insecure Offenders: Rebellious Youth and the Welfare State* (London, 1963).

Gardiner, R., *In Northern Europe 1930* (London, 1930).

Gardiner, R., *Reconstruction in Silesia* (London, 1930).

Gardiner, R., *World Without End: British Politics and the Younger Generation* (London, 1932).

Gardiner, R., *England Herself: Ventures in Rural Restoration* (London, 1943).

Gardiner, R., *Love and Memory: A Garland of Poems, 1920–1960* (Dorset, 1960).

George, W. L., *A London Mosaic* (London, 1921).

Gosling, R., 'Dream Boy', *New Left Review*, 3 (May–June 1960), pp. 33–4.

Gosling, R., *Lady Albemarle's Boys* (Fabian Pamphlet, 1961).

Gosling, R., *Sum Total* (London, 1962).

Gotsch-Trevelyan, K., *Unharboured Heaths* (London, 1934).

Graye, E., *The Fascinating Flapper* (London, 1926).

Hall, S., 'Politics of Adolescence?', *Universities and Left Review*, 6 (Spring 1959), pp. 2–4.

Hall, S., 'Absolute Beginnings', Review of Colin MacInnes and Mark Abrams, *Universities and Left Review*, Autumn 1959, pp. 17–25.

Hall, S., 'Student Journals', *New Left Review*, 7 (January–February 1961), pp. 50–1.

Hall, S., 'The Hippies: An American Moment' (University of Birmingham, CCCS Stencilled Paper, 1968) reprinted in J. Nagel (ed.), *Student Power* (London, 1969), pp. 170–202.

Hamblett, C. and Deverson, J., *Generation X* (London, 1964).

Hargrave, J., *A Short History of the Kibbo Kift* (typescript, 1924).

Hargrave, J., *The Confession of the Kibbo Kift* (London, 1927).

Henriques, B. L. Q., *The Indiscretions of a Magistrate: Thoughts on the Work of the Juvenile Court* (London, 1951).

Hoggart, R., *The Uses of Literacy: Aspects of Working-Class Life with Special Reference to Publications and Entertainments* (London, 1957).

Hoggart, R., 'We Are the Lambeth Boys', *Sight and Sound*, Vol. 28, No. 3 (Summer–Autumn 1959), pp. 164–5.

Hoggart, R., Review of R. Gosling, *Sum Total* (1962), *New Statesman*, November 1962, p. 788.

Hoggart, R., *Higher Education and Cultural Change: A Teacher's View* (The 44th Earl Grey Memorial Lecture, Newcastle, 1965).

Hoggart, R., 'Proper Ferdinands?' in *The Permissive Society: The Guardian Inquiry* (London, 1969).

James, A. E., *Her Majesty the Flapper* (London, 1912).

Jephcott, P., *Girls Growing Up* (London, 1942).

Jephcott, P., *Rising Twenty: Notes on some Ordinary Girls* (London, 1948).

Jephcott, P., *Some Young People* (London, 1954).

Jessel, S., 'Mr Mick Jagger Speaks His Mind', *The Times*, 1 August 1967, p. 8.

Johnson, P., 'The Menace of Beatlism', *New Statesman*, 28 February 1964, pp. 326–7.

Keynes, M. N., *The Problem of Boy Labour in Cambridge* (Cambridge, 1911).

Kidson, F. and Neal, M., *English Folk Song and Dance* (Cambridge, 1915).

Llewellyn Smith, H. et al. (eds), *The New Survey of London Life and Labour*, Vol. VIII (London, 1934).

Lymington, Viscount, *A Knot of Roots: An Autobiography* (London, 1965).

McCartney, I., *Break of Day* (London, 1932).

MacClure, V., *How to be Happy in London* (London, 1926).

Morgan, B., *The Flapper's Daughter* (London, 1935).

Morison, S. E., *Harvard College in the Seventeenth Century, Part II* (Cambridge, Massachusetts, 1936).

Mortimer-Granville, J., *Youth: Its Care and Culture: An Outline of Principles for Parents and Guardians* (London, 1880).

Mowat, C. L., *Britain Between the Wars, 1918–1940* (1955; reprinted London, 1968).

Nagel, J. (ed.), *Student Power* (London, 1969).

Newton, F. (Eric Hobsbawm), 'Beatles and Before' *New Statesman*, 8 November 1963, p. 673.

Newton, F., 'Beats and Beatles', *New Statesman*, 17 January 1964, p. 82.

Newton, W. D., *Phillip and the Flappers* (London, 1918).

O'Brien, F., 'The Trade in Dublin', *The Bell*, Vol. 1, No. 2 (November 1940), pp. 6–15.

O'Brien, F., 'The Dance Halls', *The Bell*, Vol. 1, No. 5 (February 1941), pp. 44–52.

O'Connor, J., 'The Juvenile Offender', *Studies*, Vol. LII, No. 52 (1963), pp. 69–96.

Parsons, T., 'Age and Sex in the Social Structure of the United States' (1942) reprinted in T. Parsons, *Essays in Sociological Theory* (New York, 1954), pp. 89–103.

Paul, L., *Angry Young Man* (London, 1951).

Pethick-Lawrence, E., *My Part in a Changing World* (London, 1938).

Raison, T. (ed.), *Youth in New Society* (London, 1966).

Rowntree, B. S. and Lavers, G. R., *English Life and Leisure: A Social Study* (London, 1951).

Rowse, A. L., *Politics and the Younger Generation* (London, 1931).

Samuel, R., 'Dr Abrams and the End of Politics', *New Left Review*, 5 (September–October 1960), pp. 2–9.

Senex, 'The New Girl', *Irish Monthly*, Vol. 54 (1926), pp. 738–44.

Shute, N., *We Mixed our Drinks: The Story of a Generation* (London, 1945).

Stedman Jones, G., 'The Meaning of the Student Revolt' in A. Cockburn and R. Blackburn (eds), *Student Power: Problems, Diagnosis, Action* (Harmondsworth, 1969), pp. 25–56.

Trevor-Roper, H. R., *Archbishop Laud* (1940; reprinted London, 1965).

Trevor-Roper, H. R., *The Last Days of Hitler* (1947; reprinted London, 1995).

Tuite, H., *The Southdown Flapper* (London, 1926).

Wells, E. M., 'The Dance-Board', *The Bell*, Vol. 1, No. 3 (December 1940), pp. 77–80.

Wilson, J., 'Teenagers' in L. Deighton, *Len Deighton's London Dossier* (Harmondsworth, 1967), ch. 1.

Winslow, T. and Davidson, F. P. (eds), *American Youth: An Enforced Reconnaissance* (Harvard, 1940).

Wolfe, T., 'The Noonday Underground' in T. Wolfe, *The Mid-Atlantic Man and Other New Breeds in England and America* (London, 1968), pp. 99–112.

Wyndham, H., *Nights in London: Where Mayfair makes Merry* (London, 1926).

Zweig, F., *The Student in the Age of Anxiety: A Survey of Oxford and Manchester Students* (London, 1963).

Secondary sources

(a) Books and articles

Acker, K., 'All Girls Together', *Weekend Guardian*, 3 May 1997, p. 12.

Addison, P. and Jones, H. (eds), *A Companion to Contemporary Britain, 1939–2000* (Oxford, 2005).

Alexander, S., 'Becoming a Woman in London in the 1920s and 1930s', in M. Shiach (ed.), *Feminism and Cultural Studies* (Oxford, 1999), ch. 10.

Ali, T., *Street Fighting Years: An Autobiography of the Sixties* (London, 1987).

Andersen, C., *Jagger Unauthorised* (London, 1993).

Andrews, G. et al. (eds), *New Left, New Right and Beyond: Taking the Sixties Seriously* (London, 1999).

Anstruther, I., *Oscar Browning: A Biography* (London, 1983).

Badman, K. and Rawlings, T., *Quite Naturally the Small Faces* (London, 1997).

Bailey, V., *Delinquency and Citizenship: Reclaiming the Young Offender, 1914–1948* (Oxford, 1987).

Barnard, S., *The Rolling Stones: Street Fighting Years* (London, 1993).

Barnes, R., *Mods!* (London, 1991).

Beaven, B., *Leisure, Citizenship and Working-Class Men in Britain, 1850–1945* (Manchester, 2005).

Beddoe, D., *Back to Home and Duty: Women Between the Wars, 1918–1939* (London, 1989).

Bell, D., *Acts of Union: Youth Culture and Sectarianism in Northern Ireland* (London, 1990).

Ben-Amos, I. K., *Adolescence and Youth in Early Modern England* (London, 1994).

Best, A., (ed.), *Water Springing from the Ground: An Anthology of the Writings of Rolf Gardiner* (Dorset, 1972).

Bingham, A., ' "Stop the Flapper Vote Folly": Lord Rothermere, the Daily Mail, and the Equalisation of the Franchise 1927–1928', *Twentieth Century British History*, Vol. 13, No. 1 (2002), pp. 17–37.

Bingham, A., *Gender, Modernity and the Popular Press in Interwar Britain* (Oxford, 2004).

Birt, J., *The Harder Path: The Autobiography* (London, 2002).

Black, L. and Pemberton, H. (eds), *An Affluent Society? Britain's Postwar 'Golden Age' Revisited* (Aldershot, 2004).

Blackstone, T. et al., *Students in Conflict: LSE in 1967* (London, 1970).

Blake, A. (ed.), *Living Through Pop* (London, 1999).

Booker, C., *The Neophiliacs: The Revolution in English Life in the Fifties and Sixties* (1969; reprinted London 1992).

Boyes, G., *The Imagined Village: Culture, Ideology and the English Folk Revival* (Manchester, 1996).

Bramwell, A., *Ecology in the 20th Century: A History* (Newhaven, CT, 1989).

Breward, C., *The Culture of Fashion: A New History of Fashionable Dress* (Manchester, 1995).

Brigden, S., 'Youth and the English Reformation', *Past and Present*, 95 (May 1982), pp. 36–67.

Brooke, C. N. L., *A History of the University of Cambridge, Vol. IV, 1870–1990* (Cambridge, 1993).

Brown, T., *Ireland: A Social and Cultural History* (London, 1981).

Buckley, C. and Fawcett, H., *Fashioning the Feminine: Representation and Women's Fashion from the Fin de Siècle to the Present* (London, 2002).

Butterfield, H., *The Discontinuities between the Generations in History: Their Effect on the Transmission of Political Experience* (Cambridge, 1971).

Callaghan, J., *Time and Chance* (London, 1987).

Cannadine, D., *G. M. Trevelyan: A Life in History* (London, 1992).

Ceadel, M., 'The "King and Country" Debate, 1933: Student Politics, Pacifism and the Dictators', *Historical Journal*, Vol. 22, No. 2 (1979), pp. 397–422.

Chase, M., 'Rolf Gardiner: an Interwar, Cross-Cultural Case Study' in B. J. Hake and S. Marriott (eds), *Adult Education between Cultures* (Leeds, 1992), ch. 11.

Chase, M., 'North Sea and Baltic: Historical Conceptions in the Youth Movement and the Transfer of Ideas from Germany to England in the 1920s and 1930s', in S. Berger, P. Lambert und P. Schumann (eds), *Historikerdialoge: Geschichte, Mythos und Gedachtnis im deutsch-britischen kulturellen Austausch 1750–2000* (Vandenhoeck and Ruprecht, 2002), pp. 309–30.

Childs, M. J., *Labour's Apprentices: Working-Class Lads in Late Victorian and Edwardian England* (London, 1992).

Cockett, R., 'The New Right and the 1960s: the Dialectics of Liberation' in G. Andrews et al. (eds), *New Left, New Right and Beyond: Taking the Sixties Seriously* (London, 1999), ch. 6.

Cohen, S., *Folk Devils and Moral Panics: The Creation of the Mods and Rockers* (1972; reprinted Oxford, 1980).

Cohn, N., 'Carnaby Street' in P. Hewitt (ed.), *The Sharper Word: A Mod Anthology* (London, 2002), pp. 34–6.

Colls, R., *Identity of England* (Oxford, 2002).

Connell, K. H., 'Peasant Marriage in Ireland: its Structure and Development since the Famine', *Economic History Review,* Second Series, Vol. XIV, No. 3 (1962), pp. 502–23.

Connell, K. H., 'Catholicism and Marriage in the Century after the Famine' in K. H. Connell, *Irish Peasant Society: Four Historical Essays* (Oxford, 1968; reprinted Blackrock, 1996), ch. 4.

Cowling, M., *Religion and Public Doctrine in Modern England* (Cambridge, 1980).

Cox, P., *Gender, Justice and Welfare: Bad Girls in Britain, 1900–1950* (Basingstoke, 2003).

Crane, D., *Fashion and Its Social Agendas: Class, Gender and Identity in Clothing* (London, 2000).

Crouch, C., *The Student Revolt* (London, 1970).

Cutforth, R., *Later than we Thought: A Portrait of the Thirties* (London, 1976).

Dahrendorf, R., *LSE: A History of the London School of Economics and Political Science, 1895–1995* (Oxford, 1995).

Davies, A., *Leisure, Gender and Poverty: Working-Class Culture in Salford and Manchester, 1900–1939* (Buckingham, 1992).

Davies, A., 'Street Gangs, Crime and Policing in Glasgow during the 1930s: the case of the Beehive Boys', *Social History*, Vol. 23, No. 3 (October 1998), pp. 251–67.

Davies, J., 'It's Like Feminism, But You Don't Have to Burn Your Bra: Girl Power and the Spice Girls' Breakthrough 1996–7' in A. Blake (ed.), *Living Through Pop* (London, 1999), ch. 10.

Davis, J., *Youth and the Condition of Britain: Images of Adolescent Conflict* (London, 1990).

Delany, P., *The Neo-Pagans: Friendship and Love in the Rupert Brooke Circle* (London, 1987).

Donnelly, M., *Sixties Britain: Culture, Society and Politics* (London, 2005).

Doyle, B., ' "More than a dance hall, more a way of life": Northern Soul, Masculinity and Working-Class Culture in 1970s' Britain' in A. Schildt and D. Siegfried (eds), *Between Marx and Coca-Cola: Youth Cultures in Changing European Societies, 1960–1980* (Oxford, 2006), ch. 14.

Drakeford, M., *Social Movements and their Supporters: The Green Shirts in England* (London, 1997).

Dyhouse, C., *Students: A Gendered History* (London, 2006).

Ellis, C., 'The Younger Generation: the Labour Party and the 1959 Youth Commission', *Journal of British Studies*, Vol. 41, No. 2 (April 2002), pp. 199–231.

Faithfull, M., *Faithfull* (London, 1994).

Fass, P., *The Damned and the Beautiful: American Youth in the 1920s* (Oxford, 1977; reprinted in paperback 1979).

Fielding, S., *Labour and Cultural Change* (Manchester, 2003).

Fink, C., et al. (eds), *1968: The World Transformed* (Cambridge, 1998).

Foster, R. F., *Modern Ireland, 1688–1988* (London, 1988).

Fowler, D., *The First Teenagers: The Lifestyle of Young Wage-earners in Interwar Britain* (London, 1995).

Fowler, D., *Patterns of Juvenile and Youth Crime in Northern Ireland, 1945–2000* (Belfast, 2001).

Fraser, M., *Children in Conflict* (London, 1973).

Fraser, R. et al., *1968: A Student Generation in Revolt* (London, 1988).

Gitlin, T., *The Sixties: Years of Hope, Days of Rage* (New York, 1993).

Golden, A. L., *The Spice Girls* (New York, 1997).

Gosling, R., *Personal Copy: A Memoir of the Sixties* (London, 1980).

Gould, T., *Inside Outsider: The Life and Times of Colin MacInnes* (London, 1983).

Gould T. (ed.), *Absolute MacInnes: The Best of Colin MacInnes* (London, 1985).

Graves, R. and Hodge, A., *The Long Weekend: A Social History of Great Britain 1918–1939* (1940; reprinted London, 1995).

Grayson, R., 'Mods, Rockers and Juvenile Delinquency in 1964: the Government Response', *Contemporary British History*, Vol. 12, No. 1 (Spring 1998), pp. 19–47.

Green, J., *All Dressed Up: The Sixties and the Counterculture* (1998; reprinted London, 1999).

Green, M., *Children of the Sun: A Narrative of Decadence in England since 1918* (1977; reprinted London, 1992).

Griffiths, P., *Youth and Authority: Formative Experiences in England, 1560–1640* (Oxford, 1996).

Griffiths, R., *Fellow Travellers of the Right: British Enthusiasts for Nazi Germany, 1933–39* (Oxford, 1980).

Grunenberg, C. and Harris, J. (eds), *Summer of Love: Psychedelic Art, Social Crisis and Counterculture in the 1960s* (Liverpool, 2005).

Grunhut, M., *Juvenile Offenders Before the Courts* (Oxford, 1956).

Hall, S. and Whannel, P., *The Popular Arts* (London, 1964).

Halsey, A. H. (ed.), *Twentieth Century British Social Trends* (London, 2000).

Harrison, B., 'College Life, 1918–1939' in B. Harrison, *The History of the University of Oxford, Vol. VIII: The Twentieth Century* (Oxford, 1994), ch. 4.

Harrison, B. (ed.), *The History of the University of Oxford, Vol. VIII: The Twentieth Century* (Oxford, 1994).

Harrod, T., *The Crafts in Britain in the 20th Century* (Newhaven, CT, 1999).

Hassall, C., *Rupert Brooke: A Biography* (London, 1964).

Haste, C., *Rules of Desire: Sex in Britain: World War I to the Present* (London, 1992).

Hastings, S., *Rosamond Lehmann* (London, 2002).

Haye, A. de la, 'The Dissemination of Design from Haute Couture to Fashionable Ready-to-wear during the 1920s', *Textile History*, Vol. 24, No. 1 (Spring 1993), pp. 39–48.

Hendrick, H. *Images of Youth: Age, Class, and the Male Youth Problem, 1880–1920* (Oxford, 1990).

Hennessy, P., *Having It So Good: Britain in the Fifties* (London, 2006).

Hewitt, P. (ed.), *The Sharper Word: A Mod Anthology* (London, 1999).

Hill, J., *Sport, Leisure and Culture in Twentieth Century Britain* (Basingstoke, 2002).

Hoggart, R., 'Schools of English and Contemporary Society', Inaugural Lecture, University of Birmingham, reprinted in R. Hoggart, *Speaking to Each Other: Essays, Vol. 2* (Harmondsworth, 1970).

Hoggart, R., 'The Student Movement and Its Effects in the Universities' in S. Armstrong (ed.), *Decade of Change*, Society for Research into Higher Education, Annual Conference Papers (Surrey, 1979), pp. 3–10.

Hoggart, R., 'Lambeth Boys', *Sight and Sound*, Vol. 54, No. 2 (Spring 1985), pp. 106–9.

Hoggart, R., *An Imagined Life: Life and Times, 1959–1991* (Oxford, 1992).

Hoggart, R., *Between Two Worlds: Essays* (London, 2001).

Holbrook, D., *Creativity and Popular Culture* (London, 1994).

Holloway, D. (ed.), *The Sixties: A Chronicle of the Decade* (London, 1992).

Horn, P., *Women in the 1920s* (Stroud, 1995).

Horton, E. M., *Youth on the Prow: A Flapper's View of the Life and Events during the Years 1921–1932* (Oxford, 1994).

Horwood, C., *Keeping Up Appearances: Fashion and Class Between the Wars* (Stroud, Gloucs., 2005).

Hotchner, A. E., *Blown Away: The Rolling Stones and the Death of the Sixties* (London, 1990).

Howard, A., *Rab: The Life of R. A. Butler* (London, 1987).

Howarth, T. A. B., *Cambridge Between Two Wars* (London, 1978).

Humphries, S., *Hooligans or Rebels? An Oral History of Working-Class Childhood and Youth, 1889–1939* (Oxford, 1981).

Humphries, S., *A Secret World of Sex: Forbidden Fruit: The British Experience, 1900–1950* (London, 1988).

Inglis, I. (ed.), *The Beatles, Popular Music and Society: A Thousand Voices* (London, 2000).

Jackson, A., *Ireland, 1688–1998: Politics and War* (Oxford, 1999).

Jarvis, M., *Conservative Governments, Morality and Social Change in Affluent Britain, 1957–64* (Manchester, 2005).

Jenvey, S., 'Sons and Haters: Ulster Youth in Conflict', *New Society*, 20 July 1972, pp. 125–7.

Jones, S. G., *Workers at Play: A Social and Economic History of Leisure, 1918–1939* (London, 1986).

Keogh, D., *The Vatican, the Bishops and Irish Politics, 1919–39* (Cambridge, 1986).

Kershaw, I., *Hitler, 1936–45: Nemesis* (London, 2000).

Kidd, H., *The Trouble at LSE* (Oxford, 1969).

Langhamer, C., *Women's Leisure in England, 1920–60* (Manchester, 2000).

Langhamer, C., 'Love and Courtship in Mid-Twentieth Century England', *Historical Journal*, Vol. 50, No. 1 (2007), pp. 173–96.

Latham, A. J., *Posing a Threat: Flappers, Chorus Girls and other Brazen Performers of the American 1920s* (Hanover, NH, 2000).

Lawton, J., *1963: Five Hundred Days: History as Melodrama* (London, 1992).

Leach, E. E., 'Vicars of Wannabe: Authenticity and the Spice Girls', *Popular Music*, Vol. 20, No. 2 (May 2001), pp. 143–67.

Lee, J. J., *Ireland, 1912–1985: Politics and Society* (Cambridge, 1989).

Leech, K., *Youthquake: The Growth of a Counter-Culture through Two Decades* (London, 1973).

Lester, P., *Spice Girls* (London, 1997).

Levy, S., *Ready, Steady, Go!: Swinging London and the Invention of Cool* (London, 2002).

Lowe, M. A., *Looking Good: College Women and Body Image, 1875–1930* (Maryland, 2003).

Lubenow, W. C., *The Cambridge Apostles, 1820–1914: Liberalism, Imagination, and Friendship in British Intellectual and Professional Life* (Cambridge, 1998).

MacDonald, I., *Revolution in the Head: The Beatles Records and the Sixties* (London, 1994).

Makela, J., *John Lennon Remembered: Cultural History of a Rock Star* (New York, 2004).

Martin, W., *The New Age Under Orage: Chapters in English Cultural History* (Manchester, 1967).

Marwick, A., 'Youth in Britain, 1920–1960: Detachment and Commitment', *Journal of Contemporary History*, Vol. 5, No. 1 (1970), pp. 37–51.

Marwick, A., *The Sixties: Cultural Revolution in Britain, France, Italy and the United States, c.1958–c.1974* (Oxford, 1998).

Marwick, A., 'Youth Culture and the Cultural Revolution of the Long Sixties' in A. Schildt and D. Siegfried (eds), *Between Marx and Coca-Cola: Youth Cultures in Changing European Societies, 1960–1980* (Oxford, 2006), ch. 1.

Matless, D., *Landscape and Englishness* (London, 1998).

McKibbin, R., *Classes and Cultures: England, 1918–1951* (Oxford 1998).

Mellers, W., *Twilight of the Gods: The Beatles in Retrospect* (London, 1973).

Melman, B., *Women and the Popular Imagination in the Twenties* (London, 1988).

Middlemas, K. and Barnes, J., *Baldwin: A Biography* (London, 1969).

Montgomery, J., *The Twenties* (1957; reprinted London, 1970).

Moore-Colyer, R. J., 'Back to Basics: Rolf Gardiner, H. J. Massingham and "A Kinship in Husbandry" ', *Rural History*, Vol. 12, No. 1 (2001), pp. 85–108.

Moore-Colyer, R. J., 'Rolf Gardiner, English Patriot and the Council for the Church and Countryside', *Agricultural History Review*, Vol. 49 (2001), pp. 187–209.

Moore-Colyer, R. J., 'A Northern Federation?: Henry Rolf Gardiner and British and European Youth', *Paedagogica Historica*, Vol. 39, No. 3 (June 2003), pp. 305–24.

Moran, J., 'Milk Bars, Starbucks and the Uses of Literacy' in *Cultural Studies*, Vol. 20, No. 6 (November 2006), pp. 552–73.

Morgan, A., *Harold Wilson* (London, 1992).

Morgan, K., *The People's Peace: British History, 1945–1990* (Oxford, 1990).

Muncie, J., 'The Beatles and the Spectacle of Youth' in I. Inglis (ed.), *The Beatles, Popular Music and Society: A Thousand Voices* (London, 2000), ch. 3.

Murden, J., 'Psychedelic Liverpool?' In C. Grunenberg and J. Harris (eds), *Summer of Love: Psychedelic Art, Social Crisis and Counterculture in the 1960s* (Liverpool, 2005), ch. 13.

Norman, P., *Shout! The True Story of The Beatles* (London, 1981).

Norman, P., *The Stones* (London, 1984).

Nott, J., *Music for the People: Popular Music and Dance in Interwar Britain* (Oxford, 2002).

O'Connell, S., 'From Toad of Toad Hall to the "Death Drivers" of Belfast: An Exploratory History of Joyriding', *British Journal of Criminology*, 46 (2006), pp. 455–69.

O'Mahony, D., and Deazley, R., *Juvenile Crime and Justice* (Belfast, 2000).

Osgerby, B., *Youth in Britain since 1945* (Oxford, 1998).

Osgerby, B., 'Youth Culture' in P. Addison and H. Jones (eds), *A Companion to Contemporary Britain, 1939–2000* (Oxford, 2005), ch. 8.

Osgerby, B., ' "Seized by Change, Liberated by Affluence': Youth Consumption and Cultural Change in Postwar Britain' in H. van Nierop (ed.), *Twentieth Century Mass Society in Britain and the Netherlands* (Oxford, 2006), ch. 11.

Palacios, J., *Lost in the Woods: Syd Barrett and the Pink Floyd* (London, 1998).

Pattison, R., *The Triumph of Vulgarity: Rock Music in the Mirror of Romanticism* (Oxford, 1987).

Pearson, G., *Hooligan: A History of Respectable Fears* (London, 1983).

Pimlott, B., *Harold Wilson* (London, 1992).

Plumb, J. H., *In the Light of History* (London, 1972).

Plumb, J. H., 'Secular Heretics' in J. H. Plumb, *In the Light of History* (London, 1972), Pt II, ch. 1.

Pumphrey, M., 'The Flapper, the Housewife and the Making of Modernity', *Cultural Studies*, Vol. 1, No. 2 (May 1987), pp. 179–94.

Rawlings, T., *Mod: A Very British Phenomenon* (London, 2000).

Reiman, R. A., *The New Deal and American Youth: Ideas and Ideals in a Depression Decade* (Athens, GA, 1992).

Reynolds, D. (ed.), *Christ's: A Cambridge College over Five Centuries* (London, 2004).

Reynolds, S., *Rip It Up and Start Again: Post-Punk 1978–84* (London, 2005).

Rock, P., 'The Teddy Boy' in V. Bogdanor and R. Skidelsky (eds), *The Age of Affluence: Britain, 1955–1964* (London, 1970), ch. 9.

Rorabaugh, W. J., *Berkeley at War: The 1960s* (New York, 1989).

Rosen, M., *Popcorn Venus: Women, Movies and the American Dream* (New York, 1973).

Rossinow, D., *The Politics of Authenticity: Liberalism, Christianity and the New Left in America* (Columbia, New York, 1998).

Rowbotham, S., *A Century of Women: The History of Women in Britain and the United States* (London, 1997).

Ryan, L., *Gender, Identity and the Irish Press, 1922–1937* (Lampeter, 2002).

Ryan, L., 'Locating the Flapper in Rural Irish Society: the Irish Provincial Press and the Modern Woman in the 1920s' in A. Heilmann and M. Beetham (eds), *New Woman Hybridities: Femininity, Feminism and International Consumer Culture, 1880–1930* (London, 2004), ch. 5.

Sandbrook, D., *Never Had It So Good: A History of Britain from Suez to The Beatles* (London, 2005).

Sandbrook, D., *White Heat: A History of Britain in the Swinging Sixties* (London, 2006).

Savage, J., *England's Dreaming: Sex Pistols and Punk Rock* (1991; second edition, London, 2001).

Savage, J., *Teenage: The Creation of Youth 1875–1945* (London, 2007).

Schaffner, N., *Saucerful of Secrets: The Pink Floyd Odyssey* (New York, 1991).

Schildt A. and Siegfried D. (eds), *Between Marx and Coca-Cola: Youth Cultures in Changing European Societies, 1960–1980* (Oxford, 2006).

Schofield, C., *Jagger* (London, 1983).

Sebag Montefiore, S., 'Spice Girls Back Sceptics on Europe', *Spectator*, 14–21 December 1996, p. 17.

Sinfield, A., *Literature, Politics, and Culture in Postwar Britain* (Berkeley and Los Angeles, 1989).

Smith, S. R., 'The London Apprentices as Seventeenth-Century Adolescents', *Past and Present*, 61 (November 1973), pp. 149–61.

Smyth, J., 'Dancing, Depravity and All That Jazz: the Public Dance Halls Act of 1935', *History Ireland*, Vol. 1, No. 2 (Summer 1993), pp. 51–4.

Sohn, A., 'Between the Wars in France and England' in F. Thebaud (ed.), *A History of Women in the West*, Vol. V (London, 1994).

Spalding, F., *Gwen Raverat: Friends, Family, and Affections* (London, 2001), ch. 9.

Spice Girls, *Girl Power* (London, 1996).

Springhall, J., *Youth, Empire and Society: British Youth Movements, 1883–1940* (London, 1977).

Springhall, J., *Coming of Age: Adolescence in Britain, 1860–1960* (Dublin, 1986).

Stevenson, E., *Babbitts and Bohemians: From the Great War to the Great Depression* (1967; reprinted London, 1998).

Stevenson, J., *British Society, 1914–45* (1984; reprinted Harmondsworth, 1986).

Stone, D., *Responses to Nazism in Britain, 1933–1939* (Basingstoke, 2003).

Street, J., 'Youth Culture and the Emergence of Popular Music' in T. Gourvish and A. O'Day (eds), *Britain since 1945* (London, 1991), ch. 14.

Street, J., 'Youth Culture' in P. Johnson (ed.), *Twentieth Century Britain: Economic, Social and Cultural Change* (London, 1994), ch. 26.

Taylor, A. J. P., *Essays in English History* (London, 1976).

Taylor, A. J. P., *A Personal History* (London, 1983).

Taylor, L. and Nelson, S., 'Young People and Civil Conflict in Northern Ireland' in *Conference on Young People in Northern Ireland: Three Papers* (Belfast, 1977).

Thorpe, A., *Britain in the Era of Two World Wars, 1914–1945* (London, 1994).

Tinkler, P., 'Red Tips for Hot Lips: Advertising Cigarettes for Young Women in Britain, 1920–70', *Women's History Review*, Vol. 10, No. 2 (2001), pp. 249–72.

Tinkler, P., 'Rebellion, Modernity and Romance; Smoking as a Gendered Practice in Popular Young Women's Magazines, Britain 1918–1939', *Women's Studies International Forum*, Vol. 24, No. 1 (2001), pp. 111–22.

Todd, S., *Young Women, Work, and Family in England, 1918–1950* (Oxford, 2005).

Todd, S., 'Young Women, Work and Leisure in Interwar England', *Historical Journal*, Vol. 48, No. 3 (September 2005), pp. 789–809.

Todd, S., 'Flappers and Factory Lads: Youth and Youth Culture in Interwar Britain', *History Compass*, 4/4 (2006), pp. 715–30.

Todd, S., 'Breadwinners and Dependants: Working-Class Young People in England, 1918–1955', *International Review of Social History*, 52 (2007), pp. 57–87.

Trentmann, F., 'Henry Rolf Gardiner (1902–1971)', in B. Harrison (ed.), *Oxford Dictionary of National Biography* (ODNB), Vol. 21 (Oxford, 2004), pp. 427–9.

Watkinson, M. and Anderson, P., *Crazy Diamond: Syd Barrett and the Dawn of Pink Floyd* (London, 1993).

Whiteley, S., *Women and Popular Music: Sexuality, Identity and Subjectivity* (London, 2000).

Whyte, J. H., *Church and State in Modern Ireland* (Dublin, 1971).

Williamson, P., *Stanley Baldwin: Conservative Leadership and National Values* (Cambridge, 1999).

Wills, A., 'Delinquency, Masculinity and Citizenship in England, 1950–1970', *Past and Present*, No. 187 (May 2005), pp. 157–85.

Wilson, B., *The Youth Culture and the Universities* (London, 1970).

Wilson, E., *Adorned in Dreams: Fashion and Modernity* (London, 1985).

Woollacott, A., *On Her Their Lives Depend: Munitions Workers in the Great War* (London, 1994).

Wright, P., *The Village that Died For England: The Strange Story of Tyneham* (London, 1995).

Yellis, K. A., 'Prosperity's Child: Some Thoughts on the Flapper', *American Quarterly*, Vol. 21, No. 1 (Spring 1969), pp. 44–64.

Zdatny, S., 'The Mode "à la Garçonne" and the Meaning of Hair', unpublished paper delivered at the Social History Conference, Roehampton Institute, London, January 1993.

Zdatny, S. (ed.), *Hairstyles and Fashion: A Hairdresser's History of Paris, 1910–1920* (Oxford, 1999).

(b) Unpublished theses

Craven, J., 'Redskins in Epping Forest: John Hargrave, the Kibbo Kift and the Woodcraft Experience', unpublished Ph.D. thesis, University of London, 1999.

Horn, A., 'Juke Boxes and Youth Culture in Britain, 1945–1960', unpublished Ph.D. thesis, University of Lancaster, 2004.

Mertens, M. J., 'Early Twentieth Century Youth Movements, Nature and Community in Britain and Germany', unpublished Ph.D. thesis, University of Birmingham, 2000.

(c) Miscellaneous (songs, reports, websites etc.)

Interpol, Song and Lyrics of 'Obstacle 1' (2004?).

Keane website www.keaneshaped.co.uk/faq/

The Last Poets, 'The Revolution Will Not Be Televised' (1968).

The Spice Girls' website www.spicegirls.com

University of Birmingham, Centre for Contemporary Cultural Studies, *Annual Report*, 1968–9.

University of Birmingham Centre for Contemporary Cultural Studies, Unpublished Research Reports, Periodicals Section, Cambridge University Library at L200.b.301.

Who Was Who, 1971–1980 (London, 1989).

Wohlgemuth, K., 'Teen interview from October 1965', www. readysteadyball.co.uk

Index